HUMAN RIGHTS TECTONICS

HUMAN RIGHTS TECTONICS

Global Dynamics of Integration and Fragmentation

Edited by
Emmanuelle Bribosia
Isabelle Rorive

in collaboration with
Ana Maria Corrêa

intersentia
Cambridge – Antwerp – Chicago

Intersentia Ltd
Sheraton House | Castle Park
Cambridge | CB3 0AX | United Kingdom
Tel.: +44 1223 370 170 | Fax: +44 1223 370 169
Email: mail@intersentia.co.uk
www.intersentia.com | www.intersentia.co.uk

Distribution for the UK and Ireland:
NBN International
Airport Business Centre, 10 Thornbury Road
Plymouth, PL6 7PP
United Kingdom
Tel.: +44 1752 202 301 | Fax: +44 1752 202 331
Email: orders@nbninternational.com

Distribution for Europe and all other countries:
Intersentia Publishing nv
Groenstraat 31
2640 Mortsel
Belgium
Tel.: +32 3 680 15 50 | Fax: +32 3 658 71 21
Email: mail@intersentia.be

Distribution for the USA and Canada:
Independent Publishers Group
Order Department
814 North Franklin Street
Chicago, IL 60610
USA
Tel.: +1 800 888 4741 (toll free) | Fax: +1 312 337 5985
Email: orders@ipgbook.com

Human Rights Tectonics. Global Dynamics of Integration and Fragmentation

Artwork on cover: Valérie Lenders

ISBN 978-1-78068-613-4
D/2018/7849/75
NUR 828

British Library Cataloguing in Publication Data. A catalogue record for this book is available from the British Library.

FOREWORD

Human rights law scholarship is flourishing. Today's mid-career human rights law scholars in Europe vividly remember the birth and early childhood of their discipline. Throughout the 1990s, many law faculties were creating their first human rights chair and many academic human rights centres were founded. Gradually, 'human rights law' came to be seen as a discipline in its own right rather than as a part of constitutional law or public international law. In the meantime, the discipline of human rights law has moved to the next level, characterised by increased specialisation. Especially when it comes to research, not so many legal scholars of human rights identify as 'generalists', covering the entire field of human rights law. Indeed, both the proliferation of the output of some of the human rights monitoring bodies (in particular the European Court of Human Rights (ECtHR)) and the expansion of scholarship in this field have made it impossible for any single scholar to be completely up to date with all developments and insights. As a result, most scholars self-identify as experts in one or more sub-fields of human rights law, such as privacy law, free speech, minority rights or ECtHR case law. This is a positive development, testifying to the increasing maturity of the discipline and leading to ever more sophisticated insights. Yet at the same time, there is a risk that a focus on the trees might obscure the wood. As the human rights landscape expands, a holistic view becomes more, not less, relevant, and the same holds true for the study of the interactions and connections between different features in that landscape. This is an argument in favour of cherishing a degree of 'generalism' in human rights law scholarship, and a call for experts in sub-disciplines to occasionally reflect on the positioning of the contents of their box of choice within the broader field.

It may be argued that such a reflection is also relevant for those actors who play a crucial role in interpreting human rights law and who are by definition situated within their respective boxes, that is to say, supranational human rights monitoring bodies. Each of these bodies has its own jurisdictional and/or thematic specialisation, as well as its own mandate and context. This regularly results in idiosyncratic reasoning. Yet at the same time, many supranational human rights monitoring bodies also show an awareness of the work of other such bodies and occasionally align their work with that of others.

Both the idea of scholarship adopting a holistic approach to human rights law and the idea of exploring how the different layers or nodes of human rights law communicate and interact with each other are central to the research project that provides the background to the present volume. The project 'The Global Challenge of Human Rights Integration: Toward a Users' Perspective' (2012–2017) was funded by the Belgian Federal Department of Science Policy (BELSPO). Within the framework of this project, I had the pleasure of working together with Emmanuelle Bribosia and Isabelle Rorive, the editors of this volume. Their work on the project and on this volume exemplifies how experts of a sub-field of human rights law (in this case equality and discrimination law) can contribute immensely to a holistic approach of the field. In the same vein, many other experts of specific themes (economic, social and cultural (ESC) rights, disability rights, etc.) or specific jurisdictions (the Court of Justice of the European Union (CJEU), the ECtHR, etc.) have accepted the editors' invitation to explore the dynamics of fragmentation and integration within that sub-field or between that sub-field and broader human rights law.

The result is a volume of high academic quality, in which coherence is assured by the common perspective, yet at the same time a range of current topics of human rights law is discussed. As such, it will be of interest to many scholars of human rights law.

Eva Brems

CONTENTS

LIST OF CASES

AFRICAN COURT ON HUMAN AND PEOPLES' RIGHTS

COURT OF JUSTICE OF THE EUROPEAN UNION

EUROPEAN COURT OF HUMAN RIGHTS

INTER-AMERICAN COURT OF HUMAN RIGHTS

INTERNATIONAL COURT OF JUSTICE

UN COMMITTEES

COMMITTEE ON ECONOMIC, SOCIAL AND CULTURAL RIGHTS

COMMITTEE ON THE ELIMINATION OF DISCRIMINATION AGAINST WOMEN

COMMITTEE ON THE PROTECTION OF THE RIGHTS OF ALL MIGRANTS WORKERS AND MEMBERS OF THEIR FAMILIES (CMW)

HUMAN RIGHTS COMMITTEE

CANADA

UNITED KINGDOM

UNITED STATES

LIST OF CONTRIBUTORS

Oddný Mjöll Arnardóttir
Judge at the Icelandic Court of Appeal; Research Professor at the University of Iceland

Joanna Bourke Martignoni
Senior Researcher at the Geneva Academy of International Humanitarian Law and Human Rights, Switzerland; Lecturer in Human Rights at the University of Fribourg, Switzerland

Eva Brems
Professor in the Law Faculty and Founder of the Human Rights Centre at Ghent University, Belgium; Activist on the board of several Belgian human rights NGOs

Emmanuelle Bribosia
Professor in the Law Faculty, co-founder of the Equality Law Clinic and Director of the Centre for European Law at the Université libre de Bruxelles (ULB), Belgium

Joseph Damamme
PhD candidate in the Centre for European Law at the Université libre de Bruxelles (ULB), Belgium; involved in the Equality Law Clinic at the ULB

Valeska David
PhD Researcher at Ghent University, Belgium

Olivier De Schutter
Professor of Human Rights Law and Legal Theory at the University of Louvain, Belgium; Member of the UN Committee on Economic, Social and Cultural Rights

Bruno De Witte
Professor of European Law at Maastricht University, the Netherlands; Co-director of the Maastricht Centre for European Law; Part-time Professor of Law at the European University Institute, Florence, Italy

Kristin Henrard
Professor of Human Rights, focusing on vulnerable groups, including minorities, at the Erasmus School of Law, Rotterdam, the Netherlands

Jasper Krommendijk
Assistant Professor of European Law at Radboud University, Nijmegen, the Netherlands

Adamantia Rachovitsa
Assistant Professor of Public International Law at the University of Groningen, the Netherlands

Isabelle Rorive
Professor in the Law Faculty, co-founder of the Equality Law Clinic and Director of the Perelman Centre for Legal Philosophy at the Université libre de Bruxelles (ULB), Belgium

Rhona KM Smith
Head of Law and Professor of International Human Rights at Newcastle University, United Kingdom

Dorothea Staes
Affiliated Researcher at the Université libre de Bruxelles (ULB), Belgium; Perelman Centre for Legal Philosophy at the ULB

Lorenza Violini
Professor of Constitutional Law and Director of the Department of National and Supranational Public Law at the University of Milan, Italy

INTRODUCTION TO HUMAN RIGHTS TECTONICS*

Emmanuelle Bribosia** and Isabelle Rorive***

The mass violence, countless killings and systematic extermination of certain categories of the population during the Second World War led to the development of the supranational legal protection of human rights. Since 1945, both the sources of human rights and the bodies which control them have multiplied and have superimposed themselves on the older constitutional protection systems.[1] In the last few decades, the legal landscape of these rights has become more complex and diversified without following a well-defined pattern. Protective instruments have developed following both a logic of regionalisation and a logic of specialisation, with categories of rights protected just as much as categories of people. From the common matrix of the values in the Universal Declaration of Human Rights of 1948, fundamental rights

* This book project was carried on in the framework of the IUAP project, *The Global Challenge of Human Rights Integration: Towards a Users' Perspective* (2012–2017), http://www.hrintegration.be. The authors are much indebted to Eva Brems and all partners of the IUAP project for their contributions to this research project, which inspired this collective volume and this introduction. In addition, the authors warmly thank Eimear O'Neill for the precious editing work.

** Emmanuelle Bribosia is a professor at the Law Faculty of the Université libre de Bruxelles (ULB) and the Director of the Centre for European Law (http://www.cde.ulb.be, Email: ebribo@ulb.ac.be).

*** Isabelle Rorive is a professor at the Law Faculty of the ULB and the Director of the Perelman Centre for Legal Philosophy (http://www.philodroit.be, Email: irorive@ulb.ac.be).

1 See, among others, the dossier 'Human Rights Integration: Theorizing the Multi-layered Nature of Human Rights Law' (2014) *European Journal of Human Rights* 289; E Brems, 'Should Pluriform Human Rights Become One? Exploring the Benefits of Human Rights Integration' (2014) 4 *European Journal of Human Rights* 447; E Brems, 'Smart Human Rights Integration' in E Brems and S Ouald Chaib (eds), *Fragmentation and Integration in Human Rights Law: Users' Perspectives*, Edward Elgar, Cheltenham 2018; L Hennebel and H Tigroudja, *Traité de Droit International des Droits de l'Homme*, Pedone, Paris 2016; O De Schutter, *International Human Rights Law*, 2nd edn, Cambridge University Press, Cambridge 2014; J Lacroix and J-Y Pranchère, *Le Procès des Droits de l'Homme – Généalogie du Scepticisme Démocratique*, Seuil, Paris 2016.

were deployed to shape a 'layered' architecture, whose relatively homogeneous content does not, however, form a coherent and systematic whole.[2] The resulting image is made of 'bits and pieces',[3] with overlap and overlays, most often without any hierarchical relationship.[4]

Fragmentation, extensively commented on in the context of general international law,[5] is also at work in human rights law, with certain peculiarities inherent in this area of law, which confers rights on individuals rather than providing for reciprocal rights and obligations between States. Initially, the different human rights protection systems functioned autonomously by interpreting their respective instruments of protection, whether international, regional or constitutional. With globalisation, an increasing permeability between these different systems has been observed, notably in the form of a 'global conversation' on the interpretation of human rights.[6] These different systems, influenced by various actors who favour the inter-systemic circulation of legal arguments and the use of comparative law,[7] have begun to resonate with one another. However, resonance is not always synonymous with convergence, and some lines of divergence may actually be beneficial to the effectiveness of the protection of human rights.[8]

---

2 D Staes, 'When the European Court Refers to External Instruments: Mapping and Justifications', April 2017, doctoral thesis under the supervision of I Rorive and S Van Drooghenbroeck, defended at the Université libre de Bruxelles and the Université Saint-Louis as part of the Human Rights Integration project, pp 1–10.

3 For an overview of these 'parts and pieces', see, for instance, E Brems, 'Should Pluriform Human Rights Become One?', above n 1, pp 448–450; S Turgis and J Dhommeaux, *Les interactions entre les Normes Internationales Relatives aux Droits de la Personne*, Pedone, Paris 2012, pp 37–45.

4 A Buyse, 'Tacit Citing – The Scarcity of Judicial Dialogue between the Global an the Regional Human Rights Mechanisms in Freedom of Expression Cases', in T McGonagle and Y. Donders (eds), *The United Nations and Freedom of Expression and Information: Critical Perspectives*, Cambridge University Press, Cambridge 2015, p 2 of the book chapter as it is available at SSRN: http://papers.ssrn.com/sol3/papers.cfm?abstract_id=2279350.

5 Probably the best-known study on the topic of fragmentation of international law is the Report of the Study Group of the International Law Commission: M Koskenniemi, *Fragmentation of International Law: Difficulties Arising from the Diversification and Expansion of International Law*, UN Doc A/CN.4/L.682 (13.04.2006).

6 O De Schutter, this volume, pp 3–39; E Brems, 'Smart Human Rights Integration', above n 1. For a broad review of the literature on this 'global conversation', see D Staes, above n 2, p 5.

7 E Bribosia and I Rorive, 'Anti-discrimination Law in the Global Age' (2015) 1 *European Journal of Human Rights* 3–10; L van den Eynde, 'Interpreting Rights Collectively: Comparative Arguments in Public Interest Litigants' Briefs on Fundamental Rights Issues', doctoral thesis under the supervision of J Allard and E Bribosia, November 2015, defended at the Université libre de Bruxelles; B Frydman and C Bricteux (eds), *Les Défis du Droit Global*, Bruylant, Brussels 2017.

8 E Brems, 'Smart Human Rights Integration', above n 1; E Bribosia, G Caceres and I Rorive, 'Les signes religieux au cœur d'un bras de fer : la saga Singh' (2014) *Revue trimestrielle des droits de l'homme* 495.

WHAT DO WE MEAN BY HUMAN RIGHTS TECTONICS?

Without claiming it to be a perfect scientific superposition of phenomena, the theory of plate tectonics seems to capture the essence of international and regional human rights law, which is resolutely foreign to pyramidal organisation, even in the form of complex hierarchies.[9] The geophysical activity of our planet reflects the brutality of power relations and involves movements that interlock and respond to each other, even to the point of distorting or creating matter.

The 'Pangea' hypothesis, which refers to a supercontinent that contained almost all of today's land mass,[10] symbolises a form of unity that could be embodied in the Universal Declaration of Human Rights adopted by the United Nations General Assembly in 1948. The theory of plate tectonics explains the different forces that created fracture lines and led to a 'drift' of continents. In the same way, human rights are multiple and form a fragmented legal universe. Like tectonic plates, the different strata of fundamental rights do not overlap perfectly. At the global scale, they are numerous, vary in size and are in perpetual movement.

This movement reflects developments in the protection of human rights, some of which are of such magnitude that they can be considered major upheavals. According to scientists, 'the convection drive plates tectonics through a combination of pushing and spreading apart at mid-ocean ridges and pulling and sinking downward at subduction zones'.[11] In the same way, the elaboration of new instruments of human rights protection, their mobilisation before various bodies (whether administrative, jurisdictional, quasi-jurisdictional, etc.) and the implementation of these decisions or recommendations translate into fights, battles, shocks, jolts or clashes, which are all the more significant as, at their heart, it is often human dignity which is in question.

Both the forces which characterise the dynamics of plate tectonics and the movements which create them have parables in the mechanisms of fundamental rights protection. The tectonic structures lead to a 'fracturing of the rock beyond a certain threshold of constraint'.[12] The faults thus produced are of various types,

---

9 I Rorive, *Le revirement de jurisprudence : étude de droit anglais et de droit belge*, Bruylant, Brussels 2003, paras 48–49 and the references mentioned therein.

10 Alfred Wegener forged this concept (*Die Enstehung der Kontinente und Ozeane (L'origine des continents et des océans)*, 1915). See N Bardet, 'La « valse des continents » d'Alfred Wegener : un nouveau paradigme en Sciences de la Terre', http://www.saga-geol.asso.fr/Geologie_page_conf_Wegener.html.

11 B Oskin, 'What is Plate Tectonics?', *Livescience*, 19 December 2017, https://www.livescience.com/37706-what-is-plate-tectonics.html.

12 http://www.larousse.fr/encyclopedie/divers/tectonique/96183 (our translation).

resulting in the elongation, the shortening or the breaking up of the material. In addition, where the plates meet, their relative motion determines the type of boundary, which can be *convergent*, *divergent* or *transformative*, features that are reminiscent of the movement between the fragmentation and integration of human rights.[13] A combination of 'divergent boundaries' and certain 'hot spots' can lead to a dramatic increase in the ocean crust,[14] which echoes the climate of many human rights treaties, not to mention the 'shield' zones which protect these tectonic plates, whose 'interior is theoretically unalterable',[15] in a similar fashion to non-derogable or absolute human rights.

A COMBINATION OF AN INTEGRATED AND AN ISSUE-BASED APPROACH

The fight against human rights violations remains one of the major challenges of the twenty-first century. Since 1945, the development of a regime for international human rights protection has certainly led to progress; however, the protection of human rights is too often left to the sovereignty and goodwill of States.[16] This book takes stock of the fact that the traditional approach, which consists of studying different legal judicial systems individually, does not provide adequate conceptual and normative tools to understand the evolution of human rights on a transnational scale. Stemming from the tensions between the fragmentation and integration in human rights law, this volume fosters a critical reflection on the integration of international, European and non-European human rights law in a globalised era. In doing so, it opts for a pragmatic approach in the sense that human rights law is not understood as the set of rules laid down in the treaties or inscribed in existing formal sources. Emphasis is placed here on the actual state of the law as observed from the applications received. It is about giving tools to develop strategies which fit into the lines of tension between fragmentation and integration in order to advance causes. Thus, one point of originality of this book is the way in which it attempts to address problems faced by human rights users.[17] The 12 chapters do not merely focus on the plurality of human rights sources or monitoring bodies, but also aim to identify concrete

---

13 See O De Schutter, this volume, pp 3–39.

14 http://www.larousse.fr/encyclopedie/divers/tectonique/96183.

15 Ibid.

16 B Frydman and C Bricteux (eds), above n 7, p 19.

17 E Desmet, 'Methodologies to Study Human Rights Law as an Integrated Whole from a Users' Perspective', in E Brems and S Ouald Chaib (eds), above n 1; E Brems and E Desmet, 'Studying Human Rights Law from the Perspective(s) of its Users' (2014) 8(2) *HR&ILD* 111.

issues encountered by the courts, non-judicial bodies and individuals in this highly fragmented regulatory environment. This pragmatic and user-centred perspective distinguishes the book from other notable works, which look at or foster convergence in international human rights law.[18]

Through a theoretical and case study methodology, the book analyses the impact of the fragmentation of international and regional human rights, which can cause failures in effective legal protection or, on the contrary, can strengthen it. This book is part of the research project 'The Global Challenge of Human Rights Integration: Towards a Users' Perspective'.[19] The authors, from diverse legal backgrounds, had the opportunity to present a preliminary version of their work during an international symposium, organised in Ghent in December 2015.[20] Only some of these contributions have been retained in this volume, based on their quality and their complementarity. Over the course of an editing process of several stages, with the invaluable support of Ana Maria Corrêa,[21] the various authors have agreed to update and to revisit their contributions in greater detail. We thank them wholeheartedly for their commitment to this publication.

All contributions have high relevance to the three axes that we wanted to develop: first, investigating from different theoretical angles the promises and challenges of an integrated approach to fundamental rights at the global level; second, developing an issue-based approach through a case analysis which symbolises contemporary issues of struggle in international and regional human rights law; and, third, tightening the focus on Europe by identifying particular lines of convergence and divergence on this continent.

---

18 C Buckley and A Donald, *Towards Convergence in International Human Rights Law: Approaches of Regional and International Systems*, Martinus Nijhoff Publishers, Leiden 2015; A Cançado Trindade, *International Law for Humankind: Towards a New Jus Gentium*, Martinus Nijhoff Publishers, Leiden 2010.

19 'The Global Challenge of Human Rights Integration: Towards a Users' Perspective' (Human Rights Integration – HRI) is a research network which aims to study human rights law as an integrated whole from a users' perspective. HRI is an Inter-university Attraction Pole (IAP) funded by the Belgian Science Policy Office (BELSPO). It consists of Universiteit Gent (UGent), Université libre de Bruxelles (ULB), Vrije Universiteit Brussel (VUB), Universiteit Antwerpen (UAntwerp), Université Saint-Louis-Bruxelles (USL-B) and Universiteit Utrecht (UU). See more on its website: http://www.hrintegration.be.

20 'The Global Challenge of Human Rights Integration – Towards a Users' Perspective', International Conference, 9–11 December 2015; see more details at: http://www.hrintegration.be/conferences. E Brems and E Desmet, 'Introduction: Theorizing the Multi-layered Nature of Human Rights Law' (2014) 3 *European Journal of Human Rights* 289–292; M Baumgärtel, D Staes and FJ Mena Parras, 'Hierarchy, Coordination, or Conflict? Global Law Theories and the Question of Human Rights Integration' (2014) 3 *European Journal of Human Rights* 326–354; E Brems, 'Should Pluriform Human Rights Become One?', above n 1, pp 447–470.

21 Ana Maria Corrêa is a PhD candidate at the Université libre de Bruxelles and a researcher at the Perelman Center for Legal Philosophy (http://www.philodroit.be/_Correa-Ana-Maria_).

PROMISES AND CHALLENGES OF AN INTEGRATED APPROACH TO HUMAN RIGHTS

The opening section of the book highlights the promises and challenges of an integrated approach to human rights. To start with, Olivier De Schutter identifies the integration of human rights in 'The Formation of a Common Law of Human Rights', a kind of jus commune that is part of a collective deliberation between different bodies, whether jurisdictional or otherwise, the primary characteristics of which would be to be free from any form of hierarchical relationship and left entirely to the discretion of its authors.[22] Although the factors that favour the emergence of this 'global conversation' may be well known, the focus here is on the driving force behind it: strengthening the legitimacy of each instrument of human rights protection in an international context where States remain eager to preserve their sovereignty, knowing that both the international courts and the expert bodies have developed an interpretation of human rights instruments that focuses on contextual factors rather than on literal interpretation. Today, the permeability and resonances between the different strata of human rights is such that 'human rights bodies occasionally feel compelled to justify departing from precedents established by other such bodies, as if they were part of the same legal system – more precisely, as if such precedents had more than mere persuasive authority, and were actually binding'.[23] One of the main challenges to the formation of a common law of human rights lies in the opportunistic use of foreign jurisprudence, known as 'cherry-picking'. To address this, De Schutter calls on the various human rights bodies to be more transparent, but above all more consistent. To this end, he suggests that well-established foreign jurisprudence on a controversial point creates a kind of rebuttable presumption. In other words, 'foreign precedents' should be considered presumptions 'which could be set aside if the context in which the "receiving" court operates is different'.[24] In practice, such a phenomenon is triggered by different actors bringing these precedents to the knowledge of human rights courts and bodies. These actors can be non-governmental organisations (NGOs) defending a liberal or a conservative agenda, the many figures of third-party interveners or amicus curiae, judges, lawyers, scholars, etc. This model based on a stare decisis doctrine is appealing with respect to more human rights integration. It is a promising starting point to further flesh out the reasons according to which a precedent should be departed from.

In order to go deeper into the practical aspects of the formation of a common law of human rights and to further investigate its drawbacks,

---

22 O De Schutter, this volume, pp 3–39.

23 Ibid.

24 Ibid, p 35. A procedural approach is also favoured by E Brems, 'Smart Human Rights Integration', above n 1.

the next three chapters develop the distinct positions of particular actors that are part of an integrated approach to human rights. These are UN special procedures, the African Court on Human and Peoples' Rights and non-judicial bodies such as the European Fundamental Rights Agency.

UN special procedures are particularly relevant in this respect. They are not created in connection with a specific instrument for the protection of human rights. On the contrary, they are expected to draw on all relevant sources to extract the rights and obligations that apply to a particular state or subject, such as migrants' rights. A degree of flexibility on sources and leeway on legal strategies to advance their mandate have put UN special procedures in a unique position to truly engage in an integrated approach to human rights. Relying on a broad definition of the human rights user so as to include individuals, NGOs and civil society organisations, States themselves, institutions and entities within regional and international organisations, Rhona Smith addresses the provocative question of whether UN monitoring systems are system puppets or some (or all) of their users' saviours?[25] She first stresses the extent to which these procedures stem from a highly political organisation. She then goes on to analyse various sets of interactions they have with the Human Rights Council, other intergovernmental or international fora, regional organisations, other UN human rights monitoring systems, States, NGOs and civil society, individuals or even between themselves. A body of evidence supports their contribution towards the integration of human rights systems: 'filling protection gaps in law and practice, acting as a critical friend to States and non-State actors, and raising awareness of issues and the plight of individual whose voices would otherwise not be heard'.[26] At the crossroads of various human rights layers, UN special procedures are in a prominent position to foster convergence and integration. They are still struggling to do so as they remain entangled in a UN human rights system 'beset with the problems of politicisation, backlog and limited enforcement opportunities'.[27]

In comparison to other regional courts, the African Court on Human and Peoples' Rights (ACtHPR) is in a privileged position to pursue human rights integration. This is due to two main features. First, human rights integration is part of the drafting of the African Charter on Human and Peoples' Rights (ACHPR), which gives equal weight to all three generations of human rights. In other words, the indivisibility, interdependence and inter-relation of human rights are specifically entrenched in the text of the ACHPR. Second, human rights integration is part of the interpretation of the ACHPR as the ACtHPR enjoys the jurisdiction to interpret and apply not only the ACHPR but also any other relevant human rights instrument ratified by the States concerned. Furthermore,

25 R Smith, this volume, pp 41–68.
26 Ibid, p 67.
27 Ibid, p 68.

and very significantly, explicit provisions of the ACHPR direct the ACtHPR to draw inspiration from other international instruments when interpreting the rights enshrined in the ACHPR. Reliance on judicial borrowing in the practice of the ACtHPR fosters inter-systemic dialogue and the coordination of international jurisprudence. It also 'legitimises the ACtHPR in the eyes of its constituencies and audience during the first crucial years of its functioning'.[28] Based on an extensive analysis of the ACtHPR's case law, Adamantia Rachovitsa categorises the various ways according to which the ACtHPR uses international instruments. As she convincingly argues, there is considerable room to improve the transparency and quality of the ACtHPR's methodology and reasoning. To some extent, her guidance echoes that which Olivier De Schutter provided at the global level. Finally, she discusses whether 'there is a need to balance *international* human rights integration with the specificity of the ACHPR'[29] and how this could be done. As she puts it in line with the idea of 'smart integration', developed by Eva Brems,[30] '[h]uman rights integration should not be seen and used as an interpretative "bulldozer"; rather, it should highlight difference and variety in legal standards'.[31] In other words, reliance on precedents should be weighted against distinctive regional features.

With a focus on judicial dialogue and cross-fertilisation, human rights integration issues have often put the emphasis on courts. However, there is a growing need to go beyond a paradigm of human rights in which protection is the responsibility of the judiciary alone. Lorenza Violini sheds some light on to the role of non-judicial bodies.[32] She looks not only at regional organisations, such as the European Fundamental Rights Agency, the Inter-American Commission on Human Rights and the African Commission on Human and Peoples' Rights, but also at National Human Rights Institutions (NHRIs). She highlights major lines of convergence of these non-judicial actors and discusses whether and how these bodies might develop a dialogue to share common practices and enhance coordination so as to engage in a similar process to their judicial counterparts. However, such inter-systemic interaction is still at a preliminary stage.

HUMAN RIGHTS TECTONICS THROUGH AN ISSUE-BASED APPROACH

The second part of the book reflects on four issues of social justice where human rights tectonics are at play. They all relate to legal battles which mobilise,

---

28 A Rachovitsa, this volume, p 78.
29 Ibid, p 83.
30 E Brems, 'Smart Human Rights Integration', above n 1.
31 Rachovitsa, this volume, p 84.
32 L Violini, this volume, pp 89–107.

in one way or another, the principle of non-discrimination. They disclose various tensions, fights, battles and clashes that take place at the core of human rights protection. They illustrate the movement between the fragmentation and the integration of human rights, and the many crossroads that must be navigated to overcome the boundaries between the generations of human rights, the grounds of discrimination or the various systems of human rights protection. Here, again, various dynamics comparable to the movements of tectonic plates are observable. The dialectic between convergence and divergence points towards transformative tools for developing strategies to advance human rights causes in a globalised era.

In the first case study, we explore the commonalities between several battles where commercial companies appropriate the language of fundamental rights to justify differences in treatment based on gender, sexual orientation or religious beliefs. These companies claim a form of freedom of conscience, understood as the choice of values that constitute their identity. They do so in relation to the sexual and reproductive rights of women and the equal treatment of all people regardless of their sexual orientation. Furthermore, other instances where a company's policy of neutrality sometimes targets a symbol of a minority religion uncover the extent to which the corporate image of private companies seems to be linked to a form of conscience understood as an intrinsic part of their identity. To address this multi-faceted phenomenon and in line with the general perspective of this book, we support the view that there is a genuine need for a global approach[33] to anti-discrimination law, which would help to identify new areas for producing and implementing the law which are neither national nor international. This makes it possible to unveil some driving forces between different layers of human rights.[34] Against this background, this contribution provides an analysis of some symbolic cases from either side of the Atlantic to assess how anti-discrimination law is challenged and undermined when companies or associations invoke their 'conscience'.

In recent years, intersectionality has been considered to be a fruitful approach to foster human rights integration.[35] As a second case study on anti-discrimination law, Joanna Bourke Martignoni analyses selected examples where an intersectional lens is applied to sexual and reproductive rights issues within the practice of the UN's treaty monitoring bodies:[36] 'While the concept of intersectionality has occupied centre stage in much of the gender

---

33 B Frydman, 'A Pragmatic Approach to Global Law', in H Muir Watt and D Arroyo (eds), *Global Governance Implications of Private International Law*, Oxford University Press, Oxford 2015, pp 181–200.

34 E Bribosia and I Rorive, this volume, pp 89–107.

35 E Brems, 'Should Pluriform Human Rights Become One?', above n 1, p 466.

36 J Bourke Martignoni, this volume, pp 141–162.

and postcolonial studies literature produced since the 1980s, the use of intersectional perspectives by the international human rights mechanisms has a much more recent history.'[37] The UN human rights treaty bodies have mainly relied on a single-entry approach to enforce norms prohibiting discrimination. The resulting practice of these bodies has tended to reinforce fragmentation and discursive hierarchies about which experiences of discrimination are identified and redressed by international human rights law. With the impetus of the Committee on the Elimination of Discrimination against Women, things are changing. Bourke Martignoni not only takes stock of these developments, but also reflects on the potential and limitations of intersectional approaches to sexual and reproductive rights, as well as 'the capacity of the UN human rights monitoring mechanisms to engage in the nuanced, radical and frequently contradictory analyses of inequalities and power relations that such approaches require'.[38]

Drawing on literature from political and critical socio-legal theory, Valeska David challenges another kind of legal boundary: the one between cultural identity and economic empowerment.[39] This third case study is based on a body of case law of both the European Court of Human Rights (ECtHR) and the Inter-American Court of Human Rights (IACtHR), which is frequently regarded as 'a jurisprudence of difference' related to the cultural identity, lifestyles and 'special needs' of minorities such as Roma, Travellers and indigenous peoples.[40] She argues that '[w]hile this case law has attracted extensive interest from the perspective of the "culturalisation" of human rights law,[41] less attention has been paid to the interaction between this legal phenomenon and the advancement of socio-economic equality claims'.[42] These cases are interlocked with claims over land, living conditions, housing, protection against eviction and access to and management of natural resources. David grapples with this interaction to explore whether and how far rights claims on the basis of cultural and economic disadvantage could be integrated into the legal reasoning of the ECtHR or the IACtHR. These two regional courts are more constrained by their specific legal mandate than the ACtHPR, which is urged to foster an integrated approach to human rights.[43]

The experience of persons with disabilities before the ECtHR provides a fourth case study to dig into Olivier De Schutter's account of the formation

---

37 Ibid, p 142.
38 Ibid.
39 V David, this volume, pp 163–192.
40 Ibid, p 164.
41 On this notion, see F Lenzerini, *The Culturalization of Human Rights Law*, Oxford University Press, Oxford 2014.
42 V David, this volume, p 164.
43 See A Rachovitsa, this volume, pp 89–107.

of a common law of human rights. The ECtHR refers more and more often to external instruments to support the interpretation and application of the European Convention on Human Rights (ECHR) and its Protocols.[44] In disability cases, the instruments referenced include the UN Convention on the Rights of Persons with Disabilities,[45] documents of the UN Committee on the Rights of Persons with Disabilities, judgments of national Supreme Courts on disability and recommendations of the International Labour Organization. Based on an extensive and rigorous case law analysis, Dorothea Staes and Joseph Damamme draw a typology which is guided by the idea of 'human rights integration'.[46] From a top-down view on the human rights architecture, they show that the practice of referencing other instruments enhances the harmonious coexistence of the relevant norms. A bottom-up perspective also brings to light the potential of the practice to strengthen the protection of the human rights of persons with disabilities.

HUMAN RIGHTS DYNAMICS IN EUROPE

Europe is a genuine laboratory to investigate how a new instrument of human rights protection – the Charter of Fundamental Rights of the European Union – and its mobilisation before national judges, the Court of Justice of the European Union (CJEU) and even the ECtHR blurs the lines of convergence and divergence in a multi-layered human rights system.

The dominant view in legal literature, until recently, saw the relationship between the CJEU and the ECtHR as complementary and harmonious. During the beginning of the twenty-first century, two major developments have affected this relationship: the failed accession of the EU to the ECHR following Opinion 2/13[47] and the dominant role now played by the EU's Charter of Fundamental Rights in the practice of the CJEU when human rights issues are at stake. Taking stock of these developments, Bruno De Witte points out that the CJEU operates in an environment which does not necessarily pressure it to contribute to the effective enforcement of other international human rights instruments.[48] He highlights the extent to which human rights interactions between the EU and the outside world increasingly happen beside the judicial arena in the context of the EU's external relations, 'at least at the level of policy

44 On this issue, see D Staes, above n 2.

45 Convention on the Rights of Persons with Disabilities, adopted on 24 January 2007, G.A. Res. 61/106, UN Doc. A/RES/61/106 (entered into force on 3 May 2008).

46 D Staes and J Damamme, this volume, pp 193–221.

47 CJEU (Full Court), 18 December 2014, ECLI:EU:C:2014:2454.

48 B De Witte, this volume, pp 225–241.

documents, if not always in practice'.[49] Today, in addition to being more consistent in its action, one of the main challenges the EU faces is to link its own human rights norms to the development of international norms so as to refrain from becoming a 'solo singer' rather than a 'voice' in the choir of the legal protection of human rights.

Building on De Witte's chapter, Jasper Krommendijk explores in further detail the aftermath of Opinion 2/13, which 'reflects the increasing worries of the CJEU about the sometimes far-reaching case law of the ECtHR, which could hamper the effectiveness of EU law'.[50] Based on a solid review of the case law of the CJEU after Opinion 2/13 and on previous published work looking at the interactions between both European systems, Krommendijk assesses whether this Opinion has been 'a game-changer' in the CJEU's practice of referring to the case law of the ECtHR.[51] In this respect, not only does he identify a typology of the CJEU's practice of relying on precedents of the ECtHR, but he also looks at cases where the CJEU entirely omits any fundamental rights perspective, failing even to engage with the Charter of Fundamental Rights. This extensive case law review leads him to conclude that no marked changes can be identified in the practice of the CJEU since Opinion 2/13. Amongst the various explanations for this, two are worth underlining. Primarily, it is not surprising that the CJEU 'exercises some caution and damage control' after the 'heavy blow' of Opinion 2/13.[52] Furthermore, the trend to refer less often and more unassumingly to the ECHR and the case law of the ECtHR started before Opinion 2/13 with the 'Charter-centrism idea of the EU now having its "own catalogue" of fundamental rights'.[53]

To grasp the full extent of the dynamics operating in Europe, it is critical to look at the other side of the coin, bringing the focus on to the practice of the ECtHR. The allocation of the burden of proof in cases of racial discrimination is a topical example which can deepen the discussion on convergence and divergence in international human rights law. Starting with a discussion on the trend among international courts to adopt the shared burden of proof in cases of human rights violations, Kristin Henrard zooms in on the recent case law of the CJEU on the Race Equality Directive.[54] This allows her to bring a broader perspective on the ECtHR's struggle with the application of the allocation of the shared burden of proof in cases involving racially motivated crimes. Indeed, for once, it is EU law that has been the driving force behind the expansion of

---

49 Ibid, p 236.
50 J Krommendijk, this volume, p 243.
51 Ibid, p 246.
52 Ibid, p 267.
53 Ibid, and interviews referred to in footnote 139.
54 K Henrard, this volume, pp 271–301.

the right to equality and anti-discrimination in Europe.[55] Henrard invites the ECtHR to build on its existing judicial dialogue with the CJEU to further clarify and strengthen its precedents in this matter and to reduce the national margin of appreciation.[56]

As an expression of the principle of subsidiarity, the margin of appreciation is at the core of human rights dynamics in Europe. 'It represents the normative vision of agency that larger or more centralised units should not usurp functions that smaller or more local units are able to perform well enough'.[57] It also has a functional justification related to efficiency and competence. Furthermore, as to the interpretation and application of rights, it allows flexibility and pluralism. Oddný Mjöll Arnardóttir goes beyond discussing these key elements of the margin of appreciation doctrine. Starting from the divergent views of George Letsas and Andrew Legg, she revisits the issue of whether an internal conceptual framework can be constructed to encompass the various aspects of the doctrine reflected in the case law of the ECtHR.

***

At a time when human rights are (again) 'on trial',[58] lawyers have to add their voice to that of political scientists in order to stress the robustness of the idea of human rights and to revitalise its emancipatory potential. This book is part of such a framework which posits a democratic defence of human rights. While the human rights legal landscape is still expanding, the case for an increased integration of human rights law needs to be addressed comprehensively and concrete issues faced by human rights users should not be overlooked.

With the imagery of plate tectonics in the background, this book aims to ascertain the extent to which human rights law is in perpetual construction and constant renewal. Semantically, one might bear in mind that the term plate tectonics comes from the Late Latin 'tectonicus', borrowed from the Greek 'τεκτονικός', which means belonging to carpentry or pertaining to building.[59]

55 E Bribosia and I Rorive, above n 7, p 3.

56 In this respect, Henrard's contribution is directly linked to some findings of D Staes and J Damamme, this volume, pp 193–221.

57 OM Arnardóttir, this volume, p 315.

58 J Lacroix and J-Y Pranchère, *Human Rights on Trial: A Genealogy of the Critique of Human Rights*, Cambridge University Press, Cambridge 2018.

59 See, for instance, the Collins English Dictionary.

PART I

PROMISES AND CHALLENGES OF AN INTEGRATED APPROACH TO HUMAN RIGHTS

THE FORMATION OF A COMMON LAW OF HUMAN RIGHTS

Olivier De Schutter*

1. INTRODUCTION

A silent revolution has taken place since the 1980s in the world of human rights. The revolution has two inter-related dimensions. First, in the interpretation of human rights instruments, the pendulum has shifted from a focus on literal

* Olivier De Schutter is Professor of human rights law and legal theory at the Université catholique de Louvain in Belgium, as well as at SciencesPo in Paris. Email: olivier.deschutter@uclouvain.be.

interpretation and the original intention of the drafters to a focus on contextual factors, by which the judge ensures the evolution of human rights doctrine to changing circumstances. Second, and more recently, whereas in the past the bodies tasked with the enforcement of human rights law based their assessment on the particular instrument on the basis of which they were established and that defined their jurisdiction, whether that instrument was an international treaty or a domestic legislative or constitutional instrument, they now increasingly refer to each other's case law. They were working in relative isolation from one another; they are now all participants in the shaping of the common law of human rights.

This contribution takes stock of the first of these developments and it examines in greater detail the significance of the second. It proceeds in six steps. It first describes the origins of the development of human rights law in the form of a human rights *jus commune* (2). It then distinguishes this phenomenon from other scenarios in which human rights bodies refer to one another, but where such cross-references have other justifications and thus do not illustrate the phenomenon of human rights *jus commune* as such; this is the case, in particular, where comparative law analyses make it possible to identify the emergence of a consensus on how a certain issue should be addressed (in which case the case law is treated as an empirical fact rather than as normative authority) or where one body refers to the views expressed by another body, which is established in order to provide an authoritative interpretation of the instrument applied (3). It then highlights what is specific about the development of a human rights *jus commune*, showing, in particular, how this can strengthen the legitimacy of human rights adjudication, allowing judicial and non-judicial human rights bodies to move together and faster in the protection of human rights (4).

The practice of relying on precedents set by other human rights bodies is inconsistent, however; external observers often see it as *ad hoc*, as a form of 'cherry-picking' and, therefore, ultimately as poorly justified – in fact risking undermining the legitimacy of human rights courts or expert bodies when it was intended to strengthen it (5). The chapter describes what a dialogic approach could consist in, explaining why case law 'external' to the legal system which the 'receiving' body belongs to cannot be treated as binding precedent, but nevertheless should not be simply ignored or dismissed as irrelevant (6). It ends with a brief conclusion (7).

2. INTERNATIONAL HUMAN RIGHTS TREATIES AS 'LIVING INSTRUMENTS' AND THE FORMATION OF A *JUS COMMUNE*

The debate concerning the role of courts in interpreting the text they apply in order to adapt its meaning to changing circumstances has accompanied the rise of constitutional adjudication almost since it was inaugurated. Justice John Marshall famously declared in *McCulloch v Maryland* that 'it is a constitution we are expounding' and that the constitution is an instrument which is 'to be adapted to the various crises of human affairs'.[1] As implied by this dictum, the role of courts in updating the meaning of the constitution is particularly important where the instrument is difficult to amend due to the special majorities required to that effect, and where the text bears the mark of the times when it was initially adopted; the text may then appear ill-suited to provide answers to the new questions that emerge many decades later and the burden inevitably falls on the interpreter to ensure its continued relevance.

The rise of international human rights since the Second World War simply led to this debate being transposed into a new arena. Human rights instruments, after all, often rely on highly abstract and general language, meant as much to inspire as to provide detailed guidance; they are the result of diplomatic negotiations that often lead to adopting wording that is ambiguous and chosen precisely in order to accommodate different interpretations; and, while they are meant to last, they are very rarely amended, at least as far as substantive provisions are concerned, both because of the unanimity requirement for such a revision to proceed and because they are seen to embody values that are both universal and timeless. It was therefore entirely predictable that the classic divides between those who believe the text should be read according to its original meaning and those who insist on the role of the interpreter in adapting that meaning to an evolving context – or between the partisans of an interpretation centred on the 'original intent' of the drafters and those who insist, instead, on basing the interpretation on the 'purpose' of the text (the overall philosophy of the document or the set of values, principles or objectives that the wording itself only imperfectly embodies) – should be transposed to the field of international human rights.

But this first shift is now leading to a second one, which is both more innovative and more remarkable: the practice of borrowing, from court to court, doctrines that gradually define the interpretation of human rights law.[2] The shift is from rules-based adjudication, in which the interpretation of the text takes place within the legal system in which the interpreter operates, to a form of adjudication in which the task of the court is to express the consensus that emerges from a transnational dialogue between jurisdictions as to what the appropriate interpretation of human rights should be across different legal systems.

1 17 US (4 Wheat.) 316, 407, 415 (1819).

2 The expression 'from court to court' is used here for ease of exposition; as will become clear below, the argument put forward here extends to the interpretation by human rights treaty bodies, insofar as these expert bodies exercise quasi-judicial functions.

A rule-based approach to interpretation is fully compatible with a certain form of judicial activism, for instance, where the court prioritises 'evolving meaning' over fidelity to original intent or to established precedent, or grounds interpretation in the values or objectives pursued by the document rather than in a literal understanding of its wording. Yet, however inventive (and indeed, at times, controversial) these choices may be, they are nevertheless choices made *within* the system in which the court operates – it is *this* country's history, for instance, that the court shall invoke in order to justify departing from precedent,[3] or, conversely, it is the absence of a competing jurisprudence within *this* court that will justify holding firm to another precedent despite the strong criticism it may have given rise to.[4]

Instead, what is specific and new to the kind of interpretation that is now becoming dominant is that the answers to the questions of interpretation that arise are sought *outside* the legal system in which the court operates: the regional human rights jurisdiction, for instance, shall seek inspiration from how other regional or international courts have addressed the problem it is confronted with, and the constitutional court shall look at what foreign courts have done in situations similar to that which it faces. Human rights law looks less like a body of rules that were adopted by a 'principal' (the framers of the constitution, the governments having negotiated the treaty) for the court, the 'agent', to apply as faithfully as possible; it looks more like a natural language that evolves incrementally, by the succession of judgments that may be seen as 'speech acts', each of which contributes to the general development of the language of human rights.

The classic understanding of interpretation is vertical: whether the emphasis was on a textual (or 'literal') reading, on the search for the 'original intent' or on fidelity to the 'spirit' of the rule, rule application operates from the top down, from the body of rules and principles applicable to the particular case at hand. Although this formalistic understanding has been widely denounced as a myth, as it ignores the creative role of judicial interpretation,[5] it nevertheless remains

---

3 See, e.g., *Lawrence and Garner v Texas*, 539 US 558 (2003) (noting that 'there is no longstanding history in this country of laws directed at homosexual conduct as a distinct matter', as one of the reasons why the precedent established in *Bowers v Hardwick*, 478 US 186 (1986), where the Court upheld a Georgia statute making it a criminal offence to engage in sodomy, should be overruled).

4 See, e.g., *Planned Parenthood of Southeastern Pa. v Casey*, 505 US 833 (1992).

5 This was, of course, at the heart of the critique of the Legal Realists in the early twentieth century in the United States. It was also central to the school of 'free interpretation' led by François Gény in France, and it was to a large extent a characteristic of the Interessenjurisprudenz promoted in Germany by Rudolf von Jhering. The literature on these different schools of jurisprudence is too overwhelming to be cited. In the United States, Benjamin Cardozo's book of 1921, *The Nature of the Judicial Process*, Yale University Press, New Haven, as well as Karl Llewellyn's *Bramble Bush: On Our Law and its Study*,

at the heart of the judicial function and, as its founding fiction, the main source of its legitimacy; this is what Dworkin referred to when, in a famous article published in 1977, he referred to the postulate of the 'single right answer'.[6] Instead, with the new interpretative technique that has emerged, the legitimacy of the court is grounded in the fact that it is part of a human rights community of interpretation that, collectively, has concluded that a certain solution provides a better 'fit' with the values embodied in human rights law than other, competing solutions. The 'right answer' in this approach is the product of a process of collective deliberation – of a conversation in which various judicial and quasi-judicial bodies engage as quasi-equals. It is more about invention than it is about discovery. And it is always provisional, since the criterion of what is 'right' is permanently shifting.

Both international and regional jurisdictions or expert bodies and domestic courts take part in the dialogue leading to the emergence of the human rights *jus commune*. The important consequence that follows is that human rights law increasingly develops as a hybrid between constitutional law and international law. Even when they do not apply international human rights treaties directly, domestic courts apply the bills of rights included in their constitutions by taking into account the fact that such bills of rights derive from the Universal Declaration of Human Rights,[7] and thus should be read in accordance with the interpretative consensus on human rights that emerges across various jurisdictions. By doing so, they aggrandise their power, freeing themselves from the strictures of their own domestic tradition of constitutional interpretation. At the same time, international courts supervising compliance with human rights treaties feel empowered to set aside rules of interpretation or doctrines of international law in the name of the unique character of human rights.[8] For

---

New York, Oceana Publishing 1930 and *The Common Law Tradition: Deciding Appeals*, Little, Brown & Co., Boston and Toronto 1960, are perhaps the most representative. R von Jhering's *Der Kampf ums Recht*, originally published in 1872, Frankfurt am Main, Klostermann, and François Gény's *Méthodes d'interprétation et sources en droit positif*, LGDJ, Paris, 2nd ed 1919, summarise the views of these authors on judicial interpretation.

6 R Dworkin, 'No Right Answer?' in PMS Hacker and J Raz (eds), *Law, Morality, and Society: Essays in Honour of HLA Hart*, Clarendon Press, Oxford 1977, pp 58–84.

7 For an early overview of the influence of the Universal Declaration of Human Rights on domestic constitutions, see H Hannum, 'The Status of the Universal Declaration of Human Rights in National and International Law' (1995/1996) 25 *Georgia Journal of International and Comparative Law* 287, 292–316.

8 On the specific nature of human rights treaties in international law, see *inter alia* E Schwelb, 'The Law of Treaties and Human Rights' (1973–1975) 16 *Archiv des Völkerrechts* 14; M Craven, 'Legal Differentiation and the Concept of the Human Rights Treaty in International Law' (2000) 11 *European Journal of International Law* 489. See also, more generally, on the deviations from classic international law that result from the rise of human rights T Meron, *Human Rights and Humanitarian Norms as Customary Law*, Clarendon Press, Oxford 1989.

instance, the extent to which reservations to treaties may be authorised and the consequences that are attached to reservations being found invalid shall take into account the specific nature of human rights treaties.[9] Similarly, the fact that we operate in the specific field of human rights shall lead the principle according to which the State cannot be bound beyond what it has consented to, whether by ratifying a treaty or by failing to oppose the formation of a customary rule of international law, to be given lesser weight.[10] The chief justification for carving out this specificity of human rights treaties is that the primary aim of such treaties is not to establish reciprocal rights and duties between States, but rather

9 See, on the status of reservations to human rights treaties (also referred to as treaties of a 'humanitarian' nature), International Court of Justice, Reservations to the Convention on the Prevention and Punishment of the Crime of Genocide, Advisory Opinion (28 May 1951), ICJ Rep 1951, p 19; Inter-American Court of Human Rights, Advisory Opinion OC-2/82 of 24 September 1982 on the effect of reservations on the entry into force of the American Convention on Human Rights (Articles 74 and 75), Series A, No. 2; European Court of Human Rights, *Belilos v Switzerland*, no. 10328/83, ECHR 1988; Human Rights Committee, General Comment No. 24: Issues relating to reservations made upon ratification or accession to the Covenant or the Optional Protocols thereto, or in relation to declarations under Article 41 of the Covenant, 4 November 1994 (CCPR/C/21/Rev.1/Add.6).

10 The cases of *Demir and Baykara v Turkey*, no 34503/97, ECHR 2008, and of *International Federation for Human Rights (FIDH) v France* before the European Committee of Social Rights (Complaint No. 14/2003, decision on the merits of 8 September 2004), provide illustrations of this. In *Demir and Baykara*, the Grand Chamber of the European Court of Human Rights concluded that Article 11 of the European Convention on Human Rights protected the right of public servants to form unions and to collective bargaining, a novel interpretation which, the Court stated, seeks to 'take account of the perceptible evolution in such matters, in both international law and domestic legal systems' (§153). The Court cited, among other sources, Article 6 §2 of the European Social Charter, which 'affords to all workers, and to all trade unions, the right to bargain collectively, thus imposing on the public authorities the corresponding obligation to promote actively a culture of dialogue and negotiation in the economy, so as to ensure broad coverage for collective agreements' (§49). This provision was referred to despite Turkey having deliberately chosen not to accept it as part of its commitments under the European Social Charter (States acceding to the European Social Charter select among its provisions, within certain parameters, those that they will accept as binding). Rather similarly, in *FIDH v France*, the European Committee of Social Rights decided to extend the protection of the right to social and medical assistance (under Article 13 of the Revised European Social Charter) and the right of children and young persons 'to grow up in an environment which encourages the full development of their personality and of their physical and mental capacities' (under Article 17 of the same instrument) to children of undocumented migrants, despite the fact that according to paragraph 1 of the Appendix to the Revised Social Charter, these provisions apply to foreigners 'only in so far as they are nationals of other Parties lawfully resident or working regularly within the territory of the Party concerned'. The European Committee of Social Rights justifies setting aside this restriction to the scope of application ratione personae of the Charter by the consideration that the European Social Charter 'was envisaged as a human rights instrument to complement the European Convention on Human Rights' (§27) and that such a restriction, 'in the circumstances of this particular case … treads on a right of fundamental importance to the individual since it is connected to the right to life itself and goes to the very dignity of the human being. Furthermore, the restriction in this instance impacts adversely on children who are exposed to the risk of no medical treatment' (§30).

to grant to individuals under the jurisdiction of the States parties rights that they may assert against the State, just as individuals are protected by constitutional protections in domestic law. This was already noted by the International Court of Justice in its 1951 Advisory Opinion on Reservations to the Convention on the Prevention and Punishment of the Crime of Genocide:

> In such a convention [such as the 1948 Convention on the Prevention and Punishment of the Crime of Genocide, adopted for a purely humanitarian and civilising purpose] the contracting States do not have any interests of their own; they merely have, one and all, a common interest, namely, the accomplishment of those high purposes which are the raison d'être of the convention. Consequently, in a convention on this type one cannot speak of individual advantages or disadvantages to States, or of the maintenance of a perfect contractual balance between rights and duties.[11]

In other words, it is the quasi-constitutional nature of human rights treaties that allows their application to deviate from the classic approach of international law. Because it brings this quasi-constitutional nature of human rights treaties to the fore, the formation of a human rights *jus commune* reinforces the tendency for human rights to establish themselves as a separate regime of international law, one which increasingly borrows its methodology, including its methods of interpretation, from domestic constitutional law.[12]

3. CROSS-JURISDICTIONAL DIALOGUE: A TYPOLOGY OF SCENARIOS

Though it is visible in the practice of both international bodies and domestic courts, this shift occurs at different levels and in different institutional settings. Therefore, there exists a certain confusion about the phenomenon – what it consists of and what are the specific challenges and opportunities it presents.

---

11 International Court of Justice, Reservations to the Convention on the Prevention and Punishment of the Crime of Genocide, Advisory Opinion, 28 May 1951, p 15, at p 23.

12 Both for this reason and because they have developed their own specialised institutions, human rights therefore provide a good illustration of the problem of fragmentation of international law into a number of self-contained regimes, each with its own norms and dispute-settlement mechanisms, and relatively autonomous both vis-à-vis each other and vis-à-vis general international law. On this debate, see in particular B Simma, 'Self-Contained Regimes' (1985) 16 *Netherlands Yearbook of International Law* 111; and the Report of the Study Group of the International Law Commission (chaired by Martti Koskenniemi), Fragmentation of International Law: Difficulties Arising from the Diversification and Expansion of International Law, UN doc. A/CN.4/L.702, 18 July 2006 (also reproduced in the Report on the work of the fifty-eighth session (1 May–9 June and 3 July–11 August 2006) of the International Law Commission to the UN General Assembly, Official Records, sixty-first session, Supplement no. 10 (A/61/10), Chapter 12).

In order to understand the formation of the common law of human rights and to assess its consequences, it may be useful to distinguish this specific phenomenon from other situations in which human rights bodies may rely in their reasoning on a doctrine developed by another such body. Indeed, depending on the context, other rationales may provide a better explanation for such a practice and may therefore raise a different set of questions. It is with the formation of a human rights *jus commune* that we are concerned here. But in order to highlight this specific phenomenon, we must first refer to three other scenarios in which case law developed by one jurisdiction influences another jurisdiction, even in the absence of a hierarchical link between the two, but which falls outside our inquiry.

3.1. COMPARATIVE LAW ANALYSIS AS A MEANS OF IDENTIFYING AN EMERGING CONSENSUS

A first situation in which comparative analysis may be relied on, leading one court to ground its reasoning on the position adopted by other courts having faced a similar question of interpretation, is where a regional or international court, in its interpretation of a human rights treaty, takes into account the views expressed by domestic courts in the States parties to the specific treaty concerned. This is a common practice of the European Court of Human Rights, which routinely relies on the emerging 'European consensus' in support of its dynamic interpretation of the European Convention on Human Rights (ECHR) by referring to the jurisprudence of the highest courts of the domestic legal orders of the Council of Europe Member States.[13]

The practice is not without its pitfalls. The European Court of Human Rights may be accused of manipulating the information collected as, in identifying this 'European consensus', it does not feel bound to follow any mathematical average. It may appear to the external observer that the Court uses a comparative law analysis to arrive at a pre-conceived conclusion. Nevertheless, it generally serves to enhance the 'substantive legitimacy' of its decision; in other words,

13 For a systematic analysis, see C Rozakis, 'The European Judge as a Comparatist' (2005) 80 *Tulane Law Review* 257; or, more recently, K Dzehtsiarou, 'Does Consensus Matter? Legitimacy of European Consensus in the Case Law of the European Court of Human Rights' (2011) 3 *Public Law* 534; K Dzehtsiarou, *European Consensus and the Legitimacy of the European Court of Human Rights*, Cambridge University Press, Cambridge 2015. Like the article foreshadowing its conclusions (K Dzehtsiarou and L Lukshevich, 'Informed Decision-Making: The Comparative Endeavours of the Strasbourg Court' (2012) 30 *Netherlands Quarterly of Human Rights* 272), this volume builds on an empirical study, based in particular on a number of interviews with judges of the European Court of Human Rights and members of the Court's registry, to document the role of comparative law analysis in the jurisprudence of the Court.

its acceptability by the States parties to the Convention and thus the standing of the Court in the eyes of governments.[14] Indeed, basing the interpretation of an international treaty on such comparative analysis finds some support in the Vienna Convention on the Law of Treaties, which lists among the considerations that may guide the interpretation of international treaties 'any subsequent practice in the application of the treaty which establishes the agreement of the parties regarding its interpretation'.[15]

Though this practice certainly constitutes a remarkable example of the use of comparative law in international jurisprudence, it does not illustrate, strictly speaking, the shift towards a human rights *jus commune*. When an international mechanism established by a treaty refers to the practices of the States bound by the said treaty, such references remain internal to the system under which the mechanism operates; it is not equivalent to a court borrowing from sources external to that system. It therefore lies outside the scope of our inquiry.

3.2. DOMESTIC COURTS REFERRING TO THE INTERPRETATION OF A SPECIALISED MONITORING BODY ESTABLISHED UNDER A HUMAN RIGHTS INSTRUMENT FOR THE APPLICATION OF THAT INSTRUMENT

A second situation occurs where a domestic court takes into account the case law of a regional or international monitoring body – whether judicial or not – established in order to supervise compliance with a treaty to which the forum State is a party. This situation too should not be seen as illustrating the formation of a human rights *jus commune*. By taking as authoritative the interpretation provided by the regional or international monitoring body, the domestic court simply seeks to avoid engaging the responsibility of the State of which it is an organ.[16] For the national courts of the Council of Europe Member States, for instance, the case law emanating from the European Court of Human Rights simply provides the latest and the most authoritative reading of the ECHR.

---

14 Such 'substantive legitimacy' may be distinguished from the 'procedural legitimacy' that is grounded on the fact that the court follows certain rules related to the decision-making process; both differ from 'outcome legitimacy', which stems from the fact that the particular solution adopted by the court is seen as appropriate and workable in practice. On these different sources of legitimacy of international decision-making, see TM Franck, 'Why a Quest for Legitimacy?' (1987) 21 *UC Davis Law Review* 535, 543; K Dzehtsiarou and L Lukshevich, above n 13, pp 275–278.

15 Article 31 §3 (b) of the Vienna Convention on the Law of Treaties (signed on 23 May 1969 and in force since 27 January 1980, UNTS, vol 1155, p 331).

16 For a detailed exposition in the context of the ECHR, see O De Schutter, 'La coopération entre la Cour européenne des droits de l'homme et le juge national' (1997) *Revue belge du droit international* 21.

It is thus the best predictor of how that court would assess whether or not a violation has occurred in the case presented before the national authorities; by ignoring the jurisprudence of the European Court of Human Rights or by treating it as a mere source of inspiration rather than as authoritative, the domestic judge would quite deliberately run the risk of violating the Convention.[17]

In this situation, reference to international jurisprudence is not so much a matter of choice as it is a matter of duty; although we do see one court borrowing a solution from another court, this occurs within the supervisory system established by the human rights treaty in question. The distinction between such a situation and the formation of a human rights *jus commune* is not always clear-cut, however. First, where the authoritative nature of the jurisprudence emanating from the monitoring bodies established under the international instrument concerned is contested, as is the case for many human rights treaty bodies set up by the core United Nations human rights instruments or for the International Labour Organization (ILO) expert committees (the Committee on Freedom of Association and the Committee of Experts on the Application of Convention and Recommendations), the pronouncements from such monitoring bodies shall be treated as merely persuasive; they will be seen not as constraining the domestic court, but rather as expressing one view that the said court may (or may not) choose to seek inspiration from.[18]

---

17 Protocol No. 16 to the Convention for the Protection of Human Rights and Fundamental Freedoms, signed on 2 October 2013, provides for the highest courts and tribunals of the Contracting Parties to be able to request the European Court of Human Rights to give advisory opinions on questions of principle relating to the interpretation or application of the rights and freedoms defined in the ECHR or the protocols thereto. The Protocol thus acknowledges the authoritative nature of the interpretation provided of the ECHR by the European Court of Human Rights.

18 The debate concerning the weight to be given to concluding observations or final views adopted by the UN human rights treaty bodies remains lively. The Committee on International Human Rights Law and Practice of the International Law Association found that domestic courts afford 'considerable weight' to the interpretation of human rights treaties by the expert bodies that these treaties establish (see its Final Report on the Impact of the Work of the United Nations Human Rights Treaty Bodies on National Courts and Tribunals, adopted at the 2004 Berlin Conference). Particularly in countries where international law is considered to be directly applicable under relatively loose conditions, this tendency may be further strengthened by the position adopted in recent years by the International Court of Justice (see, in particular, the Advisory Opinion on the Legal Consequences of the Construction of a Wall in the Occupied Palestinian Territory, where the Court stated that it would in principle consider, in its interpretation of human rights treaties, the views expressed by the expert bodies established under such treaties (Advisory Opinion of 9 July 2004, ICJ Reports 2004, 136, paras 108–110); and the *Case of Ahmadou Sadio Diallo*, in which the International Court of Justice established a presumption that it would, in principle, follow the interpretation given by such expert bodies to the treaties concerned (International Court of Justice, *Case of Ahmadou Sadio Diallo (Republic of Guinea v Democratic Republic of Congo)*, judgment of 30 November 2010, §66)).

Second, in dualist domestic legal systems, which deny the competence of the domestic courts to apply directly international human rights law, international human rights law (and the jurisprudence developed at the international level) shall be treated as little more than as a guide to the interpretation of domestic constitutional or legislative provisions. It is to the extent that domestic rules can be interpreted in accordance with the requirements imposed on the State under international law instruments that courts may take such instruments into account; such was, for instance, the status of the ECHR before the British courts prior to the adoption of the 1998 Human Rights Act,[19] and such is still largely the case in international human rights law in general in Canada.[20]

---

19 See, e.g., *Salomon v Commissioner for Customs and Excise* (1967) 2 QB 116, 143 (international treaties as a source of interpretation of domestic legislation adopted in order to implement the said treaties in the domestic legal order); *R v Secretary of State for the Home Department, ex parte Brind* (1990) 1 All ER 469, 477 ('when the terms of primary legislation are fairly capable of bearing two or more meanings and the court, in pursuance of its duty to apply domestic law, is concerned to divine and define its true and only meaning ... various prima facie rules of construction have to be applied ... To these can be added, in appropriate cases, a presumption that Parliament has legislated in a manner consistent, rather than inconsistent, with the United Kingdom's treaty obligations' (Lord Donaldson MR)), although, as cautioned by Lord Bridge in the proceedings on appeal of this judgment, 'the presumption whereby the courts prefer [the interpretation] which avoids conflict between our domestic legislation and our international treaty obligations is a mere canon of construction which involves no importation of international law into the domestic field' (*Brind and Others v Secretary of State for the Home Department* (1991) 1 All ER 720). For attempts to systematise the case law, see P Duffy, 'English Law and the European Convention on Human Rights' (1980) *International and Comparative Law Quarterly* 585; or C Warbrick, 'Rights, the European Convention on Human Rights and English Law' (1994) *European Law Review* 34. For an overview, see O De Schutter, *Fonction de juger et droits fondamentaux*, Bruylant, Brussels 1999, pp 282–291.

20 See in particular *A.G. Canada v A.G. Ontario* (The Labour Conventions Case), 937 AC 355 (PC); *Bancroft v University of Toronto* (1986) 24 DLR (4th) 620 (Ont. H.C.); *Re Vincent and Minister of Employment and Immigration* (1983), 148 DLR (3rd) 385 (FCA); *Reference re Public Service Employee Relations Act (Alta.)* [1987] 1 SCR 313. For instance, in *R v Keegstra* ([1990] 3 SCR 697 (judgment of 13 December 1990)), a case concerning the compatibility with freedom of expression of the criminalisation of hate propaganda to which we return below, the Supreme Court of Canada considers the prescriptions imposed under the International Convention on the Elimination of All Forms of Racial Discrimination (ICERD) and the International Covenant on Civil and Political Rights, two instruments to which Canada is a party, simply to note that these treaties 'demonstrate that the prohibition of hate-promoting expression is considered to be not only compatible with a signatory nation's guarantee of human rights, but is as well an obligatory aspect of this guarantee' (Dickson CJ for the majority). Though the Supreme Court remarked that 'the international human rights obligations taken on by Canada reflect the values and principles of a free and democratic society, and thus those values and principles that underlie the Charter itself' and that 'international human rights law and Canada's commitments in that area are of particular significance in assessing the importance of Parliament's objective under s. 1 [of the Charter, which requires that restrictions to the rights and freedoms be justified]', absent from the reasoning of the Court is any clear commitment to follow the requirements of these instruments as well as the jurisprudence of its monitoring bodies, unless they converge with the prescriptions of the Charter; indeed, the ICERD and the ICCPR are treated no differently

In monist legal systems, which treat directly applicable international law as equivalent to domestic rules, there is generally no need to rely on such a doctrine of conform interpretation, although this obviously can help harmonise the understanding of human rights as stipulated in national legislative or constitutional instruments with that of international instruments to which the State is a party; indeed, such a practice is occasionally prescribed in the domestic constitution.[21]

Third, situations may occur in which the domestic court has a certain degree of discretion to exercise as to the interpretation to give to the human rights treaty invoked by the alleged victim (for instance, because the 'authoritative' interpretation provided by the international supervisory body is ambiguous) and then turns to comparative law to assess the answer of other domestic courts confronted with the same question. The 2010 *Cadder* case provides an illustration of this.[22] The UK Supreme Court was asked in that case to re-examine the earlier position of the British courts concerning the right of a person detained by the police to have access to a lawyer upon being first questioned. The European Court of Human Rights had affirmed such a right for the first time in the *Salduz* case of 2008, where it found a violation of Article 6 §3 (c) of the ECHR (the right to legal assistance), in conjunction with Article 6 §1 (the right to a fair trial), on account of the applicant's lack of legal assistance while he was in police custody.[23] The European Court of Human Rights concluded that, in principle, 'access to a lawyer should be provided as from the first interrogation of a suspect by the police, *unless* it is demonstrated in the light of the particular circumstances

---

in the Supreme Court's judgment than the ECHR, despite the fact that Canada is a party to the former instruments and not to the latter. That international human rights instruments should be treated as mere sources of inspiration for the interpretation of the Canadian Charter is a broadly held view; it is perhaps telling that, in his dissenting opinion to Keegstra, McLachlin J refers to the ICERD and the ICCPR to distinguish the Canadian Charter's approach to freedom of expression as being specific: 'The guarantees of free expression in those documents explicitly permit a wide variety of limitations on free expression – limitations which the person asserting the right of free expression must observe. By contrast, the Canadian guarantee of free expression is more comprehensive.' On the relationship of the United Kingdom and Canada to international human rights law, see generally CPM Waters, *British and Canadian Perspectives on International Law*, Martinus Nijhoff Publishers, Leiden 2006.

21 For instance, Article 10 para 2 of the 1978 Spanish Constitution provides that: 'The principles relating to the fundamental rights and liberties recognized by the Constitution shall be interpreted in conformity with the Universal Declaration of Human Rights and the international treaties and agreements thereon ratified by Spain.' Similarly, Article 39 of the 1996 Constitution of South Africa (in force since 4 February 1997) provides that: 'When interpreting the Bill of Rights, a court, tribunal or forum … (b) must consider international law.'

22 Supreme Court of the United Kingdom, *Cadder (Appellant) v Her Majesty's Advocate (Scotland) (Respondent)* [2010] UKSC 43 (judgment of 26 October 2010).

23 *Salduz v Turkey*, no. 36391/02, ECHR 2008.

of each case that there are compelling reasons to restrict this right' (emphasis added). 'The rights of the defence', it stated, 'will in principle be irretrievably prejudiced when incriminating statements made during police interrogation without access to a lawyer are used for a conviction.'[24] The UK Supreme Court therefore had to decide which weight was to be given to the *Salduz* jurisprudence and, taking into account the 'unless' formula of the European Court, whether safeguards provided for the detainee in Scotland that the European Court of Human Rights by definition could not have considered in *Salduz* could compensate for the absence of a lawyer during the first interrogation.

In answering the first question, the UK Supreme Court recalled that, under section 2(1) of the Human Rights Act 1998, British courts deciding a question arising in connection with a Convention right must 'take into account' any decision of the European Court of Human Rights. This principle had been reiterated in the case law of the Supreme Court itself (or, as it was then, the House of Lords),[25] although that same court did not hesitate to depart from precedents set in Strasbourg where it considered that the British legal system had been misunderstood or where the specificities of the common law had not been considered.[26] But perhaps more noteworthy is that the Supreme Court sought guidance from the case law that followed the *Salduz* judgment in other Member States of the Council of Europe: prompted by an amicus brief submitted by the non-governmental organisation JUSTICE, it referred specifically to the position of the Dutch Supreme Court, as well as to the position of the highest judicial bodies in France, including the Constitutional Council (Conseil constitutionnel), and concluded from this comparative analysis that 'if Scotland were not to follow the example of the others it would be almost alone among all the [Council of Europe] member states in not doing so'.[27]

In the *Cadder* case, therefore, comparative law served to support reliance of the UK Supreme Court on the jurisprudence of the European Court of Human Rights, insofar as such an analysis demonstrated the authority that such jurisprudence had exercised on other supreme judicial tribunals in Europe. Again, however, this scenario does not illustrate the formation of a human rights *jus commune* as such, as the product of judicial dialogue across jurisdictions. Rather, it represents a hybrid: it is still the ECHR, as made applicable before British courts under the Human Rights Act, that is the source applied,

24 Ibid, §55.

25 See *R (Alconbury Developments Ltd) v Secretary of State for the Environment, Transport and the Regions* [2001] UKHL 23, [2003] 2 AC 295, para 26 (per Lord Slynn of Hadley); *R (Anderson) v Secretary of State for the Home Department* [2002] UKHL 46, [2003] 1 AC 837, para 18 (per Lord Bingham of Cornhill).

26 See *Cadder*, §45.

27 Ibid, §49.

and it is because foreign jurisdictions had to interpret the Convention (rather than similarly worded norms from their domestic legal systems) that they are cited as authorities.

3.3. INTERNATIONAL COURTS REFERRING TO THE INTERPRETATION OF THE SPECIALISED MONITORING BODY ESTABLISHED UNDER A HUMAN RIGHTS INSTRUMENT FOR THE APPLICATION OF THAT INSTRUMENT ITSELF

Our third situation is in a way the reverse of the previous one. It occurs when an international court with a general competence (i.e., with a jurisdiction not limited to any particular international instrument) takes into account the interpretation given to a human rights treaty by the monitoring body specifically established to supervise compliance with that treaty. Consider again the position adopted by the International Court of Justice in the *Ahmadou Sadio Diallo* case.[28] Mr Diallo was a Guinean businessman who had filed various claims against the Democratic Republic of Congo (DRC), where he had located his activities, as well as against a company of which the DRC was a shareholder. He had been arrested, detained and subsequently expelled by the authorities of the DRC. The Republic of Guinea alleged that this had led to the violation of a number of rules of international law, including various provisions of human rights treaties to which both States were parties: the expulsion of Mr Diallo was denounced as a breach of Article 13 of the International Covenant on Civil and Political Rights (ICCPR),[29] as well as of Article 12, paragraph 4, of the African Charter on Human and Peoples' Rights,[30] and his arrest and detention were said to have violated Article 9, paragraphs 1 and 2 of the Covenant, and Article 6 of the African Charter. In addition, Mr Diallo was alleged to have suffered conditions of detention amounting to inhuman or degrading treatment as prohibited by international law.

In assessing the claims of the Republic of Guinea, the International Court of Justice first provides its own interpretation of the Covenant. It then adds, however, that its reading 'is fully corroborated by the jurisprudence of the Human Rights Committee established by the Covenant to ensure compliance with that instrument by the States parties' and which since it was created

28 The case was referred to above, n 18.

29 International Covenant on Civil and Political Rights, opened for signature in New York on 16 December 1966, in force on 23 March 1979 (UNTS, vol 999, p 171).

30 African Charter on Human and Peoples' Rights, opened for signature on 27 June 1981, in force on 21 October 1986 (OAU Doc CAB/LEG/67/3 rev 5, 21 ILM 58 (1982), UNTS, vol 1520, p 217).

'has built up a considerable body of interpretative case law, in particular through its findings in response to the individual communications which may be submitted to it in respect of States parties to the first Optional Protocol, and in the form of its "General Comments".[31] This 'case law', the Court notes, should be given great weight in the interpretation of the ICCPR:

> Although the Court is in no way obliged, in the exercise of its judicial functions, to model its own interpretation of the Covenant on that of the Committee, it believes that it should ascribe great weight to the interpretation adopted by this independent body that was established specifically to supervise the application of that treaty. The point here is to achieve the necessary clarity and the essential consistency of international law, as well as legal security, to which both the individuals with guaranteed rights and the States obliged to comply with treaty obligations are entitled.[32]

The World Court takes a similar approach to the African Charter on Human and Peoples' Rights, its interpretation of which is corroborated by the jurisprudence of the African Commission on Human and Peoples' Rights.[33]

Whereas this attitude of the International Court of Justice is certainly such as to favour legal certainty by ensuring a consistent interpretation of the instruments binding upon States, it would not qualify as illustrating the phenomenon of human rights *jus commune* as such. Here we do not have a situation in which one instrument, applicable to the case presented before a monitoring body, is read in the light of the interpretation given to another instrument by another body with which there exists no institutional link. No transplantation or borrowing from one system to another has taken place; what the example illustrates is simply that a division of labour is gradually emerging between various mechanisms that are tasked with the interpretation of the same legal instrument.

In the judgment it delivered in the *Ahmadou Sadio Diallo* case, however, the Court goes further:

> [It] also notes that the interpretation by the European Court of Human Rights and the Inter-American Court of Human Rights, respectively, of Article 1 of Protocol No. 7 to the (European) Convention for the Protection of Human Rights and Fundamental

---

31 International Court of Justice, *Case of Ahmadou Sadio Diallo* (*Republic of Guinea v Democratic Republic of Congo*), judgment of 30 November 2010, §66.

32 Ibid.

33 See ibid, §67: 'when the Court is called upon … to apply a regional instrument for the protection of human rights, it must take due account of the interpretation of that instrument adopted by the independent bodies which have been specifically created, if such has been the case, to monitor the sound application of the treaty in question. In the present case, the interpretation given above of Article 12, paragraph 4, of the African Charter is consonant with the case law of the African Commission on Human and Peoples' Rights established by Article 30 of the said Charter'.

> Freedoms and Article 22, paragraph 6, of the American Convention on Human Rights – the said provisions being close in substance to those of the Covenant and the African Charter which the Court is applying in the present case – is consistent with what has been found in respect of the latter provisions.[34]

In contrast to the reliance on the case law of the Human Rights Committee and of the African Commission on Human and Peoples' Rights, these references do illustrate the contribution of the International Court of Justice to the emergence of a human rights *jus commune*. Neither the ECHR nor the American Convention on Human Rights was applicable to the case before it. Yet the International Court of Justice refers to these instruments, and to the interpretation given to them by specialised courts, because of the similarity of language and because these instruments derive – as do the ICCPR and the African Charter – from the Universal Declaration of Human Rights. That is the common law of human rights.

4. DEVELOPING THE HUMAN RIGHTS *JUS COMMUNE*

In contrast to the three situations which the previous section has outlined, it is indeed the formation of a human rights *jus commune* as such that we witness where international courts of expert bodies refer to one another simply as a means to strengthen the legitimacy of the views they express, although they belong to different systems and apply different treaties. Therefore, for ease of expression, reference shall be made here to 'foreign jurisprudence'. The phrase serves to indicate that human rights *jus commune*, properly conceived, consists in one human rights body borrowing from the interpretation of human rights law by another body, in the absence of any formal link between the two bodies concerned. The borrowing jurisdiction and the source jurisdiction operate separately from another. Thus, in the kind of scenario explored here, the 'receiving' human rights body seeks inspiration in, or feels bound by, the interpretation made of a human rights norm by another human rights body, which faced a similar question of interpretation in a different material and institutional context. How 'binding' should such an interpretation be for the 'receiving' body, or should the authority of such interpretation be merely persuasive? Which difficulties would the 'receiving' body face if it endeavoured to follow such an interpretation?

To provide an illustration, consider how human rights bodies gradually affirmed a duty of States parties to comply with the provisional measures recommended by the judicial or quasi-judicial bodies established under

[34] Ibid, §68.

human rights treaties, when such bodies receive individual applications or communications from individuals allegedly at risk. The major international human rights treaties are silent about the possibility for these bodies to grant such interim measures. However, the idea has progressively emerged that this power of human rights bodies is inherent in their jurisdiction and that it should be recognised in the name of the effectiveness of the protection of human rights. This development is almost entirely the combined result of expert bodies asserting a power they were not explicitly attributed under the treaties establishing them, and of the strength of the human rights *jus commune*.

The 1984 Convention against Torture and Other Cruel, Inhuman or Degrading Treatment or Punishment provided the departure point.[35] When, acting in accordance with Article 18(2) of the Convention, the Committee against Torture adopted its Rules of Procedure, it included Rule 108 §9, enabling it to adopt provisional measures in proceedings brought by individuals alleging a violation of the Convention against Torture.[36] In the case of *Cecilia Rosana Núñez Chipana v Venezuela*, it took the view that non-compliance with such provisional measures should be considered a violation of the Convention, as:

> the State party, in ratifying the Convention and voluntarily accepting the Committee's competence [to examine individual communications] under article 22, undertook to cooperate with it in good faith in applying the procedure. Compliance with the provisional measures called for by the Committee in cases it considers reasonable is essential in order to protect the person in question from irreparable harm, which could, moreover, nullify the end result of the proceedings before the Committee.[37]

Acting under the ICCPR, the Human Rights Committee followed this lead. Under Rule 92 of its rules of procedure, which the Human Rights Committee adopted in accordance with Article 39(2) of the ICCPR, the Human Rights Committee

---

35 Convention against Torture and Other Cruel, Inhuman or Degrading Treatment or Punishment, signed in New York on 10 December 1984, in force on 26 June 1987 (UNTS, vol 1465, p 85).

36 See Rule 108 §9 of the Rules of Procedure (CAT/C/3/Rev 3) (13 July 1998). This is now Rule 114(1) in the most recently update version of the Rules of Procedure (CAT/C/3/Rev.6) (1 August 2014): 'At any time after the receipt of a complaint, the Committee, a working group, or the Rapporteur(s) on new complaints and interim measures may transmit to the State party concerned, for its urgent consideration, a request that it take such interim measures as the Committee considers necessary to avoid irreparable damage to the victim or victims of alleged violations.'

37 Committee against Torture, *Cecilia Rosana Núñez Chipana v Venezuela*, final views of 10 November 1998, Communication No 110/1998 (CAT/C/21/D/110/1998). Article 22 of the Convention against Torture and Other Cruel, Inhuman or Degrading Treatment or Punishment describes the competence of the Committee to receive and consider communications from or on behalf of individuals subject to the jurisdiction of States parties to the Convention who claim to be victims of a violation by a State party of the provisions of the Convention, provided that the State concerned has made a declaration to that effect.

'may, prior to forwarding its views on the communication to the State party concerned, inform that State of its views as to whether interim measures may be desirable to avoid irreparable damage to the victim of the alleged violation'.[38] In the case of *Dante Piandiong, Jesus Morallos and Archie Bulan v The Philippines*, which it decided in 2000, the Human Rights Committee considered that a refusal of a State to comply with such measures, 'especially by irreversible measures such as the execution of the alleged victim or his/her deportation from the country, undermines the protection of Covenant rights through the Optional Protocol [providing for the possibility of individual complaints filed by alleged victims of violations of the ICCPR]'.[39] It has repeated this statement subsequently,[40] confirming its view that the States parties to the Covenant could be under an obligation to comply with the interim measures indicated by the Committee. Just like the Committee against Torture, the Human Rights Committee did so despite the fact that the power to adopt such interim measures was not attributed to the Committee under the text of the Covenant itself.

As long as these statements remained those of expert bodies, whose authority to deliver binding statements to the States parties remains contested, they may not have attracted much attention. In 2005, however, in the case of *Mamatkulov and Askarov v Turkey*, the European Court of Human Rights itself considered for the first time in a final judgment that a refusal by a State party to the ECHR to comply with an interim measure indicated by a Chamber of the Court or its President on the basis of Article 39 of the Rules of the Court constitutes a violation of Article 34 of the Convention, which imposes an obligation on the Contracting Parties 'not to hinder in any way the effective exercise' of the right to individual application.[41] This represented a shift in attitude from the part of the Court. In its previous case law, while finding that there existed a general practice of States parties to the Convention to comply with such interim measures, the Court fell short from identifying the emergence of a rule of a customary nature in the application of the ECHR.[42]

---

38 Rules of Procedure of the Human Rights Committee (CCPR/C/3/Rev10) (11 January 2012).

39 Human Rights Committee, final views adopted on 19 October 2000 on Communication no. 869/1999 (CCPR/C/70/D/869/1999), Annual Rep I, p 181.

40 See, e.g., Human Rights Committee, *Weiss v Austria*, Communication no. 1086/02, final views of 8 May 2003 (CCPR/C/77/D/1086/2002).

41 *Mamatkulov and Askarov v Turkey*, no. 46827/99, ECHR 2005.

42 See, e.g., *Cruz Varas v Sweden*, no. 15576/89, §100, ECHR 1991: 'The practice of Contracting Parties in this area shows that there has been almost total compliance with Rule 36 indications [indications given by the European Commission of Human Rights or its President that, in the interests of the proceedings, the parties should refrain from adopting certain measures, based on Rule 36 of the Rules of Procedure of the European Commission of Human Rights]. Subsequent practice could be taken as establishing the agreement of Contracting States regarding the interpretation of a Convention provision (see, mutatis mutandis, [*Soering v United Kingdom*, no. 14038/88, §103, ECHR 1989], and Article 31 §3 (b) of the Vienna Convention of 23 May 1969 on the Law of Treaties) but not to create new rights and obligations

Indeed, there was good reason for the Court to be cautious. Although in *Mamatkulov and Askarov v Turkey*, the Court cited in support of its position the practice both of the International Court of Justice and that of the Inter-American Court of Human Rights, the Rules of the European Court of Human Rights are adopted by the plenary Court.[43] They are thus not agreed upon by the States parties to the Convention. Their status therefore differs markedly from that of Article 41 of the Statute of the International Court of Justice,[44] which the *LaGrand (Germany v United States)* judgment of 27 June 2001 interpreted as imposing on the States parties to a dispute before the Court an obligation to comply with the provisional measures indicated under that provision, despite the vague character of the wording of that provision.[45] Nor may Article 39 of the Rules adopted by the European Court of Human Rights be considered equivalent to Article 63(2) of the American Convention on Human Rights, which provides explicitly for a power of the Inter-American Court of Human Rights to adopt provisional measures 'in cases of extreme gravity and urgency, and when necessary to avoid irreparable damage to persons'. Both the Statute of the International Court of Justice and the American Convention on Human Rights are international treaties to whose terms the States parties have agreed. In contrast, no equivalent clause exists in the ECHR. In *Mamatkulov and Askarov v Turkey*, the Court nevertheless considered that the precedents set by the Committee against Torture and the Human Rights Committee authorised it to consider, like these expert bodies, that the obligatory character of interim measures should be considered as a condition of the effectiveness of the protection provided to the individual by a system of individual communications. It stated:

> The Court observes that the ICJ, the Inter-American Court of Human Rights, the Human Rights Committee and the Committee against Torture of the United Nations,

---

which were not included in the Convention at the outset ... In any event, as reflected in the various recommendations of the Council of Europe bodies [calling upon the States parties to the Convention to agree to recognising the Court a power to adopt provisional measures of a binding character], the practice of complying with Rule 36 indications cannot have been based on a belief that these indications gave rise to a binding obligation ... *It was rather a matter of good faith co-operation with the Commission in cases where this was considered reasonable and practicable*' (emphasis added). For comments, see, e.g., R Bernhardt, 'Interim Measures of Protection under the European Convention on Human Rights' in R Bernhardt (ed), *Interim Measures Indicated by International Courts*, Berlin, Springer Verlag 1994, p 102; R St J McDonald, 'Interim Measures in International Law, with Special Reference to the European System for the Protection of Human Rights' (1992) 52 *Zeitschrift für ausländisches öffentliches Recht und Völkerrecht* 703.

43 See, in its current version, Article 25(d) ECHR.

44 3 Bevans 1179; 59 Stat 1031; TS 993 (1945).

45 Article 41 of the Statute of the International Court of Justice provides: '1. The Court shall have the power to indicate, if it considers that circumstances so require, any provisional measures which ought to be taken to preserve the respective rights of either party. 2. Pending the final decision, notice of the measures suggested shall forthwith be given to the parties and to the Security Council.'

> although operating under different treaty provisions to those of the Court, have confirmed in their reasoning in recent decisions that the preservation of the asserted rights of the parties in the face of the risk of irreparable damage represents an essential objective of interim measures in international law. Indeed it can be said that, whatever the legal system in question, the proper administration of justice requires that no irreparable action be taken while proceedings are pending.

The episode provides a clear example of human rights bodies developing a doctrine, motivated perhaps by the need to ensure an effective protection of human rights, but which is difficult to reconcile with an orthodox (some might say conservative) view of international law.

That this development was made possible by a number of human rights bodies moving in the same direction and, in part, legitimising their interpretative inventivity by referring to one another's case law seems hardly contestable. Indeed, the pressure to transpose solutions developed in one system into another system is such that human rights bodies occasionally feel compelled to justify departing from precedents established by other such bodies, as if they were part of the same legal system – more precisely, as if such precedents had more than mere persuasive authority and were actually binding. Thus, in *Kindler v Canada*, which it was presented with in 1991, the Human Rights Committee went out of its way to explain what distinguishes the situation it was confronted with from the situation that had given rise to the judgment the European Court of Human Rights adopted on 7 July 1989 in *Soering v United Kingdom*. In this latter case, the European Court of Human Rights had concluded that the extradition to the United States of Jens Soering would expose him to inhuman treatment, contrary to Article 3 ECHR, the equivalent to Article 7 ICCPR. Like Soering, Kindler was a fugitive who was threatened with extradition to the United States, where he feared he would face the death penalty. Should the Human Rights Committee follow the assessment of the European Court of Human Rights in a judgment delivered just a few years earlier? The Committee believed not:

> In determining whether, in a particular case, the imposition of capital punishment could constitute a violation of article 7, the Committee will have regard to the relevant personal factors regarding the author, the specific conditions of detention on death row, and whether the proposed method of execution is particularly abhorrent. In this context the Committee has had careful regard to the judgment given by the European Court of Human Rights in the *Soering v United Kingdom* case [European Court of Human Rights, judgment of 7 July 1989.] It notes that important facts leading to the judgment of the European Court are distinguishable on material points from the facts in the present case. In particular, the facts differ as to the age and mental state of the offender, and the conditions on death row in the respective prison systems. The author's counsel made no specific submissions on prison conditions in Pennsylvania [the US state where Kindler was facing prosecution; Soering was to be

> prosecuted in West Virginia], or about the possibility or the effects of prolonged delay in the execution of sentence; nor was any submission made about the specific method of execution. The Committee has also noted in the *Soering* case that, in contrast to the present case, there was a simultaneous request for extradition by a State where the death penalty would not be imposed [Germany, of which Jens Soering was a national, had requested that he be extradited to that country rather than returned to the United States, where he had committed a crime].[46]

To thus distinguish the case of *Kindler* from that of *Soering* is not to deny the authoritative value of the decision of the European Court; rather, it is the opposite – it is to acknowledge its weight as precedent. Yet, there is no institutional link between the Human Rights Committee and the European Court of Human Rights, hierarchical or otherwise; the only link that binds the two bodies is that they apply treaties which are both inspired by the Universal Declaration of Human Rights and thus use similar wording.

It is this kind of mutual borrowing that we are growing accustomed to. Indeed, the practice has become so widespread that it is almost institutionalised and has occasionally been codified, for instance, in the South African post-apartheid Constitution[47] or in the 1981 African Charter of Human and Peoples' Rights.[48] The reasons for this development are obvious enough. In addition to the replication of language from the Universal Declaration of Human Rights in

---

46 Human Rights Committee, *Kindler v Canada*, Comm No. 470/1991, decision of 30 June 1993, §15.3.

47 Article 39(1) of the 1996 Constitution of South Africa was already referred to above (n 21). The full provision reads: 'When interpreting the Bill of Rights, a court, tribunal or forum (a) must promote the values that underlie an open and democratic society based on human dignity, equality and freedom; (b) must consider international law; and (c) may consider foreign law.' Article 35(1) of the Interim Constitution of 1993 used even more explicit wording: 'In interpreting the provisions of [Chapter 3 on fundamental rights] a court of law shall promote the values which underlie an open and democratic society based on freedom and equality and shall, where applicable, have regard to public international law applicable to the protection of the rights entrenched in this Chapter, and may have regard to comparable foreign case law.'

48 Article 60 of the African Charter provides that the African Commission on Human and Peoples' Rights shall 'draw inspiration from international law on human and peoples' rights, particularly from the provisions of various African instruments on Human and Peoples' Rights, the Charter of the United Nations, the Charter of the Organisation of African Unity, the Universal Declaration of Human Rights, other instruments adopted by the United Nations and by African countries in the field of Human and Peoples' Rights, as well as from the provisions of various instruments adopted within the Specialised Agencies of the United Nations of which the Parties to the present Charter are members'. Article 61 in turn prescribes that the Commission 'shall also take into consideration, as subsidiary measures to determine the principles of law, other general or special international conventions, laying down rules expressly recognised by Member States of the Organisation of African Unity, African practices consistent with international norms on Human and Peoples' Rights, customs generally accepted as law, general principles of law recognised by African States as well as legal precedents and doctrine'.

a large number of constitutions and in various regional human rights treaties, they include the much-improved accessibility of case law through the internet, particularly as regards the case law of supreme courts or constitutional courts, since the early 1990s; the growing role of non-governmental organisations before regional or international courts, acting as amici curiae, which appear particularly keen to present the court with detailed comparative law analyses, in which the most progressive jurisprudence is presented in a digestible form; the desire of human rights bodies (whether judicial or not) not to be seen as providing a weaker level of protection than that provided by other, similar bodies; and, finally, a simple principle of judicial economy, leading human rights bodies to seek inspiration from solutions developed elsewhere, since such solutions are presumed to have been based on carefully weighed considerations and, perhaps, to have induced at least some reliance either by individuals or by States so that not following precedents established by other, 'foreign' courts deserves at least a special justification. These various circumstances have been well articulated elsewhere and, as such, there is no need to revisit them here.[49] Rather, the next section will ask whether the judicial method that this leads to is workable and what challenges still have to be addressed.

5. THE PROBLEM OF CONSISTENCY IN THE FORMATION OF THE HUMAN RIGHTS *JUS COMMUNE*

The challenges associated with the formation of a common law of human rights fall into two categories. Some of these challenges concern the use of case law as a source of law, how the doctrine of precedent may constrain judges and whether there is a principled way to rely on distinctions to adapt general principles to specific cases. All legal system face these challenges, although they have been discussed more explicitly in common law jurisdictions where the binding character of judicial precedent is acknowledged openly rather than abided to in secret. But other challenges concern the practice by which we have defined the human rights *jus commune*, in which one 'borrowing' jurisdiction treats as persuasive, or to a certain extent binding, an interpretation provided by a 'source' jurisdiction, which is external to the system in which the receiving mechanism operates. As long as such practice remains ad hoc and unsystematic, it may undermine the legitimacy of decision-making in the very process of seeking to strengthen it. But can a proper methodology be designed for such borrowing to develop in a more principled manner?

---

49 C McCrudden, 'A Common Law of Human Rights?: Transnational Judicial Conversations on Constitutional Rights' (2000) 20 *Oxford Journal of Legal Studies* 499.

The practice of the European Court of Human Rights illustrates the problem.[50] Two examples are considered here. The first example concerns the use, in the case law of the Court, of the views expressed on questions of interpretation by the ILO expert bodies or by the European Committee of Social Rights, operating under the European Social Charter. The second example concerns the relationship between the Court and the Human Rights Committee, where the ICCPR includes provisions very similar, if not identical, to those of the ECHR.

5.1. DEVELOPING THE HUMAN RIGHTS COMMON LAW IN THE AREA OF WORKERS' RIGHTS

In the well-known case of *National Union of Rail, Maritime and Transport Workers v United Kingdom*, the European Court of Human Rights was asked whether the statutory ban on secondary industrial action was a disproportionate interference with the freedom of association recognised under Article 11 ECHR.[51] In denouncing such interference, the applicant union referred, in particular, to the recognition of the right to strike by the Committee on Freedom of Association and the Committee of Experts on the Application of Conventions and Recommendations, two expert bodies established within the ILO, which had based their conclusions in this regard on Articles 3 and 10 of the Freedom of Association and Protection of the Right to Organise Convention, 1948 (No. 87),[52] an instrument ratified by the United Kingdom.[53]

The European Court of Human Rights also took note of the position of the European Committee of Social Rights, the body of experts in charge of supervising compliance with the European Social Charter, which – like the ILO bodies – had taken issue at the British rules concerning 'solidarity' strikes. Article 6 §4 of the European Social Charter provides that 'with a view to ensuring

[50] On the practice of the European Court of Human Rights, see D Staes, 'When the European Court Refers to External Instruments: Mapping and Justifications', doctoral thesis under the supervision of I Rorive and S Van Drooghenbroeck, April 2017, defended at the Université libre de Bruxelles and the Université Saint-Louis as part of the Human Rights Integration project.

[51] *National Union of Rail, Maritime and Transport Workers v United Kingdom*, no. 31045/10, ECHR 2014.

[52] UNTS, vol 68, p 17.

[53] As regards secondary industrial action (or 'sympathy' strikes), the ILO Committee of Experts had noted in particular that 'a general prohibition of this form of strike action could lead to abuse, particularly in the context of globalization characterized by increasing interdependence and the internationalization of production, and that workers should be able to take such action, provided that the initial strike they are supporting is itself lawful'. (*Giving globalisation a human face*, International Labour Office, 2012, at para 125, cited in *National Union of Rail, Maritime and Transport Workers v United Kingdom*, above, n 51, §30). Similarly, the Committee on Freedom of Association considered this form of industrial action to be protected by international labour law: see ibid, §31.

the effective exercise of the right to bargain collectively', the States parties to the Charter that have accepted this clause recognise 'the right of workers and employers to collective action in cases of conflicts of interest, including the right to strike, subject to obligations that might arise out of collective agreements previously entered into'. On the basis of this provision, the European Committee of Social Rights had criticised the United Kingdom for not ensuring immunity from dismissal of workers engaging in secondary industrial action (so-called 'sympathy strikes', in solidarity with workers of another enterprise), relying in that regard on the conclusions reached by the ILO Committee of Experts.[54]

But which weight, if any, is to be given to these findings? In the case of *Demir and Baykara v Turkey* referred to above,[55] another case concerning the implication for unions of freedom of association, the Court had stated that: 'The consensus emerging from specialised international instruments and from the practice of Contracting States may constitute a relevant consideration for the Court when it interprets the provisions of the Convention in specific cases.'[56] '[I]n defining the meaning of terms and notions in the text of the Convention', the Court explained:

> [It] can and must take into account elements of international law other than the Convention, the interpretation of such elements by competent organs, and the practice of European States reflecting their common values. The consensus emerging from specialised international instruments and from the practice of Contracting States may constitute a relevant consideration for the Court when it interprets the provisions of the Convention in specific cases.[57]

The Court had taken the bold step, in *Demir and Baykara*, of imposing on Turkey an interpretation of Article 11 ECHR that extended the right to form trade unions to municipal civil servants and that derived from freedom of association a right to collective bargaining. The Court developed this interpretation by taking into account other instruments of international law to

---

54 European Committee of Social Rights, Conclusions XIII-1 (1993) and Conclusions XIX-3 (2010), cited in the *National Union of Rail, Maritime and Transport Workers v United Kingdom* judgment, above, n 51, §§36–37.

55 See above, n 10.

56 *Demir and Baykara v Turkey*, above, n 10, §85. For an extensive discussion of the *Demir and Baykara* case under this angle, see J Arato, 'Constitutional Transformation in the ECtHR: Strasbourg's Extensive Recourse to External Rules of International Law' (2012) 37 *Brooklyn Journal of International Law* 349–387. See also C Barrow, '*Demir and Baykara v Turkey*: Breathing Life into Article 11' (2010) 4 *European Human Rights Law Review* 419–423; and KD Ewing and J Hendy, 'The Dramatic Implications of *Demir and Baykara*' (2010) 39(1) *Industrial Law Journal* 2–51 (also addressing the broader ramifications of the judgment before English courts and for the relationships with economic freedoms protected under EU law).

57 Ibid, *Demir and Baykara v Turkey*.

guide its interpretation of this clause,[58] without limiting itself to the instruments ratified by the State concerned:

> it is not necessary for the respondent State to have ratified the entire collection of instruments that are applicable in respect of the precise subject matter of the case concerned. It will be sufficient for the Court that the relevant international instruments denote a continuous evolution in the norms and principles applied in international law or in the domestic law of the majority of member States of the Council of Europe and show, in a precise area, that there is common ground in modern societies.[59]

The implications of this approach were remarkable. Although Article 11(2) ECHR states that the guarantee of freedom of association 'shall not prevent the imposition of lawful restrictions on the exercise of these rights by members of the armed forces, of the police or of the administration of the State', the Court considered that 'the restrictions imposed on the three groups mentioned in Article 11 are to be construed strictly'. Such restrictions could affect the 'exercise' of the right to organise, but not its 'very essence'; moreover, 'it is incumbent on the State concerned to show the legitimacy of any restrictions to such persons' right to organise'.[60] In support of this reading, it cited Article 5 of the European Social Charter and Article 22 ICCPR, both of which allow the States parties to restrict the exercise of the right to freedom of association of members of the armed forces and of the police, but without referring to members of the administration of the State, as well as ILO Convention No. 87 on Freedom of Association and Protection of the Right to Organise, Article 2 of which provides that all workers, without distinction whatsoever, have the right to establish and to join organisations of their own choosing.[61]

In addition, the Court considered that by annulling ex nunc a collective agreement concluded by a Turkish union of municipal civil servants, the Turkish courts had violated the right to freedom of association; it saw the right to bargain collectively with the employer as 'one of the essential elements' of the right to form and to join trade unions for the protection of one's interests as set forth in Article 11 ECHR, an interpretation that the Court had refused to give in the past but that it felt compelled to reconsider 'having regard to the developments in labour law, both international and national, and to the practice

---

58 Ibid, §76: 'Being made up of a set of rules and principles that are accepted by the vast majority of States, the common international or domestic law standards of European States reflect a reality that the Court cannot disregard when it is called upon to clarify the scope of a Convention provision that more conventional means of interpretation have not enabled it to establish with a sufficient degree of certainty.'

59 Ibid, §86.

60 Ibid, §97.

61 Ibid, §§37 and 100.

of Contracting States in such matters'.[62] As remarked above,[63] it is noteworthy that, to reach this conclusion, the Court took into account in particular Article 6 §2 of the European Social Charter, although this is a provision of the Charter that Turkey had not accepted in the à la carte system of the Charter. Though this paragraph of the Charter does not as such oblige authorities to enter into collective agreements, the Court relied on the meaning attributed to it by the European Committee of Social Rights, to the effect that 'States which impose restrictions on collective bargaining in the public sector have an obligation, in order to comply with this provision, to arrange for the involvement of staff representatives in the drafting of the applicable employment regulations'.[64] In other words, following this extensive interpretation of Article 11 ECHR in the light of other international instruments, Turkey was in effect bound to comply with a requirement of the European Social Charter that it had deliberately not consented to, as interpreted by a committee of experts which read into the relevant provision a guarantee that this provision was silent about.

When, a little more than five years later, the European Court of Human Rights was again faced with a new question of interpretation of Article 11 ECHR, it could have taken a similar approach, in order to protect the right of unions to resort to 'secondary strikes', by reading freedom of association as protected under the ECHR in the light of international case law related to union's rights. Instead, it took the view in *National Union of Rail, Maritime and Transport Workers v United Kingdom* that:

> the negative assessments made by the relevant monitoring bodies of the ILO and European Social Charter are not of such persuasive weight for determining whether the operation of the statutory ban on secondary strikes in circumstances such as those complained of in the present case remained within the range of permissible options open to the national authorities under Article 11 of the Convention.[65]

The Court arrived at this conclusion after noting that the review it performs has a 'distinct character ... compared with that of the supervisory procedures of the ILO and the European Social Charter' insofar as:

> The specialised international monitoring bodies operating under those procedures have a different standpoint, shown in the more general terms used to analyse the ban on secondary action. In contrast, it is not the Court's task to review the relevant domestic law in the abstract, but to determine whether the manner in which it actually affected the applicant infringed the latter's rights under Article 11 of the Convention.[66]

62 Ibid, §154.
63 See above, n 10.
64 *Demir and Baykara v Turkey*, above, n 10, §149.
65 *National Union of Rail, Maritime and Transport Workers v United Kingdom*, above, n 51, §98.
66 Ibid.

In other words, according to the judgment of the Court in *National Union of Rail, Maritime and Transport Workers*, whereas the ILO bodies and the European Committee of Social Rights assessed the British legal system in the abstract, all that was required from the European Court of Human Rights was to examine whether a violation of the ECHR occurred in the particular case it was presented with, without it being necessary to adopt a position on the full range of hypothetical situations that might occur in the future. This would justify the Court in departing from the findings of these other bodies, even when faced with a similar question of interpretation as regards the scope of the protection of workers freedom of association. Although the wordings of the respective instruments are not identical – from the very vague formulations of Articles 3 and 10 of the ILO (No. 87) Freedom of Association and Protection of the Right to Organise Convention to the comparatively far more precise wording of Article 6 of the European Social Charter, with Article 11 ECHR located somewhere in between – it is not these textual divergences that the European Court of Human Rights invoked to justify departing from the readings of the ILO Committee of Experts and the European Committee of Social Rights; rather, it relied on the respective functions of these bodies and its own.

It is therefore rather ironic that in *National Union of Rail, Maritime and Transport Workers*, the Court explicitly pledged to be consistent as regards its importation, as a guide to the interpretation of the Convention, of assessments made by other international and regional human rights bodies (including but not limited to bodies established within the framework of the Council of Europe). The United Kingdom argued that the ILO Committee of Experts was 'not formally competent to give authoritative interpretations to ILO Conventions'[67] and that nor could the assessment of the European Committee of Social Rights under the collective complaints procedure be treated as authoritative 'since, despite the independence and expertise of its members, the ECSR did not possess judicial or quasi-judicial status'.[68] In response, the European Court of Human Rights emphasised the role of these expert bodies in providing an interpretation of the ILO instruments concerned or of the European Social Charter respectively, and it noted that: 'It would be inconsistent with [the method adopted in *Demir and Baykara*] for the Court to adopt in relation to Article 11 an interpretation of the scope of freedom of association of trade unions that is much narrower than that which prevails in international law.'[69] Yet, by emphasising that the nature of the review performed by the Court is distinct from that of these expert bodies, the Court made it clear that it refuses to be bound by any assessments such bodies may have made of a domestic legal

67 Ibid, §96.
68 Ibid, §94.
69 Ibid, §76.

system under consideration, since its examination only focuses on the specific facts before it, rather than on the compatibility of that legal system as a whole with the requirements of the Convention.

Of course, it may well be that the *National Union of Rail, Maritime and Transport Workers* case did not provide the European Court of Human Rights with an ideal opportunity to question the restrictions imposed on unions' resort to 'solidarity strikes' under the British legislation, since the 'substance' of the freedom of association of the unions did not appear to be affected in the circumstances of that case; indeed, the unions were not deprived of any means to effectively influence social dialogue. Nevertheless, the hesitations of the Court and the awkward combination of a pledge to interpret the Convention consistently with general international human rights law, and a (not particularly plausible) attempt to explain why the views of the ILO experts and the European Committee on Social Rights could be disregarded, provide a good illustration of the main problem facing the formation of human rights *jus commune*: the problem of consistency. But how real is this 'problem'? And should it not rather be seen as a symptom of our inability to define an intermediate ground between recognising that case law borrowed from external sources can have binding authority (which it obviously could not) and dismissing such case law as little more than providing information to the Court that it may freely disregard if it does see the solution as fit for its own purposes?

5.2. INTERACTING WITH THE HUMAN RIGHTS COMMITTEE

We may take as our departure point another example, by asking how the European Court of Human Rights has been referring to the case law of the Human Rights Committee in recent years. In *Bayatyan v Armenia*, the Grand Chamber of the Court was asked to decide whether a conscientious objector, refusing to perform a military service on religious grounds, could be prosecuted.[70] Since Article 4 §3 (b) ECHR excludes from the scope of 'forced or compulsory labour' prohibited by Article 4 §2 'any service of a military character or, in case of conscientious objectors in countries where they are recognised, service exacted instead of compulsory military service', it had traditionally been assumed that the Member States of the Council of Europe could refuse to provide for a right to conscientious objection without violating the Convention; that was the position expressed by the European Commission of Human Rights since the 1966 case

[70] *Bayatyan v Armenia*, no. 23459/03, ECHR 2011. For a comment, see P Muzny, '*Bayatyan v Armenia*: The Grand Chamber Renders a Grand Judgment' (2012) 12 *Human Rights Law Review* 135–147.

of *Grandrath v Federal Republic of Germany*.[71] In effect, freedom of religion, recognised under Article 9 ECHR, was nullified as far as conscientious objection to performing a military service was concerned; the issue was considered exclusively under the provision of the Convention referring to conscientious objectors, which dealt with forced labour.

In *Bayatyan v Armenia*, however, the Court changed its view and for the first time explicitly recognised a right to conscientious objection. A major reason for this change was the evolution of the position of the Human Rights Committee. The Committee had traditionally assumed that Article 8 ICCPR implicitly acknowledged that the States parties to the Covenant could refuse to recognise conscientious objection to military service.[72] In a General Comment it adopted in 1993 on freedom of religion, however, it noted that whereas the Covenant 'does not explicitly refer to a right to conscientious objection', such a right 'can be derived from article 18, inasmuch as the obligation to use lethal force may seriously conflict with the freedom of conscience and the right to manifest one's religion or belief'.[73] When, in 2004, it was confronted with the claims of two Jehovah's Witnesses who were prosecuted for having refused to perform their military service, it confirmed its willingness to depart from its previous approach. It reasoned that since Article 8 ICCPR seemed to implicitly acknowledge that the States parties to the Covenant could refuse to recognise conscientious objection to military service,[74] this provision 'itself neither recognizes nor excludes a right of conscientious objection', and the claims it was presented with were therefore to be assessed 'solely in the light of article 18 of the Covenant', which guarantees freedom of religion.[75] On the basis of that rule, it concluded that the refusal to establish a procedure for the recognition of religious conscientious objectors was a disproportionate interference with freedom of religion.

In *Bayatyan v Armenia*, the European Court of Human Rights followed the same approach, using wording borrowing directly from that of the Human

---

71 *Grandrath v Federal Republic of Germany*, no. 2299/64, Commission report of 12 December 1966, ECHR Yearbook, vol 10, p 626.

72 Article 8 ICCPR prohibits forced and compulsory labour. However, §3 of this provision excludes from this notion 'any service of a military character … and, in countries where conscientious objection is recognized, any national service required by law of conscientious objectors'. The Committee implied from this formulation that the States parties to the ICCPR had a choice whether or not to allow for conscientious objection on the grounds of religion to justify a refual to perform a military service: see Human Rights Committee, *L.T.K. v Finland*, Communication no 185/1984, CCPR/C/25/D/185/1984, decision of 9 July 1985.

73 Human Rights Committee, General Comment No. 22: The right to freedom of thought, conscience and religion (Art. 18) (CCPR/C/21/Rev.1/Add.4, 27 Sept. 1993), para 11.

74 See above, n 73.

75 Human Rights Committee, *Yeo-Bum Yoon and Myung-Jin Choi v Republic of Korea*, Joined Communications nos 1321–1322/2004 (CCPR/C/88/D/1321–1322/2004), decision of 23 January 2007.

Rights Committee.[76] Citing the *Demir and Baykara* judgment of 2008, the Court noted in this regard that:

> in defining the meaning of terms and notions in the text of the Convention, the Court can and must take into account elements of international law other than the Convention and the interpretation of such elements by competent organs. The consensus emerging from specialised international instruments may constitute a relevant consideration for the Court when it interprets the provisions of the Convention in specific cases.[77]

The Court provided a detailed description of the evolution that the Human Rights Committee went through in the 1990s in the part of the judgment where it offers its own assessment.[78] Although that factor in itself may not have been decisive, it nevertheless seems to have had an important weight.

This, however, does not mean that the Court will align itself with the position of the Committee whenever the latter has provided an interpretation of provisions of the ICCPR with a wording similar to that of the ECHR. The famous cases concerning the wearing of headscarves provide an illustration of this. In six decisions it adopted on 30 June 2009, the European Court of Human Rights declared inadmissible as manifestly ill-founded applications filed against France, which alleged that the application of the French law of 2004 prohibiting the wearing of religious insignia in public schools[79] resulted in a violation of freedom of religion and freedom of expression, protected under Articles 9 and 10 ECHR.[80] Though the position of the Court was predictable once we consider its former case law on this issue,[81] it is nevertheless remarkable that this

---

76 The Court referred to para 23 of the *travaux préparatoires*, where it was noted that 'the clause relating to conscientious objectors [sub-paragraph (b) of Article 4 §3] was intended to indicate that any national service required of them by law would not fall within the scope of forced or compulsory labour. As the concept of conscientious objection was not recognised in many countries, the phrase "in countries where conscientious objection is recognised" was inserted'. In the Court's opinion, the *travaux préparatoires* thus confirm that 'the sole purpose of sub-paragraph (b) of Article 4 §3 is to provide a further elucidation of the notion "forced or compulsory labour". In itself, it neither recognises nor excludes a right to conscientious objection and should therefore not have a delimiting effect on the rights guaranteed by Article 9' (§100).

77 *Bayatyan v Armenia*, above, n 70, §102.

78 Ibid, §105.

79 Law n° 2004–228 as of 15 March 2004 framing, in application of the principle of secularism, the use of signs or garments displaying religious affiliation in public schools, colleges and high schools.

80 The cases of *Ranjit Singh* and *Jasvir Singh*, no. 27561/08 and 25463/08 concerned pupils wearing a keski (substituting a turban); the cases of *Aktas* (no. 43563/08), *Gamaledynn* (no. 18527/08), *Bayrak* (no. 14308/08) and *Ghazal* (no. 29134/08) concerned Muslim pupils wearing a bonnet (substituting a headscarf).

81 In the *Dogru* and *Kervanci* judgments of 4 December 2008 (nos 31645/04 and 27058/05 respectively), the Court had already taken the view that France had remained within its margin of appreciation by adopting this legislation.

position is in complete disregard of the Concluding Observations concerning France adopted by the Human Rights Committee a year earlier[82] – and which, anecdotally, it would confirm again in an individual decision in 2012.[83]

Other such disagreements have occasionally emerged between the European Court of Human Rights and the Human Rights Committee.[84] This would not constitute a problem if the two bodies not only applied different instruments, but also applied instruments containing different provisions, imposing different sets of obligations on the States parties. Here, however, we are faced with instruments that, in areas such as freedom of religion, use almost exactly the same wording derived from the Universal Declaration of Human Rights. In addition to inviting forum-shopping by individuals alleging to be victims of violations,[85] such divergences are problematic for a number of reasons. They undermine the legitimacy of both the bodies concerned, as the authority of the views they express is challenged. They are a source of legal uncertainty for the domestic courts and, generally, for the States parties; although in principle

82 Concluding Observations of the Human Rights Committee, France (CCPR/C/FRA/CO/4) (2008), para 23 (concluding that France 'should re-examine Act No. 2004/228 of 15 March 2004 in light of the guarantees of article 18 of the Covenant concerning freedom of conscience and religion, including the right to manifest one's religion in public as well as private, as well as the guarantee of equality under article 26').

83 In the case of *Bikramjit Singh v France*, the Human Rights Committee was presented with the case of a Sikh adolescent who was denied access to school in France because he insisted on wearing a keski (a sort of mini-turban covering the long uncut hair considered sacred in the Sikh religion). The Committee considered that France had not provided 'compelling evidence that by wearing his keski the author would have posed a threat to the rights and freedoms of other pupils or to order at school' and had not sought to find a solution to accommodate all interests at stake (Human Rights Committee, *Bikramjit Singh v France*, Communication no. 1852/2008, decision of 1 November 2012).

84 See, e.g., concerning the refusal to allow a Sikh to provide a photograph for an identity document on which he wears a turban, the contrasting views of the Human Rights Committee in *Ranjit Singh v France* (concerning a residence permit) (Communication no. 1876/2009, decision of 22 June 2011) or in *Mann Singh v France* (concerning a passport) (Communication no. 1928/2010, decision of 19 June 2013) on the one hand, and of the European Court of Human Rights in *Mann Singh v France* (no. 24479/07, inadmissibility decision of 13 November 2008) (concerning a driver's licence) on the other hand. In these cases, the Human Rights Committee concluded that France had not provided an acceptable justification for the interference with freedom of religion, whereas in *Mann Singh v France*, the European Court of Human Rights considered that the restriction imposed by France was not disproportionate. On these cases, see E Bribosia, G Caceres and I. Rorive, 'Les signes religieux au cœur d'un bras de fer: la saga Singh' (2017) *Revue trimestrielle des droits de l'homme* 495.

85 See on this risk the detailed and prescient study by Laurence R Helfer, 'Forum Shopping for Human Rights' (1999) 148 *University of Pennsylvania Law Review* 285. The cases referred to above provide an illustration: after having failed to convince the European Court of Human Rights to find a breach of Article 9 ECHR after France had denied him the right to appear on a driver's license wearing his Sikh turban, Mann Singh successfully filed a communication with the Human Rights Committee, this time alleging that the refusal of the French authorities to allow him to appear on the photograph of his passport wearing a turban violated Article 18 ICCPR.

it is the protection most favourable to the individual that should prevail, this principle may be difficult to apply in practice in those situations where rights conflict with one another (and the State frequently puts forward the protection of the rights of others to justify certain interferences). Moreover, as far as political authorities are concerned, such a conclusion is not obvious; in reality, the executive or the legislature may feel that, since human rights bodies established at the international level cannot agree among themselves, the State is free to choose the attitude that suits it best.

The broader point, however, is that the European Court of Human Rights gives the impression that it has been inconsistent as regards the weight it affords (or not) to the interpretation given by the Human Rights Committee of provisions of the ICCPR that rely on a wording similar to that of the ECHR. For instance, whereas the Court justified the evolution of its case law in *Baytayan* by the similar evolution that took place in the jurisprudence of the Human Rights Committee, it almost entirely ignored the views expressed by the Committee in the above mentioned cases concerning freedom of religion, and it failed to relate to the position of the same Committee in the second *Hirst* case concerning the right to vote of convicted detainees in the United Kingdom.[86] In *A and Others v United Kingdom*, it refers to the interpretation given by the Committee to Article 4 ICCPR, the derogation clause under the Covenant, as expressed by General Comment No. 29 on Article 4 of the ICCPR (24 July 2001). It then explains that the requirement imposed by the Human Rights Committee under Article 4 ICCPR – that the measures derogating from the Covenant be 'temporary' – does not apply as such under Article 15 ECHR, although nothing in the wording of these respective clauses suggests why their interpretation should be different.[87]

86 *Hirst v United Kingdom*, no 74025/01, ECHR 2005. In its General Comment No. 25 of 12 June 1996, the Human Rights Committee had stated: 'If conviction for an offence is a basis for suspending the right to vote, the period of suspension should be proportionate to the offence and the sentence. Persons who are deprived of liberty but who have not been convicted should not be excluded from exercising the right to vote' (para 14). Although the Court refers to the position of the Human Rights Committee where it lists 'relevant international materials' (§§26–27), it does not consider that view in the remainder of its judgment.

87 *A and Others v United Kingdom*, no. 3455/05, §178, ECHR 2009. In fact, the Court is rather ambiguous as to whether or not it shares the view of the Human Rights Committee, according to which the requirement that the measures adopted be 'strictly necessary' to respond to the exigencies of the situation imply that such measures be temporary in nature: 'While the United Nations Human Rights Committee has observed that measures derogating from the provisions of the International Covenant on Civil and Political Rights must be of "an exceptional and temporary nature" ... the Court's case-law has never, to date, explicitly incorporated the requirement that the emergency be temporary, although the question of the proportionality of the response may be linked to the duration of the emergency. Indeed, the cases ... relating to the security situation in Northern Ireland, demonstrate that it is possible for a "public emergency" within the meaning of Article 15 to continue for many years. The Court does not consider that derogating measures put in place in the immediate aftermath of the al-Qaeda attacks in the United States of America, and reviewed on an annual basis by Parliament, can be said to be invalid on the ground that they were not "temporary".'

Such apparent inconsistencies should concern us. They risk undermining the legitimacy of reliance on comparative analysis in human rights law, the operation at the heart of the formation of human rights *jus commune*. A more principled approach seems desirable. But is it possible?

6. FROM A FORMALISTIC TO A DIALOGIC APPROACH

The view that is taken here is that the proper role of foreign human rights jurisprudence should be to force human rights bodies to be more reflexive about their interpretation of human rights law. Foreign jurisprudence should not be treated as binding, as it does not have such authority; nor, however, should it be treated as a mere source of inspiration, with only persuasive authority that could be ignored if the 'receiving' court finds it inconvenient to follow. Rather, because such foreign jurisprudence does create certain expectations, it should be seen as establishing a presumption, but one that is rebuttable: the interpretation provided in one instance should in principle be followed in later instances, unless there are strong (and principled) reasons to depart from the precedent. The integrity of the human rights system as a whole will benefit from thus being disciplined.

Prior precedents should not be ignored. Nor, however, should they discourage the quest for alternative interpretations of the requirements of human rights, where the balance of interests weighs in favour of a different reading of human rights rather than in favour of respecting legitimate expectations and preserving legal certainty. Indeed, if human rights bodies were to act as if they were bound to follow the precedents set by their peers, the order in which cases are presented for settlement, as well as the fora where they are settled, would take on a decisive importance: human rights litigation would become a strategic game for some repeat players, particularly non-governmental advocacy organisations, although in the majority of cases, it would be mere chance – which facts are ripe for adjudication first and before which court – that would ultimately decide the outcome. Therefore, the proposal is not to treat such precedents as binding, as in the classic doctrine of stare decisis – which in effect would mean forcing the 'receiving' court to rely on the technique of distinctions, classic in common law adjudication, so as to justify not following a precedent – but to see such precedents as mere presumptions, which could be set aside if the context in which the 'receiving' court operates is different.

This does not rule out that inconsistencies shall persist between different human rights bodies operating under different instruments and in different legal regimes, even where the provisions applied are similarly worded. Much as such inconsistencies are dissatisfying for the logical mind, they are to a large extent inevitable. Yet, that is not to imply that human rights bodies can simply ignore each other's jurisprudence. This would deprive these bodies of an important tool to improve the quality of decision-making and of an important source of judicial economy. It would also soon lead to the formation of a cacophony that would delegitimise the reference of human rights as a universal and timeless language. The default position is therefore for each human rights monitoring body to take into account the case law developed in other fora, where such case law is based on similarly worded instruments, and to treat such case law as persuasive (though not binding) authority, which can be given a certain weight in the deliberation. Thus conceived, the dialogue between human rights jurisdictions can contribute to a more reflexive jurisprudence – one that is better informed by how similar situations have been dealt with elsewhere and one that, where such solutions do indeed exist and have been leading to satisfactory outcomes, accepts the burden of justifying any deviation from such solutions.

This is true where a particular doctrine is developed in one forum and where the question arises of whether a similar doctrine should be adopted in another forum facing a similar issue. But it is equally true where one monitoring body has assessed a specific situation (such as a measure adopted by a State) and another body is subsequently asked to perform a similar assessment. Where, as in the examples above, the European Court of Human Rights and the Human Rights Committee adopt opposing views as to the acceptability of the restrictions imposed by France on religious freedom, this threatens the legitimacy of human rights law due to the specific pedigree of this branch of law, which presents itself as grounded in a certain concept of human dignity. That is bad enough. But it is perhaps even worse that the respective bodies do not feel obliged to respond to one another's views and thus do not seize upon such divergences as an opportunity to improve the overall quality of their decision-making. There are certainly disadvantages to a human rights court adopting a deferential position, in which it feels bound to follow the precedent set by a foreign court (or, more broadly, a monitoring mechanism located outside the system in which the borrowing court operates). But the opposite position, in which a court simply disregards such precedents, is equally problematic from the point of view of the progress of law; it leads to each system of protection becoming self-referential and increasingly rigid and dogmatic in the solutions it prescribes.

7. CONCLUSION

It is perhaps the Supreme Court of Canada that best embodies the dialogic attitude that moves us beyond the dilemma. In the case of *R v Keegstra*, the Court was asked to decide whether a teacher, who was prosecuted in the province of Alberta under hate propaganda legislation (section 319(2) of the Criminal Code) for communicating anti-semitic statements to his students, could invoke freedom of expression (as guaranteed under section 2 of the Canadian Charter of Rights and Freedoms) in order to escape liability: Mr Keegstra had vilified the Jews in class and had told his classes that 'Jewish people seek to destroy Christianity and are responsible for depressions, anarchy, chaos, wars and revolution', and that they had 'created the Holocaust to gain sympathy'.[88] Those questioning the constitutionality of the criminalisation of hate speech in Canada were seeking to rely, in particular, on the case law of the United States Supreme Court, based on the First Amendment to the United States Constitution.[89] What value, if any, should be attached to such a reference? Speaking for the majority of the Court, Chief Justice Dickson saw fit to explain 'the reasons why or why not American experience may be useful' in addressing a question arising under the Canadian Charter of Rights and Freedoms:

> In the United States, a collection of fundamental rights has been constitutionally protected for over two hundred years. The resulting practical and theoretical experience is immense, and should not be overlooked by Canadian courts. On the other hand, we must examine American constitutional law with a critical eye, and in this respect La Forest J. has noted in *R. v Rahey*, [1987] 1 S.C.R. 588, at p. 639: 'While it is natural and even desirable for Canadian courts to refer to American constitutional jurisprudence in seeking to elucidate the meaning of Charter guarantees that have counterparts in the United States Constitution, they should be wary of drawing too ready a parallel between constitutions born to different countries in different ages and in very different circumstances …'
>
> Canada and the United States are not alike in every way, nor have the documents entrenching human rights in our two countries arisen in the same context. It is only common sense to recognize that, just as similarities will justify borrowing from the American experience, differences may require that Canada's constitutional vision depart from that endorsed in the United States … I am unwilling to embrace various categorizations and guiding rules generated by American law without careful consideration of their appropriateness to Canadian constitutional theory. Though I have found the American experience tremendously helpful in coming to my own conclusions regarding this appeal, and by no means reject the whole of the First Amendment doctrine, in a number of respects I am thus dubious as to the applicability of this doctrine in the context of a challenge to hate propaganda legislation … Far from requiring a less solicitous protection of Charter rights and freedoms, such independence of vision protects these rights and freedoms in a different way … [I]n my view the international commitment to eradicate hate propaganda and, most importantly, the special role given equality and multiculturalism in the Canadian Constitution necessitate a departure from the view, reasonably prevalent in America at present, that the suppression of hate propaganda is incompatible with

---

88 *R v Keegstra* [1990] 3 SCR 697 (judgment of 13 December 1990).

89 The leading case is *Beauharnais v Illinois*, 343 US 250 (1952), although the case has been distinguished many times at different levels of jurisdiction, and its authority is now seriously weakened as a result (see, e.g., *Garrison v Louisiana*, 379 US 64 (1964); *Ashton v Kentucky*, 384 US 195 (1966); *New York Times Co v Sullivan*, 376 US 254 (1964); *Brandenburg v Ohio*, 395 US 444 (1969); and *Cohen v California*, 403 US 15 (1971)).

> the guarantee of free expression. [Moreover, the role of section 1 of the Canadian Charter of Rights and Freedoms, which prescribes that the rights and freedoms of the Charter are 'subject only to such reasonable limits prescribed by law as can be demonstrably justified in a free and democratic society', a provision that has no exact equivalent in the US Constitution] may well demand a perspective particular to Canadian constitutional jurisprudence when weighing competing interests. If values fundamental to the Canadian conception of a free and democratic society suggest an approach that denies hate propaganda the highest degree of constitutional protection, it is this approach which must be employed.

This position is consistent with the role United States constitutional law has played, in other contexts, in Canadian Charter jurisprudence.[90] It is neither deferential to the case law developed outside Canada nor dismissive of such case law. The jurisprudence of the US Supreme Court, we are told, should be considered carefully because of the wisdom it embodies: 'over two hundred years' of accumulated 'practical and theoretical experience' cannot be simply overlooked by the Canadian courts. Nor should such jurisprudence be controlling, however, where the overall structure and spirit of the Canadian Charter of Rights and Freedoms points to an opposite solution.[91]

---

90 For instance, *Re BC Motor Vehicle Act* [1985] 2 SCR 486, per Lamer J, at p 498 (the use of the substantive/procedural dichotomy in approaching the content of the 'principles of fundamental justice' under section 7 of the Canadian Charter of Rights and Freedoms, which stipulates that 'Everyone has the right to life, liberty and security of the person and the right not to be deprived thereof except in accordance with the principles of fundamental justice ... is largely bound up in the American experience with substantive and procedural due process. It imports into the Canadian context American concepts, terminology and jurisprudence, all of which are inextricably linked to problems concerning the nature and legitimacy of adjudication under the U.S. Constitution. That Constitution, it must be remembered, has no section 52 [of the Canadian Constitution, which provides that "any law that is inconsistent with the provisions of the Constitution is, to the extent of the inconsistency, of no force or effect"] nor has it the internal checks and balances of ss 1 and 33. We would, in my view, do our own Constitution a disservice to simply allow the American debate to define the issue for us, all the while ignoring the truly fundamental structural differences between the two constitutions').

91 In the dissenting opinion appended to *Keegstra*, McLachlin J (joined by Sopinka J) does not disagree with the general approach of the majority towards the constitutional case law of the US Supreme Court. He considers, however, that the Canadian understanding of freedom of expression is closer to that of the United States than to the approach embodies in international or European human rights instruments ('Perhaps the experience most relevant to Canada is that of the United States, since its Constitution, like ours, places a high value on free expression, raising starkly the conflict between freedom of speech and the countervailing values of individual dignity and social harmony. Like s 2(b) [of the Charter of Rights and Freedoms, which guarantees freedom of thought, belief, opinion and expression], the First Amendment guarantee is conveyed in broad, unrestricted language, stating that "Congress shall make no law ... abridging the freedom of speech, or of the press" ... [In contrast,] protection for free expression under [Article 10 ECHR] has at times been decidedly lukewarm, as befits an international instrument which is designed to limit as little as possible the sovereignty of the nations that signed it').

It is thus that we should conceive of the dialogic relationship between human rights bodies, both domestic and international. These monitoring mechanisms are not connected institutionally to one another. Yet, they influence each other by expressing views that each must take into account. The duty to consider such views follows from the fact that the various instruments – whether they are domestic legislation or catalogues of rights in national constitutions, or international or regional human rights treaties – share the same origin in the Universal Declaration of Human Rights. Given the similarity of language and the commonality of origin, it seems inevitable that such influence will make itself felt. Indeed, it would be odd if counsels arguing their case before domestic or international tribunals, as well as non-governmental organisations intervening as amici curiae, did not rely on comparative law analysis to build their argument. This is to be welcomed, to the extent that it leads to a more richly argued case law in each forum – a case law better informed by the range of solutions that have been explored elsewhere, by the advantages or disadvantages of each, and by the various sensitivities or philosophical approaches that may provide them with a justification. Through the formation of a human rights *jus commune* thus conceived, we may hope for an adequate equilibrium point between the dangers of homogeneity and the pitfalls of dispersion and cacophony.

UN SPECIAL PROCEDURES

System Puppets or User's Saviours?

Rhona KM Smith*

1. INTRODUCTION

Following the establishment of the UN Human Rights Council, the then Secretary-General, Kofi Annan, termed the UN special procedures the 'crown jewel' in the UN system.[1] Earlier, a report to the former Commission stated that they were 'the essential cornerstone of United Nations efforts to promote and protect human rights'[2] and Surya Subedi, a former rapporteur,

* Dr Rhona Smith is Head of Law and Professor of International Human Rights at Newcastle University in the UK. This chapter is written in her academic capacity and nothing herein necessarily reflects the views of the United Nations or any special procedures mandate holders. Email: rhona.smith@newcastle.ac.uk. Text completed June 2017.

1 Kofi Annan, 'Address to Mark International Human Rights Day in New York City' UN Doc SG/SM/10788, 8 December 2006.

2 *Rationalisation of the Work of the Commission* ('Selebi Report'), UN Doc E/CN.4/1999/104, at para 17.

simply considers them 'the public face of the UN human rights system'.[3] They certainly occupy a unique position. Appointed by the UN Human Rights Council, each mandate reports annually to the Council and/or the General Assembly. The terms of the mandate may dictate the actual work undertaken or leave it open to the appointee. 'special procedures' is the generic term applied to the special mechanisms of the former Commission on Human Rights (now the UN Human Rights Council) by which individual experts are appointed to examine particular human rights issues, monitor specific countries or territories, develop specific guidelines or consider specific violations of human rights and fundamental freedoms. The mandates to which they are appointed are not dependent on treaties for their authority,[4] but rather draw support from the terms of the UN Charter. This provides a degree of flexibility on sources (as they are not bound to particular treaties) and, as a consequence, special procedures can use whichever legal arguments and strategies best advance their mandate, embodying a truly integrated approach. Unsurprisingly, a range of users can and do engage with the special procedures.

For the purposes of this chapter, the working definition proposed by Ellen Desmet is widely construed: '[a] human rights user is any individual or composite entity who engages with (uses of) human rights'.[5] Individuals, non-governmental organisations (NGOs) and civil society organisations, States themselves and institutions and entities within regional and international organisations are included. Users across Desmet's four categories are included – rights claimants, rights realisers, supportive users (e.g. advocates, defenders and NGOs) and judicial users (courts and tribunals, including, for the purposes of this chapter, UN monitoring systems).[6] The question addressed is: are they system puppets or some (or all) of their users' saviours? In order to determine the answer, the system of special procedures will first be outlined and the key literature identified, analysing the reality of their autonomy. A broader discussion of engagement of special procedures with different users demonstrates the support available to the UN and beyond through these mechanisms.

2. THE UN SPECIAL PROCEDURES

From ad hoc individual experts appointed to examine particular issues or to represent the Secretary-General in specific countries, a web of independent

3 S Subedi, 'Protection of Human Rights through the Mechanism of UN Special Rapporteurs' (2011) 33 *Human Rights Quarterly* 201, 209.

4 The treaty bodies, in contrast, by definition derive their authority from the treaties by which they are established.

5 E Desmet, 'Analysing Users' Trajectories in Human Rights: A Conceptual Exploration and Research Agenda' (2014) 8 *Human Rights and International Legal Discourse* 121, 125.

6 Ibid, pp 129–131.

experts arguably unparalleled in any system has emerged to form the contemporary UN special procedures. When the UN Human Rights Council inherited the UN special procedures from the former UN Commission on Human Rights in 2006, a process of review, rationalisation and improvement was undertaken.[7] No State argued against the continuation of the procedures, though there was debate on many aspects of the system as it stood.[8] For example, attempts were made to rein in the work of the procedures, not least through elaboration of the Code of Conduct.[9]

As history attests, the special procedures emerged relatively unscathed from this review process. Indeed, numbers of both thematic and country mandates have increased under the Human Rights Council. Even the Belarus mandate, controversially discontinued when the Council was created, was re-established in 2013.[10] One report models growth on the actual 2009–2013 increase as opposed to the 1980–2013 growth rate, predicting a total of, respectively, 100 or 80 mandates within about 15 years.[11] Hurst Hannum suggests reviewing the need for more mandates in light of General Assembly Resolution 41/120 (which concerned human rights treaties) and posits the idea of a general rule with mechanisms mostly ceasing after six years of operation, albeit with a few exceptions, arguing that all mandates should be viewed as finite rather than open-ended.[12]

---

7 Human Rights Council Resolution 5/1 *Institution-building of the United Nations Human Rights Council*, section II, paras 54–64.

8 Academic contributions to this debate include the special edition (2011) 15(2) *International Journal of Human Rights*, edited by S Subedi (then UN Special Rapporteur on the situation of human rights in Cambodia), S Wheatley, A Mukherjee and S Ngane; J Gutter, 'Special Procedures and the Human Rights Council' (2007) 7 *Human Rights Law Review* 93; T Piccone, 'Catalysts for Rights: The Unique Contribution of the UN's Independent Experts on Human Rights Brookings', Brookings Institute, 2010; R Smith, 'From "Crown Jewel" to "Frankenstein's Monster": "Reviewing, Rationalizing and Improving" the Role of the UN Special Procedures' (2011) 17 *Australian Journal of Human Rights* 33.

9 Human Rights Council Resolution 5/2 *Code of Conduct for Special Procedures Mandate-Holder of the Human Rights Council*. Note that a subsequent draft was introduced by China, Cuba and the Russian Federation – UN Doc A/HRC/11/L.8 – which was perceived by rapporteurs and other States to threaten the independence of mandate holders. The final draft was modified following State lobbying. Particular State criticism was focused on reports by the then Special Rapporteur on extrajudicial, summary or arbitrary executions (Philip Alston; see UN Doc A/HRC/11/2) and the then Special Rapporteur on the promotion and protection of the right to freedom of opinion and expression (Frank La Rue; see UN Doc A/HRC/11/4). The final draft (June 2009) confines itself to recalling that it is incumbent on special procedures mandate holders to exercise their functions in full respect for and strict observance of their mandates (at para 2).

10 Mandate re-established by Human Rights Council – UN Doc A/HRC/RES/20/13.

11 M Limon and T Piccone, Human Rights Special Procedures: Determinants of Influence, Understanding and Strengthening the Effectiveness of the UN's Independent Human Rights Experts, Universal Rights Group and Brookings, 2014, p 9.

12 H Hannum, 'Reforming the Special Procedures and Mechanisms of the Commission on Human Rights' (2007) 7 *Human Rights Law Review* 73, 79–82.

Currently, there are 12 country mandates[13] and 44 thematic mandates.[14] Of the thematic mandates, there are six working groups,[15] each with representatives from the five principal regional groupings, the remainder being individual mandates. The oldest mandates still in existence are Palestine[16] and Myanmar[17] for country mandates, the Working Group on Enforced and Involuntary Disappearances[18] and the Special Rapporteur on extrajudicial, summary or arbitrary executions[19] for thematic mandates.

Although this chapter considers special procedures generally, individual mandates, as opposed to Working Groups, will be the primary focus. There are two sets of individual mandate holders: those country mandate holders who focus on one territory or country, albeit usually on all aspects of human rights, and can be charged with monitoring and reporting to the Council, advising the State and offering/facilitating technical assistance in a capacity-building role; and those thematic mandates who often face the total impossibility (given the logistical constraints) of following and reporting on one issue, right or freedom throughout all UN Member States' territories.[20] Of course, some thematic

---

13 Belarus, Cambodia, the Central African Republic, the Democratic People's Republic of Korea, Eritrea, Iran, Mali, Myanmar, Somalia, Sudan and the Palestinian territories. The twelfth, on the Syrian Arab republic, was established in 2011, but only becomes operational when the commission of inquiry ends – UN Doc A/HRC/RES/S-18/1. For a current list, see http://spinternet.ohchr.org/_Layouts/SpecialProceduresInternet/ViewAllCountryMandates.aspx (accessed 26 June 2017).

14 The most recent additions are the right to privacy (HRC res 28/16), the enjoyment of human rights for persons with albinism (HRC res 28/6), protection against violence and discrimination based on sexual orientation and gender identity (HRC res 32/2) the right to development (HRC res 33/14) and, in June 2017, non-discrimination against persons with leprosy (A/HRC/35/L.14). For a full list, see http://spinternet.ohchr.org/_Layouts/SpecialProceduresInternet/ViewAllCountryMandates.aspx?Type=TM (accessed 26 June 2017).

15 The working groups are the Working Group on Enforced or Involuntary Disappearances (established in 1980 by the Commission on Human Rights, E/CN.4/RES/1980/20/XXXVI), the Working Group on Arbitrary Detention (established in 1991 by Economic and Social Council Resolution E/CN.4/RES/1991/42), the Working Group of Experts on People of African Descent (UN Doc E/CN.4/RES/2002/68), the Working Group on the Use of Mercenaries as a Means of Violating Human Rights and Impeding the Exercise of the Right of Peoples to Self-determination (UN Doc E/CN.4/RES/2005), the UN Working Group on the Issue of Human Rights and Transnational Corporations and Other Business Enterprises (UN Doc A/HRC/RES/17/4, established in 2011 following the adoption of the guiding principles) and the newest, the Working Group on the Issue of Discrimination Against Women in Law and in Practice (UN Doc A/HRC/RES/15/23).

16 Commission on Human Rights resolution E/CN.4/RES/1993/2A in 1993.

17 Commission on Human Rights resolution E/CN.4/RES/1992/58 in 1992.

18 Commission on Human Rights resolution E/CN.4/RES/1980/20/(XXXVI) in 1980.

19 Economic and Social Council resolution E/RES/1982/35 in 1982.

20 As discussed below, some thematic mandates are required to elaborate guidelines with cognisance taken of the global reality. See, for example, NM M'Jid, 'Reflections on a Six-Year Tenure as UN Special Rapporteur on the Sale of Children, Child Prostitution, and Child Pornography' (2014) 38 Fletcher Forum of World Affairs.

mandate holders are charged with developing frameworks and guidelines,[21] making a unique contribution to the integrated legal framework.

Special procedures are required to be first and foremost independent. The post requires functioning at the highest diplomatic level. As a consequence, this can preclude autobiographical papers emerging on the reality of the role, although with academic appointees, it is perhaps inevitable that there is a literature emerging during and after service reflecting on the experiences of being a mandate holder.[22] There are also a growing number of researchers and doctoral students examining facets of this anomalous area of human rights monitoring and protection.[23] However, special procedures remain a relatively infrequent subject of analysis in academic literature.[24] The available literatures shall be drawn upon to gain further insight into the reality of the role in practice.

---

21 Examples include the *Guiding Principles on Business and Human Rights*, drafted by John Ruggie, UN Doc A/HRC/17/31, annex, adopted in HRC res 17/4, available at http://www.ohchr.org/Documents/Publications/GuidingPrinciplesBusinessHR_EN.pdf (accessed 26 June 2017); the 1998 *Guiding Principles on Internal Displacement* UN Doc E/CN.4/1998/53/Add.2 developed by Francis Deng; and Cephas Lumina's *Guiding Principles on Foreign Debt and Human Rights* UN Doc A/HRC/20/23, presented in June 2012 and endorsed in resolution 20/10. The Special Rapporteur on minority issues produced *Language Rights of Linguistic Minorities: A Practical Guide for Implementation* in 2016, a handbook available at http://www.ohchr.org/EN/Issues/Minorities/SRMinorities/Pages/LanguageRights.aspx (accessed 26 June 2017). The Working Group on the use of mercenaries as a means of violating human rights and impeding the exercise of the right of peoples to self-determination is working on guidelines for private military and security companies; see its report in 2016, UN Doc A/HRC/33/43.

22 A non-exhaustive list includes M Kirby, 'UN Special Procedures: Reflections on the Office of the UN Special Representative for Human Rights in Cambodia' (2010) 11 *Melbourne Journal of International Law* 491; S Subedi, 'The UN Human Rights Mandate in Cambodia: The Challenge of a Country in Transition and the Experience of the Special Rapporteur for the Country' (2011) 15 *International Journal of Human Rights* 249; N Rodley, 'On the Responsibility of Special Rapporteurs' (2011) 15 *International Journal of Human Rights* 319; PS Pinheiro, 'Being a Special Rapporteur: A Delicate Balancing Act' (2011) 15 *International Journal of Human Rights* 162; Y Erturk and B Purkayastha, 'Linking Research, Policy and Action: A Look at the Work of the Special Rapporteur on Violence against Women' (2012) 60 *Current Sociology* 142; P Leurprecht, 'Cambodge – L'interminable attente de justice' (2013) 2 *Revue Québécoise de Droit International*; N Maalla M'Jid, 'Reflections on a Six-Year Tenure as UN Special Rapporteur on the Sale of Children, Child Prostitution, and Child Pornography' (2014) 38 *Fletcher Forum of World Affairs* 39. Many thematic rapporteurs also write extensively on their thematic area of expertise.

23 See, for example, J Gutter, *Thematic Procedures of the United Nations Commission on Human Rights and International Law: In Search of a Sense of Community*, Intersentia, Antwerp 2006; M Lempinen, *Challenges Facing the System of Special Procedures of the United Nations Commission on Human Rights*, Abo Akademi Institute for Human Rights, Turku 2001; J Naples-Mitchell, 'Perspectives of UN Special Rapporteurs on Their Role: Inherent Tensions and Unique Contributions' (2011) 15 *International Journal of Human Rights* 232; T Piccone, above n 8; L Smyth, 'Country-Specific Mandate-Holders: The Role of the Special Rapporteur on the Situation of Human Rights in Cambodia' (2014) 14 *Melbourne Journal of International Law* 1.

24 Key books include J Gutter, above n 23; I Nifosi, *The UN Special Procedures in the Field of Human Rights*, Intersentia, Antwerp 2006; B Ramcharan, *The Protection Roles of UN Human Rights Special Procedures*, Martinus Nijhoff, Leiden 2009; T Piccone, *Catalysts*

Independence brings benefits and can be exploited by mandate holders to source a range of legal authorities, depending on the circumstances. All aspects of the fragmented legal universe can be drawn on: national law, regional law, international law and a range of guidelines and policies. The Working Group on Business and Human Rights, for example, is tasked with advancing the application of the Guiding Principles on Business and Human Rights. These are soft law, developed by a former mandate holder, the Secretary-General's Special Representative, John Ruggie.[25] Perusing annual reports and the communications to governments and other actors demonstrate the range of sources that mandate holders research or request further information on. Special procedure mandate holders have also elected to engage with customary laws,[26] national laws[27] and regional laws,[28] as well as international human rights and humanitarian laws,[29] alone, in combination or in a comparative dimension. These multiple layers of human rights form the foundation of their work. Arguably, this fragmented legal universe can strengthen special procedure work as it enables innovative solutions

for Rights: The Unique Contribution of the UN's Independent Experts on Human Rights, Brookings Institute, Washington DC 2010; H Cantu Rivera (ed), *The Special Procedures of the Human Rights Council*, Intersentia, Antwerp 2015.

25 Above n 23.

26 For example, looking at indigenous peoples' traditional rights in relation to land in communications of the Indigenous Peoples' mandate – Communication BLZ 2/2015 to Belize on customary land tenure.

27 For example, see 'Effective Promotion of the Declaration on the Rights of Persons Belonging to National or Ethnic, Religious and Linguistic Minorities', UN Doc A/67/293 (2012) on the role of national institutions and mechanisms; or Communications such as OL EGY 14/2016 from Mandates of the Special Rapporteur on the promotion and protection of the right to freedom of opinion and expression, the Special Rapporteur on the rights to freedom of peaceful assembly and of association and the Special Rapporteur on the situation of human rights defenders offering a human rights analysis of a new 2016 Egyptian law on NGOs or JOL DEU 2/2016 from mandates of the Special Rapporteur on the promotion and protection of the right to freedom of opinion and expression, the Special Rapporteur on the situation of human rights defenders and the Special Rapporteur on the independence of judges and lawyers of the 2016 draft law amending Germany's existing regulations on the surveillance of communications between non-German citizens.

28 The Special Rapporteur on migrants, for example, has worked with the European Union. Critiquing their laws and policies and how they affect migrants seeking to enter the EU, for example, see his 2013 thematic study 'Regional Study: management of the external borders of the European Union and its impact on the human rights of migrants', UN Doc A/HRC/23/46, associated documentation, http://www.ohchr.org/EN/Issues/Migration/SRMigrants/Pages/RegionalThematicStudy.aspx (accessed 26 June 2017) and, more recently, a joint March 2017 press statement on the new EU regulations, http://www.ohchr.org/EN/NewsEvents/Pages/DisplayNews.aspx?NewsID=21330&LangID=E (accessed 26 June 2017).

29 See, for example, 'Report of the Special Rapporteur on extrajudicial, summary or arbitrary executions on the right to life and use of force by private security providers in law enforcement contexts', UN Doc A/HRC/33/51, which commenced operation decades before the UN Convention on Enforced Disappearances was drafted.

to be advanced, ensuring that no one is left behind and that States and non-State actors can better respect, protect and promote human rights everywhere. On the flipside, much depends on the individual mandate holder or the knowledge of the Office of the United Nations High Commissioner for Human Rights (OHCHR) desk officer/s tasked with supporting the mandate. This also means that the approach to the fragmented legal norms can change with the terms of mandate holders. This is part of the double-edged sword of total independence, though it offers opportunities for strengthening human rights integration.

In theory, such a potentially integrated approach to human rights should render procedures more accessible to all stakeholders. The reality suggests that this is not necessarily so: different users interact with special procedures and, indeed, with individual mandate holders in different ways. Awareness of these interactions and relationships fosters an understanding of how special procedures can contribute to a more integrated human rights. Are they used by the system for diverse reasons or do they represent hope for those with limited other options for claiming rights and freedoms?

3. SYSTEM PUPPETS?

It is indisputable that the UN special procedures are appointed by, and are answerable to, the UN Human Rights Council. In that sense, they are a product of the political system of the UN. All mandates report annually to the UN and the renewal of mandates (triennially for thematic mandates and annually for country mandates)[30] is dependent on intergovernmental consensus. Although this indicates a degree of dependence on the Council, they remain steadfastly outside the UN system due to the 'constitutional' independence of all mandate holders.

Officially, all mandate holders are independent of the UN, States and government. The *Manual of Operations* makes clear that:

> Mandate-holders are selected on the basis of their expertise and experience in the area of the mandate, personal integrity, independence and impartiality and objectivity. The independent status of the mandate-holders is crucial in order to enable them to fulfil their functions in all impartiality.[31]

---

30 Though note exceptions in, for example, the case of Cambodia (UN Doc A/HRC/RES/30/23, A/HRC/36/32) currently with biennial renewals.

31 Manual of Operations of the Special Procedures of the Human Rights Council, August 2008, available http://www.ohchr.org/Documents/HRBodies/SP/Manual_Operations2008.pdf, accessed 26 June 2017 at para 11.

On appointment, mandate holders take an oath to that effect.[32] During the Commission and early Council era, appointments were arranged by an almost 'Byzantine' process, in the words of one experienced rapporteur, relating his appointment following an unexpected telephone invitation for the Burundi mandate and similarly later in respect of Myanmar.[33] He had never visited either country before his appointment, though, perhaps surprisingly, that is not uncommon for country mandates even today.[34] With the advent of the Human Rights Council's reforms, there is evidence that the appointment process has been rendered more transparent and the independence (or otherwise) of candidates more visible.[35] Special procedures are thus increasingly 'outside human rights experts',[36] coming from outside the UN and intergovernmental system.

To emphasise this independence, mandate holders give their time voluntarily and receive no payment. They only receive travel (flights are directly booked by the OHCHR) and a per diem allowance to cover their accommodation, food and ancillary expenses when on mission. There is no honorarium available for the time spent on mission or the hours spent otherwise on communications, preparation, reporting and research. Many mandate holders lose earnings or earning potential when engaged in UN work and there is no support for those mandate holders travelling with dependants.[37] Such a lack of funding can deter potentially excellent candidates from allowing themselves to be considered for appointment. Looking at the backgrounds of appointees, the majority are full-time academics or at least in some way affiliated to universities.[38]

---

32 Code of Conduct, above n 7, Article 5: 'I solemnly declare that I shall perform my duties and exercise my functions from a completely impartial, loyal and conscientious standpoint, and truthfully, and that I shall discharge these functions and regulate my conduct in a manner totally in keeping with the terms of my mandate, the Charter of the United Nations, the interests of the United Nations, and with the objective of promoting and protecting human rights, without seeking or accepting any instruction from any other party whatsoever.'

33 PS Pinheiro, above n 22, pp 163–164.

34 Very few country mandate holders have experience within the country prior to their appointment. Whilst this may ensure absolute independence and a lack of preconceived ideas, it can also bring challenges.

35 Note the controversy over the Palestinian country mandate renewal in 2014 – Professor Christina Cerna was the unanimous choice of the Consultative Group of the Human Rights Council, yet was not appointed. The President of the Council interviewed additional candidates and recommended the appointment of a different candidate. See the President's list, approved by the Council, and Report of Consultative Group with recommendations to the President of the Human Rights Council, Part III (Remaining individual thematic and country mandates), both available at http://www.ohchr.org/EN/HRBodies/SP/Pages/HRC25.aspx (accessed 26 June 2017).

36 I Nifosi, above n 24, p 73.

37 For example, those mandate holders with small children or other dependants have to pay for their care and support, or pay for them accompanying the mandate holder on mission.

38 Review of backgrounds of current mandate holders, http://www.ohchr.org/EN/HRBodies/SP/Pages/Introduction.aspx (accessed 26 June 2017). There has been little change compared to Limon and Piccone's report (above n 11, at 14), which found that 56% of mandate holders on 17 January 2014 were working in academia/research.

This gives mandate holders a degree of financial stability whilst discharging their mandates. Some universities support rapporteurs in terms of time, money, research assistance and so forth; others do not.[39] The second-largest group are those with backgrounds in NGOs and civil society. Obviously, there can be a blurring of divisions in any such classifications – some mandate holders have academic and NGO affiliations and may have even worked in government. Many current mandate holders and many of those applying for mandates have served in different roles within the UN – for example, previous experience in treaty bodies or with other mandates or commissions of inquiries.[40] Such an accumulation of expertise has definite advantages in understanding the UN systems and processes. However, there is a risk of this breeding a degree of complacency insofar as some mandate holders understand from the outset which battles are just not worth fighting and how best to work with the system.[41] Rapporteurs also approach relationships with the UN system differently: some present themselves as working completely outwith the UN and as having no links other than reporting and logistical support to it, while others present themselves as UN experts. Much can depend on the particular viewpoint of the individual and the specific circumstances of time and place.

Mandates are dependent on the UN, particularly the OHCHR, for logistical and administrative support. Thematic mandates are supported by one and a fraction full-time assistants serving in the UN Secretariat at OHCHR Geneva. Some mandates have two or more full-time staff. In contrast, country mandates are supported by a fractional desk officer who has extensive responsibilities for a broad geographical area, often in addition to a number of related tasks. Some country mandates benefit from an in-country OHCHR office, though most do not.[42] Technically funding for special procedures is protected as it flows from the main budget, not the comparatively miniscule OHCHR budget.[43]

---

39 Attempts are under way to document all external support in money or kind provided to mandate holders: http://www.ohchr.org/EN/HRBodies/SP/CoordinationCommittee/Pages/Disclosureofexternalfundsreceivedbymandate-holders.aspx (accessed 26 June 2017).

40 For example, Paulo Sergio Pinheiro, mentioned above, has held two country mandates, one thematic mandate and is now the appointee to the Syrian country mandate; Michael Kirby, the former Cambodian mandate holder, sat on the Democratic People's Republic of Korea (DPRK) Commission of Inquiry; Vitit Muntarbhorn has served the DPRK country mandate, the thematic mandate on sale of children, child prostitution and child pornography, chaired the International Commission of Inquiry on Côte d'Ivoire, was a Commissioner on the Syria Commission of Inquiry and until then was Independent Expert on protection against violence and discrimination based on sexual orientation and gender identity.

41 For example, Joanna Naples-Mitchell has interviewed consecutive mandate holders; see above n 23.

42 The Cambodia Office of the High Commissioner for Human Rights is indelibly tied to the mandate, both being established in the Paris Peace Accords; see S Subedi, above n 22, at 262.

43 For an overview of the OHCHR budget, see 'OHCHR's Funding and Budget', http://www.ohchr.org/EN/AboutUs/Pages/FundingBudget.aspx (accessed 26 June 2017).

Nevertheless, each mandate holder is only supported for two missions a year (biannual country visits can be a challenge when monitoring fast-paced changes in one country or trying to cover the whole UN membership), mandated reporting to the Human Rights Council (and/or General Assembly) and attendance at the annual meeting of special procedures in Geneva. Special rapporteurs do not undertake missions alone. Visits are facilitated by the OHCHR country or regional office (where applicable) and rapporteurs are accompanied by OHCHR staff on all visits, including the desk officer or assistant from Geneva. In this way, the organisation of missions is dependent on the UN/OHCHR and the mandate holder can be made to feel like a puppet in the system, irrespective of the wording of the *Manual of Operations* concerning the mandate holder driving the planning of missions. On the other hand, without the support of the OHCHR staff, it would be difficult, if not impossible, for rapporteurs to navigate the complexities of authorisations preceding any mission.

What can be clearly stated is that special procedures are not puppets of any specific human rights regime. Although completely based in the UN system and working only within UN Member States and recognised territories, they embrace the fragmented legal universe, drawing support from whichever system seems appropriate. This means working with diverse national laws and using relevant regional laws as well as soft law. It is undoubtedly a contribution to integrated human rights.

Looking beyond the UN, there are arguments for special procedures being regarded as puppets of other stakeholders. The media is a contentious example. Undoubtedly, the media is a potent force in many countries and its power and reach can be successfully employed by special procedures. Investigative journalism and strong reporting can be a credible source of information. However, many governments refute comments which they attribute to the media (rightly or wrongly), and the Code of Conduct itself precludes communications based solely on media reports in an attempt to assuage State concerns.[44] Some individuals engage extensively with the media,[45] run their own websites and use social media, including Twitter accounts and Facebook pages.[46] Other mandate holders adopt a lower profile. Limon and Piccone reflect on the online presence

44 Above n 9, at Article 9(e).

45 In 2016, there were 322 press releases and 42 media statements issued by mandate holders: *Report on the Twenty-third Annual Meeting of Special Rapporteur/Representatives, Independent Experts and Chairpersons of Working Groups on Special Procedures of Human Rights*, UN Doc A/HRC/34/34 (hereinafter Annual Report), para 12.

46 For some examples, see UN Special Rapporteur on the rights to freedom of assembly and of association (http://freeassembly.net); two former rapporteurs on the right to food (http://www.righttofood.org and http://www.srfood.org); the former UN Special Rapporteur on the situation of human rights in the Islamic Republic of Iran (http://shaheedoniran.org) (all accessed 30 October 2015). It is also acknowledged that not all UN Member States permit Facebook and Twitter, so there may be issues of accessibility in relation to any such interactions.

and public profile of mandate holders between 2011 and 2013,[47] suggesting that clearer guidance should be agreed in order to minimise 'flash points'.[48] The transition from rapporteurs with backgrounds in foreign ministries, diplomacy and government arguably contributes to the unresolved tension.

NGOs appear to consider special procedures as high-profile 'mouthpieces' for their work and concerns. This is sometimes a benefit and sometimes a challenge. Undoubtedly, special procedures have a global platform to raise concerns (the Human Rights Council and/or the General Assembly), albeit that this is subject to time constraints. Strong media profiles can also be attractive to NGOs. Certainly, tensions can arise when special procedures do not appear to NGOs to act strongly or quickly enough when presented with apparent evidence of human rights violations. However, the options for action available to special procedures requires adherence to diplomatic practices. Accordingly, they are not well suited to the modern world of instant communications. Press statements can be issued relatively quickly.[49]

For both press/media and NGOs, it is difficult to argue that special procedures are puppets. The independence and impartiality of the role leaves each mandate holder with the choice as to how to respond to issues raised by NGOs and on the extent to which he or she interacts with the press (and, indeed, with NGOs).

Ultimately, the special procedures stem from a highly political organisation and body. There is no escaping the fact they are appointed by and report to States. Despite this, the independence and impartiality of the discharge of mandates offers considerable protection against rapporteurs being forced to dance to anyone's tune. Adherence to such a high level of neutrality in practice depends in part on the individual approach and perspective of each mandate holder. Although special procedures can appear to be puppets of different stakeholders at different times, there is no consistency and, with the turnover of appointments, it is fair to say that mandate holders are not a successful embodiment of a system puppet.

4. USER'S SAVIOURS?

Before there can be an analysis of whether the special procedures are user's saviours, it is necessary to determine who the users are. This enables the main

47 M Limon and L Piccone, above n 11, at 32–33, though note also the Manual of Operations guidance.

48 The issue has been subsequently discussed in annual meetings of special procedures and chairpersons of working groups.

49 Note, for example, the press statement issued in May 2015: 'A central role for a civil society is the only way to guarantee inclusive post-2015 development goals', available at http://www.ohchr.org/EN/NewsEvents/Pages/DisplayNews.aspx?NewsID=15970&LangID=E (accessed 26 June 2017).

strands of the web of interactions to be traced and evaluated. The broad definition of human rights users, drawn from Ellen Desmet's work, is outlined above.[50] Specifically looking at special procedures, during country missions, rapporteurs usually meet with government actors (key for many country visits, especially for country mandates), the diplomatic community (again particularly with country mandates), NGOs/civil society, the press and individuals, including victims. They also meet and work with regional organisations, intergovernmental fora and other UN human rights monitoring bodies. Their interaction spans the breadth of 'users' and includes rights claimants, rights realisers, supportive users and, when engaging with courts and tribunals (which is generally necessary when considering the adequacy of remedies or infringements of rights or determining the robustness of the protection of rights in a State), judicial users. Understanding each set of interactions opens up the following question: to what extent are they 'used' by each, the use being anywhere on the scale from positive to negative?

4.1. INTERACTIONS WITH THE HUMAN RIGHTS COUNCIL

The Human Rights Council itself is a user of the special procedures. By virtue of establishing (or renewing) a mandate, the Council is deploying independent expertise to further its own objectives, given that it was established explicitly with responsibility 'for promoting universal respect for the protection of all human rights and fundamental freedoms for all'.[51] With respect to specific functions, the General Assembly requires the Council inter alia to promote advisory services, capacity building and technical assistance, to serve as a dialogue on thematic issues, to promote the full implementation of human rights obligations within States, to respond promptly to human rights emergencies and to make recommendations for promoting and protecting human rights.[52] It is evident that special procedures contribute to this, rendering assistance, whether this be technical assistance and capacity building, drafting guidelines, reviewing State performance against one or more human rights standards or otherwise. Although the Council has expanded the number and range of mandates, care must be taken to ensure that special procedures are not regarded as a panacea for the ills of the international human rights regime; they are not and they cannot be such. Special procedures are but a tool within the toolkit available to the Council to address human rights concerns. Independence and impartiality can be a double-edged sword: on the one hand, special procedures do not

50 Above n 5.
51 General Assembly Resolution 60/251 Human Rights Council at para 2.
52 Ibid, at para 5 (a, b, d, f and i).

necessarily 'review to order' – rather, they use their own discretion to shape the interpretation and application of their mandate; on the other hand, special procedures can fill gaps in capacity within the Council itself by injecting expertise on specific issues and countries. Sometimes the Council has requested special procedures to work together on particular issues – the Democratic Republic of Congo is an example.[53] However, that was arguably an attempt to secure a country mandate through a combination of resources and expertise in thematic mandates.[54] There is a difference between special procedures being deployed for specific projects and those with more general mandates. Combining the two does not necessarily produce results. Nevertheless, it is evident that the Council is increasingly using special procedures for fact-finding missions, commissions of inquiry and sensitive human rights issues.

One facet of the work of the Council in which use of special procedure reports is mandated, but where more use of the special procedures arguably could be made, is in universal periodic review. At present, the contribution of special procedures is limited to their comments being extracted into the 'compilation prepared by the Office of the High Commissioner for Human Rights of the information contained in the reports of treaty bodies, special procedures, including observations and comments by the State concerned, and other relevant official United Nations documents'.[55] There have been calls for greater involvement of special procedures, especially country mandate holders, in the Council's universal periodic review process.[56] Most special procedures would welcome such a development and could provide an expert evidence-based counterpoint to the sometimes more politicised and diplomatic contributions of States. Some special procedures on country visits do choose to act in part as a follow-up mechanism, taking States to task on progress against accepted recommendations. During meetings with governments, efforts taken to address points raised by other States during the review process and even voluntary commitments offered by a State can freely be raised. This is potentially more realistic for country mandates as not all thematic issues are addressed in universal periodic review reports, although in general it raises the challenges of independence, as special procedures are not per se follow-up mechanisms to the Council review process.

---

53 Human Rights Council Resolution 13/22, in which the Council invited six special procedures mandate holders and the Special Representative of the Secretary-General for children and armed conflict to report on the development of the situation in the Democratic Republic of the Congo. For their third joint report, see the 2011 *Third Joint Report of Seven United Nations Experts on the Situation in the Democratic Republic of the Congo*, UN Doc A/HRC/16/68.

54 The special procedures involved indeed recommended the establishment of a country mandate – ibid, para 16 (conclusions).

55 Human Rights Council Resolution 5/1 *Institution-Building of the United Nations Human Rights Council*, at para 15(b).

56 M Limon and T Piccone, above n 11; S Subedi, above n 22, at p 262.

Being a special rapporteur is, as Pinheiro reflects, 'a delicate balancing act'[57] and care must be taken that the 'crown jewel' of the human rights system does not become 'Frankenstein's monster'.[58] Experienced rapporteur and former UN treaty body member Professor Philip Alston wrote warning against the Human Rights Council permitting States to limit the autonomy of UN special procedures.[59] Attempts to rein in the use of powers beyond a narrow interpretation of the Code of Conduct inevitably threatens the autonomy of the rapporteurs, the very essence of their existence which so often allows them to do the work they do. Nevertheless, there can be no doubt that the Human Rights Council uses special procedures – the Council creates and renews/discontinues mandates and, to that extent, can deploy them as it sees fit. Special procedure mandate holders are not necessarily consulted by the Council in advance of decisions on their mandates and this can give rise to tensions. However, the use made of their reports is inconsistent and inevitably influenced by politics.

4.2. INTERACTIONS WITH OTHER INTERGOVERNMENTAL/ INTERNATIONAL FORA

The OHCHR website lists interactions of the special procedures with 'other intergovernmental fora': the UN Security Council and Commission on the Status of Women; and the African Union.[60] The African Union will be considered below (see section 5). Since late 2013, the UN Secretary-General has spearheaded a Human Rights Up Front initiative,[61] committing the UN to prioritising human rights and responses to 'impending catastrophes'.[62] By virtue of this, there should be heightened awareness of, and emphasis on, human rights throughout the UN system, almost 'human rights mainstreaming'. Irrespective of the 'scattered, terse, even cryptic' mentions of human rights in the UN Charter,[63] there is no denying that human rights have been an identified international issue for the 70 years of the UN's existence though the comparative lack of engagement with

57 PS Pinheiro, above n 22.

58 L Sunga, 'What Effect if Any Will the UN Human Rights Council Have on Special Procedures?' in G Alfredsson, J Grimheden, B Ramcharan and A Zayas (eds), *International Monitoring Mechanisms: Essays in Honour of Jakob Th Moller*, 2nd ed, Brill, Leiden 2009, p 178.

59 P Alston, 'Hobbling the Monitors: Should UN Human Rights Monitors Be Accountable?' (2011) 2 *Harvard International Law Journal* 561.

60 Activities with the other intergovernmental bodies; see http://www.ohchr.org/EN/HRBodies/SP/Pages/Engagementwithotherintergovernmentalfora.aspx (accessed 26 June 2017).

61 See generally https://www.un.org/sg/en/content/ban-ki-moon/human-rights-front-initiative (accessed 26 June 2017).

62 The launch statement is available at https://www.un.org/sg/en/content/ban-ki-moon/human-rights-front-initiative (accessed 26 June 2017).

63 H Steiner, P Alston and R Goodman, *International Human Rights in Context: Law, Politics and Morals*, 3rd ed, Oxford University Press, Oxford 2008, p 135.

human rights per se remains a systemic problem. When UN special procedures interact with intergovernmental/international fora, this can contribute to a better understanding of human rights norms. It can also foster human rights integration, providing cross-cutting analyses and even promulgating solutions to problems.

Within the Security Council, 'Arria Formula'[64] meetings were initiated in 1992 and named for the then Ambassador of Venezuela who posited the concept. They are informal confidential discussions which allow the Security Council to invite individuals, including mandate holders, to share ideas and engage in discussions. By way of example, in May 2014, the Special Rapporteur on the human rights of internally displaced persons held an 'Arria Formula' meeting with the Security Council and engaged with subsequent follow-up discussions.[65] The UN Commission on the Status of Women has particular interests in certain mandates and reports are brought to it. For example, the new Working Group on discrimination against women in law and practice is requested to make its reports available to the Commission on the Status of Women.[66] Similarly, the Special Rapporteur on violence against women gives an oral report annually to the Commission.

Special procedures interact directly with fora and organisations relevant to their mandates, though such work is not always well received by the body concerned. Thus, for example, Philip Alston, the Special Rapporteur on extreme poverty and human rights, reported to the General Assembly (Third Committee) in October 2015 on the World Bank and the disconnect he identified between its rhetoric on human rights and the reality of its legal policy, policy analysis, operations and safeguards, which did not reflect a human rights-based approach in reality.[67] The World Bank was identified by him as the 'single most important international agency' for a mandate looking at extreme poverty and human rights.[68] Unsurprisingly, the World Bank refutes many of the findings.

---

64 See 'Background Note of the "Arria Formula" Meetings of the Security Council Members', available at http://www.un.org/en/sc/about/methods/bgarriaformula.shtml (accessed 26 June 2017).

65 Report of the twenty-first annual meeting of special rapporteurs, representatives, independent experts and working groups of the special procedures of the Human Rights Council, including updated information on the special procedures, UN Doc A/HRC/28/41, at para 21; see also the work of the Special Rapporteur on Trafficking in persons, especially women and children, who participated in an open debate in the Security Council in June 2016 on conflict-related sexual violence, Annual Report, UN Doc A/HRC/34/34, para 32.

66 Human Rights Council Resolution 13/23, para 21.

67 'Extreme Poverty and Human Rights', UN Doc A/70/274, submitted in accordance with Human Rights Council Resolution 26/3.

68 'Extreme Poverty and Human Rights', UN Doc A/70/274, at para 2. See also P Alston, 'World Bank: A Human Rights-Free Zone?' *Open Democracy*, 20 October 2015, https://www.opendemocracy.net/openglobalrights/philip-alston/world-bank-human-rights-free-zone (accessed 26 June 2017).

Other special procedures work with other organisations – the Special Rapporteur on cultural rights works closely with UNESCO; the Special Rapporteur on the sale and exploitation of children can work with UNICEF; the Special Rapporteur on slavery may interact with the International Labour Organization (ILO) and so on. Other mandates work directly with specific fora. Examples include the UN Forum on Minority Issues, which is guided by the Special Rapporteur on minority issues,[69] and the Economic and Social Council's UN Permanent Forum on Indigenous Issues,[70] which is a high-level advisory body mandated to address several aspects of the rights of indigenous peoples and obviously can complement the work of the Special Rapporteur on the rights of indigenous peoples.

Overall, the broader UN system is a selective user of the special procedures. However, human rights and the special procedures within that system are a small part of the broader UN system, so this is not surprising. More use of special procedure reports could strengthen Human Rights Up Front and help nurture a more holistic system-wide approach to human rights within the UN.

5. INTERACTIONS WITH REGIONAL ORGANISATIONS

Special procedures also work with their counterparts from other organisations. Both the African Union and the Organization of American States operate systems of special procedures, whilst the Organization for Security and Co-operation in Europe (OSCE) has a number of designated thematic experts. It should be noted that only the UN deploys country mandates, though other organisations send independent experts to investigate and report on specific country situations.

The 2012 Addis Ababa road map guides the first initiative of cooperation between the UN special procedures and the African Union. In January 2012, a dialogue between special procedure mandate holders of both organisations was held in Addis Ababa: nine UN Human Rights Council and seven AU African Commission of Human and Peoples' Rights mandate holders attended, along with representatives of the organisations and from civil society. At the conclusion of the meeting, agreement was reached on a road map for greater cooperation.[71] This included agreement that there would be regular and systematic modalities for sharing information between the two organisation's procedures,

---

69 Established Human Rights Council Resolution 6/15 (2007); see also http://www.ohchr.org/EN/HRBodies/HRC/Minority/Pages/ForumIndex.aspx (accessed 26 June 2017).

70 Established by ECOSOC Resolution 2000/22; see also https://www.un.org/development/desa/indigenouspeoples (accessed 26 June 2017).

71 *Dialogue between Special Procedures Mandate-Holders of the UN Human Rights Council and the African Commission on Human and Peoples Rights: Road Map, Addis Ababa*, 2012, available at http://www.ohchr.org/Documents/HRBodies/SP/SP_UNHRC_ACHPRRoad%20Map.pdf (accessed 26 June 2017).

and that a working group would develop synergies and develop joint actions.[72] Since then, a number of joint statements have been adopted and there have been meetings and regular discussions between mandate holders. The 2014 review was positive, with all parties reaffirming their commitment to implementing the Road Map and enhancing cooperation.[73] Further dialogues on implementation of the review have been ongoing. An example of cooperation is perhaps the UN Independent Investigation on Burundi, which drew on the expertise of three independent experts – two UN Special Rapporteurs and one African Union Special Rapporteur – reporting in 2016.[74]

The model has been extended globally. The Inter-American Commission on Human Rights (IACHR) uses a system of thematic rapporteurs who also sometimes work with UN special procedures. There is evidence of cooperation on specific issues. With regard to the (still) ongoing detention of individuals by the USA in Guantanamo Bay facilities, the IACHR joined with four UN special procedures to call on the US government to respect and guarantee the life, health and personal integrity of detainees.[75] Similarly, there were various activities organised jointly by Dinah Shelton and James Anaya, respectively the former IACHR and UN Rapporteurs on indigenous peoples.[76] In June 2017, the UN Special Rapporteurs on the rights of indigenous peoples (Victoria Tauli Corpuz), on human rights defenders (Michel Forst) and on the environment (John Knox) joined with the IACHR Rapporteur on Indigenous Peoples (Francisco Jose Eguiguren Praeli) to denounce attacks on indigenous and environmental rights in Brazil.[77] Such activities are ad hoc and are not explicitly mandated. However, pooling resources and combining forces does add strength to any arguments and findings. For other examples, see the 2016 joint declaration of the Special Rapporteur on the right to freedom of opinion and expression with media representatives of the Organization for Security and Cooperation in Europe, the Inter-American Commission on Human Rights

72 Ibid, paras 1 and 2.

73 *Consultation between Special Procedures Mandate-Holders of the UN Human Rights Council and the African Commission on Human and Peoples' Rights: Review Addis Ababa Road Map*, Luanda, April 2014.

74 Investigation established during the UN Human Rights Council Special Session on Burundi – UN Doc A/HRC/S-24 of 17 December 2015 and reported back to the Council in September 2016 (UN Doc A/HRC/33/37).

75 Press release, Geneva and Washington DC, 1 May 2013, http://newsarchive.ohchr.org/en/NewsEvents/Pages/DisplayNews.aspx?NewsID=13859&LangID=E (accessed 26 June 2017).

76 See, for example, the joint seminar on the protection of the rights of indigenous peoples, held in June 2010, press release from the OAS, available at http://www.cidh.org/Comunicados/English/2010/58-10eng.htm (accessed 26 June 2017).

77 'Indigenous and Environmental Rights under Attack in Brazil, UN and Inter-American Experts Warn', 8 June 2017, http://www.ohchr.org/EN/NewsEvents/Pages/DisplayNews.aspx?NewsID=21704&LangID=E (accessed 26 June 2017).

and the African Commission on Human and Peoples' Rights on freedom of expression and countering violent extremism.[78] Given the restrictions in funding in particular, melding work with regional equivalents seems a logical progression and facilitates wider user engagement when appropriate.[79] There are also benefits for more integration of human rights, with the different levels cooperating in furtherance of a more unitary approach. Certainly, special procedures can and do draw on the work of regional bodies when appropriate, particularly those regional organisations with human rights foci: the Council of Europe, the African Union and the Organization of American States.

Whilst there is regional interaction, it is not so feasible to regard these regional organisations as 'users' of the UN special procedures. Perhaps it would be more appropriate to regard the interactions as collaborations.

6. INTERACTIONS WITH OTHER UN HUMAN RIGHTS MONITORING SYSTEMS

Arguably the work of special procedures should be complementary to that of treaty bodies. Nigel Rodley, who has served as the Special Rapporteur on Torture (1993–2001) and from 2001 served on the Human Rights Committee, considers the two systems to be 'highly complementary',[80] though notes that this is in part due to mutual respect and discussions obviating any potential overlap.[81] With the expansion in treaty bodies (and crucially ratification of core treaties), there is more potential for overlap between special procedures and treaty bodies, laying the groundwork for integration of approaches and consolidation of international human rights. Some clearly coexist – the Committee on Enforced Disappearances and the Working Group on Enforced or Involuntary Disappearances (the newest treaty body and the oldest working group), for example, now collaborate and coordinate their work on eradicating enforced disappearances.

78 http://www.ohchr.org/EN/NewsEvents/Pages/DisplayNews.aspx?NewsID=19915&LangID=E (accessed 26 June 2017).

79 It will not always be politically advisable or personally desirable for these sorts of joint statements.

80 N Rodley, 'The United Nations Human Rights Council, its Special Procedures, and its Relationship with the Treaty Bodies: Complementarity or Competition?' in K Boyle (ed), *New Institutions for Human Rights Protection*, Oxford University Press, Oxford 2009, p 73. See also his earlier article on the same topic, 'United Nations Human Rights Treaty Bodies and Special Procedures of the Commission on Human Rights: Complementarity or Competition?' (2003) 25 *Human Rights Quarterly* 882.

81 He notes an example whereby the UN Human Rights Committee and the Working Group both received a case, the Working Group transmitting it to the Committee: K Boyle (ed), above n 80, at p 64.

During country visits, special procedures can raise issues noted under concluding observations. Special Rapporteur decisions to request invitations to visit a particular country can be influenced by treaty body reports, drawing on the work of treaty-monitoring bodies. Conversely, special procedures can feed back to treaty bodies following State visits on a country's ratification plans or other issues. Treaty bodies can use reports of rapporteurs when drafting lists of issues or engaging in interactive dialogues with States during the treaty-reporting process. Rapporteurs can also contribute their expertise to general discussion days or thematic comments within the workload of the treaty bodies. (It should obviously be remembered that treaty body members are also independent experts.)

To an extent, both sets of experts use each other's body of work, fostering integration. There is most clearly overlap when thematic mandates are reporting on topics covered by treaties and when country mandates are reviewing compliance with treaties generally (rather than specifically as the treaty bodies do).[82] Individuals have served on both systems, reinforcing this complementarity. Both systems work to achieve better protection and promotion of human rights by using independent experts reviewing State performance.

As with universal periodic review (discussed above), there is potential for the synergies between the systems to be exploited where both parties choose to do so. There are obvious parallels and, ultimately, all systems aim at strengthening the protection of human rights.

7. INTERACTIONS WITH STATES OUTSIDE THE FOREGOING

Although States are obviously key stakeholders, if not the key stakeholders with which special procedures interact, Naples-Mitchell highlights the inherent tension arising from the 'competing needs to treat States as partners and as adversaries'.[83] This is particularly pertinent when States are considered other than as Human Rights Council actors. Country missions are central to the work of rapporteurs, especially those with country mandates, though not all country mandate holders enjoy access to the State under review.[84] Ramcharan regards the

---

82 Treaty bodies usually examine State compliance article by article; special procedures are more eclectic in their selection of rights and freedoms.

83 J Naples-Mitchell, above n 23, at 236.

84 Virtually every country mandate has at times been refused invitations to visit States; see, for current examples, the DPRK and Eritrea – Vitit Muntarbhorn *Report of the Special Rapporteur on the situation of human rights in the Democratic People's Republic of Korea*, Vitit Muntarbhorn, the first mandate holder reflecting on six years without an invitation to visit the country UN Doc A/HRC/13/47 and the latest report by the current mandate

role of special procedures in fact-finding as 'among their strongest contributions to the protection of human rights'.[85] No country visit can take place without an official invitation issued by the putative host State.[86] If no invitation to visit is forthcoming, negotiations can take place between the permanent mission in Geneva and OHCHR staff members in pursuit of securing an invitation.[87] Even once an invitation is issued, the State must be aware of its responsibilities, including fully facilitating the visit of the rapporteur (freedom of movement, freedom of inquiry, assurances of no reprisals against those meeting special rapporteurs and appropriate security arrangements).[88] When the necessary guarantees cannot be made, a planned mission may be cancelled. Often the cancellation or postponement of a country visit gives great publicity to an issue – two high-profile examples of such non-visits were the planned joint visit to the US Guantanamo Bay detention facilities[89] and the cancelled visit of the UN Special Rapporteur on the human rights of migrants to Australia in September 2015.[90]

---

holder, Tomas Ojea Quintana, *Report of the Special Rapporteur on the situation of human rights in the Democratic People's Republic of Korea*, UN Doc A/HRC/34/66, para 31; *Report of the Special Rapporteur on the situation of human rights in Eritrea, Sheila B. Keetharuth*, UN Doc A/HRC/35/39, para 8. Security concerns can also be an issue – see *Report of the Independent Expert on the Situation of Human Rights in Somalia, Bahame Tom Nyanduga*, UN Doc A/HRC/27/71, at para 2, though he undertook a mission in 2016 – see *Report of the Independent Expert on the Situation of Human Rights in Somalia, Bahame Tom Nyanduga*, UN Doc A/HRC/33/64, para 2. Both these States have been subject to commissions of inquiry which arguably heightens the tension between the UN and the states concerned, both the then rapporteurs served on 'their' country's commission.

85 B Ramcharan, above n 24, at p 153.

86 T Piccone (above n 8) and M Limon and T Piccone (above n 11) review the number of invitations issued pursuant to requests. At the end of June 2017, there were 117 standing invitations. For an up-to-date list, see http://spinternet.ohchr.org/_Layouts/SpecialProceduresInternet/StandingInvitations.aspx (accessed 26 June 2017).

87 Special procedures cannot force States to issue invitations and some countries do not engage with rapporteurs, whether country (recent examples are the DPRK, Iran, Eritrea) or thematic, though note that the DPRK invited the Special Rapporteur on the rights of persons with disabilities to visit in May 2017 – for an end of mission press statement, see http://www.ohchr.org/EN/NewsEvents/Pages/DisplayNews.aspx?NewsID=21610&LangID=E (accessed 26 June 2017).

88 For the terms of reference for fact-finding missions, see UN Doc E/CN.4/1998/45.

89 Statement issued 31 October 2005 by Leandro Despuoy, Special Rapporteur on the independence of judges and lawyers, Paul Hunt, Special Rapporteur on the right of everyone to the enjoyment of the highest attainable standard of health, Asma Jahangir, Special Rapporteur on freedom of religion and belief, Manfred Nowak, Special Rapporteur on torture and other cruel, inhuman or degrading treatment or punishment, and Leila Zerrougui, Chairperson Rapporteur of the Working Group on Arbitrary Detention, ultimately declining the qualified invitation issued by the USA; see UN Doc E/CN.4/2006/120, para 3.

90 Francois Crepeau, Special Rapporteur on the human rights of migrants, statement postponing visit to Australia scheduled for September/October 2015, available at http://un.org.au/2015/09/26/official-visit-to-australia-postponed-due-to-protection-concerns/#more-6974 (accessed 26 June 2017).

Exceptionally, entry without permission has been attempted, as Naples-Mitchell records with respect to Palestine.[91]

Country mandates by definition must try to engage with States. They can be classified as 'item 4' or 'item 10' in the Human Rights Council's agenda: the former means that the territory has a human rights situation that requires the Council's attention, while the latter is more related to technical assistance and capacity building. There can be overlaps with mandates addressed under agenda item 10 actually having a strong role in terms of monitoring matters of concern to the Council. Either way, the role involves monitoring human rights in a country and subsequently reporting findings to the Council. Some countries accept the mandates and agree in advance to the renewal resolution; indeed, some ask for a mandate to be established. However, other States refuse to cooperate with country mandates and refute outright their establishment/imposition.[92] It should be noted that country mandates are distinct from Commissions of Inquiry, which the Council can also establish. There is some degree of overlap with the salient country rapporteur generally being appointed to serve on any commission. This was the case for the Democratic Peoples' Republic of Korea and then rapporteur Marzuki Darusman,[93] Syria and appointed rapporteur Paulo Pinheiro,[94] Eritrea and rapporteur Sheela Keetharuth.[95]

There is potential for country visits to be of great use to States, especially when technical assistance is being delivered or a mandate holder is gathering information on themes to assist States implementing human rights. For States seeking to promote human rights in third countries, deploying special procedures offers a mechanism to investigate, report and assist. In such a way, these states are users. However, for those States being reviewed by special procedures, the 'use' of the guidance and assistance on offer is variable. The High Commissioner

---

91 Richard Falk, former Special Rapporteur on the situation of human rights in the Palestinian territories, considers the consequential refusal of entry into Israel as a profile-raising success – J Naples-Mitchell, above n 23, at 238. He was detained for three days then expelled from the country.

92 The DPRK has not invited mandate holders to visit. The country also rejected the recent Commission of Inquiry: the Special Rapporteur was a member of the Commission, and the former Secretary-General's Special Representative on Cambodia was Chair – report, see below. For an analysis, see M Kirby, 'Special Edition' (2014) 15 *Asia-Pacific Journal of Human Rights and Law* 1.

93 For further information, see *Report of the Commission of Inquiry on Human Rights in the Democratic People's Republic of Korea*, UN Doc A/HRC/25/63; and for more information, see http://www.ohchr.org/EN/HRBodies/HRC/CoIDPRK/Pages/CommissionInquiryonHRinDPRK.aspx (accessed 26 June 2017).

94 For details of the commission, chaired by the putative country rapporteur, see http://www.ohchr.org/EN/HRBodies/HRC/IICISyria/Pages/IndependentInternationalCommission.aspx (accessed 26 June 2017).

95 *Report of the Commission of Inquiry on Human Rights in Eritrea*, UN Doc A/HRC/29/42, 4 June 2015. For further information, see http://www.ohchr.org/EN/HRBodies/HRC/CoIEritrea/Pages/commissioninquiryonhrinEritrea.aspx (accessed 26 June 2017).

for Human Rights publicly commented in September at the opening meeting of the Human Rights Council that criticism is not a threat to sovereignty, stating that: 'Sovereignty cannot be damaged by carefully evaluated commentary.'[96] Nevertheless, many States do regard any criticism as an assault on their sovereignty and thus as contrary to the principles of the UN. In the main, such an approach taken by States under review seems to strengthen rather than weaken the resolve of mandate holders, with alternative means being found to obtain evidence.

8. INTERACTIONS BETWEEN THEMSELVES

As has been noted, special procedures work together when the Council so requests, or through engagement on common interests with regional entities. There is, however, a degree of integration inter se – the evolution of the annual meetings of special procedures[97] and the strengthening of the Coordinating Committee have supported this.[98] All special procedure mandate holders and chairs of working groups are supported to meet annually to discuss common areas of concern and share experiences.[99] Press statements can be issued on behalf of all special procedures – this obviously accords considerable weight of expertise. Special procedures also often issue joint communications and urgent appeals, something that is encouraged by the *Manual of Operations*.[100] For example, in 2016, 455 out of 526 communications issued were joined by other special procedures.[101] Working together, when appropriate, promotes integration as diverse approaches are brought together, to the potential benefit of all. Country mandate holders can benefit from the specific expertise of thematic mandates. Mandate holders often privately notify each other of other non-official visits they are undertaking and, indeed, the two mandate holders may collaborate unofficially as regards the content of reports, terminology and so on.

---

96 For the full statement, see http://www.ohchr.org/EN/NewsEvents/Pages/DisplayNews.aspx?NewsID=16414&LangID=E (accessed 26 June 2017).

97 The Vienna Declaration and Programme of Action adopted by the World Conference on Human Rights underlined the importance of preserving and strengthening the system of Special Procedures and specified that the procedures and mechanisms should be enabled to harmonise and rationaliSe their work through periodic meetings: UN Doc A/CONF.157/23, Part II, para. 95.

98 This Committee was established in 2005 and now reports annually to the Human Rights Council, which adds further to information sharing and integration: http://www.ohchr.org/EN/HRBodies/SP/CoordinationCommittee/Pages/CCSpecialProceduresIndex.aspx (accessed 26 June 2017). For the most recent report, see Annual Report, UN Doc A/HRC/34/34, above n 45.

99 Information on the annual meetings is available at http://www.ohchr.org/EN/HRBodies/SP/AMeeting/Pages/AnnualMeeting.aspx (accessed 26 June 2017). The 24th annual meeting was held in June 2017.

100 Manual of Operations, above n 23.

101 See Annual Report, above n 45, at para 8.

From the perspective of integrated human rights, the Annual Report to the Human Rights Council notes that in 2016, three mandate holders specifically focused on integrating gender perspectives in their thematic areas, including in relation to the right to food,[102] the prohibition of torture and cruel, inhuman and degrading treatment,[103] and the realisation of the human rights to water and sanitation.[104] The sustainable development goals were another common sub-theme. Whilst both of these pursue UN agendas, the diverse independent expert reviews offer unique insights and can lead to greater integration by widening the understanding of sustainable development goals or gender perspectives.

Although not 'users' in the sense given in this chapter (though arguably they are supportive users), special procedures benefit from the support of each other and clearly act together, pulling and sharing resources when it is appropriate to do so.

9. INTERACTIONS WITH NGOs AND CIVIL SOCIETY

Special procedures interact quite extensively with NGOs and civil society. For some mandates, NGOs are a principal source of information, while for others they are a source of verification of credibility of information. Most country missions include meetings with such stakeholders and frequently reporting activities in Geneva or New York also include briefings with civil society entities. The Human Rights Council itself has strengthened the engagement of NGOs and recognises the participation of NGOs in many ways.[105] NGOs, for example, can contribute to the stakeholders' report for universal periodic review, and can comment on and otherwise participate in the interactive dialogue with Special Procedures in Council. NGOs of course are also increasingly engaged with the treaty bodies, not least with the compilation and submission of shadow reports. An entire chapter in the *UN Civil Society Handbook* is dedicated to special procedures to raise awareness of the opportunities presented.[106]

Accredited NGOs have a range of opportunities to participate formally in the Human Rights Council dialogues and to run side-events during reports of special procedures. NGOs can also call for new mandates. A recent example is

---

102 *Report of the UN Special Rapporteur on the Right to Food*, UN Doc A/HRC/31/51.

103 *Report of the Special Rapporteur on Torture and Other Cruel, Inhuman or Degrading Treatment or Punishment*, UN Doc A /HRC/31/57.

104 *Report of the Special Rapporteur on the Human Right to Safe Drinking Water and Sanitation*, UN Doc A/HRC/33/49.

105 NGOs can be accredited to the Human Rights Council if they have consultative status with the UN Economic and Social Council – see ECOSOC Resolution 1996/31 (see also http://www.esango.un.org, accessed 26 June 2017).

106 Chapter 6; for the handbook, see http://www.ohchr.org/EN/AboutUs/CivilSociety/Documents/Handbook_en.pdf (accessed 26 June 2017).

the establishment of the Special Rapporteur on privacy – a joint NGO statement from 95 organisations picked up the call of the General Assembly and urged the Human Rights Council to create the new mandate.[107] This mandate was established in June 2015.

Non-accredited NGOs can also engage with special procedures. Perhaps this is most evident during information gathering when special procedures can take evidence from any credible source. This obviously includes NGOs and civil society groups. Similarly, when on mission, special procedures can and do meet with a variety of stakeholders, especially on field trips. Local civil society groups and NGOs are a particularly useful source of national information. When there is no OHCHR country office, NGOs arguably have a potentially even greater role as information providers balancing and illuminating State reports and claims. The mix of material drawn up sets the work of rapporteurs apart. Of course, many complaints are brought to the attention of the special procedures by NGOs.

NGOs are often the most avid users of the special procedures. Nevertheless, paradoxically NGOs can be their strong critics. Accessibility to procedures is limited, with most of the world's NGOs and civil society groups being unaware of the possibilities offered by special procedures, whether in terms of highlighting issues, developing standards, negotiating with States or even addressing violations. Of course, if all NGOs and civil society organisations sought to engage fully with the special procedures, the current system simply could not cope.

10. INTERACTIONS WITH INDIVIDUALS

Special procedures also interact with individuals, although, as users, individuals are probably the least engaged group. Human rights, as a body of legal and policy standards, aim at guaranteeing individual rights and freedoms. Individuals should thus be beneficiaries of the special procedures' work and in that sense 'users'. Individuals tend to engage with special procedures through country missions and external fora (for example, the Special Rapporteur on the right of indigenous peoples can interact with the Permanent Forum on Indigenous Peoples, which advises the Economic and Social Council,[108] and the Forum on Minority Issues is convened by the Special Rapporteur on minority issues).[109]

---

107 For the text, see Joint NGO Oral Statement to the Human Rights Council 28th Ordinary Session, 'Call to Establish a UN Special Rapporteur on the Right to Privacy', delivered by Andrew Smith, Article 19; for the text, see https://www.icj.org/wp-content/uploads/2015/03/Advocacy-HRC28-Privacy-JointOralStatement-2015.docx (accessed 26 June 2017).

108 Established by ECOSOC Resolution 2000/22; for an overview, see http://undesadspd.org/IndigenousPeoples.aspx (accessed 26 June 2017).

109 Human Rights Council Resolution 6/15; for more information, see http://www.ohchr.org/EN/HRBodies/HRC/Minority/Pages/ForumIndex.aspx (accessed 26 June 2017).

where information gathering occurs and victim testimonies may be heard. Individuals may also petition mandate holders, though this is not frequently utilised. In 2016, the special procedures addressed a total of 526 communications to 119 States.[110]

The first thematic Commission mechanism, the Working Group on Enforced or Arbitrary Disappearances, established a procedure for dealing with urgent reports requiring immediate attention.[111] Reports received are sent to the ministry of foreign affairs of the country concerned for comment. All special procedures can receive communications from individuals or from groups. According to the *Manual of Operations*[112] and Code of Conduct,[113] special procedures can issue letters of allegation and urgent appeals, and, of course, can send general letters. The latter can be addressed to non-State actors or can be used for requesting specific information. Article 9 of the Code of Conduct prescribes the admissibility criteria that the Special Rapporteur should employ when considering communications. These are broadly similar to those of the treaty bodies: the communication should not be manifestly unfounded or politically motivated; it should have a factual description of the alleged violation; it should not be abusive; it should be submitted by victims or others acting in good faith with reliable knowledge of violations; and, particularly relevant in so many instances, any communication cannot be exclusively based on reports disseminated in the mass media. Today the Quick Response Desk of the OHCHR acts as a focal point.[114] Received communications are forwarded to the rapporteur for a decision. If action is to be taken, then the desk officers draft the communication in conjunction with the rapporteur and coordinate support amongst other rapporteurs. (As noted above, rapporteurs often act together in relation to such communications.) UN country teams and the relevant desk officers in Geneva are also involved in the process. These letters of allegation follow a set format.[115] Urgent appeals are restricted to time-sensitive alleged violations of human rights involving loss of life or life-threatening situations.[116]

Working groups traditionally receive the highest levels of communications,[117] but can have high-impact situations. For example, the Working Group on Arbitrary Detention recorded the release of 17 individuals and 230 military

110 Annual Report, above n 45, at para 8.

111 For the revised method of work, see UN Doc A/HRC/WGEID/102/2 (2014).

112 Manual of Operations, above n 31.

113 UN Human Rights Council Resolution 5/2, Articles 9 and 10.

114 Manual of Operations, above n 31, at para 31.

115 From ibid, para 47.

116 Code of Conduct, above n 9, Article 10; Manual of Operations, above n 31, at paras 43 et seq.

117 According to the 2016 statistics, in 2016 the Working Group on Enforced or Involuntary Disappearances, for example, transmitted 801 cases of enforced disappearances, 389 of which were under the urgent action procedure – Annual Report, above n 45, at para 10.

officers in 2014.[118] However, when looking across all mandates, Piccone queries the effectiveness of communications.[119] He notes slow responses by States to letters from rapporteurs and regional variations in non and low responses to letters from rapporteurs, African States generally being the least likely to respond.[120] However, many special procedures would agree that it is not infrequent that a positive change is noted following a communication, albeit that there is no explicit causal connection between the action and the communication and there remains no formal response from the State. Therefore, the statistics do not give a true reflection of the importance and impact of this mechanism. There are also follow-up possibilities – the special procedures can raise issues on country visits, special procedures and OHCHR staff can follow up in Geneva with permanent representatives, and, of course, there is the possibility (in theory) of follow up in universal periodic review, with States picking up on negative or non-responses when questioning a State under review.[121] However, this raises the issue of the non-involvement of special procedures with Universal Periodic Review (UPR), as discussed above. The Working Group on Arbitrary Detention, it should be noted, has now implemented a more formal follow up system for its communications.

Victim testimonies can be particularly potent and represent another way for individuals to interact with rapporteurs directly. (It should be noted that meetings with victims are not necessarily reported in formal reports to the Human Rights Council or the media – protection of individuals is paramount.) Alison Aggarwal, research assistant to the former rapporteur on adequate housing, writes convincingly on the impact of victims testimonies in shaping the work of her rapporteur: 'listening to women's experiences [was] integral to his exploration of a broad and inclusive approach to women's right to adequate housing'.[122] Ramcharan discusses the 'painstaking efforts' of mandate holders 'to act for the protection of those at risk of serious violations of human rights'.[123] Few rapporteurs would disagree with this.

Individuals should be able to use the special procedures to enhance the protection and promotion of their rights. However, the reality is that for most

---

118 *Report on the Twenty-First Annual Meeting of Special Rapporteurs/Representatives, Independent Experts and Working Groups of the Special Procedures of the Human Rights Council, Including Updated Information on the Special Procedures*, A/HRC/28/41, at para 8.

119 T Piccone, above n 8, at p 20; see also M Limon and T Piccone, above n 11, at p 30 for updated figures. This excludes the principal Working Groups which receive communications.

120 T Piccone, above n 8, at p 22.

121 In the first cycle, there is no evidence of this happening. The most common recommendations concerning special procedures were to extend standing invitations to all special procedures or to respond to requests for visits made publicly by special rapporteurs (thematic or country). Review of all first-cycle working group reports, on file with the author.

122 A Aggarwal, 'UN Special Rapporteur on Adequate Housing: Emerging Gendered Norms for the Right to Adequate Housing' (2004) 10 *Australian Journal of Human Rights* 8.

123 B Ramcharan, above n 24, at p 152.

of the world's people, the special procedures remain relatively inaccessible. Of course, moving the communication process online has alleviated this to some extent, but the number of letters from individuals (as opposed to through NGOs) is remarkably small,[124] although an explosion in the number of communications would break the capacity of the present system.

11. CONCLUSIONS: PUPPETS OR SAVIOURS?

Clearly special procedures retain a rather special role within the web of mechanisms available for promoting and protecting human rights. Majat Maalla M'Jid highlights the 'unique platform' offered by her former mandate (on the sale of children, child prostitution and child pornography) to raise awareness, knowledge and understanding, monitor respect, address allegations and advocate for implementation.[125] Similar views are expressed by other mandate holders.[126] Such a platform inevitably brings with it challenges and responsibilities. To the greatest extent, resolving and addressing such challenges and responsibilities depends as much on the personality, skills and views of the individual mandate holder as on the Human Rights Council and the UN Member States. For such a unique and special role to depend almost entirely on the holders volunteering their time, skills and energies is perhaps the crux of the issue – they are a pro bono resource, so the actual performance of each mandate holder depends to an extent on the time and energy that each individual mandate holder is willing and able to dedicate to this work. The dwindling resources of the UN itself compound the problem as the logistical, administrative and research support to fully support mandates is, at times, simply not available. Nevertheless, special procedures can and do make a difference. They contribute towards the integration of human rights systems, filling protection gaps in law and practice, acting as a critical friend to States and non-State actors, and raising awareness of issues and the plight of individual whose voices would otherwise not be heard. Interacting with any and all stakeholders and working across legal systems are specific features of UN special procedures.

There is evidence of a range of entities trying to use the special procedures for their own political or financial ends. Sometimes this works for the improvement of human rights; sometimes it does not. The 'use' made of special procedures by a range of actors is inconsistent and eclectic. For specific users such as the Human Rights Council, the system seems to be increasingly perceived as a way of

124 The treaty body system also receives comparably few individual communications.

125 N Maalla M'Jid, above n 22, at p 48.

126 See, inter alia, S Subedi, above n 3; PS Pinheiro, above n 22; quotes in J Naples-Mitchell, above n 23; quotes in M Limon and T Piccone, above n 11.

outsourcing work, albeit that this can and does result in high-quality independent returns. For other users, the system is more 'hit and miss': special procedures can diffuse tensions, clarify State obligations and even ameliorate suffering, but not across the board. Time and funding preclude much immediate impact 'on the ground', though longer-term succour is apparent when their policy and legal recommendations are realised by States and organisations. More funding could increase the range of individuals who can accept mandates and could extend the work undertaken. However, some aspects of their uniqueness would be lost if there was further standardisation or mainstreaming. Special procedures have multifaceted roles and seem to be regarded differently by different users at different times. Perhaps, after all, despite the challenges encountered, UN special procedures can be the saviours of a UN human rights system beset with the problems of politicisation, backlog and limited enforcement opportunities.

THE AFRICAN COURT ON HUMAN AND PEOPLES' RIGHTS

A Uniquely Equipped Testbed for (the Limits of) Human Rights Integration?

Adamantia Rachovitsa*

1. INTRODUCTION

International human rights law is embedded within international law that is fragmented by design. At the same time, human rights law itself forms a fragmented universe, on account of both its multilevel architecture and governance – comprising universal, regional and subregional levels of protection – and the (over-)specialisation of the field. Against this background, human rights integration is seen as a means to mitigate certain challenges associated

* Assistant Professor of Public International Law, Faculty of Law, University of Groningen, the Netherlands. Email: a.rachovitsa@rug.nl.

with this fragmentation. Human rights integration may also be an opportunity to restore focus on the user(s) of the human rights system and on the arguments that can be employed with the aim of framing an individual's claim and calling for the highest possible level of protection across different regimes and specialities.[1]

Within the confines of positive law, human rights integration can be pursued on three different levels/stages: first, when States draft a human rights treaty; second, when an international court or other international body interprets that treaty; and third, when the treaty is applied.[2] Human rights integration is, accordingly, constrained by the limitations attached to these three different tasks. In this regard, this chapter argues that the African Court on Human and Peoples' Rights (ACtHPR) is uniquely situated to pursue human rights integration. This is due to three distinctive features pertaining to the African Charter on Human and Peoples' Rights (ACHPR)[3] and the ACtHPR's mandate. First, the indivisibility, interdependence and inter-relation of human rights are not merely underlying principles and postulates, but are specifically entrenched in the text of the ACHPR; the ACHPR provides civil and political rights alongside economic, social and cultural rights and peoples' rights. Second, the ACtHPR enjoys the jurisdiction to interpret and apply not only the ACHPR but also any other relevant human rights instrument ratified by the State(s) concerned. Hence, the ACtHPR enjoys a considerably broader mandate ratione materiae vis-à-vis other international human rights courts. Third, the ACtHPR is specifically directed by Articles 60 and 61 of the ACHPR to draw inspiration from other international instruments when interpreting the rights envisaged in the ACHPR.

This chapter discusses two out of these three distinctive features in connection with human rights integration. The analysis on the ACtHPR's jurisdiction merits separate discussion and it will not be covered in this chapter. Consequently, this chapter focuses on human rights integration in the drafting of the ACHPR (section 2) and human rights integration when the ACtHPR interprets the ACHPR (section 3). Although the ACHPR and the practice of the African Commission on Human and Peoples' Rights (hereinafter 'the African Commission' or 'the Commission') have attracted the attention of international scholars, it is surprising that not much has been written since the ACtHPR

1 E Brems, 'Should Pluriform Human Rights Become One? Exploring the Benefits of Human Rights Integration' (2014) 4 *European Journal of Human Rights* 447.

2 Interestingly, domestic courts have a different and more expansive (vis-à-vis international courts) role in pursuing human rights integration. See A Rachovitsa, 'Treaty Clauses and Fragmentation of International Law: Applying the More Favourable Protection Clause in Human Rights Treaties' (2016) 16 *Human Rights Law Review* 77, 81–83.

3 Adopted 27 June 1981, entered into force 21 October 1986, Organisation of African Unity, CAB/LEG/67/3 rev. 5, 21 ILM 58 (1982).

started to develop its case law.[4] The analysis herein provides the first assessment of how the ACtHPR has addressed these issues in its existing jurisprudence.[5]

2. HUMAN RIGHTS INTEGRATION IN THE DRAFTING OF THE ACHPR AND THE POTENTIAL OF THE AFRICAN HUMAN RIGHTS *CORPUS JURIS*

The ACHPR is a unique treaty, according equal weight to all three generations of human rights: it provides civil and political rights; economic, social and cultural rights; and also peoples' rights. Economic, social and cultural rights include the right to work under equitable and satisfactory conditions (Article 15), the right to health (Article 16), the right to education (Article 17) and the right to a healthy environment (Articles 23 and 24). Peoples' rights encompass the right to self-determination (Articles 20 and 22) and the right to dispose of natural resources (Article 21). Another characteristic of the ACHPR is its emphasis on the duties of the individual towards the community and the State (Article 29). At the same time, the ACHPR omits certain rights (e.g. there is no right to privacy under the ACHPR) and it envisages fewer safeguards compared with other human rights treaties, as can be seen from the poor drafting of the provisions concerning criminal procedure before and during trial (Articles 6 and 7), the limited scope of the right to vote (Article 13), the introduction of claw-back clauses and the vague language of the limitation clauses.[6]

The role of the ACtHPR (and the African Commission) is critical for developing the special features of the ACHPR and the rights provided therein. This role is marked not only by the novelty of economic, social and cultural rights and peoples' rights being justiciable and adjudicated by and before an international human rights court, but also the potential for construing the inter-relatedness and indivisibility of human rights in more effective – and perhaps new – ways. To this end, human rights integration can be relevant

4 For two recent studies, see JD Mujuzi, 'The African Court on Human and Peoples' Rights and its Protection of the Right to a Fair Trial' (2017) 16 *Law & Practice of International Court and Tribunals* 187, 198; and F Viljoen, 'Understanding and Overcoming Challenges in Accessing the African Court on Human and Peoples' Rights' (2018) 67 *International & Comparative Law Quarterly* 63.

5 More specifically, the ACtHPR has finalised, in the exercise of its contentious jurisdiction, 40 cases: 18 were declared inadmissible, three were struck off the docket, 16 were decided on their merits (two of which were decided jointly) and three were judgments on the interpretation of the ACtHPR's rulings. Information available at http://www.african-court.org/en/index.php/cases/2016-10-17-16-18-21#finalised-cases (accessed 23 October 2017).

6 C Heyns, 'The African Regional Human Rights System: In Need of Reform?' (2001) 2 *African Human Rights Law Journal* 155, 161; E Brems, *Human Rights: Universality and Diversity*, Martinus Nijhoff Publishers, The Hague 2001, pp 116–117, 126–128, 133–136.

both as an interpretative argument and/or principle (or rather, perhaps, as a set of interpretative arguments and/or principles) and as an outcome of that interpretation process, in two distinct ways. First, human rights integration can be relevant in terms of making international law and human rights responsive to African circumstances and in advancing the African human rights *corpus juris*.[7] The Commission has begun to develop the contours of a regional human rights culture and the ACtHPR should build on this.[8] Second, and conversely, one needs to bear in mind the possible subsequent contribution of the African *corpus juris* to the progressive development of international law.[9]

On certain occasions, the African Commission's interpretations have been characterised as either 'very progressive' or 'dangerously loose' constructions of the Charter.[10] For example, the Commission read the right to housing and the right to food into the ACHPR, even though these are not provided therein. The Commission's reasoning was grounded on the fact that the right to housing and the right to food are inseparably linked to the dignity of human beings and are essential for the enjoyment and fulfilment of other rights, such as the rights to property, health and family life.[11] Turning to another issue, in the *Social and Economic Rights Action Center (SERAC) and Center for Economic and Social Rights (CESR) v Nigeria* case, the Commission made certain important pronouncements concerning peoples' rights by articulating the collective nature of such rights in light of the ACHPR's provisions. The case concerned the protection of the Ogoni people from the adverse effects of oil exploration in the Niger Delta. Forced evictions were found to constitute a violation of the right to housing enjoyed by the Ogoni people as a *collective right*.[12] Moreover, the Commission accepted the applicants' allegation linking Article 4 on the right

---

7 African Commission on Human Rights, *Social and Economic Rights Action Center (SERAC) and Center for Economic and Social Rights (CESR) v Nigeria*, App. No. 155/96, 27 October 2001 §68.

8 R Murray, 'A Comparison between the African and European Courts of Human Rights' (2002) 2 *African Human Rights Law Journal* 195, 219; I Bantekas and L Oette, *International Human Rights Law and Practice*, 2nd ed., Cambridge University Press, Cambridge 2016, p 281; M Mutua, 'The African Human Rights Court: A Two-Legged Stool?' (1999) 21 *Human Rights Quarterly* 342, 362.

9 See also AK Perrin, 'African Jurisprudence for Africa's Problems: Human Rights Norm Diffusion and Norm Generation through Africa's Regional International Court' (2015) *American Society International Law Proceedings* 32. On the contribution of the International Court of Justice and the European Court of Human Rights to the development of international law, see respectively H Lauterpacht, *The Development of International Law by the International Court*, Steven & Sons Limited, London 1958, pp 37–40; and JG Merrills, *The Development of International Law by the European Court of Human Rights*, 2nd ed., Manchester University Press, Manchester 1993.

10 I Bantekas and L Oette, above note 8, pp 279–280.

11 *SERAC and CESR v Nigeria* §§60, 65.

12 Ibid §63.

to life and integrity of the person to the life of the *Ogoni society as a whole.* The Commission went on to find that Nigeria had violated Article 4 with respect not only to specific individuals in Ogoniland, but also to the Ogoni community as a whole.[13] This was an innovative approach for 2001 and even vis-à-vis the progressive case law of the Inter-American Court of Human Rights (IACtHR) on indigenous peoples' rights established in 2007 in the *Saramaka* judgment.[14]

The ACtHPR, for its part, has not yet had many opportunities to develop the distinctive rights provided in the ACHPR.[15] The ACtHPR has decided, as of 30 October 2017, 16 complaints on their merits involving the following States: Côte d'Ivoire (one case), Kenya (one case), Libya (one case), Senegal (one case), Malawi (one case), Rwanda (one case), Burkina Faso (two cases) and Tanzania (eight cases). The subject matter of the complaints mostly concerned well-established civil and political rights, including the right to political participation and the question of whether the prohibition of independent candidature violates an applicant's right to participate in public affairs;[16] the right to equal protection under the law in the context of assessing the impartiality and independence of electoral bodies;[17] the right to freedom of expression in connection with the right to effective remedy[18] and the question of whether criminal defamation statutes are a proportionate and necessary restriction on freedom of expression;[19] the right to life;[20] the right to be free from arbitrary deprivation of liberty;[21] the right to be free from torture;[22] and several aspects of the right to a fair trial (e.g. the right to be heard and to defend oneself, the right to be tried within a reasonable time, to free legal assistance and to the pronouncement of a judgment in open court).[23]

---

13 Ibid §67.

14 *Saramaka People v Suriname*, Judgment on Preliminary Objections, Merits, Reparations and Costs, Series C, No. 17, 28 November 2007, §171.

15 There is one case concerning indigenous peoples' rights (*African Commission on Human and Peoples' Rights v Republic of Kenya*, App. No. 006/2012, Judgment on Merits, 26 May 2017) and it will be discussed in section 3.3.

16 *Tanganyika Law Society and Legal and Human Rights Centre and Reverend Christopher R. Mtikila v United Republic of Tanzania*, App. Nos 009 & 011/2011, Judgment on Merits, 14 November 2013.

17 *Actions pour la Protection des Droits de l'Homme (APDH) v Republic of Cote d'Ivoire*, App. No. 001/2014, Judgment on Merits, 18 November 2016.

18 *Abdoulaye Nikiema, Ernest Zongo, Blaise Ilboudo & Burkinabe Human and Peoples' Rights Movement v Burkina Faso*, App. No. 013/2011, Judgment on Merits, 28 March 2014.

19 *Lohé Issa Konaté v Burkina Faso*, App. No. 004/2013, Judgment on Merits, 5 December 2014.

20 *The African Commission on Human and Peoples' Rights v Libya*, App. No. 002/2013, Judgment on Merits, 3 June 2016.

21 Ibid.

22 *Alex Thomas v United Republic of Tanzania*, App. No. 005/2013, Judgment on Merits, 20 November 2015; *The African Commission on Human and Peoples' Rights v Libya.*

23 Ibid, *Alex Thomas*; *Wilfred Onyango Nganyi and 9 Others v United Republic of Tanzania*, App. No. 006/2013, Judgment on Merits, 18 March 2016; *Mohamed Abubakari v United Republic of Tanzania*, App. No. 007/2013, Judgment on Merits, 3 June 2016; *Christopher Jonas v United Republic of Tanzania*, App. No. 011/2015, Judgment on Merits, 28 September 2017.

These are the first years of the ACtHPR's functioning and in due time the alleged violations and the countries concerned will become more varied.[24]

3. THE INTERPRETATIVE USE OF RELEVANT INTERNATIONAL INSTRUMENTS AS A MEANS TO PURSUE HUMAN RIGHTS INTEGRATION

The interpretative use of relevant international instruments not only tells us about the ACtHPR's openness to other standards in general, but can also be a means to pursue human rights integration. The use of other international instruments implicates the ACtHPR in the construction of an international and regional *corpus juris* on human rights. Moreover, the use of other international instruments and the views of other bodies in the process of interpretation mitigate the risk of conflicting or diverging interpretations of similar or identical treaty provisions. This is particularly important in light of the ACtHPR's distinctively broad contentious jurisdiction. Pursuant to Article 3(1) of the Protocol: 'The jurisdiction of the Court shall extend to all cases and disputes submitted to it concerning the interpretation and application of the Charter, this Protocol *and any other relevant Human Rights instrument ratified by the States concerned*' (emphasis added).[25] The risk of divergent interpretations of other human rights treaties when the ACtHPR engages with, interprets and applies these treaties is an issue which has not been addressed by either the ACHPR or the Protocol.[26] At the same time, however, one should not over-emphasise the fragmentation of international jurisprudence or the divergence of views of the international bodies entrusted with monitoring human rights treaties. These matters can be mitigated (as will be discussed below) to a great extent, in the course of interpretation, by being aware of and taking into account the views of other international bodies and courts. The discussion below addresses the

---

24 This was also the case with the Commission, which now addresses more diverse questions concerning armed conflict, oil extraction, collective rights, indigenous peoples and mass expulsions. See I Bantekas and L Oette, above note 8, pp 277–279.

25 Protocol to the African Charter on Human and Peoples' Rights on the Establishment of the African Court on Human and Peoples' Rights (adopted 10 June 1998, entered into force 25 January 2004). The Protocol was replaced by the Protocol on the Statute of the African Court of Justice and Human Rights on 1 July 2008 merging the African Court on Human and Peoples' Rights and the Court of Justice of the African Union into one single court. See, in general, F Viljoen, *International Human Rights Law in Africa*, 2nd ed., Oxford University Press, New York 2012, pp 435–439.

26 Separate Opinion of Vice-President Fatsah Ouguergouz in *Tanganyika Law Society* §16; F Viljoen, above note 25, p 438; GJ Naldi and K Magliveras, 'Reinforcing the African System of Human Rights: The Protocol on the Establishment of a Regional Court of Human and Peoples' Rights' (1998) 16 *Netherlands Quarterly of Human Rights* 431, 436.

following issues: how the ACtHPR engages with international instruments in its reasoning; the quality of its judicial reasoning in terms of legal methodology (section 3.1); the different uses of these instruments and their impact on the interpretation of the ACHPR (section 3.2); and, finally, the development of the specificity of the ACHPR and the African human rights corpus juris in the pursuit of international human rights integration (section 3.3).

Articles 60 and 61 ACHPR concern the use of other international law instruments in interpreting the ACHPR. Article 60 provides that:

> The Commission shall draw inspiration from international law on human and peoples' rights, particularly from the provisions of various African instruments on Human and Peoples' Rights, the Charter of the United Nations, the Charter of the Organisation of African Unity, the Universal Declaration of Human Rights, other instruments adopted by the United Nations and by African countries in the field of Human and Peoples' Rights, as well as from the provisions of various instruments adopted within the Specialised Agencies of the United Nations of which the Parties to the present Charter are members.

Article 61 refers only to the consideration of other rules as *subsidiary* measures to determine principles of law, and its scope is restricted to treaties, practices, customs, general principles, legal precedents and doctrine *originating from or accepted by African States*.[27] Article 60 is therefore of a more general scope and has a more global outlook in terms of the instruments that may be taken into account in the process of interpretation. Articles 60 and 61 are interesting examples of the pursuit of human rights integration at the international and regional levels respectively.[28] Other human rights treaties, including the International Covenant on Civil and Political Rights (ICCPR),[29] the International Covenant on Economic, Social and Cultural Rights (ICESCR),[30] the European Convention on Human Rights (ECHR)[31] and the Inter-American Convention on Human Rights (IACHR),[32] do not contain equivalent clauses. This suggests that the drafters of the ACHPR specifically chose to include these guidelines supporting human rights integration.

27 Article 61 reads: 'The Commission shall also take into consideration, as subsidiary measures to determine the principles of law, other general or special international conventions, laying down rules expressly recognised by Member States of the Organisation of African Unity, African practices consistent with international norms on Human and Peoples' Rights, customs generally accepted as law, general principles of law recognised by African States as well as legal precedents and doctrine.'

28 E Brems, above note 6, p 94.

29 Adopted on 16 December 1966, entered into force on 23 March 1976, 999 UNTS 171.

30 Adopted on 16 December 1966, entered into force on 3 January 1976, 993 UNTS 3.

31 Concluded 4 November 1950, entered into force 3 September 1953, ETS 5.

32 Concluded 21 November 1969, entered into force 18 July 1978, OAS Treaty Series No 36.

3.1. THE CONSIDERATION OF RELEVANT INTERNATIONAL INSTRUMENTS AND VIEWS AND JUDGMENTS OF OTHER INTERNATIONAL BODIES OR COURTS

The interpretative directions envisaged in Articles 60 and 61 are addressed to both the African Commission and the ACtHPR.[33] Article 60 paves the way for the ACtHPR to draw inspiration from and use instruments that are not binding. The provision makes specific mention of international law on human and peoples' rights, and goes on to provide a non-exhaustive list ('particularly from') including non-binding instruments such as the Universal Declaration on Human Rights (UDHR) or instruments adopted by UN specialised agencies. Therefore, the ACtHPR is able to use non-binding instruments or even treaties that are not ratified by the State concerned as interpretative aids.[34] This conclusion is further supported by the fact that when the drafters of the ACHPR and the Protocol did intend to introduce the requirement for a treaty to have been ratified by the State(s) concerned, they did so explicitly.[35] Interestingly, Article 60 ACHPR has looser requirements compared with Article 31(3)(c) of the Vienna Convention on the Law of Treaties (VCLT) concerning the consideration of relevant rules of international law applicable in the relations between the parties.[36] The interpretative principle embodied in Article 31(3)(c) VCLT specifically requires: (a) *rules*, strongly suggesting that it excludes non-binding instruments; and (b) that these rules be *applicable in the relations between the parties*, which means that at least the State concerned (if not all contracting parties to the treaty under interpretation) should have ratified the other treaty.[37] Consequently, Article 60 is

---

33 *Tanganyika Law Society* §107.4; *African Commission on Human and Peoples' Rights v Republic of Kenya* §108. Individual judges in their opinions also refer to Articles 60 and 61. See Partly Dissenting Opinion of Vice-President, Justice Elsie N Thompson in *Mohamed Abubakari* §4. Cf C Heyns, above note 6, p 169, who argues that Articles 60 and 61 are not addressed to the ACtHPR.

34 E Brems, above note 6, p 95.

35 See Article 3(1) of the Protocol referring to an 'instrument ratified by the States concerned' and Article 61 of the Charter referring to 'general or special international conventions, laying down rules expressly recognised by Member States of the Organisation of African Unity'.

36 Article 31(3)(c) VCLT reads: 'There shall be taken into account, together with the context … any relevant rules of international law applicable in the relations between the parties.' See J Pauwelyn, *Conflict of Norms in Public International Law*, Cambridge University Press, New York 2003, p 256; B Rudolf, 'Unity and Diversity in the Settlement of International Disputes' in A Zimmermann and R Hofmann (eds), *Unity and Diversity in International Law*, Duncker & Humbolt, Berlin 2006, p 389, at pp 391–392.

37 For a useful overview of the question of the meaning of 'applicable in the relations between the parties', see R Gardiner, *Treaty Interpretation*, Oxford University Press, Oxford 2010, pp 269–275; J Pauwelyn, above note 36, pp 257–263. Cf U Linderfalk, 'Who are "the Parties"? Article 31(3)(c) of the 1969 Vienna Convention and the "Principle of Systemic Integration" Revisited' (2008) LV *Netherlands International Law Review* 343.

a lex specialis interpretative rule and it allows the ACtHPR to take a greater range of norms of international law into account than Article 31(3)(c) VCLT does.

The ACtHPR rarely invokes Articles 60 and 61 ACHPR in an explicit fashion.[38] Still, the ACtHPR regularly draws inspiration from a variety of treaties and non-binding instruments following the similar, long-standing practice of the African Commission.[39] These include general human rights treaties, both global (e.g. the ICCPR[40] or the ICESCR)[41] and regional (e.g. the ECHR[42] or the IACHR);[43] specialised treaties of a regional scope, such as the Cultural Charter for Africa;[44] and non-binding instruments ranging from the UDHR[45] and the UN General Assembly (UNGA) Declaration on the Rights of Indigenous Peoples[46] to the work of the UN Special Rapporteur on Minorities[47] or the 1988 UN Principles for the Protection of All Persons under Any Form of Detention or Imprisonment.[48]

In addition to international treaties, the ACtHPR gives extensive discussion to the views of UN bodies and the jurisprudence of other international human rights courts. In this way, it holds the appropriate and up-to-date interpretation of a treaty as this has been developed by the body entrusted with monitoring it.[49] For instance, the ACtHPR takes into consideration General Comments by the UN Human Rights Committee (HRC) and the ICESCR Committee as authoritative statements on the interpretation of the provisions of the respective UN treaties.[50]

---

38 The ACtHPR explicitly used the provisions in *Tanganyika Law Society* §107.4; *African Commission on Human and Peoples' Rights v Republic of Kenya* §108.

39 I Bantekas and L Oette, above note 8, p 279.

40 *Tanganyika Law Society* §76; *Lohé Issa Konaté* §9; *Alex Thomas*; *Mohamed Abubakari*; *Actions pour la Protection des Droits de l'Homme*; *Abdoulaye Nikiema and Others*.

41 *Frank David Omary* §76; *African Commission on Human and Peoples' Rights v Republic of Kenya* §2.

42 *Tanganyika Law Society* §§82.1, 106.2–106.5; *Lohé Issa Konaté* §§147–154, 158–163; *Alex Thomas* §§95–98, 104, 116, 118–119, 146; *Wilfred Onyango Nganyi* §§136–154, 172–178; *The African Commission on Human and Peoples' Rights v Libya* §95; *Mohamed Abubakari* §§27, 158, 224; *Actions pour la Protection des Droits de l'Homme* §§64, 134, 148.

43 *Tanganyika Law Society* §§82.1, 106.2–106.5; *Lohé Issa Konaté* §§147–154, 158–163; *Alex Thomas* §§95–98, 104; *Wilfred Onyango Nganyi* §179; *Actions pour la Protection des Droits de l'Homme* §95.

44 *African Commission on Human and Peoples' Rights v Republic of Kenya* §178.

45 *Frank David Omary* §§74, 76; *Alex Thomas* §45.

46 *African Commission on Human and Peoples' Rights v Republic of Kenya* §§126–131.

47 Ibid §§105–106.

48 *The African Commission on Human and Peoples' Rights v Libya* §92.

49 However, this is not always the case, since in certain instances the ACtHPR did not (explicitly) refer to the HRC's views regarding the interpretation of the ICCPR. In particular, the ACtHPR did not discuss the HRC, General Comment 32, 'Article 14, Right to equality before courts and tribunals and to fair trial', UN Doc CCPR/C/GC/32 23 August 2007 regarding the understanding of Article 14(3)(d) ICCPR in *Alex Thomas* §§90–91. See JD Mujuzi, above note 4, p 198.

50 *Tanganyika Law Society* §107.4; *African Commission on Human and Peoples' Rights v Republic of Kenya* §181.

This is a commendable practice since it mitigates, to a significant extent, the risk of diverging interpretations of the same or similar treaty provisions, both when the ACtHPR exercises its jurisdiction to interpret and apply another human rights treaty[51] and when the ACtHPR takes another treaty into account as an aid to its interpretation of the ACHPR.

More generally, cross-referencing and judicial borrowing[52] offer the ACtHPR the opportunity to benefit from the substantial experience of other international courts on procedural issues. When addressing the question of the exhaustion of domestic remedies, the ACtHPR gives due regard not only to the existing practice of the African Commission[53] but also to the jurisprudence of the IACtHR and the European Court of Human Rights (ECtHR).[54] The ACtHPR has consulted and referenced the 2013 *El Salvador/Honduras v Nicaragua* judgment by the International Court of Justice (ICJ) in order to clarify the admissibility requirements for an application for a review of a judgment.[55] The jurisprudence of the ECtHR has been a valuable guide for the Court in deciding whether it enjoys jurisdiction to scrutinise a national authority's assessment of the admissibility of evidence.[56] The practice of judicial borrowing serves the ACtHPR in two ways: first, it fosters dialogue and the coordination and convergence of international jurisprudence; and second, it legitimises the ACtHPR in the eyes of its constituencies and audience during the first crucial years of its functioning.[57] Notably, it is not only the ACtHPR that relies, for example, on the persuasive force of the case law of the ECtHR and the IACtHR,

---

51 The ACtHPR regularly finds violations of other human rights treaties and orders the respondent States to comply with their respective obligations. For example, the ACtHPR found a violation of the ICCPR in *Alex Thomas* §124; a violation of the African Charter on Democracy, Elections and Governance (adopted on 30 January 2007, entered into force on 15 February 2012); the Economic Community of West African States (ECOWAS) Revised Treaty (adopted 24 July 1993, entered into force 23 August 1995, 2373 UNTS 233) in *Lohé Issa Konaté* §§164, 167, 170; and the ECOWAS Protocol on Democracy and Good Governance supplementary to the Protocol relating to the Mechanism for Conflict Prevention, Management and Resolution (Protocol A/SP1/12/01, adopted December 2001) in the *Actions pour la Protection des Droits de l'Homme* case §§135, 151.

52 B Pirker, 'Interpreting Multi-sourced Equivalent Norms: Judicial Borrowing in International Courts' in T Broude and Y Shany (eds), *Multi-sourced Equivalent Norms in International Law*, Hart Publishing, Oxford 2011, p 93.

53 *Tanganyika Law Society* §82.1; *Actions pour la Protection des Droits de l'Homme* §§93–94.

54 *Tanganyika Law Society* §82.1; *Actions pour la Protection des Droits de l'Homme* §95.

55 *Frank David Omary* §52.

56 *Mohamed Abubakari* §§25–27.

57 R Murray, above note 8, p 219; Y Shany, *Questions of Jurisdiction and Admissibility before International Courts*, Cambridge University Press, Cambridge 2016, p 7. See also EF Mac-Gregor, 'What Do We Mean When We Talk about Judicial Dialogue? Reflections of a Judge of the Inter-American Court of Human Rights' (2017) 30 *Harvard Human Rights Journal* 89, 100.

but also the respondent States.[58] Therefore, the consideration and use of other international instruments, through cross-referencing and judicial borrowing, are a particularly useful 'currency' before the ACtHPR.

3.2. THE DIFFERENT USES OF OTHER INTERNATIONAL INSTRUMENTS AND THE INTERPRETATIVE IMPACT ON THE CONSTRUCTION OF THE ACHPR

The interpretative principle contained in Article 60, allowing the ACtHPR to 'draw inspiration' from other human rights instruments, does not give a concrete indication of how the ACtHPR may use a given instrument or what the interpretative impact on its construction of the ACHPR may be. These are important considerations for assessing the ACtHPR's reasoning and, more generally, for understanding human rights integration. Three main ways in which the ACtHPR uses external sources to interpret the ACHPR are discussed below.

First, the ACtHPR has a regular practice of comparing the text of the ACHPR to other human rights treaties. It is common practice for all international courts and bodies to have recourse to other treaties in order to ascertain the ordinary meaning of certain terms contained in the treaty under interpretation.[59] International judges are inclined to employ such a 'comparative reading', especially during the initial stage of the interpretation process, without necessarily invoking a specific legal basis.[60] Likewise, the ACtHPR does not elaborate on the legal basis for this interpretative practice – either Article 60 ACHPR or Article 31(1) VCLT with regard to interpreting a treaty in good faith and identifying the common use of a term by States in international law would suffice.[61] The ACtHPR prefers to justify its practice by stating that the provisions

---

58 Tanzania's arguments in *Tanganyika Law Society* §103 drew on judgments by the IACtHR; Burkina Faso discussed the jurisprudence of the ECtHR in *Lohé Issa Konaté* §127.

59 As far as the ICJ is concerned, see *Case Concerning the Application of the Convention on the Prevention and Punishment of the Crime of Genocide (Bosnia and Herzegovina v Serbia and Montenegro)*, Judgment on Merits, 26 February 2007, ICJ Rep 2007, p 43 §162; B Peters, 'Aspects of Human Rights Interpretation by the UN Treaty Bodies' in H Keller and G Ulfstein (eds), *United Nations Human Rights Treaty Bodies: Law and Legitimacy*, Cambridge University Press, Cambridge 2012, p 29, available at http://papers.ssrn.com/sol3/papers.cfm?abstract_id=2013298.

60 R Gardiner, above note 37, p 283; B Simma and T Kill, 'Harmonising Investment Protection and International Human Rights: First Steps towards a Methodology' in C Binder et al (eds), *International Investment Law for the 21st Century*, Oxford University Press, New York 2009, p 678, at pp 683–686.

61 R Gardiner, above note 37, pp 282–284; F Breman, 'Treaty "Interpretation" in a Judicial Context' (2004) 29 *Yale Journal International Law* 315, 318; U Linderfalk, above note 37, p 364; J Pauwelyn, above note 36, p 256.

of both the ECHR and the IACHR are similar to those of the ACHPR,[62] or that the protection provided for a particular right is more detailed under the ICCPR.[63]

Second, it is interesting how the similarity or dissimilarity of the ACHPR compared to another treaty is invoked to support an expansive or a restrictive interpretation respectively of a right under the ACHPR. This is important in cases in which the ACtHPR does not merely present a comparative overview of treaty provisions, but also defines the scope of protection of the rights under the ACHPR by reference to other instruments. To give an example, given that Article 14(3)(d) ICCPR explicitly includes the right to free legal aid as an inherent element of the right to a fair trial,[64] is the ACtHPR to construe Article 7(1)(c) ACHPR on the right to a fair trial, which lacks such a provision, as including the right to free legal aid? Should the ACtHPR use an a contrario argument in this instance, thereby excluding the right to legal aid from the scope of Article 7 ACHPR, or should it use a 'by analogy' argument supporting human rights integration and, consequently, read the right to free legal aid into the right to a fair trial under the ACHPR? The ACtHPR's general approach is to pursue international human rights integration by reading more detailed and effective standards of human rights into the ACHPR's scope. The ACtHPR established in a series of cases that the right to a fair trial includes the right to free legal assistance, and its reasoning was grounded in its interpretation of Article 7(1)(c) ACHPR in light of Article 14(3)(d) ICCPR.[65] This has served to strengthen the weak safeguards under the ACHPR in the area of criminal procedure before and during trial.[66] On another occasion, the ACtHPR read Article 66(2)(c) of the Revised Economic Community of West African States (ECOWAS) Treaty on the rights of journalists and Article 9 ACHPR on freedom of expression together, incorporating the guarantees of the former into the protective scope of the latter.[67] Furthermore, in *Lohé Issa Konaté*, which concerned the question of whether the harsh criminal penalties for defamation imposed on the applicant by Burkina Faso represented a disproportionate interference with his right to freedom of expression, the ACtHPR pursued a very restrictive construction of the ACHPR's claw-back clause.[68] The ACtHPR held that the phrase 'within the law' must be interpreted in a manner that does not subject the rights envisaged in the ACHPR to the domestic law of States parties. It did so by interpreting

62 *Alex Thomas* §§97–98.
63 Ibid §89; *Wilfred Onyango Nganyi* §166.
64 *Alex Thomas* §88.
65 Ibid; *Wilfred Onyango Nganyi* §165; *Mohamed Abubakari* §138.
66 C Heyns, above note 6, 159.
67 *Abdoulaye Nikiema and Others* §180.
68 Article 9(2) reads: 'Every individual shall have the right to express and disseminate his opinions *within the law*' (emphasis added).

Article 9 ACHPR with reference to international standards, including Article 19 ICCPR and the views thereon of the HRC,[69] the practice of the African Commission,[70] and the case law of the ECtHR and the IACtHR.[71] Although this is, in principle, a welcome development in the direction of a growing convergence among international bodies when interpreting limitation and claw-back clauses, it raises the question of what the permissible impact of human rights integration should be within the confines of interpretation.[72] The ICCPR, the IACHR and the ECHR do not contain similar clauses and therefore one might argue that they cannot qualify as appropriate comparators to justify the 'neutralisation' of the claw-back clauses provided in the ACHPR. In fact, the only other human rights treaty which includes similar claw-back clauses is the Revised Arab Charter,[73] but the ACtHPR chose to make no reference to it.[74] This underscores the inherent risk of selectiveness when determining which other treaties are to be taken into account when interpreting the ACHPR.

A third way that the ACtHPR uses international instruments is by integrating detailed criteria articulated by other international bodies and courts into its own analysis and jurisprudence. Such criteria are employed to define legal terms and to support the progressive development of the *corpus juris* of human rights law. In *Wilfred Onyango Nganyi*, the ACtHPR, in seeking to establish the meaning of 'trial within a reasonable time' under Article 7(1)(d) ACHPR, made recourse to the criteria of reasonableness developed throughout the extensive case law of the ECtHR.[75] In *Alex Thomas*, the jurisprudence of the ECtHR and the views of the HRC were invaluable guides for the ACtHPR in deciding whether a delay in the appeal proceedings before national courts met the threshold of 'severity' required for an alleged violation of inhuman treatment to be substantiated.[76] In *African Commission on Human and Peoples' Rights v Republic of Kenya*, the ACtHPR addressed the issue of whether the Ogiek are an indigenous population.[77] The elements of the definition of 'indigenous people' were

69 *Lohé Issa Konaté* §128.

70 Ibid §129.

71 Ibid §§147–154, 158–163.

72 D Shelton, 'International Decisions' (2015) 109 *American Journal of International Law* 635; cf A Rachovitsa, 'The Principle of Systemic Integration in Human Rights Law' (2017) 66 *International & Comparative Law Quarterly* 557, 567–568. For a similar approach by the African Commission, see I Bantekas and L Oette, above n 8, p 279.

73 League of Arab States, Revised Arab Charter on Human Rights (adopted 22 May 2004, entered into force 15 March 2008), reprinted in (2005) 12 IHRR 893.

74 The Vice-President of the ACtHPR, in a separate opinion issued in another case, pointed out this problematic issue, but concluded, in line with the ACtHPR and with no further explanation, that the ACHPR should be interpreted in the same spirit as the ICCPR. See Separate Opinion of Vice-President Fatsah Ouguergouz in *Tanganyika Law Society* §§29–31.

75 *Wilfred Onyango Nganyi* §§136–154.

76 *Alex Thomas* §§146–147.

77 *African Commission on Human and Peoples' Rights v Republic of Kenya.*

discussed on the basis of the criteria developed in the work of the Commission through its Working Group on Indigenous Populations and the UN Special Rapporteur on minorities, which, according to the ACtHPR, generally reflect the current normative standards in international law for identifying indigenous populations.[78]

The overall impact of other international human rights instruments in the ACtHPR's case law should not be under-stated. The ACtHPR relies heavily on other treaties and the judgments of other international courts in its interpretation of the ACHPR. However, it does not appear willing to acknowledge openly that other instruments are given substantial weight in its reasoning. It insists on proclaiming that: 'The Court is fortified in its reasoning by the decision of the African Commission, the ECtHR and the IACtHR, which are courts of similar jurisdiction.'[79] It frames the consideration of external instruments and case law as serving a secondary role and merely reaffirming an interpretation reached via other means. Yet, in practice, the systematic and lengthy references to other international instruments and jurisprudence, and their impact on the ACtHPR's construction of the ACHPR, suggest otherwise.

As a final note, there is considerable room to improve the transparency and quality of the ACtHPR's methodology and reasoning. A good start for the ACtHPR might be invoking Articles 60 and 61 ACHPR in an explicit fashion and elaborating on the legal bases for the different uses of international instruments. Also, it cannot go unnoticed that the VCLT rules on treaty interpretation (Articles 31–33) rarely, if ever, feature in the ACtHPR's judgments. It is curious that a newly established court such as the ACtHPR does not engage at all with the VCLT. Invoking the VCLT is a powerful way to enhance an international court's legitimacy, not to mention the quality of its judicial reasoning. Other international courts, including the ICJ, the ECtHR and the IACtHR, invoke and use the VLCT almost automatically.[80] Even in instances in which a court invokes and applies the specialised interpretative rules contained in its own constitutive treaty, it still employs the VCLT on a complementary basis.[81] The VCLT's rules

---

78 Ibid §108.

79 *Alex Thomas* §§95–98. See also *Wilfred Onyango Nganyi* §§169–179.

80 LB de Chazournes, AM Law Rosa and MM Mbengue, 'Article 18' in O Corten and P Klein (eds), *The Vienna Conventions on the Law of Treaties: A Commentary*, Oxford University Press, Oxford 2011, p 804 at p 820.

81 For example, the IACtHR in its legal reasoning employs a series of legal bases for legitimising the use of other treaties in the interpretation process. These bases include the construction of the IACHR within the system of which it forms part, the need for an evolutive interpretation of human rights, the principle of the *corpus juris* of human rights protection, Article 31(3) VCLT and Article 29(b) IACHR. See, for instance, *Yakye Axa Indigenous Community v Paraguay*, Judgment on Merits, Reparations and Costs, Series C, No. 125, 17 June 2005 §§125, 126, 128. For a general discussion, see GL Neuman, 'Import, Export and Regional Consent in the Inter-American Court of Human Rights' (2008) 19 *European Journal International Law* 101; A Rachovitsa, above note 2, pp 88–96.

of interpretation are part of a 'common language' that all judges speak, and the ACtHPR should participate with its own 'voice'.

3.3. NURTURING THE SPECIFICITY OF THE ACHPR: HUMAN RIGHTS INTEGRATION AS ALTERNATIVE ARGUMENTS?

The ACtHPR's systematic reliance on the case law of the ECtHR and the IACtHR raises the question of whether such an influence is (or could be) disproportionate. The crux of the matter is whether there is a need to balance *international* human rights integration with the specificity of the ACHPR and, if so, how? International human rights integration means reading the ACHPR in light of global and other regional human rights standards; at the same time, however, the specificity of the ACHPR vis-à-vis global international instruments and treaties (e.g. the ICCPR) and other regional treaties such as the ECHR and IACHR must be preserved. Although international human rights integration does not exclude regional human rights integration, these are two different arguments which may sometimes point in different interpretative directions. Heyns argues that the broad jurisdiction of the ACtHPR poses a risk to the specificity of the ACHPR, because the ACHPR will become just one of a number of treaties for the ACtHPR.[82] Nonetheless, in this author's opinion, this risk is more likely to materialise as a result not of the ACtHPR's broad jurisdiction, but of the manner in which the ACtHPR construes the ACHPR and its specificities in the context of interpretation.

Conceptualising the development of the ACHPR within the context of international human rights law is a challenging task for the ACtHPR, an international court that is still comparatively young. On the one hand, it is reasonable to expect the ACtHPR to take into serious consideration, and benefit from, the long-standing jurisprudence of other regional human rights courts. On the other hand, coordination and convergence with global and other regional standards should not come at the expense of neglecting the development of a regional (African) human rights understanding, the contours of which have already been established by the African Commission.[83] This specificity can be observed in the unique and special characteristics of human rights in the ACHPR and the local legal reality in States parties to the ACHPR, and it raises the possibility of different interpretations of specific human rights (compared with how the same rights are interpreted under other treaties) should different

[82] C Heyns, above n 6, p 167.

[83] I Bantekas and L Oette, above n 8, p 281. See also AK Perrin, above note 9, pp. 32–33.

contexts require it.[84] Human rights integration should not be seen and used as an interpretative 'bulldozer'; rather, it should highlight difference and variety in legal standards. Pursuing and nurturing an African *corpus juris*, when necessary, is compatible with the European consensus argument articulated by the ECtHR and with the international and regional *corpus juris* interpretative tool put forward by the IACtHR.[85]

These considerations need to be duly appreciated in the ACtHPR's legal reasoning. Interpretative tools and principles are not mere technicalities, but reflect and articulate the ACtHPR's approach. In this regard, human rights integration gives rise to different and equally valid arguments depending, among other things, on how an international body selects and uses relevant international instruments when construing its constitutive instrument. For instance, when the ACtHPR is in the process of discerning the ordinary meaning of a provision in the ACHPR, its starting point and primary focus should be the text of the ACHPR, without resorting prematurely to the case law of the ECtHR regarding the interpretation of an equivalent right under the ECHR, as was the case in *Wilfred Onyango Nganyi*.[86] Moreover, the ACtHPR should engage in its reasoning with both the global and other regional standards in a balanced and consistent manner – especially if the State concerned is bound by the aforementioned global standard(s).[87] Otherwise, the ACtHPR runs the risk of 'Europeanising' or 'Inter-Americanising' its jurisprudence[88] in the sense of over-emphasising the relevance and influence of other regional human rights treaties. One should also be mindful that the criteria developed by the jurisprudence of other international courts need to be tailored and applied in light of local circumstances and the legal reality in African countries. In the *Mohamed Abubakari* case, the fact that the judgment was not delivered publicly should have been given more weight in the assessment of the alleged violation of the right to a fair trial under the ACHPR, since, unlike in Europe, it is not common practice in many African States to have immediate access to the text of the judgment.

---

84 R Higgins, 'A Babel of Judicial Voices? Ruminations from the Bench' (2006) 55 *International & Comparative Law Quarterly* 791, 795.

85 M de Pauw, 'The Inter-American Court of Human Rights and the Interpretive Method of External Referencing' in Y Haeck, O Ruiz-Chiriboga and C Burbano-Herrera (eds), *The Inter-American Court of Human Rights: Theory and Practice, Present and Future*, Intersentia, Cambridge 2015, p 3 at pp 20–22.

86 JD Mujuzi, above n 4, p 218.

87 This was a point underlined in the Partly Dissenting Opinion of Vice-President Justice Elsie N Thompson in *Mohamed Abubakari* §§9–10 and the Dissenting Opinion of Judge Rafâa Ben Achour in *Mohamed Abubakari* §§15–17.

88 JD Mujuzi, above n 4, pp 218–219.

Finally, it is likely that a preoccupation with the relevance of the (semi-) judicial practice of other international bodies could hinder the realisation of the ACtHPR's potential for developing the specificities of the ACHPR and the African *corpus juris*.[89] An obvious area of interest is how the ACtHPR will address peoples' rights under the ACHPR given the fact that the latter is markedly different from the ECHR and the IACHR. As discussed in section 2, the African Commission in the *SERAC and CESR v Nigeria* case paved the way for the acknowledgement of the right to property, the right to housing and the right to a dignified life as *collective* human rights. Nonetheless, the ACtHPR is hesitant to follow this approach. In the 2017 judgment on the *African Commission on Human and Peoples' Rights v Republic of Kenya* case, the ACtHPR gave an affirmative answer to the question of whether the Ogiek are an indigenous population.[90] It also held that the expulsion of the Ogiek from their ancestral lands, against their will and without prior consultation, violated their communal ownership rights under the right to property. Still, the ACtHPR left it unclear as to whether this violation was pronounced with regard to the individual members of the Ogiek or the Ogiek as a collective group (or even both).[91] The ACtHPR reserved its judgment on reparations and, consequently, it remains to be seen whether it will recognise the entire community as a victim of human rights violations entitled to reparations.[92] The ACtHPR's overall position concerning the alleged violation of the community's right to decent survival is rather disappointing. The applicants argued that limited access to and removal from their ancestral home threatened to destroy the community's way of life and infringed their right to decent survival, thereby constituting a violation of Article 4. The ACtHPR highlighted the distinctive features of the ACHPR by underlining that '[c]ontrary to other human rights instruments, the ACHPR establishes the link between the right to life and the inviolable nature and integrity of the human being'[93] and that violations of economic, social and cultural rights may engender conditions unfavourable to a decent life. However, it held that the sole fact of eviction and the deprivation of specific rights did not amount to a violation of Article 4 ACHPR and that although some members of the Ogiek had died, no causal connection had been established between the evictions and those deaths.[94] The ACtHPR's assessment may be fair and sound in light of the specific circumstances of the case. Even so, one cannot but emphasise that the ACtHPR

89 For a comprehensive discussion, see J Gilbert, 'Litigating Indigenous Peoples' Rights in Africa: Potential, Challenges and Limitations' (2017) 66 *International & Comparative Law Quarterly* 657.

90 *African Commission on Human and Peoples' Rights v Republic of Kenya* §112.

91 Ibid §§128–131.

92 Ibid §223. The judgment on reparations is currently pending.

93 Ibid §152.

94 Ibid §§152–155.

failed to examine and assess the impact of the overall circumstances and the violations of other rights on the decent survival of the Ogiek as a people rather than merely on the decent survival of individual members. In this judgment, the ACtHPR took into account the practice of the African Commission, the views and General Comment of the ICESCR Committee and the case law of the IACtHR. Nonetheless, the practice of other bodies is of limited relevance to the ACtHPR's development of the more promising provisions of the ACHPR. The ACtHPR needs to chart new territory, with the potential to surpass even the groundbreaking – but controversial by the standards of the IACHR – 2015 judgment in the *Kaliña and Lokono Peoples v Suriname* case regarding the recognition of the collective juridical personality of populations.[95]

4. CONCLUSIONS

This chapter has focused on certain uniquely drafted features of the ACHPR and the Protocol thereto as they have been interpreted and applied by the ACtHPR in connection with human rights integration. The analysis demonstrated that human rights integration is fostered by, and dependent upon, the drafting and design of a human rights treaty. It was argued that, where appropriate, divergence in treaty design should be understood as contextual difference. Human rights integration should evaluate such instances carefully and should accommodate them in legal reasoning. In this sense, human rights integration is not a single argument, but rather consists of different possible arguments depending on the explicit and implicit choices made in the process of interpretation. The discussion demonstrated how human rights integration can and should be relevant in supporting convergence on a regional or universal level (or both). In the case of the ACtHPR, human rights integration highlights (and at the same time justifies) different arguments and interpretative directions concerning the advancement of an African human rights *corpus juris* and/or the convergence of the ACHPR with other regional and universal human rights treaties.

The ACtHPR is very receptive to using other international instruments in interpreting the ACHPR. This is a practice that merits careful study, for two distinct reasons. First, the interpretative use of other international instruments and views of other bodies helps avoid some of the difficulties associated with the

95 See *Kaliña and Lokono Peoples v Suriname*, Judgment on Merits, Reparations and Costs, Series C, No 309, 2511.2015, §§107–114; Partially Dissenting Opinion of Judge Alberto Pérez Pérez in *Kaliña and Lokono Peoples v Suriname* §9; and commentary by L Lixinski, 'International Decisions: Case of the *Kaliña and Lokono Peoples v Suriname*' (2017) 111 *American Journal of International Law* 147, 152.

ACtHPR's broad jurisdiction. Second, the use of other international instruments and the practice of judicial borrowing in general are the means by which the ACtHPR construes the international and regional *corpus juris* on human rights. The discussion demonstrated that the ACtHPR integrates more detailed human rights standards into the ACHPR's scope by reading the ACHPR in light of a variety of international treaties and other instruments. Although this is, in principle, a welcome practice; it is important not to lose sight of the question of what the appropriate impact of human rights integration should be within the confines of interpretation. In this respect, there is the question as to whether and, if so, to what extent the varying formulations of human rights across different treaties preclude the convergence of standards and, accordingly, dictate the preservation of the specificity of a human rights treaty provision. There is also the issue of how the ACtHPR will calibrate its case law in order to develop the distinctive features of the ACHPR and construe an African human rights *corpus juris* while embedding them in international human rights law. How the ACtHPR assesses the relevance of the jurisprudence and views of other regional courts and bodies on human rights to the interpretation of the ACHPR, and the influence they should exert, will also be crucial.

This brings us to the final point, which relates to the quality of the ACtHPR's reasoning. Legal reasoning is not merely a matter of technicality or semantics; it is the means by which all of the foregoing considerations are put into practice and, therefore, it is a factor in evaluating the ACtHPR's overall contribution to international law.[96] The ACtHPR should be more transparent with regard to acknowledging the significant influence of other international treaties and instruments, and the views of other international bodies and courts on its case law. Transparency may also be improved by explicitly invoking the principles of interpretation under the ACHPR (Articles 60 and 61) and by engaging with, and using, the VCLT rules on treaty interpretation (Articles 31–33). It is expected that the subject matter of the complaints that are brought before the ACtHPR in future will be more diverse, and therefore the ACtHPR will have the opportunity to clarify and develop the specificities of the ACHPR.

[96] See JG Merrills, above note 9, p 21. See also H Lauterpacht, above note 9, pp 37–40.

THE ROLE OF NON-JUDICIAL BODIES IN HUMAN RIGHTS IMPLEMENTATION

Lorenza VIOLINI*

1. INTRODUCTION

The classic means of protecting human rights, through independent and impartial courts, while indispensable in a democratic society based on the rule of law, may not always be sufficient for ensuring, at the national level, that human rights are fully respected by national authorities.[1]

* Full Professor of Constitutional and Comparative Constitutional Law, Faculty of Law, University of Milan. Email: Lorenza.violini@unimi.it.

1 Non-judicial Means for the protection of human rights at the National level, Council of Europe's Directorate General on Human Rights (May 1998), quoted by G DE BURCA, 'New Modes of

The above statement by the Council of Europe (CoE), which dates from 1998, expresses an early awareness of the need to go beyond a paradigm of human rights where protection is monopolised by the judiciary,[2] at least within the States of the CoE.

Almost 20 years later, the need for such a paradigm shift, towards a system where various non-judicial bodies work beside and even before courts to prevent human rights violations and monitor human rights implementation, is still relevant and concerns the global arena of human rights protection.

The awareness of this is neither new nor recent: this was the idea underpinning the creation of the Fundamental Rights Agency of the EU (FRA), as fostered by Alston and Weiler[3] in their seminal contribution on the need to establish a monitoring body of fundamental rights protection within the EU legal framework. Indeed, this was expected to be a turning point in Europe's protection of human rights policy, which finally seemed to be conceived not only as an ex post and ad hoc activity (through the role of the judiciary), but also as an ex ante and preventive action, through the operation of a non-judicial body committed to monitoring and identifying issues of concern.

Currently, we can say that a real paradigm shift never happened; in practice, the role of non-judicial bodies has been limited by the still-dominant role given to courts in the protection of rights. However, the need expressed by the CoE and leading scholars still remains. Starting from this unresolved issue of human rights protection mechanisms, this chapter aims to take the first step towards diverting the scholar's attention from the judicial protection of human rights and refocusing it on the role of agencies and institutions (non-judicial bodies) as human rights actors in the global arena.

This attempt cannot but start from a definition of what is meant by non-judicial bodies acting in human rights protection at the national, supranational and international levels. As the field of research is extremely wide, the analysis will focus on regional organisations such as the FRA, the Inter-American Commission on Human Rights (IACHR) and the African Commission on Human and Peoples' Rights (ACHPR); some remarks will

---

Governance and the Protection of Human Rights' in P Alston and O De Schutter (eds), *Monitoring Fundamental Rights in the EU*, Hart Publishing, Oxford 2005, p 32.

2 A similar view was expressed in M Nowak, 'National Institutions for the Promotion and Protection of Human Rights' in P Alston and O de Schutter, above note 1, p 93: 'The idea of promoting national human rights institutions is based on the conviction that courts are only one of the several mechanisms for the promotion and protection of human rights. In order to prevent future human rights violations and to establish a genuine culture of human rights, awareness-raising through human rights education and advocacy, preventive visits to place of detention, advisory services and similar non-judicial mechanisms seem to be as important as judicial review of alleged violations in the past.'

3 P Alston and JHH Weiler, 'An "Ever Closer Union" in Need of a Human Rights Policy' (1998) 9 *European Journal of International Law* 658.

also be dedicated to national human rights institutions (NHRIs), since they provide a useful insight into the central issue of the independence of those organisations.

This chapter analyses a selection of non-judicial bodies and the tools employed by them, as well as the institutional guarantees they enjoy, in order to highlight convergences and divergences of non-judicial action at the national, supranational and international levels in the new global landscape. The assessment of converging features in the field can be the basis for mutual sharing of working methods, good practices and experiences; it could also assist in strengthening the coordination of common efforts and multiple links aimed at creating global networks.

The analysis will conclude with the ultimate fundamental question that we aim to address: whether non-judicial bodies will be capable of becoming fundamental actors of human rights protection, engaging in a dialogue among themselves to share common practice and outcomes, similar to the well-known dialogue among courts. This will prompt our research even further: if it is quite clear that the role of non-judicial bodies is complementary to that of courts, would it be possible to foster a dialogue between courts and such bodies in order to strengthen the global protection of human rights?

2. NON-JUDICIAL RIGHTS PROMOTION AND JUDICIAL PROTECTION AS ESSENTIAL ELEMENTS OF A FULLY FLEDGED HUMAN RIGHTS SYSTEM

Moving to the relationship between non-judicial rights promotion and judicial protection, the main question is whether they should be considered competitors or cooperators.

Within the European landscape, the evolution of the judicial protection of fundamental rights has been extensively examined, whereas the non-judicial promotion has received little attention from legal and non-legal scholars.[4] Therefore, scholarly efforts specifically devoted to examining the two levels in relation to each other are still lacking, even though the need to integrate courts and agencies was already highlighted at the end of the twentieth century by Alston and Weiler. These two leading scholars have in fact underlined the necessity for the European Union (EU) to adopt a comprehensive human rights policy.

[4] Among the most recent works on the judicial protection of human rights in Europe, see M Cartabia and S Ninatti, 'Fundamental Rights in the European Court of Justice and the European Court of Human Rights' in S Douglas-Scott and N Hatzis (eds), *Research Handbook on EU Law and Human Rights*, Edward Elgar, Cheltenham 2017, pp 211–225;

They emphasised 'the need for more systematic and reliable information, the need to identify institutional responsibility for upholding human rights, the need to be able to hold those in power accountable, the need for a system of checks and balances, and the need for more openness and transparency'.[5] The authors called for the establishment of an agency dedicated to the collection of relevant data, which would be the basis for the development of a comprehensive human rights policy.

This suggestion of Alston and Weiler was followed in the first decade of the new century by the European institutions. They created the FRA by Council Regulation (EC) No 168/2007 of 15 February 2007, laying out the agency's functions and structure. The tasks attributed to the FRA by Article 4 of the Founding Regulation are: (1) the collection, recording, dissemination and analysis of data and the development of methods and standards to improve the comparability of such data; (2) the performance of, or cooperation in, scientific research and surveys; (3) the issue of opinions on specific topics, at its own initiative or at the request of the EU institutions; (4) the issue of an annual report on fundamental rights issues and of thematic reports; and (5) the promotion of dialogue with civil society.

In other parts of the world, similar phenomena might be observed. Since protection and promotion are perceived as essential aspects of a consistent rights policy, several examples were put in place both in Africa and America. In all these areas, policy-makers created monitoring systems in order to reinforce court decisions, hoping that such bodies could become allied with the judicial protection of rights, performing a preventive control on the violation of human rights by the national authorities. The two entities together can significantly contribute to creating a sound policy for enhancing the value and the effectiveness of human rights;[6] however, this can be considered a sort of wishful thinking, since in the history of non-judicial bodies (e.g., of the IACHR), only a few cases were submitted to the Inter-American Court of Human Rights (ICHR) during

W Sandholtz, 'Expanding Rights: Norm Innovation in the European and Inter-American Courts' in A Brysk and M Sthol (eds) *Expanding Human Rights: 21st Century Norms and Governance*, Edward Elgar, Cheltenham 2017, pp 156–176. As examples of the few contributions on the non-judicial promotion of human rights, see A von Bogdandy, J von Bernstorff and C Mak, 'The EU Fundamental Rights Agency within the European and International Human Rights Architecture: The Legal Framework and Some Unsettled Issues in a New Field of Administrative Law' (2009) 46 *Common Market Law Review* 1035; and P Alston and JHH Weiler, above note 3.

5 P Alston and JHH Weiler, above note 3, 661.

6 For details and references about the inter-American human rights system, see P Carozza, 'The Anglo-Latin Divide and the Future of the Inter-American System of Human Rights' (2015) 5 *Notre Dame Journal Of International and Comparative Law* 1; J Contesse, 'Contestation and Deference in the Inter-American Human Rights System' (2016) 79 *Law and Contemporary Problems* 2; L Cappuccio, 'La Corte interamericana e la protezione dei

the early years of its activities by the IACHR. This situation remained for many years until the reform related to the proceeding was set.

3. NON-JUDICIAL BODIES: A SURVEY

This section provides an overview of various kinds of non-judicial bodies acting in the field of human rights at the national and regional (international) levels. As a premise, it is worth noting that the structure and functions of non-judicial bodies vary widely among jurisdictions, thus making it difficult for them to engage in dialogue similar to that in the area of judicial protection of fundamental and human rights.[7]

3.1. HUMAN RIGHTS INSTITUTIONS AT THE NATIONAL LEVEL

Despite the existence of national non-judicial bodies dealing with human rights since, at least, the beginning of the second half of the twentieth century, the adoption of the so-called Paris Principles by the UN General Assembly with Resolution 48/134 of 20 December 1993 has set the tone for the establishment of new NHRIs[8] and for the reform of existing ones. The United Nations (UN) has played a significant role in the establishment of NHRIs by means of 'standard setting, capacity building, network facilitating, and membership granting'.[9] As evidence of the success of this UN strategy, it should be noted that independent human rights bodies have been established not only in well-consolidated democracies, but also in developing economies, like Tunisia and Egypt.[10]

According to the Paris Principles, NHRIs, created by the constitution or by statute, 'shall be vested with competence to promote and protect human rights'

diritti fondamentali: una bussola per gliStati' in L Cappuccio, A Lollini and P Tanzarella (eds), *Le Corti Regionali tra Stati e Diritti. I Sistemi di Protezione dei Diritti Fondamentali Europeo, Americano e Africano a Confronto*, Editoriale Scientifica, Napoli 2012, pp 133–144. For the African system, see A Lollini, 'La Corte africana dei diritti dell'uomo e dei popoli e il "nuovo" sistema regionale di protezione dei diritti fondamentali', in ibid, pp 203–230.

7 For a recent and interesting contribution on this point, see A Müller, *Judicial Dialogue and Human Rights*, Cambridge University Press, Cambridge 2017.

8 See K Meuwissen, 'NHRIs and the State: New and Independent Actors in the Multi-layered Human Rights System?' (2015) 15 *Human Rights Law Review* 441, 443.

9 S Cardenas, 'Emerging Global Actors: The United Nations and National Human Rights Institutions' (2003) 9 *Global Governance* 23, 28.

10 In both cases, the role of the NHRIs is highly significant: e.g., the Tunisian Human Rights Commission must be consulted on draft laws affecting human rights, can conduct investigations into violations of human rights and is required to deliver an annual report to the National Assembly, which, in turn, must discuss it in a plenary session.

and be entrusted with a very broad mandate. Among other competences, they should be able to submit to the government, upon request or independently, opinions, recommendations, proposals and reports on any matter regarding human rights and publicise them. Moreover, NHRIs should stimulate the ratification of international instruments and be involved in the formulation of programmes to increase public awareness. Specific principles are dictated with regard to NHRIs entrusted with quasi-jurisdictional competence: they should be able to seek amicable settlements, hear complaints and petitions or transmit them to other competent authorities, and, most importantly, they should be able to 'make recommendations to the competent authorities, especially by proposing amendments or reforms of laws, regulations and administrative practices, especially if they have created the difficulties encountered by the persons filing petitions to assert their rights'. The institutional functions are guaranteed by a specific set of principles on the composition of the institution and the appointment of its members, which will be analysed in section 4.

In order to ensure the networking of NHRIs, an International Coordinating Committee for National Human Rights Institutions (ICC) was established in 1993 and was tasked, inter alia, with the accreditation of national institutions. As of May 2017, there are 121 NHRIs accredited by the ICC, 78 of which have acquired A-Status (i.e., they are considered fully compliant with the Paris Principles).

When considering the different types of institutional structures of the NHRIs, it is worth noting that the classification of such institutions is not straightforward. The ICC, for instance, lists six types on its website: (1) human rights commissions; (2) human rights ombudsman institutions; (3) hybrid institutions; (4) consultative and advisory bodies; (5) institutes and centres; and (6) multiple institutions. However, Linos and Pegram[11] group NHRIs into two categories: human rights commissions, organised as a multimember council and generally (but not exclusively) tasked with advisory functions; and human rights ombudsmen, whose powers of investigation make them able to more effectively deal with individual complaints.

3.2. NON-JUDICIAL BODIES IN THE FRAMEWORK OF REGIONAL ORGANISATIONS DEALING WITH HUMAN RIGHTS

Human rights monitoring functions are entrusted to institutions acting at the regional level in Europe, America and Africa. We can divide such non-judicial

---

11 K Linos and T Pegram, 'Interrogating Form and Function: Designing Effective National Human Rights Institutions' (2015) 8 *Danish Institute for Human Rights: Matter of Concern Human Rights Research Paper Series*, p. 10 ff.

bodies into two groups: on the one side, those with common roots in the original institutional structures of the CoE, the now-abolished European Commission of Human Rights, the IACHR, part of the Organization of American States (OAS) and the ACHPR, now acting under the umbrella of the African Union; and on the other side, the FRA, an independent administrative agency that complies with the Paris Principles.

The IACHR was established by the OAS Charter, which entered into force in 1951. It was originally designed to promote the protection of human rights (as set out in the Charter) and to serve as a consultative organ of the OAS in such matters. In the framework designed by the OAS Charter, the IACHR had no jurisdictional or quasi-jurisdictional functions; however, according to the American Convention on Human Rights of 1969, two human rights regimes involving the IACHR exist: one originally created by the OAS Charter and another, involving a smaller number of States, in which the IACHR also exercises quasi-judicial functions, acting as a first-instance organ for complaints from individuals and States parties, filtering the cases to be submitted to the Inter-American Court of Human Rights. The IACHR is composed of seven members elected by the General Assembly of the OAS from a list of candidates proposed by the governments of Member States, each of which can propose up to three candidates, who may be nationals of the States proposing them or of any other Member State of the OAS. The members of the Commission are elected for a four-year term and can be re-elected only once.[12]

The functions of the Inter-American Commission are laid out in Article 41 of the American Convention on Human Rights and can be summarised as follows:[13] (1) developing awareness of human rights; (2) making recommendations to the governments of Member States; (3) carrying out studies and issuing reports; (4) requesting information from Member States; (5) responding to inquiries made by Member States on matters related to human rights and providing them with advisory services; (6) taking action on petitions and other communications (this function is exercised only with regard to States which have ratified the ACHR; and (7) submitting an annual report to the General Assembly of the OAS.

On the other side of the Atlantic, on the African continent, the ACHPR was created in 1981 by the African Charter on Human and Peoples' Rights and was tasked with monitoring functions. In 2004, it also acquired quasi-jurisdictional functions for a limited number of countries, according to the Protocol to the African Charter on Human and Peoples' Rights on the Establishment of an African Court on Human and Peoples' Rights. The African Commission is composed of 11 members elected by secret ballot by the Assembly of Heads

12 See www.oas.org (accessed 26 October 2017).

13 See L Cappuccio, above n 6.

of State and Government, chosen from a list of persons nominated by the States parties, each of which can nominate two candidates. The members of the Commission are elected for six years and can be re-elected.[14]

The functions of the ACHPR are detailed in Article 45 of the African Charter on Human and Peoples' Rights,[15] which tasks the Commission with: (1) collecting documents, undertaking studies and research, organising conferences and disseminating information regarding human and peoples' rights; (2) giving its views and making recommendations to governments; (3) formulating principles and rules 'aimed at solving legal problems relating to human and peoples' rights and fundamental freedoms'; (4) cooperating with other African and international institutions concerned with the promotion and protection of human and peoples' rights; (5) 'ensur[ing] the protection of human and peoples' rights'; (6) interpreting the Charter at the request of the States parties or the OAS institutions; and (7) performing other tasks entrusted to it by the Assembly of Heads of State and Government.

The functions of the IACHR and the African Commission are similarly laid out in their respective founding instruments, and one would therefore expect them to converge. However, the two Commissions diverge inasmuch as their practical impact depends on the history of the regions and on the socio-economic context. The divergence is even stronger due to the fact that the rights enshrined in the relevant international instruments are not identical: for example, the African Charter encompasses a wider catalogue of rights (and duties) which are peculiar to the African continent and can be traced back to 'the human values [which] in pre-colonial times in Africa were … recognized and observed according to African socialism, African family values, and customs and traditions'.[16] Furthermore, different political contexts give rise to different types of human rights violations. For this reason, despite their common origin, there is significant divergence in the effectiveness of the functions of regional non-judicial bodies.

In the framework of the CoE, since the dissolution of the European Commission on Human Rights in 1998,[17] there has been no single body tasked

---

14 See www.achpr.org (accessed 26 October 2017).

15 Space limitations do not permit us here to explain how the IACHR has been working in practice since its creation. More references and details about can be found in A Lollini, above n 6.

16 DDC Don Nanjira, 'The Protection of Human Rights in Africa: The African Charter on Human and Peoples' Rights' in J Symonides (ed), *Human Rights: International Protection, Monitoring, Enforcement*, Ashgate, Aldershot 2003, p 219.

17 M Tardu, 'The European Systems for the Protection of Human Rights' in J Symonides (ed), above n 16, p 139. The entry into force of Protocols 9 and 11 provided the suppression of the European Commission of Human Rights. In order to rationalise the procedure for enforcement of rights, admitting direct individual complaints, without the prior assent of the national governments involved, the functions of the Commission were assumed by the European Court of Human Rights.

with promoting and monitoring functions. However, the Commissioner for Human Rights, created in 1999, is entrusted to promote education in, awareness of and respect for human rights, as embodied in the human rights instruments of the CoE, complementing the role of supervisory bodies created by the various human rights instruments of the CoE.

As the Commissioner cannot receive individual complaints, he or she cannot be considered an ombudsman. Instead, according to Article 3 of Resolution (99) 50 of the CoE Commissioner for Human Rights, adopted by the Committee of Ministers on 7 May 1999, the Commissioner shall: (1) promote education and awareness regarding human rights and contribute to the promotion of their effective observance; (2) provide advice and information on the protection of human rights and the prevention of human rights violations, cooperating with NHRIs or encouraging their establishment; (3) facilitate the activities of national ombudsmen; (4) identify possible shortcomings in the law and practice of Member States concerning compliance with human rights and promote the effective implementation of these standards; (5) address reports concerning specific matters to the Committee of Ministers or to the Parliamentary Assembly and the Committee of Ministers and submit an annual report; (6) respond to requests made by the Committee of Ministers or the Parliamentary Assembly; and (7) cooperate with other international institutions for the promotion and protection of human rights.

The CoE and its institutions[18] share with the EU the task of protecting human rights. In 2007, the EU framework was complemented by the creation of the FRA. As noted by Von Bogdandy and Von Bernstorff,[19] 'within the EU administrative landscape [the FRA] is to be classified as an information agency', while 'at the same time, the Agency tends toward the UN standardized model of independent national human rights institutions'. The institutional structure of the FRA consists of: a management board, which is composed of independent experts (one appointed by each Member State, two representatives of the European Commission and one expert appointed by the CoE) and performs planning and monitoring functions; an executive board; a scientific committee composed of 11 independent experts, who are highly qualified in the field of fundamental rights and a director.[20] Despite being structured according to the framework of the European independence agencies, the FRA is peculiar as its five-year Multiannual Framework is adopted by the Council instead of the EU Commission. Having as its institutional reference the (intergovernmental) Council rather than the Commission 'attests to the

18 Within the CoE, we have two main bodies: the European Court of Human Rights and the European Committee of Social Rights (specifically committed to social rights protection).

19 See A von Bogdandy and J von Bernstorff, above n 4, p 1047.

20 See http://www.fra.europa.eu (accessed 18 October 2017).

sensitivity of the subject matter'[21] and neutralises Member States' fears of undue interference by the EU into their internal fundamental rights policies.

4. FORMS OF NON-JUDICIAL ACTION IN THE FIELD OF HUMAN RIGHTS: AN INSIGHT INTO THE WORK OF REGIONAL ORGANISATIONS

The forms of action or, in other words, the tools employed by non-judicial bodies show a significant degree of convergence, although some of them vary in terms of their impact on the different legal systems. The reason for convergence can be attributed to the common inspiration and duties of the different non-judicial organisations, i.e., to create the cultural and factual conditions necessary to ensure effective human rights protection, as opposed to the rationale of judicial action, which aims to provide redress to individuals. This section focuses on non-judicial bodies acting within the framework of regional organisations and their basic tools: monitoring, reporting, inspection powers and quasi-judicial powers. The basic set of tools available to non-judicial bodies is, to some extent, standard. This commonality of tools shows significant convergence among non-judicial bodies, in spite of their divergence in several institutional aspects and in their relation of the political and cultural contexts.

4.1. MONITORING

Monitoring is the primary tool through which non-judicial bodies assess the level of human rights protection in a given legal system. It has been noted that monitoring 'is essentially an ambivalent concept, being potentially either preventive or repressive'.[22] In general, the monitoring function by non-judicial bodies can be exercised through data gathering (as in the case of the FRA) or direct inspections (as carried out by the IACHR). Data is mainly collected from stakeholders, which can be State authorities or civil society organisations. In some instances, monitoring might involve a periodic reporting system submitted by stakeholders, which are then reviewed by the human rights body. In general, however, the institution independently gathers data from various sources and obtains a comprehensive picture of the situation.

The outcome of monitoring activities can be varied, sometimes resulting in recommendations, but generally leading to the issuing of reports, whether general or thematic. Reports are then disseminated through networks of experts,

---

21 See A von Bogdandy and J von Bernstorff, above n 4, p 1050.

22 M Tardu, above n 17, p 138.

civil society organisations and national institutions, to reach the public and perform a lato sensu educational role.

4.2. REPORTING

Reports are the main outcomes of the activities performed by non-judicial bodies. Through them, the body can both make the product of its monitoring activity available to the public and exercise its function of increasing awareness on specific human rights issues. Reports can be either general or thematic and, when issued by bodies acting within regional organisations, they can concern specific States. In this case, they might be supplemented by recommendations to the government.

Since the FRA has no power to control the policies of a specific Member State and can only issue thematic reports dealing with a number of Member States, it also issues an annual report on the overall protection of fundamental rights in the EU.[23]

In addition to general and thematic reports, the IACHR also publishes reports directed at a specific State, usually issued after having received individual or State complaints and sometimes after carrying out State visits.[24] Such papers, however, are not automatically made public. The specific procedure of the IACHR will be analysed in the following section.

Also the ACHPR issues an annual report and analyses State reports concerning human rights. The main documents issued by the ACHPR are resolutions and guidelines.

4.3. INSPECTION POWERS

In addition to collecting data from interested parties, monitoring can be also done through inspections, which can be carried out by members of the governing body of the organisation. While the High Commissioner, which is a single-handed organ, performs on-site visits within the framework of the CoE, in the American and African systems, delegations are headed by members of the Commissions. The members of the IACHR, for example, can be directly tasked with on-site visits, a procedure that, since 1961, has been performed 95 times.[25]

23 The Archive of Annual Activity Reports is available at: http://www.fra.europa.eu (accessed 18 October 2017).

24 The Archive of Annual, Thematic and Country Reports is available at: http://www.oas.org (accessed 18 October 2017).

25 See http://www.oas.org (accessed 18 October 2017).

The procedure is provided for in Article 48 of the Inter-American Convention, which regulates individual complaints. It aims both to collect information and issue recommendations to States parties. Field missions are very important when there is no effective cooperation by the State governments, and the Commission therefore believes it is necessary to gain a first-hand account of the situation. A similar method is employed by the African Commission, which can also enact subsidiary mechanisms (special rapporteurs, committees and working groups); at the moment, there are 15 such mechanisms in place, two of which, the Special Rapporteur on Prisons, Conditions of Detention and Policing in Africa and the Working Group on Indigenous Populations/Communities in Africa, have frequently made use of local visits.[26]

In general, field missions are powerful instruments for directly assessing respect for human rights. However, the use of such forms of action is not universal; for instance, FRA, which cannot perform State-specific studies, is not entitled to carry out on-site visits either. This limitation can be linked to the division of tasks between the CoE and the EU; indeed, the former occupies the role of human rights watchdog for individual States parties, while the latter focuses on the EU. Another reason for the lack of inspection powers is the extent to which the FRA makes use of the networks it has put in place. Indeed, the overall networking system can be considered an expression of the principle of horizontal subsidiarity,[27] according to which, whenever possible, the exercise of functions of public relevance should be attributed to private sector organisations, such as NGOs. Through the use of its extensive networks, then, the FRA can, without displacing its staff, be correctly informed of the level of protection of human rights in Member States.

4.4. NETWORKING

Networking is a growing phenomenon in the field of non-judicial promotion of fundamental rights. As mentioned, in 2017, the International Coordinating Committee for National Human Rights Institutions grouped 121 NHRIs established under the Paris Principles, and it continues to organise annual meetings with their representatives. In addition, there are regional networks acting in various areas of the world (Asia and the Pacific, Europe, Africa and the Americas) that organise working groups tackling region-specific issues.

Along with these forms of coordination, there are those put in place by regional organisations. Although, as shown above, all regional non-judicial

---

26 See http://www.achpr.org (accessed 18 October 2017).

27 A Maltoni, 'The Principle of Subsidiarity in Italy: Its Meaning as a "Horizontal" Principle and its Recent Constitutional Recognition' (2002) 4(4) *ICNL*, available at http://www.icnl.org/research/journal/vol4iss4/art_3.htm (accessed 18 October 2017).

rights bodies are tasked with cooperating with human rights institutions, the one body which has focused the most on creating networks has been the EU FRA. The main networks are directly instituted by the Founding Regulation and are: (1) the network of National Liaison Officers (NLOs), defined in Article 8 as 'the main contact point[s] for the Agency in the Member State'; and (2) the Fundamental Rights Platform (FRP), a cooperation network, which, pursuant to Article 10, is 'composed of non-governmental organisations dealing with human rights, trade unions and employers' organisations, relevant social and professional organisations, churches, religious, philosophical and non-confessional organisations, universities and other qualified experts of European and international bodies and organisations'. Moreover, pursuant to Article 6, paragraph 3 of the Founding Regulation, which provides that 'the Agency may enter into contractual relations, in particular subcontracting arrangements, with other organisations, in order to accomplish any tasks which it may entrust to them', the FRA has also established the FRANET, a multidisciplinary research network composed by contractors which provide the agency with data. In addition, the agency has established a number of thematic cooperation platforms with NHRIs.[28]

As the FRA's experience suggests, dialogue and networking with experts, civil society and other non-judicial bodies are essential for these institutions to increase their ability to perform their tasks. While we can find an example of such interaction within the practice of the FRA towards NHRIs and other non-judicial bodies working in the EU legal space, a similar experience is still missing if we look at the relationship between different regional bodies (e.g., between the FRA and the ICHR). In other words, while the judicial dialogue is spreading around the world, non-judicial bodies seem to play a kind of monologue, focused on their specific regional sphere. How to transform such monologue into dialogue is one of the most challenging tasks that policy-makers and scholars involved in human rights protection will face in the years ahead.

5. CONVERGENCE AND DIVERGENCE ON THE INDEPENDENCE OF NON-JUDICIAL RIGHTS BODIES

Independence is the most significant common feature of non-judicial bodies, both at the national and international levels. Therefore, independence can be

[28] There are four thematic platforms: the CoE-FRA-Equinet-ENNHRI Platform on rights of migrants and asylum-seekers (coordinated by the FRA); the CoE-FRA-Equinet-ENNHRI Platform on hate crime (coordinated by the FRA); the CoE-FRA-Equinet-ENNHRI Operational Platform for Roma Equality (coordinated by the CoE); and the CoE-FRA-Equinet-ENNHRI Platform on advancing social and economic rights and socio-economic equality (coordinated by the CoE).

considered the most important point of convergence between the different bodies active in the field of rights promotion. Nonetheless, since the term 'independence' has different meanings, it is worth analysing the different features of independence in order to assess whether convergence really exists.

5.1. A MULTIFACETED UNDERSTANDING OF INDEPENDENCE ACCORDING TO THE PARIS PRINCIPLES

Independence is one of the requirements for NHRIs to be accredited by the ICC. In order to qualify as an independent body, the Paris Principles require:

a) that the composition of the institution be 'established in accordance with a procedure which affords all necessary guarantees to ensure the pluralist representation of the social forces (of civilian society) involved in the protection and promotion of human rights' with the presence of representatives of NGOs responsible for human rights, trade unions, social and professional organisations, 'trends in philosophical or religious thought', universities, parliament and government departments (with consultative functions only);
b) that the institution should have 'an infrastructure which is suited to the smooth conduct of its activities, in particular adequate funding' being enabled 'to have its own staff and premises, in order to be independent from the Government and not be subject to financial control';
c) that the appointment of the member 'be effected by an official act which shall establish the specific duration of the mandate', which can be renewable.

Therefore, according to the Paris Principles, independence is related to the personal qualities of the members of the institution, which should represent the plurality of trends present in societies, and to the staffing and funding of the institution itself.

As to the first aspect, independence is different from the traditional guarantee of independence of the judicial branch of government (from the legislative and executive branches). Instead of focusing on this traditional type of independence, the Paris Principles emphasise plurality in the composition of the body and expertise, both in the field of human rights and in management. For example, the members of the Management Board of the FRA, pursuant to Article 12 of the Founding Regulation, should have 'appropriate experience in the management of public or private sector organisations'.

As to the staffing and funding of the institution, the guarantee of independence can be more closely compared with the independence/sovereignty enjoyed by parliaments at the State level.

5.2. SCIENTIFIC CONSISTENCY

Along with these two traditional interpretations of independence, there is another aspect of independence which is not referenced in the Paris Principles, i.e., the agency's working methods. The reason why working methods can enhance independence is because a fact-oriented approach that is based on scientific premises and periodically controlled by a specific scientific committee (as is used by the FRA of the EU) contributes to the availability of reliable information from the agencies. In other words, the scientific consistency of the organisation's working methods is particularly relevant, as results which are obtained through a sound scientific method cannot, in principle, be disputed and should therefore be persuasive for the concerned parties.

5.3. RULES FOR THE APPOINTMENT OF THE MEMBERS OF NON-JUDICIAL BODIES

Another more traditional way to assess the independence of national and regional non-judicial bodies would be to examine how members are elected, particularly whether those who perform a controlling function in the field of human rights can be influenced by the State government which appointed them and whose activity they control. This is why it is necessary to analyse the criteria for candidates to be considered for appointment. It is worth noting that such requirements indicate different understandings of independence.

The case of the FRA is particularly interesting as the agency's two main bodies, the Management Board and the Scientific Committee, have members drawn from various categories of experts. As mentioned, members of the Management Board must have 'appropriate experience in the management of public or private sector organisations and, in addition, knowledge in the field of fundamental rights'[29] and, with regard to the persons appointed by each Member State, they should have 'high level responsibilities in an independent national human rights institution or other public or private sector organisation'.[30] As regards the members of the Scientific Committee, the Founding Regulation specifies that they should be 'eleven independent persons, highly qualified in the field of fundamental rights', appointed by the Management Board 'following a transparent call for applications and selection procedure'.[31] Moreover, they should ensure geographical representation.

---

29 Article 12.1 of Council Regulation (EC) No. 168/2007 of 15 February 2007, establishing a EU Agency for Human Rights.

30 Ibid, Article 12.1, lett. a).

31 Ibid, Article 14.1.

According to Articles 2 and 3 of the Statute of the IACHR, which was approved by the General Assembly of the OAS in 1979, the seven members of the IACHR 'shall be persons of high moral character and recognised competence in the field of human rights' representing all the Member States of the organisation and elected by the General Assembly from a list of candidates proposed by Member States.

According to Article 31 of the African Charter on Human and Peoples' Rights, the 11 members of the African Commission are 'chosen from amongst African personalities of the highest reputation, known for their high morality, integrity, impartiality and competence in matters of human and peoples' rights; particular consideration being given to persons having legal experience', elected by the Assembly of Heads of State and Government from a list compiled by State governments.

The examples of the FRA and the Inter-American and African Commissions shows that expertise in the field of human rights is the most recurrent requirement, whereas other accessory requirements may vary, ranging, as mentioned, from organisational expertise to moral character and high reputation. When considering the profiles of the current members of these institutions, the most represented category of human rights experts is university professors.[32]

5.4. THE TRANSPARENCY OF THE RESULTS OF NON-JUDICIAL BODIES

Independence is also linked to the transparency of non-judicial bodies' activities. In many cases, however, proceedings and reports on human rights violations by States are confidential. As mentioned above, the IACHR, for instance, does not publish recommendations directed at States parties unless such States do not comply. The procedure is laid out in Articles 50 and 51 of the American Convention on Human Rights. Article 50 stipulates that if, following a petition or communication alleging a violation of human rights, a settlement is not reached, the Commission shall draw up a 'report setting forth the facts and stating its conclusions' and making recommendations to be transmitted to the State concerned. This report cannot be published. However, according to Article 51, 'if, within a period of three months from the date of the transmittal ... the matter has not either been settled or submitted ... to the Court', the Commission may, by an absolute majority, 'set forth its opinion and conclusions concerning the question', making, 'where appropriate', pertinent recommendations and 'prescrib[ing] a period within which the state is to take the measures that are

32 It was not by chance that the first Chairman of the FRA Scientific Committe was the Italian Law Professor Stefano Rodotà.

incumbent upon it to remedy the situation examined'. Only when the period has expired is the Commission entitled to decide, by an absolute majority, whether to publish the report.

The complexity of the procedure and the need for qualified majorities to decide on the publication of reports bring about a substantial lack of transparency in the activity of the Commission,[33] which in principle could have an impact on its independence. Indeed, the existence of public hearings and proceedings is one of the ways in which judicial independence is demonstrated, so much so that it is required by Article 6 of the European Convention on Human Rights (ECHR) for all trials and by Article 8 ACHR for criminal trials. The transparency of proceedings and the publication of reports would be at least a partial antidote to undue external influence. Moreover, it would allow other human rights bodies, both non-governmental and public, such as NHRIs, to receive a flow of information which could help foster cooperation and dialogue among them, which would in turn promote the networking of non-judicial bodies, which we have examined above.

6. CONCLUSIONS

Shifting from description to prescription, in this last section I would like to make some conclusive remarks in support of the paradigm shift in human rights protection invoked at the beginning of this chapter.

Human rights, as well as fundamental constitutional rights, have a strong universal vocation: they belong to every human being in every nation and in every region of the world. Nonetheless, their judicial protection is influenced by different 'boundary conditions'[34] which contribute to divergence in rights interpretation and protection. Non-judicial bodies are also characterised by a high degree of fragmentation, which can be even stronger than the fragmentation experienced in the field of judicial protection. In fact, while in many cases courts share the same basic structure regarding, for example, the independence of their members[35] and the fact that all cases should be decided according to the law,

---

33 H Caminos, 'The Inter-American System for the Protection of Human Rights' in J Symonides (ed), above n 16, p 192.

34 C O'Cinneide, 'The Problematic of Social Rights: Uniformity and Diversity in the Development of Social Rights Review' in L Lazarus, C McCrudden and N Bowles (eds), *Reasoning Rights: Comparative Judicial Engagement*, Hart Publishing, Oxford 2014, pp 199 ff.

35 Of course, not all cases are the same and not all courts are independent from the other powers. During 2017, for example, the Polish Parliament approved a landmark measure that restructured the Supreme Court, putting it under the effective control of the governing party (see P Mikuli, 'An Explicit Constitutional Change by Means of an Ordinary Statute? On a Bill Concerning the Reform of the National Council of the Judiciary in Poland', *International Journal of Constitutional Law Blog*, 23 February 2017), www.iconnectblog.com.

non-judicial bodies have both converging and diverging features. They act at various levels of government under different denominations and have different institutional features, even though they are charged with comparable functions (monitoring, promotion, etc.). They are often committed to improving equality and to assessing violations of human dignity, a concept that encompasses a broad range of specific rights, which are present in virtually every charter, treaty or constitution. Therefore, despite the differences among them, they seem to converge towards a common vision of rights as a sustainable global system – according to the Sustainable Development Goals approved by the General Assembly of the UN in September 2015[36] – able to improve not only the legal status of individuals, but also the overall quality of public life.

In order to increase the sustainability of a political and legal system, a reappraisal of the judicial protection of rights in the global arena is needed. The proliferation of non-judicial bodies at every level clearly shows that the protection of human rights by courts is perceived to be inadequate. This insufficiency becomes even more problematic if we consider that, in the last decade, the social and financial turmoil created by the global economic crisis has put all developed countries under pressure. In Europe, both the EU and its Member States (or at least many of them)[37] are now committed to demonstrating their ability to design and implement reliable human rights policies to improve the quality of life of people in Europe. The achievement of this goal will require additional efforts which must be performed by all components of the State structure, in which non-judicial bodies play an important role.[38]

The promising prospect of supplementing the judicial approach with a non-judicial approach to human rights is demonstrated by the evolution of both European institutions in the field and NHRIs. On the one hand, the FRA, even if it is not always considered effective in promoting human rights protection,

36 A/RES/70/1, Resolution adopted by the General Assembly on 25 September 2015.

37 However, recently in some Member States we can see violations of fundamental rights and of the core principles of democracy. In response to this, in May 2017 the European Parliament delivered a Resolution (2017/2656 – RSP), according to which 'recent developments in Hungary have led to a serious deterioration in the rule of law, democracy and fundamental rights which is testing the EU's ability to defend its founding values'.

38 Policy-makers are aware of this task, as is shown in statements made by the President of the Commission, Jean-Claude Juncker, as well as other members of the EU Commission. Junker, in particular, shortly after his election, affirmed that there would be 'a strong political commitment from the whole College to ensure that the Charter [be] respected and complied with within all EU policies for which the Commission is responsible'. Such a commitment is not limited to European citizens: in the currently uncertain international context, the EU is increasingly being called upon to be an effective global player in the field of human rights protection, not only internally, but also beyond EU borders. Evidence of this trend can be found in recent actions taken by the EU with regard to third countries, such as the Roadmap 2014–2017 approved in the 14th EU-African Summit held in Brussels in April 2014.

has increased its influence in the field of human rights since its creation.[39] On the other hand, the establishment of NHRIs in countries dealing with processes of democratisation, such as Tunisia and Egypt, is a sign of the relevance of non-judicial rights promotion in the arena of global constitutionalism.

However, this awareness, despite being a significant step towards legal systems adjusting to higher human rights standards, is not enough. Non-judicial dialogue and interaction between human rights agencies must now be triggered, and different forms of coordination among non-judicial bodies must be fostered in order to share information, exchange working methods and promote mutual cooperation, thus contributing to the overall sustainability of human rights protection.

---

39 See GN Toggenburg, 'The Role of the New EU Fundamental Rights Agency: Debating the "Sex of Angels" or Improving Europe's Human Rights Performance?' (2008) 3 *European Law Review* 385; L Violini, 'The Impact of the Charter of Fundamental Rights on European Union Policies and Legislation' in G Palmisano (ed), *Making the Charter of Fundamental Rights a Living Instrument*, Martinus Nijhoff, Brill 2015.

PART II

HUMAN RIGHTS TECTONICS THROUGH AN ISSUE-BASED APPROACH

WHY A GLOBAL APPROACH TO NON-DISCRIMINATION LAW MATTERS

Struggling with the 'Conscience' of Companies*

Emmanuelle BRIBOSIA** and Isabelle RORIVE***

1. INTRODUCTION

On 6 October 2017, the Trump Administration expanded the range of employers and insurers that can invoke religious or moral beliefs in order to avoid birth

* This contribution follows the developments detailed in E BRIBOSIA, G CACERES and I RORIVE, 'Le droit de la non-discrimination aux prises avec la conscience des entreprises' in A-G GAGNON and P NOREAU (eds), *Constitutionnalisme, droits et diversité : Mélanges en l'honneur de J. Woehrling*, Thémis, Montréal 2017, pp 419–460. This research was funded by the Interuniversity Attraction Poles Programme (IUAP), initiated by the Belgian Science Policy Office (BELSPO). More particularly, this chapter was written within the framework of the IUAP project, *The Global Challenge of Human Rights Integration: Towards a Users' Perspective* (2012–2017), http://www.hrintegration.be. It is also supported by the French Community through the ARC project, 'Sous le signe du mérite et de la conformité culturelle. Les nouvelles politiques d'intégration des immigrés en Europe' (2012–2017).

** Professor at the Law Faculty of the Université libre de Bruxelles (ULB) and the Director of the Centre for European Law (http://www.cde.ulb.be, ebribo@ulb.ac.be).

*** Professor at the Law Faculty of the ULB and the Director of the Perelman Centre for Legal Philosophy (http://www.philodroit.be, irorive@ulb.ac.be).

control pills and other contraceptives being covered by insurance as part of preventive care under the Patient Protection and Affordable Care Act (ACA or Obamacare). While efforts to repeal the ACA entirely were unsuccessful, the Trump Administration adopted two companion interim final rules to extend the right of conscientious objection to for-profit entities that are not closely held (including publicly traded companies), as is already the case for churches and religious orders, non-profit organisations or closely held for profit entities.[1] The reaction was immediate. The American Civil Liberties Union (ACLU) filed a lawsuit against this measure, arguing 'that the interim rules violate the Establishment Clause and the Equal Protection Clause of the Constitution by authorizing and promoting religiously motivated and other discrimination against women seeking reproductive health care'. An ACLU senior staff attorney stressed that 'the federal government cannot authorize discrimination against women in the name of religion or otherwise'.[2]

Simultaneously, stories of cakes are making headlines on both sides of the Atlantic. The debate revolves around the refusal by Ashers Baking Company in Northern Ireland and Masterpiece Cakeshop Ltd in Colorado to create, in the first case, a wedding cake with the words 'Support Gay Marriage' and, in the second case, a wedding cake for a buffet in honour of same-sex couples. The Supreme Court of the United Kingdom[3] and the Supreme Court of the United States[4] agreed to hear these cases. In addition to the issue of equal access to goods and services, they both touch on the extent to which companies can invoke freedom of religion or expression in order to disregard the right of non-discrimination on the grounds of sexual orientation.

In parallel to this, the *Achbita* and *Bougnaoui*[5] judgments – delivered in March 2017 by the Court of Justice of the European Union on two preliminary

1 US Department of Health & Human Services, 'Trump Administration Issues Rules Protecting the Conscience Rights of All Americans', 6 October 2017, http://www.hhs.gov/about/news/2017/10/06/trump-administration-issues-rules-protecting-the-conscience-rights-of-all-americans.html (accessed 1 December 2017). See also US Department of Health & Human Services, 'Religious and Moral Exemptions and Accommodations for Coverage of Certain Preventive Services under the Affordable Care Act', 6 October 2017, https://www.hhs.gov/sites/default/files/fact-sheet-religious-exemptions-and-accommodations-for-coverage.pdf (accessed 1 December 2017).

2 American Civil Liberties Union, 'ACLU Filing Lawsuit Challenging Trump Administration Contraceptive Coverage Rule', 6 October 2017, http://www.aclu.org/news/aclu-filing-lawsuit-challenging-trump-administration-contraceptive-coverage-rule (accessed 1 December 2017).

3 *Lee v Ashers Baking Company Ltd and Others*, UKSC 2017/0020, http://www.supremecourt.uk/cases/uksc-2017-0020.html, pending (hearings took place on May 1 and 2, 2018).

4 *Masterpiece Cakeshop, Ltd v Colorado Civil Rights Commission*, 584 US ___ (2018) (decided on June 4, 2018).

5 ECJ, Case C-157/15, *Samira Achbita, Centrum voor gelijkheid van kansen en voor racismebestrijding v G4S Secure Solutions NV*, 14 March 2017, ECLI:EU:C:2017:203; and Case C-188/15, *Asma Bougnaoui, Association de défense des droits de l'homme (ADDH) v Micropole SA, anciennement Micropole Univers SA*, 14 March 2017, ECLI:EU:C:2017:204.

references from the Courts of Cassation of Belgium and France – were also making headlines. Even if the Court of Justice has not given companies a blank cheque to forbid the Islamic headscarf (*hijab*) in the workplace in the name of a 'neutral' brand image,[6] it is often in this way that these judgments are interpreted.[7] In any event, the guidelines laid down by the Court have been described as a 'user manual' for the legal dismissal of women wearing veils.[8]

What are the commonalities between these legal battles on either side of the Atlantic? In each case, a commercial company appropriates the language of fundamental rights (religious freedom, freedom of expression or freedom of enterprise) in order to justify differences in treatment based on gender, sexual orientation or religious beliefs.[9] These companies claim a form of 'freedom of conscience' understood as the choice of values that constitute their identity. By extension, we can refer to the 'conscience' of the companies that is challenging the right of non-discrimination reflected in many national, European and international texts, with multiple influences and interpenetrations.[10]

To address this phenomenon, we support the view that the traditional segregated approach, which studies different courts and legal orders in isolation from one another, no longer provides adequate conceptual and normative tools to fully grasp the current evolutions and challenges in this domain.[11] There is a

---

6 For commentary on these judgments, see communications by Unia (Unia), 'Affaire Achbita: enfin plus de clarté sur l'interdiction du foulard au travail', press release, 14 March 2017, http://unia.be/fr/articles/affaire-achbita-enfin-plus-de-clarte-sur-linterdiction-du-foulard-au-travail (accessed 1 December 2017) and by the Observatoire de la laïcité (Observatory for Secularism), Observatoire de la laïcité press release on the Court of Justice of the European Union's judgments of 14 March 2017 (Case C-157/15 et Case C-188/15), 14 March 2017, http://www.gouvernement.fr/sites/default/files/contenu/piece-jointe/2017/03/communique_14.03.2017_-_odl_0.pdf (accessed 1 December 2017).

7 D Bilefsky, 'Ban on Head Scarves at Work is Legal, E.U. Court Rules', *New York Times*, 14 March 2017; I Amrani, 'The Hijab Ruling is a Ban on Muslim Women', *The Guardian*, 15 March 2017; *La Repubblica*, 'Corte Giustizia Ue: vietare il velo islamico al lavoro si può' ('CJEU: Banning the Islamic Headscarf in the Workplace is Permitted'), 14 March 2017; A Sanchez, 'La justicia europea avala que las empresas prohíban el velo en el trabajo' ('The European Court Accepts the Ban by Businesses on the Headscarf in the Workplace'), *El Pais*, 14 March 2017.

8 See in particular the references cited in E Bribosia and I Rorive, 'Affaires Achbita et Bougnaoui : entre neutralité et préjugés (obs. sous C.J.U.E., Gde Ch., arrêts Achbita et Bougnaoui, 14 mars 2017)' (2017) *Revue trimestrielle des droits de l'homme* 1017, 1037.

9 On this issue, see P Oliver, 'Companies and their Fundamental Rights: A Comparative Perspective' (2015) 64 *International and Comparative Law Quarterly* 661, 674–675.

10 See in particular the report published by the International Network of Civil Liberties Organizations (INCLO), 'Drawing the Line: Tackling Tensions Between Religious Freedom and Equality', 2015, http://ccla.org/cclanewsite/wp-content/uploads/2015/09/INCLO-Report-Drawing-the-Line-EQ-vs-FoR.pdf (accessed 1 December 2017).

11 E Bribosia and I Rorive, 'Antidiscrimination Law in the Global Age' (2015) 1 *European Journal of Human Rights-Journal européen des droits de l'Homme (JEDH-EJHR)* 3; I Rorive, 'Lutter contre les discriminations' in C Bricteux and B Frydman (eds), *Les défis du droit*

genuine need for a global approach[12] to anti-discrimination law, which would help to identify new areas for producing and implementing the law which are neither national nor international. This phenomenon is triggered by various actors, such as the many third-party interveners or amicus curiae defending liberal or conservative agendas.[13] Moreover, the strategic use of comparative law in equality cases extends far beyond the process of 'legal transplants'.[14] It is not limited to the migration of constitutional ideas, which are often adapted in the new environment,[15] the cross-fertilisation of jurisprudence or judicial globalisation.[16] Rather, it allows us to become familiar with the various arguments that are put forward in support of or against a claim, and with the strategies of mobilisation and counter-mobilisation in different arenas, that is, at the national, European and international levels. The comparative approach provides the necessary distance to allow for reflection and critical thinking.

Against this background, this chapter provides an analysis of some symbolic cases from either side of the Atlantic in order to assess how anti-discrimination law is challenged and undermined when companies or associations invoke their 'conscience'. National and supranational legal cases provide an insight into what is happening on the ground. They are indicative of some salient legal battles, which are taking a global turn in a climate of 'conscience wars'.[17] Section 2 of the analysis will focus on requests for exemptions by for-profit companies. In the name of their religious freedom or conscience, these companies refuse to respect the obligation to take out group insurance contracts which cover the morning-after pill, or to contract with people because of their sexual orientation. Section 3 will evaluate the process at work when, in the name of their brand image, companies dismiss employees or refuse to hire candidates who carry visible religious symbols.

---

global, Bruylant, Brussels 2018, pp 41–61. See also E Bribosia and I Rorive, 'Chroniques – Droit de l'égalité et de la non-discrimination' (2013) 2 *JEDH-EJHR* 297; (2014) 2 *JEDH-EJHR* 205; (2015) 2 *JEDH-EJHR* 223; (2016) 2 *JEDH-EJHR* 254; (2017) 2 *JEDH-EJHR* 191.

12 B Frydman, 'A Pragmatic Approach to Global Law' in H Muir Watt and D Arroyo (eds), *Global Governance Implications of Private International Law*, Oxford University Press, Oxford 2015, pp 181–200.

13 M Tushnet, 'The Inevitable Globalization of Constitutional Law' (2009) 50(1) *Virginia Journal of International Law* 989.

14 A Watson, *Legal Transplants: An Approach to Comparative Law*, Scottish Academic Press, Edinburgh 1974.

15 S Choudhry, 'Migration as a New Metaphor in Comparative Constitutional Law' in S Choudhry (ed), *The Migration of Constitutional Ideas*, Cambridge University Press, Cambridge 2006, pp 1–36.

16 A-M Slaughter, 'Judicial Globalization' (2000) 40 *Virginia Journal of International Law* 1103, 1124.

17 S Mancini and M Rosenfeld (eds), *The Conscience Wars: Rethinking the Balance between Religion, Identity and Equality*, Cambridge University Press, Cambridge 2018.

2. WHEN BUSINESSES FIND THEIR CONSCIENCE

A recent movement has seen profit-making companies invoking a form of conscience in order to escape obligations which would run contrary to it. This trend has been particularly apparent in the area of access to reproductive care (section 2.1) and the provision of goods or services to homosexuals (section 2.2). For these companies or their owners, it is often a matter of resorting to the judicial route to replay fights lost in parliament and to obtain individual exemptions which would be generalisable to others.[18] These cases revisit the contours of freedom of conscience and religion, which is invoked – even exploited – by legal persons whose social object is not the promotion of a particular conviction, but rather the defence of a conservative moral agenda. They also push the boundary between the 'ethics' of a company and the beliefs of its leaders, at the risk of making the latter prevail over the rights of their employees or customers.

2.1. THE CONTEST BETWEEN ACCESS TO SEXUAL AND REPRODUCTIVE RIGHTS AND THE CONSCIENCE OF COMPANIES

Access to reproductive care is undoubtedly a privileged ground for appeals to conscience clauses by religious and conservative circles.[19] In many cases, this was the 'price tag' on the decriminalisation of abortion by legislative or jurisprudential means.[20] The extension of a form of 'conscientious objection' to legal persons is a more recent and controversial phenomenon.

---

18 D Nejaime and RB Siegel, 'Conscience Wars: Complicity-Based Conscience Claims in Religion and Politics' (2015) 124 *Yale Law Journal* 2516, 2543. See also INCLO, above n 10.

19 E Bribosia, I Isailovic and I Rorive, 'Objection Ladies! Taking IPPF-EN v Italy One Step Further' in E Brems and E Desmet (eds), *Integrated Human Rights in Practice: Rewriting Human Rights Decisions*, Edward Elgar, Cheltenham 2017, pp 261–288; E Bribosia and I Rorive, 'Seeking to Square the Circle: A Sustainable Conscientious Objection in Reproductive Healthcare' in S Mancini and M Rosenfeld (eds), above n 17. See also Center for Reproductive Rights, 'Conscientious Objection and Reproductive Rights. International Human Rights Standards', July 2013, http://www.reproductiverights.org/sites/crr.civicactions.net/files/documents/_Conscientious_FS_Intro_English_FINAL.pdf (accessed 1 December 2017); O'Neill Institute for National and Global Law, 'T-388/2009 Conscientious Objection and Abortion: A Global Perspective on the Colombian Experience', 2014, http://www.law.georgetown.edu/oneillinstitute/research/documents/WLWT-388-09English-FINAL.pdf (accessed 1 December 2017); BR Johnson Jr, E Kismödi, MV Dragoman and M Temmerman, 'Conscientious Objection to the Provision of Legal Abortion Care' (2013) 123 *International Journal of Gynaecology and Obstetrics* S60.

20 E Bribosia and I Rorive, above n 19.

2.1.1. The Context of 'Conscience Wars' in the United States

In the context of the United States, where access to sexual and reproductive care is extremely problematic in a number of States,[21] the *Hobby Lobby* case provided the Supreme Court with its first opportunity to decide on the relationship between the 1993 Religious Freedom Restoration Act (RFRA) and the famous Patient Protection and Affordable Care Act (Obamacare). This federal legislation, passed in 2010, requires employers with more than 50 employees to pay for contraception as part of the medical coverage offered to employees through their group insurance contract. Churches and non-profit religious organisations are expressly exempted from this; however, a broader conscience clause including employers or for-profit insurers was rejected by a very narrow majority in the Senate.[22] Several Christian business leaders[23] then turned to the courts[24] on the grounds that funding contraceptives, such as the morning-after pill, violated the prohibition on killing dictated by their faith, according to which life begins at fertilisation.

In the high-profile *Hobby Lobby* case, the Supreme Court recognised for the first time that the religious beliefs of some companies are protected by the RFRA.[25] For the Court, commercial companies that have few shareholders (closely held corporations) are considered 'persons' under the RFRA[26] and must

---

21 See in particular the ACLU report, 'Healthcare Denied: Patients and Physicians Speak out about Catholic Hospitals and the Threat to Women's Health and Lives', May 2016, http://www.aclu.org/report/report-health-care-denied?redirect=report/health-care-denied (accessed 1 December 2017).

22 Respect for Rights of Conscience Act of 2011, S.1467, 112th Congress §(3) (a) (2011). The so-called 'Blunt Amendment' was rejected by the Senate in a vote of 51 to 48, with one abstention (Blunt Amendment, No 1520, 1 March 2012).

23 The *Hobby Lobby* case involves three commercial enterprises: the Green family (*Hobby Lobby Stores Inc* and *Mardel* corporations) and the Hahn family (*Conestoga Wood Specialities Corp*). The Hobby Lobby company is comprised of arts and crafts stores; the Mardel company sells Christian books and fashion clothing and accessories; and the Conestoga Wood Specialities Corporation specialises in making doors and wooden furnishings, kitchen accessories, etc.

24 D Nejaime and RB Siegel, above n 18, p 2551.

25 *Burwell v Hobby Lobby*, 573 US 22 (2014). The decision was delivered by a narrow majority of five judges to four, revealing a political, and even gender, divide (the majority of five men were appointed by Republican presidents and the minority of three women and a man were appointed by Democratic presidents). Among the many comments on this decision, see in particular J Morri, 'Une pilule dure à avaler : La Cour suprême des États-Unis consacre l'entreprise de tendance à but lucratif' (2014) *Revue des droits de l'Homme*, http://revdh.revues.org/871 (accessed 1 December 2017); SJ Willis, 'Corporations, Taxes, and Religion: The Hobby Lobby and Conestoga Contraceptive Cases' (2013) 65 *South Carolina Law Review* 1; M Tushnet, 'Do For-Profit Corporations Have Rights of Religious Conscience?' (2013) 99 *Cornell Law Review Online* 70; SJ Levine, 'Recent Applications of the Supreme Court's Hands-off Approach to Religious Doctrine: From *Hosanna-Tabor* and *Holt* to *Hobby Lobby* and *Zubik*' in HF Lynch, IG Cohen and E Sepper (eds), *Law, Religion and Health in the United States*, Cambridge University Press, Cambridge 2017, pp 75–85.

26 *Burwell v Hobby Lobby*, above n 25, p 18.

therefore benefit from its protection in order to guarantee the religious freedom of the natural persons who run them. In addition, the infringement on religious freedom by Obamacare was deemed to be substantial: these companies faced significant fines and penalties for refusing to cover the contraceptive costs of their employees.[27] While free access to contraception is a compelling public interest in the eyes of the Court, this objective could be achieved by alternative measures that would also ensure respect for the religious beliefs of the applicant companies.[28] Thus, the Court suggests that the government or insurance provider cover the cost of contraception for employees of the closely held corporations concerned, as is the case for non-profit religious organisations.[29]

This position, defended by the majority of the US Supreme Court, is far from unanimous, as evidenced by the virulent dissent of Justice Ginsburg, joined by Justice Sotomayor,[30] and more broadly the very divided doctrine on the subject.[31] First, the analogy between commercial companies, on the one hand, and churches or religiously based non-profit organisations, on the other, is questionable.[32] Some members of Congress who voted in favour of the RFRA in 1993 reacted by withdrawing their support for this text on the grounds that this judicial interpretation disregards the will of the legislator.[33] Moreover, the fact that exemptions are limited to closely held corporations should not hide the scope of this ruling, which is in fact considerable: the company Hobby Lobby has no less than 600 stores with more than 20,000 employees and records an annual turnover of more than $3 billion.[34] Second, the exemptions granted have the de facto effect of reducing protection for the people whom the general rule was specifically intended to protect.[35] As noted by Justice Ginsburg, the provision of contraception by actors other than the employer does not have 'zero effect' on women, contrary to the opinion of the Court. The goal of Obamacare was to ensure direct access to contraception by integrating it into existing professional insurance systems.[36] The result of the *Hobby Lobby* decision is to require a

---

27 Ibid, pp 31–32.

28 Ibid, pp 39–40.

29 Ibid, pp 40–45.

30 It should be noted that the other two minority judges (Breyer and Kagan) did not join Justice Ginsburg's dissent on this point.

31 P Oliver, above n 9, 661, 674–675.

32 Dissenting opinion of Judge Ginsburg, joined by Judge Sotomayor, in *Burwell v Hobby Lobby*, above n 25, pp 16–19.

33 See Brief for United States Senators Murray, Baucus, Boxer, Brown, Cantwell, Cardin, Durbin, Feinstein, Harkin, Johnson, Leahy, Levin, Markey, Menendez, Mikulski, Reid, Sanders, Schumer, and Wyden as Amici Curiae in support of Hobby Lobby Petitioners and Conestoga Respondents, *Burwell v Hobby Lobby*, above n 25 ('[we] could not have anticipated, and did not intend, such a broad and unprecedented expansion of RFRA').

34 There are several other companies with few shareholders which have many employees, such as Mars, which has 72,000 employees, or Cargill, which employs 140,000.

35 Dissenting opinion (Ginsburg) in *Burwell v Hobby Lobby*, above n 25, p 27.

36 Ibid, p 28.

substantial number of employees to take out additional medical insurance and to navigate a series of administrative procedures in order to obtain funding from public authorities. More fundamentally, the Court did not take into account the discriminatory nature of this exemption and the undermining effect it has on women's dignity.[37] Moreover, in the wake of *Hobby Lobby*, whose ratio decidendi is limited to the cost of contraception, it is easy to see how other requests for exemptions due to religious motives could emerge, for example, in relation to vaccinations or blood transfusions. Finally, what about the red line set out by the Court, which states that, in the name of a compelling public interest to ensure equal opportunities, its ruling does not permit that commercial companies rely on the RFRA to justify racial discrimination in the name of their religious beliefs?[38] If this makes sense in the context of the institutional racial segregation in the United States, the scars of which are still visible, the decision is problematic when it considers that gender equality would be less valuable than racial equality.

The *Hobby Lobby* judgment was the beginning of a movement towards the proliferation of religious exemptions through litigation, legislation and, since the accession to power of Donald Trump, through government and administration. At the litigation level, a number of non-profit Christian corporations active in the field of education, health care or, more broadly, the provision of social services, such as the Little Sisters of the Poor, have challenged the arrangement set up by Obamacare. For them, the simple fact of having to submit a form to declare their refusal to cover the cost of contraception for their employees constitutes a substantial burden in the exercise of their religion (within the meaning of the RFRA), as it makes them complicit in the provision of contraception by a third party. These contentious initiatives, which have generated many amicus briefs, have so far seen little success before the Federal Courts of Appeal, with only the Eighth Circuit Court of Appeals having granted a request.[39] Seven of these cases

---

37 D Nejaime and RB Siegel, above n 18, pp 2579–2586. In recommendations adopted shortly after the *Hobby Lobby* judgment, the Equal Employment Opportunity Commission (EEOC), an independent federal body responsible for overseeing the implementation of anti-discrimination legislation in employment, indicated that if an employer explicitly excludes contraceptives from the employee's medical coverage, this would constitute discrimination based on sex and/or pregnancy. US Equal Employment Opportunity Commission, 'Enforcement Guidance on Pregnancy Discrimination and Related Issues', n° 915.003, 14 July 2014 updated on 25 June 2015, section I (A)(3)(d), http://www.eeoc.gov/laws/guidance/pregnancy_guidance.cfm (accessed 1 December 2017).

38 *Burwell v Hobby Lobby*, above n 25, p 46.

39 The United States Court of Appeals for the Eighth Circuit in St Louis held 'that compelling their participation in the accommodation process by threat of severe monetary penalty is a substantial burden on their exercise of religion'. It added: '[t]hat they themselves do not have to arrange or pay for objectionable contraceptive coverage is not determinative of whether the required or forbidden act is or is not religiously offensive' (*Sharpe Holdings, Inc. v Department of Health and Human Servs.*, 801 F. 3d 927, 944 (CA8 2015), http://www.scotusblog.com/wp-content/uploads/2015/09/ACA-8th-CA-ruling-on-mandate-Sharpe-Holdings.pdf (accessed 1 December 2017)).

were brought before the US Supreme Court after the death of Justice Scalia,[40] whose opinion was decisive in *Hobby Lobby*. To avoid an equal split of opinions in a Supreme Court reduced to eight justices for a year, the Court decided to kick the ball into touch.[41] It was careful not to rule on whether it can be considered a burden on religious freedom, under the RFRA, due to so-called complicity, to require a non-profit corporation to submit a form in order to refuse, on religious grounds, to pay for the cost of contraception for its employees. At most, it has confirmed the feasibility of a compromise between the parties, in which an insurer could directly cover contraception.[42] In so doing, the Court implicitly endorsed the request for accommodation of religious organisations with little regard for its impact on women's rights.[43] Shortly thereafter, in June 2016, the Supreme Court denied, by a narrow majority, the petition for a writ of certiorari in the *Stormans* case,[44] filed by Washington State pharmacists to contest a State regulation which required them to deliver emergency contraceptives. In their view, this amounted to forcing them participate in abortion, an act that was contrary to their religious beliefs. This legislation provides for a conscience clause, but for natural persons, not for a pharmacy as a whole. In their dissenting opinion, Justices Alito, Roberts and Thomas pointed out that this decision was a bad omen for religious freedom.[45]

---

40 Documents relating to this case can be consulted online: http://www.scotusblog.com/case-files/cases/zubik-v-burwell (accessed 1 December 2017).

41 *Zubik v Burwell*, 578 US ___ (2016) (*per curiam*), https://www.supremecourt.gov/opinions/15pdf/14-1418_8758.pdf (accessed 1 December 2017).

42 The concurring opinion of Justice Sotomayor and Justice Ginsburg (who insist that the Court did not decide on the merits of the case) should be noted.

43 For commentary on this Supreme Court decision in the *Zubik and Others* case, see: C Mala Corbin, 'Punting on Substantial Religious Burden, the Supreme Court Provides No Guidance for Future RFRA Challenges to Anti-discrimination Laws', 17 May 2016, http://www.scotusblog.com/2016/05/symposium-punting-on-substantial-religious-burden-the-supreme-court-provides-no-guidance-for-future-rfra-challenges-to-anti-discrimination-laws-2 (accessed 1 December 2017); C Mala Corbin, 'The Contraception Mandate Accommodated: Why the RFRA Claim in Zubik v Burwell Fails', 11 March 2016, http://papers.ssrn.com/sol3/papers.cfm?abstract_id=2746027 (accessed 1 December 2017); N Tebbe, M Schwartzman and R Schragger, 'How Much May Religious Accommodations Burden Others?', 26 July 2016, http://papers.ssrn.com/sol3/papers.cfm?abstract_id=2811815 (accessed 1 December 2017) and 'When Do Religious Accommodations Burden Others?', 26 July 2016, http://papers.ssrn.com/sol3/papers.cfm?abstract_id=2812121 (accessed 1 December 2017); JJ Craddock, 'The Case for Complicity-Based Religious Accommodations', 25 June 2017, http://papers.ssrn.com/sol3/papers.cfm?abstract_id=2992324 (accessed 1 December 2017).

44 Documents relating to this decision can be consulted online: http://www.scotusblog.com/case-files/cases/stormans-inc-v-wiesman (accessed 1 December 2017).

45 In his dissent to the denial of certiorari, Justice Alito, joined by the Chief Justice and Justice Thomas, noted that: 'This case is an ominous sign … If this is a sign of how religious liberty claims will be treated in the years ahead, those who value religious freedom have cause for great concern' (*Stormans, Inc. et al v Wiesman*, 579 US ____ (2016), p 1), http://www.supremecourt.gov/opinions/15pdf/15-862_2c8f.pdf (accessed 1 December 2017). Please note

The *Hobby Lobby* case has also prompted a proliferation of requests for religious exemptions before parliaments. Some US States, such as Arkansas[46] and Colorado,[47] have had heated debates about this, but have not specifically included commercial companies as beneficiaries of the State-sponsored Religious Freedom Restoration Acts, unlike the State of Indiana.[48] Beyond the issue of access to contraception, the adoption of these conscience clauses is seen by conservatives as a vehicle for fighting back against the legalisation of same-sex marriage.[49] In several States, the adoption of these State laws coincides with the legalisation of gay marriage and tends to protect citizens or companies from being forced to provide their services during this type of union.[50]

The rise to power of Trump and his government in 2017 has introduced an important new ally to the unravelling of sexual and reproductive rights. While attempts to repeal Obamacare have so far come up against divided legislatures,[51] the new President and his administration are deploying a series of initiatives, the legality of which is sometimes questionable, in order to fulfil his campaign promises. The right to abortion, as recognised by the Supreme Court in *Roe v Wade*,[52] is eroded by the Pain-Capable Unborn Child Protection

that at the time of writing, the dissenting opinion could not be displayed on the Supreme Court website, but could be retrieved from http://web.archive.org/web/20170903001307/https://www.supremecourt.gov/opinions/15pdf/15-862_2c8f.pdf (accessed 1 December 2017).

46 ftp://www.arkleg.state.ar.us/Bills/2015/Public/HB1228.pdf, p 3 line 32 (accessed 1 December 2017); http://www.arkleg.state.ar.us/assembly/2015/2015R/Acts/Act975.pdf (accessed 1 December 2017).

47 http://leg.colorado.gov/sites/default/files/documents/2017A/bills/2017a_1013_01.pdf (accessed 1 December 2017).

48 K Guerra and T Evans, 'How Indiana's RFRA Differs from Federal Version', *Indy Star*, 2 April 2015, https://www.indystar.com/story/news/politics/2015/03/31/indianas-rfra-similar-federal-rfra/70729888 (accessed 1 December 2017). As such, under Indiana's post-*Hobby Lobby* law, a 'person' is extended to mean 'a partnership, a limited liability company, a corporation, a company, a firm, a society, a joint-stock company, an unincorporated association' or another entity driven by religious belief that can sue and be sued.

49 See a letter dated 27 February 2015, written by 15 professors or law researchers from several universities to the Indiana Parliament, in which they detail several reservations about the RFRA, which was at the time pending before the Indiana Senate, http://web.law.columbia.edu/sites/default/files/microsites/gender-sexuality/law_professors_letter_on_indiana_rfra.pdf (accessed 1 December 2017). See also MC Dorf, 'Religious Freedom Claims in Private Litigation', *Verdict*, 8 April 2015, http://verdict.justia.com/2015/04/08/religious-freedom-claims-in-private-litigation (accessed 1 December 2017).

50 Columbia Law School, 'State & Federal Religious Accommodation Bills: Overview of the 2015–2016 Legislative Session', 20 September 2016, http://www.law.columbia.edu/sites/default/files/microsites/gender-sexuality/prpcp_exemption_overview_-_9.20.16.pdf (accessed 1 December 2017).

51 Although they hold the majority in both houses of Congress, the Republicans have so far not been able to repeal and replace Obamacare because of internal dissent. See the debates around the American Health Care Act of 2017, H.R. 1628, 115th Congress (2017–2018), http://www.congress.gov/bill/115th-congress/house-bill/1628 (accessed 1 December 2017).

52 *Roe v Wade*, 410 US 113 (1973).

Act, which criminalises abortions performed 20 weeks after fertilisation, on the grounds that the foetus would feel the pain at this stage of its development.[53] In foreign affairs, a 'global gag rule' was established by a decree on 23 January 2017: foreign non-governmental organisations (NGOs) must certify that they will neither practise nor actively promote abortion if they are to continue to receive US funding.[54] As for conscientious objections to sexual and reproductive rights, both the introduction of the Conscience Protection Act to Congress in January 2017[55] and the Department of Justice (Attorney General) Guidelines on Freedom of Religion of 6 October 2017 tend to strengthen and expand it to explicitly include 'businesses' as beneficiaries. The slogan 'Americans do not give up their freedom of religion by participating in the marketplace'[56] attests to this. Finally, on 6 October 2017, the Trump Administration extended to 'for-profit entities that are not closely held (including publicly traded companies), the conscientious objection already recognized to churches and religious orders or non-profit organizations and to closely held for profit entities'.[57] This measure was immediately challenged by the ACLU in the name of the prohibition of discrimination against women.[58]

---

53 Pain-Capable Unborn Child Protection Act, H.R. 36, 115th Congress (2017–2018) (passed by a vote of 237 to 189 on 3 October 2017), http://www.congress.gov/bill/115th-congress/house-bill/36 (accessed 1 December 2017). An identical bill was introduced in the Senate: Pain-Capable Unborn Child Protection Act, S.1922, 115th Congress (2017–2018) (referred to the Committee of the Judiciary), http://www.congress.gov/bill/115th-congress/senate-bill/1922 (accessed 1 December 2017).

54 US Presidential Memorandum Regarding the Mexico City Policy, 23 January 2017, https://www.whitehouse.gov/the-press-office/2017/01/23/presidential-memorandum-regarding-mexico-city-policy (accessed 1 December 2017). See M Redden, '"Global Gag Rule" Reinstated by Trump, Curbing NGO Abortion Services Abroad', *The Guardian*, 23 January 2017, https://www.theguardian.com/world/2017/jan/23/trump-abortion-gag-rule-international-ngo-funding (accessed 1 December 2017), as well as the response by the European Parliament: 'US "Global Gag" Anti-abortion Rule a Major Setback for Women's Health, Say MEPs', 14 March 2017, http://www.europarl.europa.eu/news/en/press-room/20170309IPR65844/us-global-gag-anti-abortion-rule-a-major-setback-for-women-s-health-say-meps (accessed 1 December 2017).

55 Conscience Protection Act of 2017, H.R. 644, 115th Congress (2017–2018) (sponsored by 122 Republican and 2 Democratic representatives), https://www.congress.gov/bill/115th-congress/house-bill/644 (accessed 1 December 2017); and Conscience Protection Act of 2017, S.301, 115th Congress (2017–2018) (sponsored by 26 Republican senators), https://www.congress.gov/bill/115th-congress/senate-bill/301 (accessed 1 December 2017). These bills have been referred to the House Committee on Energy and Commerce and to the Senate Committee on Health, Education, Labor, and Pensions.

56 US Office of the Attorney General, Memorandum for All Executive Departments and Agencies, Guidance on Federal Law Protections for Religious Liberty, 6 October 2017, http://www.justice.gov/opa/press-release/file/1001891/download (accessed 1 December 2017), p 2.

57 US Department of Health & Human Services, above n 1.

58 American Civil Liberties Union, above n 2.

2.1.2. *The Fire Smouldering in Europe*

The position taken by the US Supreme Court in the *Hobby Lobby* case and the resulting legislative and political consequences contrast with the European jurisprudence. Even though conscientious objection is still largely unregulated[59] and may therefore be a significant obstacle to women's access to reproductive care,[60] several national or supranational (quasi-)jurisdictions have given precedence to a strict interpretation of this principle. Its application is generally limited to the direct participation of the objector in the act opposed by his conscience, without extending to actions which facilitate its accomplishment. In addition, its benefit is traditionally restricted to natural persons, excluding legal persons.

In this vein, in the case of *Pichon and Sajous v France*, named after pharmacists who refused to sell contraceptive pills, the European Court of Human Rights gave a narrow interpretation of the religious freedom guaranteed under Article 9 of the European Convention on Human Rights (ECHR).[61] For the Court, religious freedom 'does not always guarantee the right to behave in public in a manner governed by that belief':[62]

> as long as the sale of contraceptives is legal and occurs on medical prescription nowhere other than in a pharmacy, the applicants cannot give precedence to their religious beliefs and impose them on others as justification for their refusal to sell such products, since they can manifest those beliefs in many ways outside the professional sphere.[63]

This reasoning excludes from the outset any idea of complicity in the accomplishment of a sin. Applied here to pharmacists who are physical persons, it is a fortiori transposable to commercial companies. Moreover, the former European Commission of Human Rights repeatedly held that Article 9 ECHR does not apply to organisations whose objective is not religiously based, for example, in the case of a private association that runs a rehabilitation centre for

---

59 See 'Report on Women's Access to Lawful Medical Care: The Problem of Unregulated Use of Conscientious Objection', Parliamentary Assembly of the Council of Europe, Social Health and Family Affairs Committee (Rapporteur: Christine McCafferty), 2010, http:/www.assembly.coe.int/committeedocs/2010/20100621_aah%202010_18.pdf (accessed 1 December 2017) (hereinafter 'McCafferty Report').

60 BM Dickens, 'The Right to Conscience' in RJ Cook, JN Erdman and BM Dickens (eds), *Transnational Abortion Rights: Case and Controversies*, University of Pennsylvania Press, Philadelphia 2014, pp 220–223.

61 *Pichon and Sajous v France*, no. 49853/99, ECHR 2001-X (inadmissible). See in particular A Lamackova, 'Conscientious Objection in Reproductive Health Care: Analysis of *Pichon and Sajous v France*' (2008) 15 *European Journal of Health Law* 7.

62 *Pichon and Sajous v France*, above n 61.

63 Ibid.

young drug addicts.[64] For the Court, this exclusion is all the more justified in the case of for-profit legal persons.[65]

With regard to the conscience clauses invoked by health-care staff in relation to access to reproductive care, the same restrictive approach to religious freedom is enshrined in several national jurisdictions. For example, the UK Supreme Court ruled that only the participation in the medical intervention of terminating a pregnancy is covered by the conscience clause contained in the Abortion Act of 1967, to the exclusion of administrative acts relating to that intervention. The conscience clause therefore does not apply to a secretary responsible for transcribing the letter referring a patient to another practitioner in order to terminate a pregnancy,[66] or to a midwife in charge of caring for a patient before or after the abortion itself.[67] In the same vein, the French Constitutional Council has limited the conscience clause to extend only to people who practise direct abortion,[68] excluding those who only facilitate its arrangement.[69] Moreover, if the French law allows for a hospital doctor to decide not to personally perform an abortion, the heads of public hospitals can no longer oppose the practice of abortion in their establishment.[70]

The condemnation of Italy by the European Committee of Social Rights in the case of *IPPF-EN v Italy* demonstrates the same trend.[71] For the Committee, the proliferation of conscientious objector doctors in public hospitals (more than 70%), supported by the organisation of hospital services, led to the violation of women's right to health and the prohibition of discrimination guaranteed by the European Social Charter. Despite the legalisation of abortion

---

64 The therapists at the centre refused to testify in court about the drug addiction of a resident, alleging a violation of their freedom of conscience. *Kontakt-Information-Therapie and Hagen v Austria*, no. 11921/86, Commission decision of 12 October 1988 (inadmissible): 'the rights primarily invoked, i.e. the right to freedom of conscience under Article 9 of the Convention and the right not to be subjected to degrading treatment or punishment (Article 3), are by their very nature not susceptible of being exercised by a legal person such as a private association. Insofar as Article 9 is concerned, the Commission considers that a distinction must be made in this respect between the freedom of conscience and the freedom of religion, which can also be exercised by a church as such'.

65 *Company X. v Switzerland*, no. 7865/77, Commission decision of 27.02.1979 (inadmissable); *Kustannus oy Vapaa Ajattelija AB and others v Finland*, no. 20471/92, Commission decision of 15 April 1996 (inadmissable). These two cases concern, respectively, an anonymous company and a limited liability company challenging the payment of an ecclesiastical tax.

66 *Janaway v Salford Area Health Authority* [1988] UKHL 17.

67 *Greater Glasgow Health Board v Doogan and Wood* [2014] UKSC 68.

68 This conscience clause is enshrined in the Code de la santé publique (Public Health Code), Article L. 2212-8.

69 *Conseil constitutionnel* (French Constitional Council), 27 June 2001, decision no. 2001-446 DC, §§11–15.

70 Code de la santé publique, Article L. 2212-8 al. 4 (since the amendment in 2001).

71 *International Planned Parenthood Federation European Network (IPPF-EN) v Italy*, Complaint no. 87/2012 (ECSR, decision adopted on 10 September 2013 and delivered on 10 March 2014).

in 1978 and the precise regulation of conscientious objection, access to abortion is not effectively guaranteed to women in Italy.[72] The case law of the European Committee of Social Rights[73] is thus in line with General Comment No. 22, adopted in July 2016 by the United Nations Committee on Economic, Social and Cultural Rights.[74] The latter stresses that in order to guarantee the right of everyone to sexual and reproductive health, States must in particular prevent private actors from imposing practical or procedural obstacles to accessing health services. More particularly:

> Where health-care providers are allowed to invoke conscientious objection, States must appropriately regulate this practice to ensure that it does not inhibit anyone's access to sexual and reproductive health care, including by requiring referrals to an accessible provider capable of and willing to provide the services being sought, and that it does not inhibit the performance of services in urgent or emergency situations.

That being so, it would be naïve to under-estimate the intensity of religious lobbies' action in this area and the risk of a backlash effect for women's rights. This is demonstrated in particular by the reversal of the 1763 European Resolution on the right to conscientious objection in lawful medical care.[75] At first, the proposed resolution came from the Social, Health and Family Affairs Committee of the Parliamentary Assembly of the Council of Europe. It was based on a report presented by Christine McCafferty, a British Labour MP, which stressed the urgent need to regulate and monitor the use of conscientious objection in health services, as women were at risk of being unable to access lawful services such as abortion and emergency contraception.[76] In 2010, the balanced framework of this resolution proposal was completely reversed with the support of a narrow majority. The result is an incoherent text, prefixing some parts of the original with unfettered rights to conscientious objection not only for individuals, but also for institutions, even though the report in its original form expressly excluded the latter. Thus, in Europe, we can also see the spectre of a conscientious objection recognised not only of natural persons, but also of legal persons, in this case the 'hospitals or institutions'.[77] The initiative of

---

72 E Bribosia, I Isailovic and I Rorive, above n 19, pp 266–269; E Bribosia and I Rorive, above n 19.

73 *Federation of Catholic Family Associations in Europe (FAFCE) v Sweden*, Complaint no. 99/2013 (ECSR decision adopted on 17 March 2015 and delivered on 17 June 2015).

74 General Comment no. 22 (2016) on the right to sexual and reproductive health (Article 12 of the International Covenant on Economic, Social and Cultural Rights), UN Doc E/C.12/GC/22, 2 May 2016, §43.

75 Parliamentary Assembly of the Council of Europe (PACE), Resolution no. 1763, 'The Right to Conscientious Objection in Lawful Medical Care', 7 October 2010, http://assembly.coe.int/nw/xml/XRef/Xref-DocDetails-EN.asp?FileID=17909 (accessed 1 December 2017).

76 McCafferty Report, above n 59.

77 PACE, above n 75.

the UK All-Party Parliamentary Pro-Life Group, which led to the adoption of a 'Report into Freedom of Conscience in Abortion Provision',[78] is in line with conservative movements in Europe. The aim is to advocate for the recognition of conscientious objection in the case of indirect participation in abortion by extending the legal notion of 'complicity' to an act which is not unlawful, but is contrary to a religious requirement. There are strong links with the rhetoric used in the United States. The 'pro-life' parliamentarians also invoke comparative law elements to support their claims, such as the adoption of the Conscience Protection Act by the US Congress in July 2016, 'which provides legal protection for doctors, nurses, hospitals and all healthcare providers who choose not to provide abortions as part of their healthcare practice and provision'.[79]

Although still limited, the success of these neo-conservative positions in Europe[80] is evidence of the risk that an extensive approach to conscience clauses may jeopardise women's effective access to their sexual and reproductive rights. Invoked by natural persons working in hospitals, the over-used notion of 'complicity' is likely to undermine these rights. Invoked by legal persons, the conscience clause could well, through a snowball effect, void these rights of their meaning.

2.2. LGBT RIGHTS AT ODDS WITH THE CONSCIENCE OF COMPANIES

Over the past decade, a notable resistance has emerged alongside the advances in LGBT rights in Europe and North America, motivated by a so-called 'traditional' conception of emotional, sexual or family life.[81] Thus, in several countries (such as the Netherlands, Canada, the United States and France), the introduction of same-sex marriage has been accompanied by requests from civil servants for exemptions on the grounds of conscience.[82] Companies are also implicated in this development.

---

78 All Party Parliamentary Pro Life Group, *A Report into Freedom of Conscience in Abortion Provision*, July 2016, http://www.conscienceinquiry.uk/wp-content/uploads/2016/12/Pro-Life-APPG-Freedom-of-Conscience-in-Abortion-Provision.pdf (accessed 1 December 2017).

79 Ibid, §115.

80 A Hodzic and N Bjelic, *Neo-Conservative Threats to Sexual and Reproductive Rights in the European Union*, CESI, 2014. This report is based in part on monitoring carried out by the European Humanist Federation, Sexual and Reproductive Rights *Are* Human Rights, EHF campaign 2013/2014.

81 D Nejaime and RB Siegel, above n 18, pp 2544 et seq; R Wintemute, 'Accommodating Religious Beliefs: Harm, Clothing or Symbols, and Refusal to Serve Others' (2014) 77(2) *Modern Law Review* 240, 253.

82 See E Bribosia and I Rorive, 'Les droits fondamentaux, gardiens et garde-fous de la diversité religieuse en Europe' in E Bribosia and I Rorive (eds), *L'accommodement de la diversité religieuse. Regards croisés – Canada, Europe, Belgique*, Peter Lang, Brussels 2015, pp 192–201; INCLO, above n 10, pp 7–23; R Wintemute, above n 81; E Bribosia and I Rorive, above n 19.

The *Obergefell v Hodges* case,[83] in which the US Supreme Court granted same-sex couples the right to marry, triggered a multitude of requests for religious exemptions. It seems that the exemptions obtained in relation to reproductive care have served as a model for these requests.[84] Beyond the RFRA and comparable legislation already in effect in a number of States, more targeted proposals providing narrower accommodations specifically relating to religious views about sex, gender and marriage have been brought before State legislatures and the US Congress. These bills aim to allow private and public actors to act in ways that would otherwise violate the law, as long as their actions are justified by a religious or moral belief about sex or marriage. In many cases, as well as allowing clergy members to refuse to officiate at same-sex weddings, these bills protect private businesses that deny essential services to individuals who do not meet a particular standard of sexual and reproductive morality.[85] These accommodation policies based on freedom of religion and conscience are likely to have a detrimental effect on the full operation of non-discrimination law.

In the last few years, there has been an emblematic series of cases in the United Kingdom, the United States and Canada relating to for-profit companies with no religious corporate objective which refuse to provide services to LGBT customers on the basis of the Christian beliefs of their managers. Major cases have involved a bed-and-breakfast owner denying double-bedded rooms to same-sex couples,[86] a photography company refusing to cover a wedding ceremony,[87] a print shop turning down an LGBT organisation's request for printed envelopes and business cards,[88] and several other situations.[89] So far, national courts have held that the denial of services based on sexual orientation is discriminatory and that this is considered unequal treatment, even if customers can get the same service elsewhere without additional cost. The crucial aspect of these cases

83 *Obergefell v Hodges*, 576 US ___ (2015).

84 D Nejaime and R B Siegel, above n 18, p 2554.

85 Columbia Law School, 'State & Federal Religious Accommodation Bills: Overview of the 2015–2016 Legislative Session', above n 50. See also the report written in the framework of the 'Public Rights / Private Conscience Project' carried out at the Centre for Gender and Sexuality of Columbia Law School: *Dignity denied: Religious exemptions and LGBT elder services*, December 2017, http://www.law.columbia.edu/sites/default/files/microsites/gender-sexuality/older-adults-religious-exemptions.pdf (accessed 20 December 2017).

86 In the United Kingdom, see, for instance, *Bull & Bull v Hall & Preddy* [2013] UKSC 73; *Black & Morgan v Wilkinson* [2013] EWCA Civ 820. In Canada, see *Eadie & Thomas v Riverbend Bed and Breakfast and others (No 2)*, 2012 BCHRT 247.

87 In the United States, see, for instance, *Elane Photography, LLC v Willock*, 309 P.3d 53 (N.M. 2013).

88 In Canada, see, for instance, *Ontario Human Rights Commission v Brockie* (No.2), (2002) 222 DLR (4th) 17.

89 More generally, see E Bribosia, G Caceres and I Rorive, 'Le droit de la non-discrimination aux prises avec la conscience des entreprises' in A-G Gagnon and P Noreau (eds), *Constitutionnalisme, droits et diversité : Mélanges en l'honneur de J. Woehrling*, Thémis, Montréal 2017, pp 419–460.

is the injury to dignity and the humiliation suffered. Beyond the impact on the individuals turned away, the harm extends to the gay and lesbian community at large, which has long experienced structural prejudice.[90]

Although the judges recognised that the religious freedom of the individuals at the head of these companies was at stake, they held that this could not justify discriminatory behaviour. The position of the company refusing the goods or services was not always dissociated from that of the owners. The exact question of whether for-profit corporations can assert religious beliefs has generally not been clearly addressed.[91] However, most rulings distinguished between the case of a business and that of a religious organisation by favouring a restrictive interpretation of existing exemptions.[92] In some cases, courts stressed that commercial activities aimed at providing services to the public were not a core but a peripheral element of freedom of religion, since this freedom could be exercised in many other ways.[93] According to the different courts, for-profit organisations that open their doors to the public should not be able to claim religious exemptions that could perpetuate structural prejudice and breach human rights. The logic of reasonable accommodation does not apply here.[94]

The controversy is not over yet. This is evidenced by two very similar cases brought before the Supreme Courts of the United Kingdom[95] and the United States,[96] each involving a wedding cake with an inscription in favour of gay marriage.

In Europe, the *Ashers Baking Company* case is set in the context of Northern Ireland, where there exists intense tension between gay rights reformers and the influential born-again Christian lobby. Unlike England, Wales and Scotland, Northern Ireland has not legalised same-sex marriage. Despite growing popular support, the ruling Democratic Unionist Party still blocks this reform.[97] This background helps to explain how an apparently banal affair quickly became

---

90 R Wintemute, above n 81, 242. On this issue, see also the report produced by INCLO, above n 10, pp 13–23.

91 Sometimes only the directors were found to have discriminated (*Bull & Bull, Brockie, Wilkinson*), sometimes they were found to have acted in concert with the company (*Riverbend, Ashers Baking*), and other times it was only the company which was found to have discriminated (*Elane Photography*). *Elane Photography, LLC v Willock*, above n 87, §59.

92 *Eadie & Thomas v Riverbend Bed and Breakfast and others*, above n 86, §141; *Black & Morgan v Wilkinson*, above n 86, §50; *Bull & Bull v Hall & Preddy*, above n 86, §38.

93 *Ontario Human Rights Commission v Brockie*, above n 88; *Bull & Bull v Hall & Preddy*, above n 86, §39; *Elane Photography, LLC v Willock*, above n 87, §3.

94 R Wintemute, above n 81, 242. See also INCLO, above n 10, pp 13–23.

95 *Lee v Ashers Baking Company Ltd and others*, above n 3.

96 *Masterpiece Cakeshop, Ltd* v *Colorado Civil Rights Commission*, above n 4.

97 S Fenton, '"My Love isn't Second-Class": The Struggle for Marriage Equality in Northern Ireland', *The Guardian*, 19 October 2017, http://www.theguardian.com/inequality/2017/oct/19/my-love-isnt-second-class-struggle-marriage-equality-northern-ireland-dup (accessed 1 December 2017).

a 'high-profile case' on the national scene. With the support of the Northern Ireland Equality Commission,[98] Gareth Lee, a gay man associated with the volunteer-led LGBT organisation Queer Space, won a case before the District Court which challenged the refusal by Ashers Baking Company to ice a cake with the words 'support gay marriage' and the Queer Space logo. Ashers Baking Company claimed the message was contrary to its Christian beliefs. According to the District Judge, there is a distinction between the management of Ashers Baking Company, who can claim deep and sincere religious beliefs, and the company itself, which, according to the case law of the European Court of Human Rights, cannot avail itself of the benefit of freedom of religion.[99] In the District Judge's opinion, the denial of service amounted to direct discrimination not only on the basis of sexual orientation, but also political opinion.[100] As to the free speech issue, the District Judge ruled that the act of icing a cake did not force the respondents to promote or support gay marriage. On appeal, the Attorney General of Northern Ireland defended, contrary to the original ruling, that this was a case of 'forced speech' contrary to Article 10 ECHR.[101] To support this argument, the appellants relied on the Canadian case, *Brockie v Ontario Human Rights Commission*,[102] which decided that printing envelopes or business cards for a company which represented gay and lesbian interests did not amount to defending the LGBT cause and did not violate the freedom of religion or expression of the company's manager. However, the Ontario Superior Court of Justice argued that other acts could undermine the core elements of religious freedom and could therefore be denied, such as material that conveyed a message proselytising or promoting the gay and lesbian lifestyle or ridiculing one's religious beliefs.[103] The Court of Appeal in Belfast did not follow this line of reasoning. It ruled that: 'It was not suggested that there was any approbation of the message on the face of the cake … The fact that a baker provides a cake for a particular team or portrays witches on a Halloween cake does not indicate any support for either.'[104] Direct discrimination based on sexual orientation took place and there was no breach of the freedom of religion of the company or its directors: 'In the present case the appellants might elect not to provide a service that involves any religious or political message. What they may not do is provide

98 The support provided by the Equality Commission to the LGBT cause has been criticised for being biased. The Belfast Court of Appeal thus noted that it may have created the impression that the Commission was not interested in assisting the religious community where an issue of this sort arose (*Lee v McArthur and others* [2016] NICA 39, §106).

99 *Lee v Ashers Baking and others* [2015] NICty 2, §94 and §98.

100 Ibid, §66.

101 *Lee v McArthur and others*, above n 98.

102 Ontario Superior Court of Justice, *Brockie v Ontario (Human Rights Commission)* [2002] 22 DLR (4th) 174.

103 *Lee v McArthur and others*, above n 98, §§68–69.

104 Ibid, §67.

a service that only reflects their own political or religious message in relation to sexual orientation.'[105]

The Colorado Court of Appeals adopted a similar stance in the *Masterpiece Cakeshop* case, named after the bakery that refused to make a cake for the wedding reception of a gay couple. Requiring a bakery to bake a cake for a same-sex wedding is not 'compelled speech' or 'compelled symbolic expression': 'the act of designing and selling a wedding cake to all customers free of discrimination does not convey a celebratory message about same-sex weddings likely to be understood by those who view it'.[106] The 'Colorado Anti-Discrimination Act does not preclude Masterpiece from expressing its views on same-sex marriage – including its religious opposition to it – and the bakery remains free to disassociate itself from its customers' viewpoints'.[107]

Both the Supreme Court of the United States and more recently that of the United Kingdom have kept on their docket these two cases which address the question of the relationship between free speech and non-discrimination. In the United States, the many amici curiae in support of each of the parties[108] demonstrate the stakes involved in the high-profile *Masterpiece* case, whose outcome was expected 'to turn on the vote of Justice Anthony M. Kennedy, who is simultaneously the court's most prominent defender of gay rights and its most ardent supporter of free speech'.[109] The Trump Administration itself filed a brief urging the Supreme Court to give precedence to freedom of expression.[110] Finally, the Supreme Court reversed the decision in *Masterpiece Cakeshop v Colorado Civil Rights Commission* and issued a very narrow ruling, based on concerns specific to the case that there might have been 'religious hostility' on the part of the Colorado Civil Rights Commission.[111]

For organisations supporting the rights of LGBT people, allowing freedom of expression to prevail would be tantamount to granting a mandate to discriminate to all businesses 'that may be said to engage in expression, including florists,

---

105 Ibid, §100.

106 *Craig and Mullins* v *Masterpiece Cakeshop, Inc*, 2015COA115, 370 P.3d 272 (Colo. App. 2015), §§62–64.

107 Ibid, §72.

108 See the list of amicus curiae available online: http://www.scotusblog.com/case-files/cases/masterpiece-cakeshop-ltd-v-colorado-civil-rights-commn (accessed 1 December 2017).

109 A Liptak, 'Cake is His "Art". So Can He Deny One to a Gay Couple?', *New York Times*, 16 September 2017, https://www.nytimes.com/2017/09/16/us/supreme-court-baker-same-sex-marriage.html (accessed 1 December 2017).

110 *Masterpiece Cakeshop, Ltd* v *Colorado Civil Rights Commission*, Brief for the United States as Amicus Curiae Supporting Petitioners, http://www.scotusblog.com/wp-content/uploads/2017/09/16-111-tsac-USA.pdf (accessed 1 December 2017).

111 *Masterpiece Cakeshop, Ltd* v *Colorado Civil Rights Commission*, above n 4. Note that the decision was issued on June 4, 2018, when the proofreading stage of this book was nearly completed.

photographers, tailors, choreographers, hair salons, restaurants, jewellers, architects and lawyers'.[112] One such example is the case of *Washington v Arlene's Flowers, Inc.* involving a small business convicted of discrimination by the Supreme Court of Washington State for refusing the creation and sale of custom floral arrangements to celebrate a wedding ceremony between same-sex partners, one of whom had been a customer for a long time.[113] Many civil rights defenders stressed that it should not be forgotten that it was also in the name of religion that a South Carolina sandwich shop refused to serve African Americans in the 1960s before the Supreme Court ruled that businesses had to comply with the 1964 Civil Rights Act and its prohibition on racial discrimination.[114]

Of course, the free speech issue, which is more evident in the Northern Irish case, is not insignificant. However, nor can it be considered benign when companies invoke their religious beliefs to refuse to contract with LGBT people just as their rights are beginning to strengthen.

3. WHEN RELIGIOUS SYMBOLS ARE IN CONFLICT WITH A COMPANY'S IMAGE

Alongside this tension between freedom of religion and the prohibition of discrimination based on gender or sexual orientation, a second phenomenon manifests itself through a series of cases in which private companies dismiss or refuse to hire workers who wear visible religious symbols in the name of a brand image that sometimes calls for the religious neutrality of their employees. Again, there is tension between a freedom invoked by a commercial company and the principle of non-discrimination. The freedom of the enterprise is invoked in order to justify differences in treatment based on religious beliefs which, de facto, very often concern women.[115] Both the European Court of Human Rights (in the *Eweida* case)[116] and the US Supreme Court (in the *Abercrombie & Fitch* case)[117] set out guidelines in an attempt to reconcile the freedom of

---

112 A Liptak, above n 109.

113 *State of Washington v Arlene's Flowers, Inc*, no. 91615-2, 389 P.3d 543 (Wash. 2017) (en banc). On June 25, 2018, the US Supreme Court remanded the case to the Washington State Supreme Court for further consideration in light of its recent decision in the case of *Masterpiece Cakeshop, Ltd. v Colorado Civil Rights Commission.*

114 G Stohr, 'The Supreme Court Gets its First Test of Gay Rights since 2015', *Bloomberg*, 21 September 2017, https://www.bloomberg.com/news/articles/2017-09-21/the-supreme-court-gets-its-first-test-of-gay-rights-since-2015 (accessed 1 December 2017).

115 On this issue, see P Oliver, above n 9, 661, 674–675.

116 *Eweida and others v United Kingdom*, no. 48420/10, ECHR 2013. In this case, the Court ruled on four joint cases concerning the UK (*Eweida*, *Chaplin*, *Ladele* and *McFarlane*).

117 *Equal Employment Opportunity Commission v Abercrombie & Fitch Stores, Inc*, 575 US ___ (2015).

religion of female workers with the company's image (see section 3.1). More recently, the Court of Justice of the European Union ruled on this issue in the *Achbita* and *Bougnaoui*[118] cases, where there is a case law developing in France and Belgium on the principle of neutrality, or even secularism, which was traditionally reserved for the public sector, but is now spreading to the private sector, becoming exceedingly embedded in corporate image (see section 3.2).

3.1. THE GUIDELINES OF THE *EWEIDA* AND *ABERCROMBIE & FITCH* CASES

These two cases concern the dismissal (*Eweida*) and the non-recruitment (*Abercrombie & Fitch*) of women wearing religious symbols (a Christian cross and an Islamic headscarf respectively) deemed to be in conflict with the image the company intended to project to its clientele.

Ms Eweida, a practising Coptic Christian who was in charge of checking in passengers for the British Airways airline, was not paid because she refused to conceal the cross she wore around her neck which contravened the company's dress code. At the same time, there were accommodations in place for the Sikh turban and the Islamic veil. The English courts rejected her appeal on the grounds that wearing a visible cross is not required by the Christian religion and that its exclusion from the dress code does not therefore create any specific prejudice for Christians as a whole.[119] On the contrary, in a judgment which received much media and doctrinal attention,[120] the European Court of Human Rights upheld her claim by deciding that the United Kingdom has failed in its positive obligation to ensure the protection of the applicant's religious freedom.[121] In accordance with jurisprudence already established in the *Leyla Sahin v Turkey* judgment,[122] the Court indicated that the definition of 'manifestation' within the meaning of Article 9 ECHR implies the existence of a

118 *Samira Achbita, Centrum voor gelijkheid van kansen en voor racismebestrijding v G4S Secure Solutions NV*, 14 March 2017, ECLI:EU:C:2017:203; and *Asma Bougnaoui, Association de défense des droits de l'homme (ADDH) v Micropole SA, anciennement Micropole Univers SA*, 14 March 2017, ECLI:EU:C:2017:204.

119 *Eweida v British Airways plc* [2008] UKEAT 0123_08_2011, [2009] IRLR 78, [2009] ICR 303; *Eweida v British Airways plc* [2010] EWCA Civ 80.

120 On this issue, see G Gonzalez, 'Liberté de religion au sein de l'entreprise' in L Milano (ed), *Convention européenne des droits de l'homme et droit de l'entreprise*, Anthémis, Brussels 2016, p 60; J Ringelheim, 'Adapter l'entreprise à la diversité des travailleurs : la portée transformatrice de la non-discrimination' (2013) *JEDH-EJHR* 57; C Mathieu, S Gutwirth and P De Hert, 'La croix et les juges de la Cour européenne des droits de l'homme : les enseignements des affaires Lautsi, Eweida et Chaplin' (2013) *JEDH-EJHR* 66.

121 *Eweida and others v United Kingdom*, above n 116.

122 *Leyla Sahin v Turkey*, no. 44774/98, ECHR 2005.

sufficiently close and direct link between the act and the conviction, but that the applicant was under no obligation to establish that she acted in accordance with a command of the religion in question.[123] Moving away from the traditional approach of the European Commission of Human Rights, the Court considered that the engagement in a professional relationship does not necessarily imply a renunciation of freedom of religion, and that the possibility of changing jobs is not enough to guarantee the exercise of this freedom.[124] In the logic of reasonable accommodation to which the Supreme Court explicitly referred in the comparative law section,[125] the Court adopted a case-based approach in which it balanced the interests involved.[126] In view of the circumstances of the case (certain religious symbols were admitted by the dress code, which was subsequently abandoned by British Airways), the defence of a certain corporate image did not sufficiently justify the interference in religious freedom.

On the other hand, there was no violation of religious freedom found in the joined *Chaplin* case involving a nurse who was not allowed to wear a cross around her neck while on duty. In view of the public health and safety reasons put forward by the hospital to justify its policy, and the alternative solutions proposed for the benefit of patients (such as wearing a cross in the form of a pin attached to the uniform or slipped under a high-necked blouse), a significant margin of appreciation is given to the national decision-maker: 'The hospital officials [are] better placed to make decisions about security in their institution than the judge, who more is an international tribunal before which no one has directly testified'.[127]

In these judgments, the Court has been consistent with the jurisprudence of the United Nations Human Rights Committee, without referring to it explicitly. It is committed to applying a stricter proportionality test which has the effect of reducing the margin of appreciation of the national authorities in cases where wearing religious symbols is restricted in the name of a corporate image of a company.[128]

---

123 *Eweida and others v United Kingdom*, above n 116, §82. For a commentary, see M Pearson, 'Article 9 at a Crossroads: Interference before and after *Eweida*' (2013) 13 *Human Rights Law Review* 580.

124 *Eweida and others v United Kingdom*, above n 116, §83. See also S Oualid Chaib, 'Religious Accommodation in the Workplace: Improving the Legal Reasoning of the European Court of Human Rights' in K Alidadi, M-C Foblets and J Vrielink (eds), *A Test of Faith? Religious Diversity and Accommodation in the European Workplace*, Routledge, New York 2012, pp 33, 38–41. The European Court of Human Rights took a different stance in the case *Sindicatul 'Păstorul Cel Bun' v Romania*, no. 2330/09, ECHR 2013, §146.

125 *Sindicatul 'Păstorul Cel Bun' v Romania*, above n 124, §§48–49.

126 O De Schutter, 'Human Rights in Employment Relationships: Contracts as Power' (2013) *JEDH-EJHR* 49; J Ringelheim, above n 120, 77.

127 *Sindicatul 'Păstorul Cel Bun' v Romania*, above n 124, §94.

128 E Bribosia and I Rorive, 'Chroniques – Droit de l'égalité et de la non-discrimination' (2014/2) *JEDH-EJHR* 205; L Peroni, 'Eweida and Others v the United Kingdom (Part I): Taking Freedom of Religion More Seriously', *Strasbourg Observers*, 17 January 2013,

In the United States, the *Abercrombie & Fitch* case involved a clothing and accessories company that refused to hire a woman wearing an Islamic headscarf due to its 'Look Policy', which prohibited caps as they were considered too informal for the image of the company. For the US Supreme Court, adopting a neutral policy within the company does not circumvent the prohibition of discrimination based on religious beliefs and the duty of reasonable accommodation. Unlike European legislation, Title VII of the Civil Rights Act imposes, in the field of employment, an obligation of reasonable accommodation in matters of religion, that is, accommodation which does not give rise to *undue hardship* on the part of the employer, interpreted according to the criterion of de minimis cost.[129] The Supreme Court insisted that this legislation did not merely entail neutrality with respect to religious practices, but that it also required favourable treatment by demanding that employers do not dismiss or refuse to engage with individuals because of such practices.[130]

Regardless of the specific legal frameworks and jurisdictional approaches, it is clear that both the European Court of Human Rights and the US Supreme Court do not give a blank cheque to companies to defend their brand image. While the preservation of this image is a legitimate objective, it is examined in light of the circumstances of the case and must be assessed in respect of the harm done to the workers or candidates for employment.

3.2. THE 'USER MANUAL' OF THE *ACHBITA* AND *BOUGNAOUI* CASES

Another context entirely is that of France and Belgium, where issues surrounding the Islamic headscarf are highly controversial and have regularly been at the forefront of the media since the 1980s, whether in relation to education, employment or more widely in the public space.[131] The turn of the millennium has seen the emergence of a series of cases that have their roots in the claim – whether explicit or implicit – of a policy of neutrality by private

---

http://strasbourgobservers.com/2013/01/17/eweida-and-others-v-the-united-kingdom-part-i-taking-freedom-of-religion-more-seriously (accessed 1 December 2017); S Ouald Chaib and E Brems, 'Doing Minority Justice through Procedural Fairness: Face Veil Bans in Europe' (2013) 2 *Journal of Muslims in Europe* 23, 25.

129 On this issue, see E Bribosia, J Ringelheim and I Rorive, 'Reasonable Accommodation for Religious Minorities: A Promising Concept for European Antidiscrimination Law?' (2010) 17 *Maastricht Journal of European and Comparative Law* 137.

130 *Equal Employment Opportunity Commission v Abercrombie & Fitch Stores, Inc*, above n 117, pp 6–7.

131 For an overview of this context, see I Rorive, 'Etre et avoir l'air : une scénographie baroque des principes de neutralité et de non-discrimination. Commentaire de l'ordonnance du tribunal du travail francophone de Bruxelles du 16 novembre 2015' (2016) 4 *Administration publique (Trimestriel)* 491 and the various references cited therein.

companies (bookstores,[132] security services,[133] sale of cheap residential products, supermarkets[134]) to justify the prohibition of religious symbols (actually, the hijab) within their workforce.[135] Neutrality sometimes appears to be a means to conceal prejudices. However, when one considers the broader situation, it becomes apparent that the victims of neutrality are the Muslim women in the labour market of these two countries.

Regardless of the differences between the cases, the French and Belgian courts generally gave a very brief formal examination of the claims by the dismissed workers of a violation of freedom of religion or the prohibition of discrimination. In addition to a lack of mastery of the distinction between direct and indirect discrimination,[136] the judgments generally validated the restrictions imposed by these companies in the name of neutrality rooted in freedom of enterprise, without questioning its legitimacy and often assuming the proportionality of the redundancy measures. Finally, while all cases involved Muslim women from immigrant backgrounds, these cases were never discussed in terms of gender discrimination or even ethnic discrimination. The intersectional dimension of these exclusions[137] was therefore bypassed, as well as the prejudices and stereotypes very often at work in these situations.[138]

---

132 C. trav. Bruxelles, 15 January 2008, no. 48.695 (*Club*).

133 Soc., 9 April 2015, no. 13-19855 (*Bougnaoui* & *Micropole Univers*). For the various stages of this case, see the opinion of Advocate General E Sharpston, 13 July 2016, *Asma Bougnaoui et Association de défense des droits de l'homme (ADDH) v Micropole SA, anciennement Micropole Univers SA*, 14 March 2017, ECLI:EU:C:2017:204, §§22–27. C. trav. Anvers, 23 December 2011, no. 2010/AA/453 (*Achbita & G4S*). For a commentary on the decision of the Antwerp Labour Tribunal, see K Alidadi, 'Werkgever mag hoofddoek verbieden op basis van ongeschreven regels' (2010) 210 *Juristenkrant* 1–2.

134 Trib. trav. Tongres, 02 January 2013, no. 11/2142/A (*Hema*); Trib. trav. Bruxelles, 18 May 2015, no. 14/5803/A (*Carrefour*).

135 Almost all of these cases involve commercial companies pursuing a profit-making purpose. Only the Baby Loup nursery was a private, non-profit organisation whose mission of infant care was judged to be of general interest, but was not considered public service as such: Conseil de prud'hommes de Mantes La Jolie, no. 10/00587, 13 December 2010; Versailles, 27 October 2011, no. 10/05642; Soc. 19 March 2013, no. 11-28.845; Paris, 27.11.2013, no. 13/02981; Ass. plén., 25 June 2014, no. 13-28369. For a commentary on these cases, see G Caceres, 'Quand la religion questionne la généralité de la norme. Quelle place pour l'"accommodement raisonnable" en Europe? Étude de cas – Angleterre, France, Belgique', doctoral thesis under the supervision of E Bribosia and I Rorive, Brussels, Université libre de Bruxelles, 2016. See also R Linguelet, 'L'obligation d'aménagement raisonnable pour motif religieux en droit du travail et les ressources du droit du bien-être' (2016) *Journal des Tribunaux du Travail* 231.

136 Opinion of Advocate General J Kokott, delivered on 31 May 2016, *Samira Achbita, Centrum voor gelijkheid van kansen en voor raismebestrijding v G4S Secure Solutions NV*, 14 March 2017, ECLI:EU:C:2017:203, §40.

137 K Crenshaw, 'Demarginalising the Intersection of Race and Sex' (1989) *University of Chicago Legal Forum* 139; S Fredman, *Discrimination Law*, 2nd ed., Oxford University Press, Oxford 2011, pp 139–143.

138 On this, see ECJ, Case C-83/14, *CHEZ Razpredelenie Bulgaria AD v Komisia za zashtita ot diskriminatsia*, 16 July 2015, ECLI:EU:C:2015:480, §82 and §91.

In Belgium, Unia, the Interfederal Center for Equal Opportunities, faced with a growing number of complaints from Muslim women because of (new) neutrality requirements in labour regulations or implicitly imposed on staff, intervened to support Ms Achbita in order to convince the Belgian Court of Cassation of the interest in referring the case to the Court of Justice of the European Union for a preliminary ruling. For Unia, 'the validity of neutrality clauses (in the private sector) is unclear, as is the question of whether it involves direct or indirect discrimination'.[139] In the *Achbita* case, the Court of Justice had to determine whether the prohibition against a Muslim worker wearing a headscarf constituted direct discrimination on religious grounds where that prohibition was based on a general policy of neutrality of the business.[140]

In France, following the bitter controversies surrounding the *Baby Loup* case, named after the crèche located in the Paris suburbs that had dismissed its assistant director because of her refusal to take off her headscarf at work,[141] the question of the requirement of neutrality in the private sector has come under the political and media spotlight. With the support of the Association for the Defence of Human Rights (*Association de défense des droits de l'homme* – ADDH), the *Bougnaoui* case was also referred to the Court of Justice of the European Union by the Court of Cassation of France. The purpose here was to determine the legitimacy of an IT service provider's decision to prohibit, at the request of a client, one of its employees from wearing the veil in the workplace of the client.[142] In the wake of this, the Labour Code was amended by the El Khomri law in August 2016 to expressly authorise the inclusion of the principle of neutrality and the prohibition of religious symbols in the company's internal rules. Such restrictions must, however, be 'justified by the exercise of other fundamental rights and freedoms or by the requirements of the proper functioning of the enterprise, and (must be) proportionate to the aim pursued'.[143] This provision was introduced despite criticism from the Observatory of Secularism (*Observatoire de la Laïcité*) and the National Consultative Commission on Human Rights (*Commission nationale consultative des droits de l'homme* – CNCDH), which consider that secularism should guarantee not

139 Unia, 'Rapport annuel 2015. Le Vivre ensemble mis à l'épreuve', 2016, p 14, http://www.unia.be/fr/publications-et-statistiques/publications/rapport-annuel-2015-le-vivre-ensemble-mis-a-lepreuve (accessed 1 December 2017).

140 Cass. (Belgium), 9 March 2015, no. S.12.0062.N.

141 See the Baby Loup legal 'saga', recounted by S Hennette-Vauchez and V Valentin, *L'affaire Baby Loup ou la nouvelle laïcité*, LGDJ, Issy-les-Moulineaux 2014.

142 Cass. (France) (ch. soc.), 9 April 2015, no. 630. For a commentary, see T Dumortier et al, 'Chronique de droit des discriminations (octobre 2014–avril 2015)', *La Revue des droits de l'homme, Actualités Droits-Libertés*, 8 June 2015, 11–12, http://revdh.revues.org/1370 (accessed 1 December 2017).

143 Article L 1321-2-1 created by Law n° 2016-1088 of 8 August 2016, art. 2.

only State neutrality, but also the freedom of religion of citizens. They protested that existing legislation already imposes limits in order to 'guarantee a balance between the protection of employees' freedom of conscience and the legitimate desire to set the limits necessary for the proper functioning of the business',[144] and that this provision runs the risk of creating legal uncertainty and condoning absolute prohibitions. Besides, legal insecurity is recognised by the Ministry of Labour, Employment, Vocational Training and Social Dialogue itself, in its 'Practical Guide to Religion in Private Companies', where in January 2017 it indicates that: 'Where the reasons for the restriction are the business's image or business interests, the matter is still under debate. The case law is not definitively fixed on this point.'[145]

This difficult context indicates the extent to which the judgments of the Grand Chamber of the European Court of Justice in the *Achbita* and *Bougnaoui* cases were eagerly awaited[146] However, it is important to highlight that while this was one of the objectives of the strategic litigation developed by Unia in the *Achbita* case, the Court of Justice refrained from deciding whether a private sector company which adopts a policy of neutrality can be considered an ethos-based organisation.[147] This issue had emerged in several disputes, both in Belgium and France, particularly around the *Baby Loup* case. On this occasion, the Plenary Assembly of the Court of Cassation stated that the crèche had been wrongly categorised as an ethos-based organisation of a secular nature by the Paris Court of Appeal, since its objective was not to promote religious or philosophical convictions, but to welcome children regardless of religious belief.[148] Indeed, it would be difficult to allow a private company which introduces a policy of neutrality unrelated to its activities to benefit from the exception system introduced by Directive 2000/78 for the benefit of churches and organisations whose ethos is based on religion or belief, without distorting the interpretation of this system.[149] This was the position of Advocate General Sharpston in the

---

144 Observatoire de la laïcité and Commission consultative des droits de l'homme, 'Projet de loi de modernisation du droit du travail. Une disposition remet en cause le principe de laïcité', 19 July 2016, http://www.cncdh.fr/sites/default/files/160719_cp_art_1_pjl_travail_avec_observatoire_laicite_vdef.pdf (accessed 1 December 2017) (our translation).

145 Ministère du Travail, de l'Emploi, de la Formation professionnelle et du Dialogue social, 'Guide pratique du fait religieux dans les entreprises privées (Version employeurs)', January 2017, p 15, http://travail-emploi.gouv.fr/IMG/pdf/guide_employeurs_valide.pdf (accessed 1 December 2017).

146 For a detailed commentary on these two cases, see E Bribosia and I Rorive, above n 8, 1035.

147 Council Directive 2000/78/EC of 27 November 2000 establishing a general framework for equal treatment in employment and occupation [2000] OJ L303/16, Article 4, §2.

148 Cass. (France) (plenary), 25 June 2014, no. 13-28.369. See G Calves, 'Devoir de réserve imposé aux salariés de la crèche Baby Loup. Quelle lecture européenne du problème ?' (2014) 2 *Revue de droit du travail* 94, 100.

149 Article 4, §2 of Directive 2000/78.

Bougnaoui case, when she excluded the computer company Micropole Univers from the status of an ethos-based company due to the nature of its activities.[150]

Furthermore, if, as in the *Bougnaoui* case, a body of evidence show that stereotypes and prejudice are the reason for the dismissal, this amounts to direct discrimination. In such circumstances, the only exception is where the company can demonstrate that the duty not to wear an Islamic headscarf or any religious, political or philosophical symbols at work matches the 'genuine and determining occupational requirement' standard.[151] According to the Court of Justice, this exception should be restrictively interpreted.[152] The Court also clarified that such a requirement cannot cover subjective considerations, such as the employer's willingness to take into account the particular wishes of the customer.[153] Customer prejudices, even if they are hidden behind the requirement of neutrality, are therefore not likely to justify a discriminatory corporate policy.

This message, which a priori seems very clear, becomes more ambiguous when confronted with the reasoning in *Achbita*. Building on the *Eweida*[154] case law of the European Court of Human Rights, the Court of Justice stresses the legitimacy of a policy of neutrality in dealing with customers, anchoring it in the freedom of enterprise guaranteed in Article 16 of the Charter of Fundamental Rights. This legitimate aim is, in the view of the Court, likely to justify restrictions on religious freedom and discrimination, provided the principle of proportionality is respected.[155] The assessment of the appropriateness, necessity and proportionality of the prohibition on religious, philosophical and political symbols must be carried out by the national court on a case-by-case basis, taking into account all the interests involved. For this purpose, the Court of Justice proposes some guidelines: the policy of neutrality of the company must be coherent and systematic. Its necessity could, for example, be established if it only applies to 'front office' employees who are required to interact with customers.[156] The implementation of the latter is not without its difficulties and seems to permit the prejudices admonished by the Court to enter through the back door. How many so-called corporate neutrality policies are implemented to please customers, assuming, rightly or wrongly, that certain religious symbols

---

150 Opinion of E Sharpston in the *Bougnaoui* case, above n 133, §106.

151 Article 4, §1 of Directive 2000/78, above n 147.

152 ECJ, *Bougnaoui*, above n 118, §38.

153 Ibid, §40.

154 *Eweida and others v United Kingdom*, above n 116, §94. However, it should be noted that in this passage to which the Court of Justice refers, while the European Court of Human Rights recognises the legitimacy of enforcing a dress code in the name of a commercial image, it considers that national courts have placed too much emphasis on this when balancing the interests involved.

155 ECJ, *Achbita*, above n 118, §40.

156 Ibid, §§41–42.

are likely to 'disturb' them? Moreover, inviting the company to offer a 'back office' position instead of a dismissal may constitute a form of discrimination and encourage employers to hide the diversity present in their workforce by placing those whose religion disturbs 'in the closet'.[157]

In the *Achbita* and *Bougnaoui* judgments, the Court of Justice legitimated the implementation of a policy of neutrality by private companies under which religious, philosophical and political symbols are prohibited in the workplace. The guidelines it has developed (coherent and systematic policy, whose necessity may permit a distinction between back and front office) have been described by some as an 'instruction manual' allowing private companies to legally 'discriminate'.[158]

4. CONCLUSION

At the end of this epic transatlantic saga, what does a global approach to non-discrimination law teach us about how the 'conscience' of companies is shaking up the right to non-discrimination and coming into conflict with the prohibitions it entails?

We have seen how companies use freedom of conscience to contest the advancement of the principle of non-discrimination, both in relation to the sexual and reproductive rights of women and the equal treatment of all people regardless of their sexual orientation. As Nejaime and Siegel point out, for these companies or their owners, it is often a question of seeking judicial exemptions after certain battles have been lost in parliament and it has become difficult to advance the conservative principles which they defend through laws of general application.[159] This tendency leads to a hypertrophy of the notions of conscience and religious freedom, which are manipulated to extend to legal persons whose main object is commercial. The broad interpretation of the concept of conscience, recognised by the US Supreme Court in the momentous *Hobby Lobby* judgment and reinforced by policies implemented by Trump Administration, is not widely accepted in Europe – in fact, far from it. However, it puts pressure on the various judicial and parliamentary bodies,

---

157 By comparison, the fact that British Airways offered Ms Eweida a post without contact with the public in order to allow her to wear her Christian cross did not prevent the European Court of Human Rights from finding a violation of the Convention (*Eweida and others v United Kingdom*, above n 116, §§93–94).

158 See, for example, T Ufarte, 'La liberté de conscience des salariés face au culte de la liberté d'entreprise prôné par la CJUE : Une nouvelle guerre de religion', *La Revue des droits de l'homme, Actualités Droits-Libertés*, 16 June 2017, http://revdh.revues.org/3056 (accessed 1 December 2017).

159 D Nejaime and RB Siegel, above n 18, p 2543. See also INCLO, above n 10.

where access to sexual and reproductive rights continues to be challenged and where conservative lobbies are pushing for public and private legal entities to be granted the right of conscientious objection. The global dimension is also significant in the implementation of LGBT rights that runs up against a veiled homophobia which dons the robes of the prohibition on being complicit in sinful acts. The free speech issue in the cake cases submitted to the US and UK Supreme Courts shows how tricky it is to fight against discrimination that is rooted in the very structures of society, while at the same time protecting the fundamental freedoms which are often dubiously misappropriated.

Mirroring these cases, we decided to confront other cases where the corporate image of private companies seems to be linked, at least in part, to a form of conscience understood as an intrinsic part of their identity. How should a company's policy of neutrality be considered, particularly when it targets a symbol of a minority religion worn by women, largely of immigrant origin? Many cases in France and Belgium show great deference to freedom of enterprise. Can we be satisfied, as the Court of Justice of the European Union seems to be, with guidelines being transformed by some companies into a 'user manual' for the exclusion of women wearing the Islamic headscarf from the labour market? Should the particular context of each case not be taken into account so that examinations of the principle of non-discrimination go beyond appearances and do not hollow out the meaning of the principle by ignoring the prejudices at play? The case law of the Court of Justice of the European Union can only be reconciled with that of the European Court of Human Rights if the principle of proportionality is taken seriously, as it was in the *Eweida* judgment, where a true proportionality test was required and found that the injury suffered by an employee outweighed the protection of the corporate image. This is also the position of the US Supreme Court, which, on the basis of the reasonable accommodation mechanism, has reduced the permitted scope of dress codes linked to a company's image.

The reconciliation of the two sets of cases presented here demonstrates not only the many opportunities for businesses to use the rhetoric of fundamental rights, but also the way in which this impacts upon the protection of equality and non-discrimination.

SEXUAL AND REPRODUCTIVE RIGHTS AT THE CROSSROADS

Intersectionality and the UN Treaty Monitoring Bodies

Joanna BOURKE MARTIGNONI*

1. INTRODUCTION

This chapter analyses selected examples of the United Nations (UN) treaty-monitoring bodies' application of an intersectional lens to sexual and reproductive rights issues. While the concept of intersectionality has occupied

---

* Joanna Bourke Martignoni is a postdoctoral researcher at the Geneva Academy of International Human Rights and Humanitarian Law. Email: joanna.bourke-martignoni@graduateinstitute.ch. Parts of this analysis are based on I TRUSCAN and J BOURKE-MARTIGNONI, 'International Human Rights Law and Intersectional Discrimination' (2016) 16 *Equal Rights Review*. Research for the present chapter was also carried out within the framework of a larger research project on intersectional and multiple forms of dicrimination supported by the Swiss Network for International Studies between 2013 and 2015 (www.unifr.ch/iiedh/fr/recherche/ethique-politique-dh/snis). The views expressed in the chapter remain those of the author.

centre stage in much of the gender and postcolonial studies literature produced since the 1980s, the use of intersectional perspectives by the international human rights mechanisms has a much more recent history.

Intersectionality is both a method of observation and an action-oriented form of practice. It aims to uncover and redress forms of privilege and oppression that remain hidden from view in the single attribute analyses of inequality traditionally used by international and national human rights monitoring mechanisms.[1] The present chapter looks at the way in which the treaty-monitoring bodies are increasingly deploying the concept of intersectionality – both explicitly and implicitly – to address issues of sexual and reproductive rights.

The difficulties inherent in identifying a suitable comparator against whom the presence of discrimination or disadvantage can be assessed are highlighted. In some instances, the treaty bodies have failed to adequately address intersectional factors, such as belonging to an ethnic minority group or being a human rights defender, that have a direct bearing on the realisation of sexual and reproductive rights.[2] In other situations, exemplified in the approach taken by the majority of the Human Rights Committee (HRC) in the *Amanda Jane Mellet v Ireland* case (2016),[3] it is argued that the misuse of an intersectional comparator may potentially obscure, rather than illuminate, broader gendered power relations.

The chapter concludes with some reflections about the prospects and limitations of intersectional approaches to sexual and reproductive rights and the capacity of the UN human rights monitoring mechanisms to engage in the nuanced, radical and frequently contradictory analyses of inequalities and power relations that such approaches require.

2. THEORISING AND APPLYING INTERSECTIONAL METHODS

> Intersectionality is a form of resistant knowledge developed to unsettle conventional mindsets, challenge oppressive power, think through the full architecture of structural inequalities and asymmetrical life opportunities, and seek a more just world.[4]

---

1 VM May, *Pursuing Intersectionality, Unsettling Dominant Imaginaries*, Routledge, New York and London, 2015; N Yuval-Davis, 'Intersectionality and Feminist Politics', (2006) 13 *European Journal of Women's Studies*, 193.

2 Committee on the Elimination of Discrimination against Women (CEDAW), *AS v Hungary*, Communication No 4/2004, UN Doc CEDAW/C/36/D/4/2004, 29 August 2004; Human Rights Committee (HRC), *MT v Uzbekistan*, Communication No 2234/2013, UN Doc CCPR/C/114/D/2234/2013, 21 October 2015.

3 HRC, *Amanda Jane Mellet v Ireland*, Communication No. 2324/2013, CCPR/C/116/D/2324/2013, 9 June 2016.

4 VM May, above n 1, 1.

Scholars and activists working within the frameworks of critical race feminism and postcolonial studies have long engaged with issues of intersectional oppression.[5] These groups emphasise that gender, ethnicity, disability, age, socio-economic status and other identity characteristics are reflections of political, social and economic power constellations, which promote or limit an individual's enjoyment of rights and capabilities.[6]

This observation – that identities and power relations are multiple, dynamic and overlapping – has led to the development of intersectional models which seek to challenge the essentialist conceptions of inequality found within traditional anti-discrimination law and policies.[7] The intersectional critique argues that people cannot be defined by singular, unchanging attributes, but rather that identities are constantly being shaped and remade as a result of multiple characteristics and experiences.[8]

In rejecting the notion that individual grounds for discrimination can be easily separated from one another in terms of both their cause and effect, intersectional theories rely on a matrix framework that recognises the intricately entwined functions of both identities and power.[9]

Intersectional approaches differ from cumulative, compound or multiple conceptions of discrimination, which add together a number of grounds of discrimination as discrete, sequential and severable identity factors.[10]

---

5 See, for example, K Crenshaw, 'Mapping the Margins: Intersectionality, Identity Politics, and Violence against Women of Color' (1991) 43 *Stanford Law Review*, 1241; R Kapur, 'The Tragedy of Victimization Rhetoric: Resurrecting the 'Native' Subject in International Post-colonial Feminist Legal Politics' (2002) 15 *Harvard Human Rights Journal*, 1; C Bulbeck, *Re-orienting Western Feminisms: Women's Diversity in a Postcolonial World*, Cambridge University Press, Cambridge 1998; LM Padilla, 'Intersectionality and Positionality: Situating Women of Color in the Affirmative Action Dialogue' (1997) 66 *Fordham Law Review* 843; D Lenard Hutchinson, 'Identity Crisis: "Intersectionality", "Multidimensionality", and the Development of an Adequate Theory of Subordination' (2001) 6 *Michigan Journal of Race and Law* 285; and T Grillo, 'Anti-essentialism and Intersectionality: Tools to Dismantle the Master's House' (1995) 10 *Berkeley Women's Law Journal* 16.

6 G Quinn, 'Reflections on the Value of Intersectionality to the Development of Non-discrimination Law' (2016) 16 *Equal Rights Review* 63.

7 K Crenshaw, 'Demarginalizing the Intersection of Race and Sex: A Black Feminist Critique of Antidiscrimination Doctrine, Feminist Theory, and Antiracist Politics' (1989) 4 *University of Chicago Legal Forum*, 139; R Kapur, above n 5; and C Bulbeck, above n 5.

8 D Lenard Hutchinson, above n 5; and T Grillo, above n 5.

9 P Hill Collins, 'Learning from the Outsider Within: The Sociological Significance of Black Feminist Thought' (1986) 33 *Social Problems*; M Satterthwaite, 'Crossing Borders, Claiming Rights: Using Human Rights Law to Empower Women Migrant Workers' (2005) 8 *Yale Human Rights and Development Law Journal* 1; T Makkonen, *Multiple, Compound and Intersectional Discrimination: Bringing the Experiences of the Most Marginalized to the Fore*, Institute for Human Rights, Abo Akademi University 2000.

10 ML Andersen and P Hill Collins, *Race, Class and Gender: An Anthology*, Wadsworth Publishing, Belmont, CA 2015; T Makkonen, above n 9, p 5.

Another feature of intersectional analyses is that intra-group differences are viewed as being as important as those between groups and they further acknowledge that it is possible for individuals and groups to be simultaneously oppressed and privileged.[11] Proponents of intersectional theories and methods therefore require that these complexities, nuances and, at times, contradictions be reflected within legislation, policies and institutional practices.[12]

There is apparent consensus in academic circles and, increasingly, amongst human rights practitioners and within international organisations such as the European Union (EU) concerning the fundamental limitations of traditional, single-axis approaches to discrimination.[13] Disagreement persists, however, concerning the extent to which intersectionality-based methods are capable of providing concrete responses to the challenges that arise in responding to multifaceted experiences of inequality and oppression.[14]

For some scholars, intersectionality forms:

> [A] project of limitless scope and limited promise … It ensures that the focus of intellectual, political and legal energy is directed towards infinite elaboration of inequality subgroups, engendering a slow but steady march towards conceptual fragmentation and, ultimately, dissolution.[15]

When the individual or a small subgroup forms the unit of analysis, it is argued that it becomes increasingly difficult to design policies, strategies or legislative instruments that would advance the interests of a larger group or cohort of people.[16] Without a mechanism to objectively measure degrees of inequality, intersectional practice locks individuals and subgroups into a never-ending 'battle of oppressions' and also results in a dissipation of political and social capital due to fragmentation and competition amongst different interest groups.[17]

---

11 VM May, above n 1.

12 PYS Chow, 'Has Intersectionality Reached its Limits? Intersectionality in the UN Human Rights Treaty Body Practice and the Issue of Ambivalence' (2016) 16 *Human Rights Law Review* 453.

13 D Schiek and A Lawson, *European Union Non-discrimination Law and Intersectionality: Investigating the Traingle of Racial, Gender and Disability Dicrimination*, Routledge, Abingdon 2011; S Fredman, *Intersectional Discrimination in EU Gender Equality and Non-discrimination Law*, European Commission, Brussels 2016; F Anthias, 'Intersectional What? Social Divisions, Intersectionality and Levels of Analysis' (2012) 3 *Ethnicities* 3; G de Beco, 'Protecting the Invisible: An Intersectional Approach to International Human Rights Law' (2017) *Human Rights Law Review*, https://doi.org/10.1093/hrlr/ngx029.

14 J Conaghan, 'Intersectionality and the Feminist Project in Law' in D Cooper (ed), *Law, Power and the Politics of Subjectivity: Intersectionality and Beyond*, Routledge-Cavendish, Abingdon 2008.

15 Ibid, p 31.

16 Ibid, pp 266–267.

17 N Ehrenreich, 'Subordination and Symbiosis: Mechanisms of Mutual Support between Subordinating Systems' (2002) 71 *University of Missouri-Kansas City Law Review* 269.

Another argument invoked to refute the advantages of the practical application of an intersectionality framework centres on the claim that intersectional approaches are too complex to be effectively translated into practice within laws and policies.[18] As a result, it is asserted by these critics that intersectional methods can only work when they are confined to mapping and identifying those groups that deserve greater attention in policies and laws to redress inequalities, and providing these groups with the means to participate in law and policy-making processes.[19] In these analyses, intersectional approaches to anti-discrimination become simple observational aids rather than practical tools capable of radically changing the structures and institutions that create and reinforce intersectional forms of oppression.[20]

In relation to the point made above, human rights practitioners have also queried the value of intersectional approaches in connection with remedies.[21] Several of these commentators note that intersectional methods offer a false promise to complainants due to the fact that they have not, as yet, resulted in specific reparations that meaningfully address the root causes of inequalities and power imbalances.[22]

Such critics further maintain that institutional 'silos' and the absence of capacity within different human rights monitoring mechanisms make it virtually impossible to effectively apply intersectional methods within the existing structures and practices of international human rights law.[23] These practical difficulties, it is argued, have resulted in an ad hoc and incomplete application of intersectional analysis, thereby creating the risk of interpretive inconsistencies across jurisdictions without producing beneficial outcomes for individuals and groups that experience intersectional forms of discrimination.[24]

The following sections of the chapter outline the ambivalent engagement of the UN human rights treaty-monitoring bodies with intersectional methods. The history of the treaty bodies' adoption of intersectional thinking is

---

18 N Lykke, 'Intersectionality Analysis: Black Box or Useful Critical Feminist Thinking Technology?' in H Lutz et al (eds), *Framing Intersectionality: Debates on a Multi-faceted Concept in Gender Studies*, Ashgate, Farnham 2011, pp 207–221.

19 J Conaghan, above n 14.

20 B Tomlinson, 'Colonizing Intersectionality: Replicating Racial Hierarchy in Feminist Academic Arguments' (2013) 19 *Social Identities: Journal for the Study of Race, Nation and Culture* 254.

21 AN Davis, 'Intersectionality and International Law: Recognizing Complex Identities on the Global Stage' (2015) 28 *Harvard Human Rights Journal* 205.

22 VM May, above n 1.

23 N Taefi, 'The Synthesis of Age and Gender: Intersectionality, International Human Rights Law and the Marginalization of the Girl-Child' (2009) 17 *International Journal of Children's Rights*.

24 JE Bond, 'International Intersectionality: A Theoretical and Pragmatic Exploration of Women's Human Rights Violations' (2003) 52 *Emory Law Journal* 74.

first traced prior to a more detailed analysis of the recent work of these institutions on sexual and reproductive rights.

3. INTERSECTIONALITY COMES TO INTERNATIONAL HUMAN RIGHTS LAW

The adoption of the multilateral human rights treaties in the post-war era and the subsequent practice these instruments have inspired have broadened the reach of international anti-discrimination law. Diversification has occurred not only in terms of the definition of the acts or omissions that constitute discrimination, but also in relation to the grounds upon which discrimination must be prohibited.

The earliest of these human rights treaties, the Convention on the Elimination of All Forms of Racial Discrimination (1965), prohibits distinctions based on 'race, colour, descent, or national or ethnic origin'.[25] The International Covenant on Civil and Political Rights (ICCPR, 1966) and the International Covenant on Economic, Social and Cultural Rights (ICESCR, 1966) add an open-ended list of prohibited grounds that includes 'sex, language, religion, political or other opinion, national or social origin, property, birth or other status'.[26]

Treaty provisions on non-discrimination now routinely refer to 'other status' in order to allow the monitoring mechanisms a degree of latitude in responding to newly identified forms of inequality and oppression. The category of 'other status' has been read by the treaty bodies as including attributes such as age,[27] disability,[28] migrant or refugee status,[29] place of residence,[30] health situation,[31]

---

25 Convention on the Elimination of All Forms of Racial Discrimination, Article 1(1).

26 International Covenant on Civil and Political Rights (ICCPR), Article 2(1); and International Covenant on Economic, Social and Cultural Rights, Article 2(2).

27 Committee against Torture (CAT), General Comment No 2, Implementation of Article 2 by States Parties, UN Doc CAT/C/GC/2, 24 January 2008, paras 21–22; CAT, General Comment No 3, Implementation of Article 14 by States Parties, UN Doc CAT/C/GC/3, 13 December 2012, paras 8, 32; CEDAW, General Recommendation No 24, Women and Health, UN Doc A/54/38/Rev 1, 1999, para 24; Committee on Economic, Social and Cultural Rights (CESCR), General Comment No 6, The Economic, Social and Cultural Rights of Older Persons, UN Doc E/1996/22, 7 October 1996, para 12; and CESCR, General Comment No 20, Non-discrimination in Economic, Social and Cultural Rights, UN Doc E/C.12/GC/20, 2 July 2009, para 29.

28 HRC, General Comment No 2, Reporting Guidelines, 28 July 1981, para 13; and CEDAW, General Recommendation No 24, Women and Health, 1999, para 25.

29 Committee on the Elimination of Racial Discrimination (CERD), General Recommendation No 31, The Prevention of Racial Discrimination in the Administration and Functioning of the Criminal Justice System, UN Doc CRPD/C/GC/31, 20 August 2004.

30 CESCR, General Comment No 20, Non-discrimination in Economic, Social and Cultural Rights, UN Doc E/C.12/GC/20, 2 July 2009, para 34.

31 Ibid, para 33.

status of deprivation of liberty,[32] sexual orientation,[33] physical appearance[34] and poverty.[35]

In conjunction with this expansion of the recognised grounds of discrimination, most of the human rights treaty-monitoring bodies, including the Committee on the Elimination of Racial Discrimination (CERD),[36] the Committee on the Rights of the Child (CRC),[37] the HRC,[38] the Committee on Economic, Social and Cultural Rights (CESCR),[39] the Committee on the Rights of Persons with Disabilities (CRPD)[40] and, most significantly, the Committee on the Elimination of Discrimination against Women (CEDAW),[41] have begun to refer to forms of multiple, compound and intersectional discrimination within their work. Such discursive acknowledgement of the need to counter the essentialism that characterises the formulation of the non-discrimination

---

32 Ibid, para 27.

33 CAT, General Comment No 3, Implementation of Article 14 by States Parties, UN Doc CAT/C/GC/3, 13 December 2012, paras 8, 32.

34 CERD, Concluding Observations: The Dominican Republic, UN Doc CERD/C/DOM/CO/13–14, 19 April 2013, para 16.

35 CEDAW, Concluding Observations: Peru, UN Doc CEDAW/C/PER/CO/6, 02.022007, para 36.

36 CERD, General Recommendation No 25, Gender Related Dimensions of Racial Discrimination, 20 March 2000.

37 See, for example, Committee on the Rights of the Child (CRC), General Comment No 11, Indigenous Children and their Rights Under the Convention, UN Doc CRC/C/GC/11, 12 February 2009; CRC, General Comment No 6, Treatment of Unaccompanied and Separated Children Outside their Country of Origin, UN Doc CRC/C/GC/2005/6, 1 September 2005; and CRC, General Comment No 20 on the Implementation of the Rights of the Child During Adolescence, CRC/C/GC/20, 6 December 2016.

38 HRC, General Comment No 18, Non-discrimination, 10 October 1989. While the Committee does not expressly refer to intersectional or multiple forms of discrimination, it insists upon substantive (de facto) equality as the standard that it uses to assess State compliance with obligations under Articles 2 and 26 of the ICCPR. The Committee therefore argues that differential treatment is justified in order to redress inequalities and in para 8, it cites the example of the provisions in Article 6(5) of the ICCPR that prohibit the death sentence being carried out on pregnant women.

39 CESCR, General Comment No 20, Non-discrimination in Economic, Social and Cultural Rights, UN Doc E/C.12/GC/20, 2 July 2009, para 17: 'Some individuals or groups of individuals face discrimination on more than one of the prohibited grounds, for example women belonging to an ethnic or religious minority. Such cumulative discrimination has a unique and specific impact on individuals and merits particular consideration and remedying.' The CESCR does not go further to suggest which particular measures States must take to consider or remedy cumulative or multiple discrimination.

40 CRPD, General Comment No 3, Women and Girls with Disabilities, CRPD/GC/3, 25 November 2016.

41 CEDAW, General Recommendation No 28, Core Obligations of States Parties under Article 2 of the Convention, CEDAW/C/GC/28, 16 December 2010, para. 18; CEDAW, General Recommendation No 33, Women's Access to Justice, CEDAW/C/GC/33, 15 August 2015, para 3; CEDAW/C/GC/34, General Recommendation No 34 on the Rights of Rural Women, CEDAW/C/GC/34, 7 March 2016, para. 14.

provisions within most of the international human rights instruments appears to be gradually permeating the practice of the treaty bodies.

These ever-expanding lists of the grounds of discrimination prohibited by international human rights law would seemingly provide the treaty monitoring mechanisms with the theoretical and legal foundation for a more systematic consideration of intersectional forms of discrimination within their practice. As a general rule, however, most of the treaty bodies continue to approach discrimination as a singular phenomenon, paying little attention to the substantive rethinking of international anti-discrimination law and the broader economic and political environment that would be necessary in order to effectively capture and redress situations of intersectional inequality.[42]

4. SEXUAL AND REPRODUCTIVE RIGHTS AND SINGLE-AXIS PRACTICE: *A.S. v HUNGARY*

The following section focuses on a case in which the CEDAW did not explicitly use an intersectional framework to address sexual and reproductive rights. The consequences of this lack of analytical complexity, both in terms of its failure to acknowledge the specific axes of oppression and power relations at work, and in relation to the absence of remedies designed to confront and redress these intersectional forms of discrimination, are outlined.

In one of its earliest decisions under the Optional Protocol to the Convention on the Elimination of Discrimination against Women, the CEDAW Committee examined the coerced sterilisation of a Hungarian Roma woman, which occurred during an emergency caesarean section to deliver her stillborn foetus.[43] In her complaint, A.S. emphasised her 'extremely vulnerable situation … as a woman who would lose her child and as a member of a marginalized group of society – the Roma'.[44] She also maintained she would not have consented to the sterilisation given her 'strict Catholic religious beliefs that prohibit contraception of any kind'.[45] At the heart of her complaint was the fact that being subjected to forced sterilisation violated both her religious convictions and her interest in following Romani cultural traditions, given that 'having children is said to be a central element of the value system of Roma families'.[46]

---

42 JE Bond, above n 24, 141.

43 CEDAW, *AS v Hungary*, Communication No 4/2004, UN Doc CEDAW/C/36/D/4/2004, 29 August 2004.

44 Ibid, para 9.4.

45 Ibid, para 2.4.

46 Ibid.

The Committee's discussion on the merits of the complaint under Article 12 of the Convention, which addresses the right to health, provided an opening for it to examine the ways in which the applicant's gender and membership of the Roma community resulted in differential treatment in the context of accessing health-care services and information. The Committee did not avail itself of this opportunity and while it recalled its General Recommendation No 24 (1999) on women and health, it failed to cite the paragraph of that Recommendation in which it notes:

> there are societal factors that are determinative of the health status of women and men and vary among women themselves. For that reason, special attention should be given to the health needs and rights of women belonging to vulnerable and disadvantaged groups.[47]

This omission is particularly unfortunate, as the circumstances of the A.S. complaint would potentially have offered States parties a concrete demonstration of the kinds of measures they should be taking to address the health-related rights of women belonging to disadvantaged social groups. The gap between the rhetoric of intersectionality and its practical implementation was glaringly apparent in this instance.

As a result of this failure to consider the full range of the complainant's identity attributes, the remedies offered by the CEDAW Committee in *A.S. v Hungary*, although adequate in some respects, do not capture the specific, structural forms of discrimination experienced by Roma women in the context of sexual and reproductive health.[48] The Committee's formulation concentrates on gender as the primary axis of oppression when, in fact, it was the intersection of her situation as a member of the Roma community and as a mother that resulted in her forced sterilisation.

Despite these limitations, the *A.S. v Hungary* case is widely regarded by Roma women's rights advocates as 'ground-breaking', in that the decision indirectly raised the issue of the systemic discrimination faced by many Romani women in Hungary and throughout the region.[49] It also underscored the State's obligation to eliminate discrimination in the provision of health care and to guarantee access to reproductive and sexual health information for all.[50]

47 CEDAW, General Recommendation No 24, Article 12 of the Convention (women and health), 1999, para 6.

48 CEDAW, *AS v Hungary*, above note 43, para 11.5.

49 DL Schultz, 'Translating Intersectionality Theory into Practice: A Tale of Romani-gadže Feminist Alliance' (2012) 38 *Signs*, 37–43.

50 CEDAW, *AS v Hungary*, above note 43, para 11.5.

5. INTERSECTIONAL ANALYSIS OF SEXUAL AND REPRODUCTIVE RIGHTS

In spite of the lack of overt engagement with intersectionality by the CEDAW in its *A.S. v Hungary* decision, a number of treaty bodies have recognised the need for States parties and other actors to develop frameworks to respond to intersectional, multiple and compound discrimination in connection with sexual and reproductive rights. This interpretive guidance has primarily emerged within General Comments and Recommendations and in the Concluding Observations on States parties reports adopted by different treaty bodies.

In 2000, the CERD adopted a General Recommendation addressing the gender aspects of racial discrimination in which it acknowledged:

> Certain forms of racial discrimination may be directed towards women specifically because of their gender, such as … the coerced sterilization of indigenous women.[51]

In a similar vein, the CESCR issued a General Comment on the right to sexual and reproductive health in 2016 which recognises that 'individuals belonging to particular groups may be disproportionately affected by intersectional discrimination in the context of sexual and reproductive health'.[52] The General Comment mentions women living in poverty, trafficked and sexually exploited persons, people living with HIV/AIDS, women belonging to ethnic minorities, prisoners and lesbian, gay, bisexual and intersex persons as groups that might be particularly affected by multiple and intersectional forms of discrimination.[53] In its Concluding Observations, the CESCR has recalled the obligations of States parties to address the accessibility and availability of non-discriminatory reproductive and sexual health services for various groups – low-income and low-education families, adolescents living in rural areas, persons living with HIV/AIDS, girls from under-privileged and marginalised groups, remote and poor groups, trans and intersex persons.[54]

---

51 CERD, General Recommendation No 25, Gender Related Dimensions of Racial Discrimination, 20 March 2000, para 2. See also CERD, Concluding Observations on Colombia, CERD/C/COL/15–16 (CERD, 2016), para 32; and Concluding Observations on Paraguay, CERD/C/PRY/CO/4–6 (CERD, 2016), para 42.

52 CESCR, General Comment No 22 (2016) on the right to sexual and reproductive health, E/C.12/GC/22, 2 May 2016.

53 Ibid, paras 5 and 30–32.

54 Importantly, none of the CESCR concluding observations directly refer to intersectional discrimination, even though they do draw attention to the need to ensure the realisation of sexual and reproductive rights for specific groups. See, for example, CESCR, Concluding Observations on Honduras, E/C.12/HND/CO/2 (CESCR, 2017); Concluding Observations on Costa Rica, E/C.12/CRI/CO/5 (CESCR, 2016); Concluding Observations on Dominican

The most comprehensive application of an intersectionality-based logic within the treaty bodies' interpretive guidance appears in General Comment on Article 6 of the CRPD, which focuses on women with disabilities. In the Comment, which was adopted in 2016, the CRPD strongly advocates for the application of nuanced approaches to discrimination and notes:

> The concept of intersectional discrimination recognizes that individuals do not experience discrimination as members of a homogenous group but, rather, as individuals with multidimensional layers of identities, statuses and life circumstances. It acknowledges the lived realities and experiences of heightened disadvantage of individuals caused by multiple and intersecting forms of discrimination which requires targeted measures to be taken with respect to disaggregated data collection, consultation, policymaking, the enforceability of non-discrimination policies and the provision of effective remedies.[55]

The CRPD General Comment highlights the area of sexual and reproductive rights as being one in which women and girls with disabilities face particular barriers in the equal exercise of their rights.[56] Part B of the Comment contains numerous paragraphs that address potential violations of the sexual and reproductive rights of women and girls with disabilities, and also notes the need to take into account further identity-related features such as refugee, migrant or asylum-seeking status that may present additional limitations to the accessibility of health care, information and justice.[57] In its Concluding Observations, the CRPD drew attention to intersectional violations of sexual and reproductive rights, including forced sterilisations and forced abortions experienced by women and girls with disabilities in rural areas.[58] On several occasions,

---

Republic, E/C.12/DOM/CO/4 (CESCR, 2016), para 60(c); Concluding Observations on Former Yugoslav Republic of Macedonia E/C.12/MKD/CO/2–4 (CESCR, 2016), para 26; Concluding Observations on Angola, E/C.12/AGO/CO/4–5 (CESCR, 2016), para 52; Concluding Observations on Canada, E/C.12/CAN/CO/6 (CESCR, 2016), para 52; Concluding Observations on Northern Ireland, E/C.12/GBR/CO/6 (CESCR, 2016), para 62; Concluding Observations on Romania, E/C.12/ROU/CO/3–5 (CESCR, 2014), para 22; Concluding Observations on Germany, E/C.12/DEU/CO/5 (CESCR, 2011).

55 CRPD, General Comment on Article 6, Women and Disabilities, CRPD/C/GC/3, 25 November 2016, para 16.

56 Ibid, para 2.

57 Ibid, paras 38–46.

58 CRPD, Concluding Observations on Ukraine, CRPD/C/UKR/CO/1 (CRPD, 2015), para 47; Concluding Observations on Gabon, CRPD/C/GAB/CO/1 (CRPD, 2015), para 55; Concluding Observations on Kenya, CRPD/C/KEN/CO/1 (CRPD, 2015), paras 34 and 46; Concluding Observations on Brazil, CRPD/C/BRA/CO/1 (CRPD, 2015), para 47; Concluding Observations on the Cook Islands, CRPD/C/COK/CO/1 (CRPD, 2015); Concluding Observations on Mongolia, CRPD/C/MNG/CO/1 (CRPD, 2015).

the CEDAW has also made reference to violations of the sexual and reproductive rights of women and girls with disabilities.[59]

The CRC has consistently raised issues related to restrictions on sexual and reproductive rights and the impact of these on adolescents, in particular in connection with the stigma attached to teen pregnancy and the situation of young people living with HIV/AIDS.[60] Importantly, in its Concluding Observations on Sierra Leone in 2016, the CRC highlighted boys' lack of access to sexual and reproductive health information.[61]

The HRC has also sought to address intersectional forms of discrimination in access to sexual and reproductive rights in relation to minors and women without legal capacity, lesbian, gay, bisexual, transgender and intersex (LGBTI) persons, women in rural areas and defenders of sexual and reproductive rights.[62] The Committee on Migrant Workers (CMW) noted the need for Turkey to take measures to ensure that girls and women in transit have access to sexual and reproductive health-care services.[63]

Nearly all of the human rights treaty-monitoring bodies have issued guidance in the form of General Comments or Concluding Observations that implicitly reference intersectional or multiple forms of discrimination in relation to sexual and reproductive rights.

Aside from the CRC's mention of discrimination against boys, most of the discussions centre on the rights of women and girls and the added impact of other factors such as minority or migrant status, rural location or age. The only treaty body that consistently uses the language of intersectionality is the CEDAW; however, in practice, the other monitoring mechanisms make virtually identical recommendations concerning the measures that States parties should take in order to remedy inequalities in the enjoyment of sexual and reproductive rights.

59 CEDAW, Concluding Observations on Ukraine, CEDAW/C/UKR/CO/8 (CEDAW, 2017), para 43; Concluding Observations on Rwanda, CEDAW/C/RWA/CO/7–9 (CEDAW, 2017), para 47.

60 CRC, Concluding Observations on Bulgaria, CRC/C/BGR/CO/35 (CRC, 2016), para 44; Concluding Observations on Samoa, CRC/C/WSM/CO/2–4 (CRC, 2016), para 46; Concluding Observations on the Philippines, CRC/C/OPSC/PHL/CO/1 (CRC, 2013), para 21.

61 CRC, Concluding Observations on Sierra Leone, CRC/C/SLE/CO/3–5 (CRC, 2016), para 31.

62 HRC, Concluding Observations on Burkina Faso, CCPR/C/BFA/CO/1 (CCPR, 2016), para 19; Concluding Observations on Slovenia, CCPR/SVN/CO/3 (CCPR, 2016), para 9; Concluding Observations on Spain, CCPR/C/ESP/CO/6 (CCPR, 2016), para 13; Concluding Observations on Nicaragua, CCPR/C/NIC/CO3 (CCPR, 2008).

63 Committee on Migrant Workers (CMW), Concluding Observations on Turkey, CMW/C/TUR/CO/1 (CMW, 2016), para 42.

6. INTERSECTIONALITIES WITHIN INDIVIDUAL COMPLAINTS AND INQUIRIES

Several individual cases decided by the CEDAW and the HRC have employed intersectional methods to make findings on sexual and reproductive rights and to recommend remedies that have, in certain instances, gone beyond the individual complainant to take in broader questions of social and institutional reform.

6.1. *ALYNE DA SILVA PIMENTEL TEIXEIRA v BRAZIL*

The *Alyne* complaint was decided upon by the CEDAW in 2011.[64] The case involved the preventable death of 28-year-old Alyne da Silva Pimentel Teixeira after a private health centre failed to provide her with appropriate and timely emergency obstetric care.

The Committee determined that these omissions constituted violations of Brazil's obligations under Article 12(2) of the Convention on the Elimination of All Forms of Discrimination Against Women to ensure appropriate services in connection with pregnancy and to exercise due diligence in the regulation and monitoring of private health-care providers.[65] The Committee went on to find that the 'lack of appropriate maternal health services in the State party ... clearly fails to meet the specific, distinctive health needs of women' and therefore constituted discrimination against women under Articles 12(1) and 12(2) of the Convention.[66] It was further noted that the absence of appropriate maternal health services has a 'differential impact on the right to life of women'.[67]

In paragraph 7.7 of the decision, the Committee engages in a consideration of the 'author's claim that Ms da Silva Pimentel Teixeira suffered from multiple discrimination being a woman of African descent and on the basis of her socio-economic background'.[68] The treaty body recalls its earlier Concluding Observations on Brazil in 2007, in which it observed the existence of discrimination against women of African descent and noted that this

---

64 CEDAW, *Alyne da Silva Pimentel Teixeira (Deceased) v Brazil*, Communication No 17/2008, CEDAW/C/49/17/2008, 27 September 2011. For further details and analysis of the decision, see RJ Cook, 'Human Rights and Maternal Health: Exploring the Effectiveness of the *Alyne* Decision' (2013) 41 *Journal of Law, Medicine and Ethics* 103.

65 Ibid, CEDAW, para 7.5.

66 Ibid, para 7.6.

67 Ibid.

68 Ibid, para 7.7.

discrimination is 'exacerbated by regional, economic and social disparities'.[69] The Committee also refers to its General Recommendation No 28 (2010) on the core obligations of States parties under Article 2 of the Convention, which recognises that discrimination against women based on sex and gender is 'inextricably linked to other factors that affect women'.[70] It finishes by concluding that Ms da Silva Pimentel Teixeira was 'discriminated against, not only on the basis of her sex, but also on the basis of her status as a woman of African descent and her socio-economic background'.[71]

The reparations recommended by the Committee in the *Alyne* case included the payment of appropriate compensation to the author and the daughter of the deceased, as well as general measures to ensure safe motherhood and affordable access for all women to adequate emergency obstetric care.[72] Importantly, however, none of the recommendations mentions the obligation to adopt measures to address the underlying intersectional inequalities that led to the death of Alyne da Silva Pimentel Teixeira as a result of her maternal, ethnic and socio-economic status.

6.2. *KAREN LLANTOY HUAMÀN v PERU*

The HRC adopted its views on the complaint submitted by Karen Llantoy Huamàn in 2005.[73] The author of the communication was 17 years old when she became pregnant with a foetus that was found to be anencephalic. Despite the fact that the diagnosing doctor recommended a therapeutic abortion due to the risk that the continuation of the pregnancy posed to the complaint's life and psychological health, the director of the hospital refused to give consent. Karen Llantoy Huamàn was therefore forced to endure the severe pain and mental suffering of carrying to term and giving birth to a foetus with a known fatal abnormality.[74]

The HRC found that the State party had violated Articles 2 (right to a remedy), 7 (prohibition of torture and cruel, inhuman and degrading treatment or punishment), 17 (prohibition of arbitrary interference in private and family life) and 24 (protection of the rights of the child) of the ICCPR.[75]

---

69 Ibid.
70 Ibid.
71 Ibid.
72 Ibid, para 8.
73 HRC, *Karen Noelia Llantoy Huamàn v Peru*, Communication No 1153/2003, CCPR/85/D/1153/2003, 22 November 2005.
74 Ibid, para 6.3.
75 Ibid, para 7.

In its determination, the treaty body emphasised the 'special vulnerability' of the complainant as a 'minor girl' and noted the failure of the State party to provide her with age-appropriate medical and psychological support.[76]

While the intersections of age and gender are evoked by the HRC, the remedies decided upon do not specify the kinds of measures that the State party should take to 'ensure that similar violations do not occur in the future'.[77]

6.3. *R.P.B. v THE PHILIPPINES*

The CEDAW addressed the existence of several systems of oppression based on age, gender and disabilities in its 2014 decision in *R.P.B. v The Philippines*.[78] R.P.B., who is unable to speak and hearing-impaired, was 17 years old at the time that her neighbour allegedly raped her. She reported the incident to the police, where her sister interpreted for her using sign language. The affidavit drawn up was in Filipino. As the education system for the hearing-impaired in the Philippines is almost entirely in English, R.P.B. could not understand the affidavit, nor was she provided with an interpreter (instead relying on her sister).[79]

In her petition to the Committee, R.P.B. argued that in addition to the use of gendered myths and stereotypes about the behaviour of 'ordinary' Filipina women, her particular situation – that of being a girl and having a disability – was not taken into account. As such, there was a violation of the State's obligation to end discrimination in the legal process under Articles 1 and 2(c), (d) and (f) of the CEDAW. She also claimed that the lack of a sign-language interpreter, either at the investigative stage or at trial, violated her rights under Article 21(b) of the CRPD.[80]

In its assessment, the Committee noted that R.P.B. had suffered moral and material damages as a result of the:

> excessive duration of the trial proceedings, by the court's failure to provide her with the free assistance of sign language interpreters and by the use of the stereotypes and gender-based myths and disregard for her specific situation as a mute and deaf girl in the judgement.[81]

---

76 Ibid, paras 6.3 and 6.5.

77 Ibid, para 8.

78 CEDAW, *RPB v The Philippines*, Communication No 34/2011, CEDAW/C/57/D/34/2011, 12 March 2014.

79 Ibid, para 3.9.

80 Ibid.

81 Ibid, para 8.11.

As a result, the Committee recommended that the State provide reparation in the form of 'monetary compensation commensurate with the gravity of the violations', as well as psychological counselling and therapy for R.P.B. and her affected family members and 'barrier-free education with interpreting'.[82] More generally, it recommended that free and adequate sign-language interpretation should be provided at all stages of proceedings, that rape legislation should be reviewed and that criminal proceedings should be conducted 'in an impartial and fair manner and free from prejudices or stereotypical notions regarding the victim's gender, age and disability'.[83] In its decision, the Committee refers to its General Recommendation No 18, where it acknowledges that women with disabilities 'may face double discrimination linked to their special living conditions'.[84] Although the Committee seems to be using an additive understanding of inequalities rather than an intersectionality-based logic, the remedies ordered do go some way towards redressing the different human rights violations experienced by R.P.B as a result of forms of oppression related to her age and disability.

In its 2015 inquiry into the situation of sexual and reproductive rights in the Philippines, the CEDAW Committee recognised that different groups of women face specific, identity-based barriers to accessing sexual and reproductive health services.[85] Although the inquiry did not explicitly address intersectional discrimination, it did highlight economically disadvantaged women and adolescent girls in Manila as being of particular concern and its recommendations to the government emphasised the need to ensure that these groups of women, as well as others, have effective access to sexual and reproductive health services, including information.[86]

The jurisprudence described above highlights several key issues related to the prospects, as well as the current shortcomings, of the application of an intersectional lens to questions of sexual and reproductive rights. In both the *Alyne* and *Karen Llantoy Huamàn* cases, different treaty bodies identified intersectional discrimination on grounds including sex, ethnicity, socio-economic status and age.[87] In each of these complaints, the CEDAW and the HRC recommended that the State party make reparations to address only the gendered axis of the oppression experienced by the complaint, without examining the

82 Ibid, para 9.
83 Ibid.
84 Ibid.
85 CEDAW Committee, Summary of the Findings Concerning the Philippines under Article 8 of the Optional Protocol to the Convention on the Elimination of All Forms of Discrimination against Women, UN Doc CEDAW/C/OP.8/PHL/1, 22 April 2015.
86 Ibid, para 52(a).
87 CEDAW, *Alyne da Silva Pimentel Teixeira (Deceased) v Brazil*, above n 64; HRC, *Karen Noelia Llantoy Huamàn v Peru*, above n 73.

other underlying structural forms of discrimination and the ways in which these interacted to produce the human rights violations at issue.[88]

By contrast, in the *R.P.B.* case and its inquiry into sexual and reproductive rights in the Philippines, the CEDAW did connect reparations to the intersectional harms suffered.[89] The reparations recommended in *R.P.B.* are particularly notable in that not only do they address the situation of the complainant and her immediate right to accessible education and sign-language interpretation, but they also pave the way for institutional and systemic reforms that potentially benefit all persons with hearing impairment and all women and girls interacting with justice systems.

7. INTERSECTIONALITY TAKEN TOO FAR? *AMANDA JANE MELLET v IRELAND*

The final case discussed here is presented to demonstrate the risks of fragmentation that could arise in the application of intersectional comparators to situations in which a single-axis approach might be more effective in bringing dominant systems of oppression to light. It is argued that while intersectional methodologies may bring nuanced analyses of previously hidden experiences of discrimination to the table, it is also important not to deconstruct these to the point that they become devoid of political and explanatory power.

In its decision in the *Amanda Jane Mellet v Ireland* case under the Optional Protocol to the ICCPR, the HRC found that the State party had violated Articles 7 (torture, cruel, inhuman and degrading treatment), 17 (privacy) and 26 (non-discrimination) of the Covenant.[90] The author claimed that she had been subjected to cruel, inhuman and degrading treatment as a result of the legal prohibition of abortion in Ireland. The circumstances of the case were such that she was compelled to choose between continuing to carry a dying foetus to term or terminating her pregnancy abroad, was denied the health care and bereavement support she needed close to home and was subjected to intense social stigma.

In its finding in relation to the violation of Article 7, the Committee held that by virtue of the existing legislative framework prohibiting abortion in Ireland, 'the State party subjected the author to conditions of intense physical and mental suffering'.[91] It also noted that the author's suffering was further aggravated by the

88 See also HRC, *MT v Uzbekistan*, above n 2.

89 CEDAW, *RPB v The Philippines*, above n 78; CEDAW Committee, above n 85.

90 HRC, *Amanda Jane Mellet v Ireland*, Communication No 2324/2013, CCPR/C/116/D/2324/2013, 17 November 2016.

91 Ibid, para 7.4.

fact that she was not able to access information about appropriate options for the termination of her pregnancy from trusted medical professionals. The Abortion Information Act legally restricts the circumstances in which any individual may provide information about abortion services in Ireland or overseas and criminalises advocating or promoting the termination of pregnancy.

On the issue of the violation of the right to privacy, the Committee considered that 'the balance that the State party has chosen to strike between protection of the fetus and the rights of the woman in the present case cannot be justified'.[92] It held that the 'interference in the author's decision as to how best cope with her non-viable pregnancy was unreasonable and arbitrary in violation of article 17 of the Covenant'.[93]

Concerning the non-discrimination guarantee in Article 26 of the ICCPR, the Committee noted the author's claim that the State party's criminalisation of abortion 'subjected her to a gender-based stereotype of the reproductive role of women primarily as mothers, and that stereotyping her as a reproductive instrument subjected her to discrimination'.[94] In its determination, it found that the differential treatment to which the author was subjected in relation to other similarly situated pregnant women failed to adequately take into account her medical needs and socio-economic circumstances and 'did not meet the requirements of reasonableness, objectivity and legitimacy of purpose'.[95] As a result, it concluded that the failure of the State party to provide the reproductive health services that the author required constituted discrimination and violated her rights under Article 26 of the Covenant.

There were several concurring and dissenting opinions issued by individual members of the Committee in the case. Of particular note is the discussion of the non-discrimination provision under Article 26 in the concurring opinion of Sarah Cleveland, who held that the Committee had failed to adequately emphasise the gender-based nature of the discrimination that the author experienced as a result of the prohibition on abortion. In this regard, she noted:

> Ireland's near-comprehensive criminalization of abortion services denies access to reproductive medical services that only women need, and imposes no equivalent burden on men's access to reproductive health care. It thus clearly treats men and women differently on the basis of sex for purposes of article 26.[96]

It is important to emphasise that Sarah Cleveland's analysis stresses that the discrimination experienced by the complainant was grounded in the single

92 Ibid, para. 7.8.
93 Ibid.
94 Ibid, para. 7.11.
95 Ibid.
96 Ibid, Annex II, para 13.

axis of gender. In this case, the majority's characterisation of inequality as intersectional in nature actually served to conceal the fact that the Irish abortion ban gives rise to structural and institutional discrimination against women as a social group.

In spite of the Committee's implied focus on the 'similarly situated pregnant woman' as the relevant comparator, the remedies ordered remain broad in scope and address the situation of all women within the State party. In order to prevent similar violations in the future, the HRC states that Ireland should ensure 'effective, timely and accessible procedures for pregnancy termination in Ireland' and that health-care providers should not be prohibited from providing 'full information on safe abortion services'.[97]

The reasoning provided by the majority of the HRC in the *Amanda Jane Mellet v Ireland* case offers only a partial explanation for the systemic inequality experienced by the complainant. Through its use of a 'similarly situated pregnant woman' as the relevant comparator, the application by the Committee of an apparently intersectional logic led to the disappearance of the sex discrimination that lies at the heart of the Irish abortion ban. In the *Mellet* case, the fragmented characterisation of the complainants' identity did not lead to a restriction in terms of the scope of the remedies that were recommended by the treaty body. However, it is easy to imagine other situations in which the 'misdiagnosis' of power systems through an intersectional analysis could result in partial and ineffective reparations being offered.

8. CONCLUSIONS

The international human rights treaty-monitoring bodies are increasingly embracing the concept of intersectionality in individual complaints procedures, in their interpretive jurisprudence and within concluding observations and recommendations on periodic State reporting. However, the application of intersectional methods to the promotion and protection of sexual and reproductive rights has been piecemeal and mixed in terms of its human rights outcomes.

The examples presented in this chapter demonstrate the potential as well as the limitations of intersectionality as a theory and as a working method within the practice of the treaty bodies. An awareness of the need to ensure that a rich range of experiences is brought before judicial and quasi-judicial authorities is apparent in contemporary discussions surrounding the sexual and reproductive rights of young people, people from indigenous and minority groups and persons

97 Ibid, para 9.

with disabilities. The scope and nature of the human rights violations that arise at the intersections of different forms of discrimination can, as a result, be more effectively identified and redressed, in the process reinforcing universal, regional and national human rights guarantees.

The extension of remedies beyond the immediate, intersectional, subgroup or individual involved in a particular case may lead to new policies, procedures and legislation that address human rights issues faced by many other people. The reparations recommended by the CEDAW Committee in the *R.P.B v The Philippines* communication included country-wide provision of sign-language interpreters in legal proceedings along with a suite of policy and educational measures to respond to the gender, disability and age-based discrimination experienced by the complainant.[98]

This increased sensitivity to multiple forms of oppression can be viewed as a positive development, in that it provides a necessary counterweight to the 'single-axis' model of anti-discrimination law that is reflected in the text of the multilateral human rights treaties and in much national legislation. In this context, the adoption of intersectional methods by the international human rights system is valuable for its potential to influence the future shape of national anti-discrimination laws and policies. Many of the recommendations by treaty bodies to States have recently focused on ensuring that cases of intersectional discrimination are justiciable at the national level through, inter alia, the adoption of consolidated anti-discrimination legislation and an expansion of the mandates of national human rights institutions so that they are able to consider complaints that simultaneously invoke multiple grounds of discrimination.[99]

In practice, however, the treaty bodies still tend to rely upon an additive approach that focuses on multiple or compound discrimination rather than engaging in truly intersectional inquiries.[100] The result of this limited implementation of intersectionality is that an ever-expanding range of different subgroups is being mentioned within interpretive guidance documents and recommendations adopted by the treaty bodies. These lists of 'marginalised' and 'vulnerable' people often appear to constitute little more than ritualised processes of naming particular social groups without any development of novel or radical

---

98 CEDAW, *RPB v The Philippines*, above n 78.

99 See, for example, CEDAW, General Recommendation No 33, above n 41, para 60(c): 'provide the possibility for women to lodge claims involving multiple and intersecting forms of discrimination'.

100 J Bourke Martignoni, 'Intersectionalities, Human Rights and Climate Change' in S Jodoin et al (eds), *Routledge Handbook of Human Rights and Climate Governance*, Routledge, Abingdon 2018; PYS Chow, above n 12.

suggestions for the transformation of oppressive structures or acknowledgement of the complexities of representing intra-group diversity.[101]

Further, the spectre of fragmentation through the use of intersectional methods is apparent in the majority decision of the HRC in the *Amanda Jane Mellet v Ireland* case.[102] The application of an intersectional comparator 'similarly situated pregnant women carrying a foetus with a fatal impairment' worked to obscure the fact that gender-based discrimination was at issue and that the appropriate comparator was therefore men. On the other hand, the CEDAW Committee's erasure of the Roma identity of the complainant in the *A.S. v Hungary* decision did not capture the intersections of the racialised and gendered systems of oppression that led to her baby being stillborn and to her subsequent forced sterilisation.[103] This meant that the suggested remedies also failed to redress the institutionalised discrimination that Romani women (and mothers in particular) face in their interactions with health systems.

This decision can be distinguished from the views subsequently adopted by the same Committee in the communication by *Alyne da Silva Pimentel Teixeira v Brazil* in which it was explicitly recognised that the complainant 'was discriminated against, not only on the basis of her sex, but also on the basis of her status as a woman of African descent and her socio-economic background'.[104] Crucially, however, acknowledgement of the intersectional factors that contributed to the human rights violations experienced by Alyne da Silva Pimentel did not lead the Committee to make specific recommendations for remedies that respond to intersectional processes of oppression on the grounds of sex, ethnic origin and socio-economic status. In contrast, the HRC pursued its intersectional analysis through to the remedy stage in the case of *Karen Llantoy Huamàn v Peru*, in which the treaty body emphasised the complainant's 'special vulnerability as a minor girl' and, as a result, found a violation of Article 24 of the ICCPR.[105]

Outside of this uneven development of treaty body jurisprudence within individual cases involving sexual and reproductive rights, there is some concern that intersectional methods and approaches may, paradoxically, reinforce the essentialist and globalising tendencies of international human rights law as a form of governance.[106] As Dorothy Hodgson powerfully argues in her study

---

101 Ibid, PYS Chow. For a broader and extremely cogent formulation of a similar argument, see S Marks, 'Human Rights and Root Causes' (2011) 74 *Modern Law Review* 57.

102 HRC, *Amanda Jane Mellet v Ireland*, above n 90.

103 CEDAW, *AS v Hungary*, above n 43.

104 CEDAW, *Alyne da Silva Pimentel Teixeira (Deceased) v Brazil*, above n 64, para 7.7.

105 HRC, *Karen Noelia Llantoy Huamàn v Peru*, above n 73, para 6.5.

106 PYS Chow, above n 12; S Engle Merry, *Human Rights and Gender Violence*, University of Chicago Press, Chicago 2006.

on the debate concerning global and national women's rights movements and Maasai women's organisations in Tanzania over the issue of female genital mutilation, the use of international human rights norms and intersectional analyses to 'fetishize' particular cultural practices may 'at best mask and at worst perpetuate and aggravate … systemic inequalities and imperial relations'.[107]

In spite of the shortcomings in the currently limited and piecemeal application of intersectional methods by the UN human rights treaty-monitoring bodies, the concept of intersectionality continues to perform a valuable role in drawing attention to the need to include a wider range of experiences within the purview of international anti-discrimination law and the remedies that it provides. It is to be hoped that, in future, the treaty bodies will be bold enough to engage in the nuanced, critical and far-reaching political, social, legal and economic analyses that intersectional paradigms demand.

107 D L Hodgson, *Gender, Justice, and the Problem of Culture*, Indiana University Press, Bloomington 2017, p 124.

THE INTEGRATION OF CULTURAL AND ECONOMIC RIGHTS BY REGIONAL HUMAN RIGHTS COURTS

Valeska DAVID*

1. INTRODUCTION

Though human rights law is fragmented across distinct regimes on specific rights holders and different types of rights, in real life people experience rights in a more

* PhD Researcher, Human Rights Centre, Faculty of Law, Ghent University. Email: Valeska.David@Ugent.be. This research has been funded by the Interuniversity Attraction Poles Programme initiated by the Belgian Science Policy Office, more specifically the IAP, 'The Global Challenge of Human Rights Integration: Towards a Users' Perspective', http://www.hrintegration.be.

integrated fashion.[1] From the several identities and social positions that shape people's enjoyment of rights, this chapter concentrates on those that concern cultural identity and economic background. Albeit analytically distinguishable, in practice, the cultural and economic relations of privilege and disadvantage often operate in complex and inter-related ways, challenging policy and normative responses. This is aptly reflected in the experience of Roma, Travellers and indigenous peoples.[2] They are amongst the poorest in many countries and their identities and worldviews are widely disrespected. Their cultural and socio-economic characteristics may both operate as proxies for racial discrimination.[3] Important aspects of their struggles against discrimination, assimilation and destitution in Europe and the Americas therefore lie at the crossroads of cultural and economic inequalities.[4] Yet in law, particularly in human rights adjudication, these questions too often appear disconnected, as explained further below.

This chapter examines more than 30 judgments and decisions issued prior to 2015 by the European Court of Human Rights (ECtHR) and the Inter-American Court of Human Rights (IACtHR) on Roma, Travellers and indigenous land-related cases respectively. This body of case law is frequently regarded as 'a jurisprudence of difference'[5] – that is, case law concerned with minorities' cultural identity, lifestyles and 'special needs'. However, at the same time, the cases studied have pushed the regional courts to deal with legal claims over land, living conditions, housing, protection against eviction and access to and management of natural resources. While this case law has attracted extensive interest from the perspective of the 'culturalisation' of human rights law,[6]

1 E Brems, 'Should Pluriform Human Rights Become One? Exploring the Benefits of Human Rights Integration' (2014) 4 *European Journal of Human Rights* 447, 465.

2 The terms 'Roma' and 'Traveller' are used broadly to designate diverse groups and individuals that the international jurisprudence generally refers to as 'Gypsies'. Indigenous and tribal are similarly used in accordance to the nomenclature adopted by the Inter-American Court of Human Rights.

3 Generally speaking, discrimination by proxy arises out of classifications that do not rely on a prohibited ground, but on a usually rational ground that in practice impacts on significant numbers of those who are identified with the prohibited ground. Typical examples discussed in the literature are employers' policies rejecting applicants with all-braided hairstyles, which in practice mean to screen out a large part of black women. For a discussion of discrimination by proxy in the context of the United States, see e.g. C Gear Rich, 'Performing Racial and Ethnic Identity: Discrimination by Proxy and the Future of Title VII' (2004) 79 *NYU Law Review* 1134.

4 See e.g. Council of Europe, Commissioner of Human Rights Report, *Human Rights of Roma and Travelers in Europe*, Council of Europe, Strasbourg 2012; S Poulter, *Ethnicity, Law, and Human Tights: The English Experience*, Oxford University Press, Oxford 1998, pp 147–152. On Indigenous peoples, see e.g. R Stavenhagen, *Peasants, Culture and Indigenous Peoples: Critical Issues*, Springer, New York, 2013, pp 46–47.

5 R Sandland, 'Developing a Jurisprudence of Difference: The Protection of the Human Rights of Travelling Peoples by the European Court of Human Rights' (2008) 8(3) *Human Rights Law Review* 475.

6 On this notion, see F Lenzerini, *The Culturalization of Human Rights Law*, Oxford University Press, Oxford 2014.

less attention has been paid to the interaction between this legal phenomenon and the advancement of socio-economic equality claims. This chapter grapples with this interaction.

By looking at the aforementioned cases, the chapter explores whether and how rights claims of cultural and economic disadvantage could be integrated into the court's legal analysis. It should be noted that throughout this chapter, notions of culture and identity are used rather indistinctly. Although some doctrine distinguishes them,[7] human rights courts tend to use these terms interchangeably or in close connection to each other.[8] While any struggle against social hierarchies requires a change in cultural values, the inclusion or modification of cultural views acquires special significance to culturally defined ethnic groups like indigenous and Roma/Traveller peoples. In fact, assertions over identity and cultural rights are a key aspect of their legal and political mobilisation (notably in the case of indigenous peoples and increasingly in the case of Roma and Travellers).[9] Mindful of this, the chapter asks whether the culture/identity approach captures the socio-economic and structural dimensions of their complaints. Do human rights courts integrate these dimensions in their legal analysis and why does this matter?

In this vein, we should bear in mind that cases where cultural/identity and economic rights claims appear interlocked may pose interesting challenges to the ECtHR and the IACtHR. This is because, amongst other reasons, they may defy judicial categorical thinking, the abstraction of human rights norms and prevailing divides among them. Cultural and economic claims also tend to point at structural problems, such as widespread prejudice and unfair institutional design. Meanwhile, the ECtHR and the IACtHR are constrained not only by the cultural background in which they are inserted, but also by their legal mandate and the individual justice they are supposed to deliver.

Drawing on this case law and on literature from political and critical socio-legal theory, the chapter starts by exploring the conceptual and normative underpinnings of the interplay between cultural and socio-economic

---

7 V Bader, 'Defending Differentiated Policies of Multiculturalism' (2007) 9 *National Identity* 197, 205.

8 See e.g. ECHR, Cultural Rights in the Case Law of the European Court of Human Rights, Research Division, 2011, pp 9 ff, http://www.echr.coe.int/Documents/Research_report_cultural_rights_ENG.pdf (accessed 6 April 2017). Benhabid argues that culture has become a ubiquitous synonymous of identity: S Benhabib, *The Claims of Culture. Equality and Diversity in the Global Era*, Princeton University Press, Princeton 2002, p 1.

9 K Engle, 'On Fragile Architecture: The UN Declaration on the Rights of Indigenous Peoples in the Context of Human Rights' (2011) 22(1) *European Journal of International Law* 141, 142; K Henrard, 'The European Convention on Human Rights and the Protection of the Roma as a Controversial Case of Cultural Diversity' (2004) 5 *European Diversity and Autonomy Papers* 5, http://www.eurac.edu/en/research/autonomies/minrig/publications/Documents/EDAP/2004_edap05.pdf (accessed 6 April 2017).

inequalities. The next two sections are devoted to the examination of case law. Section 3 discusses the jurisprudence of the ECtHR in Roma and Traveller's land-use cases. Section 4 replicates the exercise with indigenous land rights cases from the IACtHR. These two sections pay particular attention to the degree to which cultural/identity and economic concerns are integrated into the legal interpretations and responses devised by the courts. This analysis is conducted in the hope of identifying limitations and opportunities for normative frameworks that could foster a more comprehensive approach to cases involving cultural and economic rights claims. These legal tools are discussed in section 5. The final section contains tentative conclusions.

2. A CONCEPTUAL AND NORMATIVE EXPLORATION OF CULTURAL AND SOCIO-ECONOMIC INEQUALITIES

Cultural and socio-economic inequalities are intertwined in many ways. Their interaction is manifested in the experience of most people experiencing structural discrimination.[10] This is also the case for indigenous peoples, Roma and Travellers. Many socio-economic measures (e.g. pensions, education, housing and wages) turn a blind eye to cultural diversity, which results in excluding or reinforcing the stigmatisation of those who do not conform to the norm.[11] Think, for instance, of fixed-residency requirements in order to access social rights, which end up excluding non-settled Roma/Travellers. At the same time, a right to social housing which does not cover family plots disregards those who are settled. Thus, depending on the context, reversing cultural devaluation and misrecognition may open up possibilities to overcome destitution, while socio-economic interventions may also assist in combating prejudices and cultural subordination.[12] None of this is surprising. After all, socio-economic ordering relies on meanings, values and representations, just as cultural expressions are influenced by socio-economic structures.[13] Socio-economic inequalities also tend to generate more homogeneous societies that misrecognise or disrespect

10 On structural discrimination, see e.g. O De Schutter and A Verstichel, 'The Role of the Union in Integrating the Roma: Present and Possible Future' (2005) 2 *European Diversity and Autonomy Papers* 27; R Saba '(Des)igualdad estructural' (2005) 11 *Derecho y Humanidades* 4.

11 S Fredman, 'Positive Duties and Socio-economic Disadvantage: Bringing Disadvantage onto the Equality Agenda' (2010) 55 *Legal Research Paper Series* 3–4.

12 N Fraser and A Honneth, *Redistribution or Recognition? A Political-Philosophical Exchange*, Verso, London 2003, pp 63–66, 83–84; R Lister, '(Mis)recognition, Social Inequality and Social Justice: A Critical Social Policy Perspective' in N Fraser and P Bourdieu (eds), *(Mis) recognition, Social Inequality and Social Justice*, Routledge, Abingdon 2007, pp 164–167.

13 Ibid, N Fraser and A Honneth, p 62; A An-Na'im, *Cultural Transformation and Human Rights*, Zed Books, London 2002, p 23.

(culturally) non-dominant groups.[14] Powerful groups generalise and naturalise their own set of values, norms and institutions, discouraging or penalising deviation.[15] Aware of this, some advocate the fostering of plurality in society instead of suppressing it, while making sure that no distinct cluster dominates above the others.[16]

In this context, one may note that legal claims grounded in the self-assertion of identity and in contesting prevailing value systems have acquired salience. This is the case for most complaints by Roma, Travellers and indigenous people before the ECtHR and the IACtHR, a phenomenon which seems to be part of the greater currency that cultural rights now hold in human rights law. As noted by Cowan, Dembour and Wilson, 'culturalist claims' are likely to carry more weight in the adjudication process. Thus, they are strategically 'used to ground and justify other kinds of claims, for example, to land, environmental protection, education, employment and even political autonomy'.[17] Challenging exclusion through culture and identity is generally referred to as the politics of recognition, difference or identity.[18] Fraser explains that 'recognition' claims mainly confront patterns of social representation or cultural domination. Acknowledging their normative traction, she also notes that such demands are often seen as divorced from 'redistribution claims' – that is, those aimed at combating destitution and economic domination.[19] She and other scholars regret this divorce, which obscures the fact that cultural subordination and socio-economic inequality are more often than not intertwined.[20]

From a normative perspective, the attention devoted to our identities relates to the 'rise' of a substantive notion of equality. This abandons a blind-justice paradigm in order to see and recognise differences among individuals and

---

14 B Parekh, 'Redistribution or Recognition: A Misguided Debate' in S May, T Modood and J Squires (eds), *Ethnicity, Nationalism and Minority Rights*, Cambridge University Press, Cambridge 2004, p 202.

15 United Nations Development Programme, *Humanity Divided: Confronting Inequality in Developing Countries*, 2013, p 264.

16 TM Scanlon, 'The Diversity of Objections to Inequality' The Lindley Lecture, University of Kansas, (22 February 1996), Lawrence, Kansas, Dept. of Philosophy, University of Kansas, 1997, 15.

17 JK Cowan, M Dembour and RA Wilson (eds), *Culture and Rights: Anthropological Perspectives*, Cambridge University Press, Cambridge 2001, p 9.

18 S Thompson, *The Political Theory of Recognition: A Critical Introduction*, Polity Press, Cambridge 2006 (analysing recognition in Charles Taylor, Axel Honneth and Nancy Fraser); IM Young, *Justice and the Politics of the Difference*, Princeton University Press, Princeton 2011, p 157; T Modood, 'Difference, Multi and Equality' in M Seymour (ed), *The Plural States of Recognition*, Palgrave Macmillan, Basingstoke 2010, p 153.

19 N Fraser and A Honneth, above n 12, p 48.

20 Ibid, p 26; B Parekh, above n 14, pp 202–209; S Fredman, 'Redistribution and Recognition: Reconciling Inequalities' (2007) 23(2) *South African Journal of Human Rights* 214, 215; B de Sousa Santos, 'Nuestra America Reinventing a Subaltern Paradigm of Recognition and Redistribution' (2001) 18(2–3) *Theory, Culture & Society* 185, 192; S Benhabib, above n 8, p 17.

social groups in order to redress power imbalances and subordination.[21] Instead of eliminating cultural differences, substantive equality aims to remove the detrimental consequences attached to them.[22] This is where cultural or identity-based rights and socio-economic rights (should) meet. Because substantive equality aims to address structural patterns of disadvantage, it introduces not only recognition, but also redistribution considerations.[23] Fredman argues that substantive equality encompasses, inter alia, recognition and redistribution. She identifies these two facets of equality with 'status-based' inequalities (which include issues of accommodating different identities) and 'socio-economic' inequalities, respectively.[24] With the exception of status discrimination in the enjoyment of socio-economic rights, recognition and redistribution claims often do not sit comfortably together and, as Fredman points out, tackling one of them may result in overshadowing the other.[25]

A conceptual and normative divide between these two strands of exclusion (cultural/socio-economic) thus seems to exist in rights discussion. To start with, it is common to regard identity issues as being governed by quite different logic from socio-economic difference or class. For example, identity-based rights would demand differential treatment and recognition of uniqueness, while socio-economic rights would emphasise our common needs, universality and equality.[26] Further, as argued by Phillips, socio-economic arrangements and the disparities they produce are generally perceived as the result of objective

---

21 S Fredman, 'Facing the Future: Substantive Equality under the Spotlight' (2010) 57 *Legal Research Paper Series University of Oxford* 6; F Ast, 'European legal frameworks responding to diversity and the need for institutional change. Indirect Discrimination as a Means of Protecting Pluralism: Challenges and Limits' in Council of Europe, *Institutional accommodation and the citizen: legal and political interaction in a pluralist society*, Trends in social cohesion n° 21, Council of Europe Publishing, 2009, p 88–89; O Fiss, 'Another Equality' (2004) 2(1) *Issues in Legal Scholarship* 1.

22 S Fredman, 'Recognition and Redistribution: Reconciling Inequalities' (2007) 23 *South African Journal on Human Rights* 216.

23 S Fredman, 'Providing Equality: Substantive Equality and the Positive Duty to Provide' (2005) 21 *South African Journal on Human Rights* 166; B Porter, 'The Crisis of ESC Rights and Strategies for Addressing it' in J Squires, M Langford and B Thiele (eds), *The Road to a Remedy: Current Issues in the Litigation of Economic, Social and Cultural Rights*, Australian Human Rights Centre, University of New South Wales Press, Kensington 2005, p 58; L Prieto Sanchís, 'Los Derechos Sociales y el Principio de Igualdad Sustancial' (1995) 22 *Revista del Centro de Estudios Constitucionales* 33.

24 S Fredman, above n 22, 214–215. In this paper the emphasis is on what she describes as the second and third elements of her multidimensional concept of equality.

25 Ibid, 219.

26 A government's reply in a case submitted to the European Committee of Social Rights clearly reflects this tension: '[The presentation made by the European Roma Rights Centre] is biased, and riddled with sometimes contradictory criticism, wavering between demands for due regard for cultural particularism and condemnation of differences in treatment in the approach to Travellers' specific requirements.' See Government's submission before the ECSR, European Roma Rights Centre v France, Complaint no 51/2008, ECSR, case document no 2, §5.

and rational choices.[27] They give the impression of being dictated by neutral criteria and by individuals' autonomy. However, group identities are usually seen quite differently. Race, gender, disability and other markers are commonly regarded as monolithic, self-contained and immutable characteristics that lie beyond our control.[28] Conversely, when the identity in question is considered to be changeable – as with religious or other 'cultural' markers – it is associated with subjectivity, volatility or even coercion, in contrast to the objective and stable character of socio-economic arrangements. Furthermore, the tension between the cultural and the economic is felt in terms of justiciability, as many socio-economic complaints remain in the non-justiciable terrain of politics.[29]

Against this background, it is submitted that insofar as culture is regarded and mobilised in the same way as other identity-based claims are, higher rates of success may follow. But this does not come without a cost. Two difficulties deserve attention here. First, as explained above, it is not rare for courts to detach cultural identity rights from related socio-economic concerns, which is quite problematic for groups like indigenous people, Roma and Travellers. Second, prevailing judicial approaches to categories such as gender and race in many instances continue to operate in an either/or scheme that prioritises one identity over others, while overlooking other social locations and their relationship with systems of inequality. As a result, cultural identity claims are similarly examined without sufficient regard for intersectionality.[30] The links between identity grounds and people's class or socio-economic status are among those typically forgotten. Moreover, it has been argued that cultural identity claims are often framed as value issues that stand in parallel to structural considerations of power and inequality, including questions of socio-economic arrangements.[31]

---

27 A Phillips, 'Equality, Pluralism, Universality: Current Concerns in Normative Theory' (2000) 2(2) *British Journal of Politics and International Relations* 248.

28 AP Harris, 'Theorizing Class, Gender, and the Law: Three Approaches' (2009) 72(4) *Law and Contemporary Problems* 39; M Barnes and E Chemerinsky, 'The Disparate Treatment of Race and Class in Constitutional Jurisprudence' (2009) 72(4) *Law and Contemporary Problems* 121–122. Examples of the preferential treatment of allegedly inherent traits can be found in the ECtHR judgment on *Bah v United Kingdom*, no 56328/07, ECHR 2011, as well as in its inadmissibility decision in *Horie v United Kingdom*, no 31845/10, ECHR 2011.

29 On the reluctance to adjudicate socio-economic rights and polycentric concerns, see the references above in n 23 and JM Woods, 'Justiciable Social Rights as a Critique of the Liberal Paradigm' (2003) 38 *Texas International Law Journal* 763.

30 See below n 130. For a more 'integrated' analysis of cultural and economic rights claims, see V David, 'Crossing Divides and Seeing the Whole: An Integrated View of Cultural Difference and Economic Disadvantage in Regional Human Rights Courts,' doctoral thesis under the supervision of E Brems, April 2018, defended at Ghent University as part of the Human Rights Integration project.

31 See e.g. IM Young, 'Structural Injustice and the Politics of Difference' in E Grabham, D Cooper, J Krishnadas and D Herman (eds), *Intersectionality and Beyond. Law, Power and the Politics of Location*, Routledge-Cavendish, Abingdon, 2009, pp 294–295; R Dhamoon, *Identity/Difference Politics: How Difference is Produced, and Why it Matters*, UBC Press,

Whether some of these difficulties affect the adjudication of Roma, Travellers and indigenous people's cases and the consequences that follow are discussed below.

3. INTEGRATING THE CULTURAL IDENTITY AND SOCIO-ECONOMIC INTERESTS OF ROMA AND TRAVELLERS BEFORE THE ECTHR

Many complaints brought by Roma and Travellers before the ECtHR concern evictions or threats of eviction. Normally eviction is grounded in the infringement of land-use regulations impeding the stationing of caravans on sites owned, rented or occupied for a lengthy amount of time by 'Gypsies' or Travellers. The restrictions on the use of land are based on environmental, visual amenity and safety considerations. In a few cases, the main issue is either access to basic public utilities by Roma living in breach of planning regulations[32] or eviction of Roma communities living in informal settlements.[33] As will become clear below, these complaints provide an interesting account of the many ways in which institutional arrangements concerning land, planning and development may overlook the needs of Roma and Travellers and, conversely, how measures aimed at protecting their cultural identity may ignore or run counter to the improvement of their socio-economic condition.[34]

From a normative point of view, Article 8 of the European Convention on Human Rights (ECHR) – the right to private and family life and respect for the home – is the overarching legal framework used by the ECtHR to rule these cases.[35] As will be seen below, although applicants have often invoked

Vancouver 2009, pp 2, 6–8; W Brown, *Regulating Aversion Tolerance in the Age of Identity and Empire*, Princeton University Press, Princeton 2008, p 20.

32 *Stenegry and Adam v France*, no 40987/05, ECHR 2007. See also *Branko Hudorovič and Aleks Hudorovič v Slovenia* and *Ljubo Novak and others v Slovenia*, nos 24816/14 and 25140/14 (pending case communicated on 8 April 2015).

33 *Yordanova and others v Bulgaria*, no 25446/06, ECHR 2012; and *Winterstein and others v France*, no 27013/07, ECHR 2013.

34 It should be noted that very similar cases to those discussed here have also been brought to the European Committee of Social Rights (ECSR), the body that monitors compliance with the European Social Charter under a collective complaint procedure. Compared to the ECtHR, the ECSR has been substantially more responsive to the plight of Roma and Travellers. Further, its approach to the rights holders and the rights at play in these cases is more integrated. Importantly, the ECSR's material competence is broader than that of the ECtHR. It covers socio-economic rights, such as the right to housing, cultural rights, the prohibition of discrimination and even a right to protection against poverty and social exclusion. See e.g. *ERRC v Greece*, Collective Complaint No 15/2003 (ECSR, 2004); *ERRC v Bulgaria*, Collective Complaint No 31/2005 (ESCR, 2006); and *ERRC v Ireland*, Collective Complaint No 100/2013 (ECSR, 2016).

35 In these cases, the Court's examination under Article 8 concentrates on whether interferences were necessary in a democratic society, which involves substantial and procedural issues.

other provisions, such as the prohibition of discrimination (Article 14 of the ECHR), the Court's analysis usually focuses on the rights contained in Article 8. These encompass the concepts of 'way of life', 'home' and procedural safeguards. The home and the private/family life limbs of Article 8 serve to capture (cultural) identity and socio-economic concerns respectively. While in practice they may be at play simultaneously, initially both limbs appeared divorced in the Court's case law. In *Buckley*, the first Strasbourg case on Roma and Travellers, the applicant claimed that the prohibition on living in her caravan on her own land, coupled with the lack of availability of alternative sites, constituted a disproportionate interference with her right to private and family life and to respect for her home. She claimed a right to settle on a safe and stable site and a right to live in a caravan and keep travelling (according to her Gypsy lifestyle) when possible. The former Commission agreed. However, the convergence between the two claims got lost in the eyes of the government and the ECtHR. For the former, the case was one of respect for the home only – something too close to 'a right to establish a home'.[36] For the Court, it was unnecessary to decide whether a cultural identity issue under the right to family/private life was at stake. Respect for the home and tackling planning and housing issues gave the State ample room for manoeuvre and displaced the cultural claim.

This 'either/or' approach was dispelled by the Grand Chamber in *Chapman*. The facts were quite similar to those in *Buckley*, but this time the ECtHR stated that more than respect for the home was at stake.[37] Living in a caravan was considered an integral part of the Roma/Traveller identity, reflecting the minority's long tradition of travelling. States eventually accepted that conclusion, although it took them a bit longer.[38]

3.1. THE CULTURAL IDENTITY DIMENSION OF ARTICLE 8 AND EXCLUSIONS ALONG THE WAY

The protection of the 'Gypsy' lifestyle considered constitutive of Roma and Traveller identity has since become a distinctive feature of this case law. It is worth recalling that the obligation to protect a 'way of life' was transposed from indigenous to Roma/Traveller cases. The former Commission applied this concept in a case concerning indigenous peoples in Norway.[39]

---

36 *Buckley v United Kingdom*, no 20348/92, ECmHR 1995, §62; *Buckley v United Kingdom*, no 20348/92, §§54–55, ECHR 1996.

37 *Chapman v United Kingdom*, no 27238/95, §73, GC ECHR 2001.

38 Governments continued to frame the case as one concerning exclusively the right to respect for home in *Chapman* and in the other cases decided in 2001. See e.g. *Chapman v United Kingdom*, above n 37, §72. The State approach clearly changed with *Connors v United Kingdom*, no 66746/01, §68, ECHR 2004.

39 *G and E v Norway*, nos 9278/81 and 9415/81, ECHR 1983.

Referring to the interference caused by a hydroelectric dam in traditional Sami areas, the Commission stated that minorities were, in principle, entitled to claim the right to respect for a particular lifestyle they could lead as part of their private life, family life or home. The United Nations (UN) Human Rights Committee endorsed a similar interpretation on the basis of Article 27 of the International Covenant on Civil and Political Rights (ICCPR).[40] In the indigenous context, protecting a 'way of life' seems to encompass symbolic/spiritual interests and issues of access to and control over material resources. However, as the following discussion suggests, such a distributive dimension has not always featured in Roma and Traveller cases.

In a set of complaints unsuccessfully submitted against the UK and led by *Chapman*, the Court recognised the vulnerable position of the Roma/Travellers and imposed a (limited) positive obligation on States to facilitate the 'Gypsy way of life'.[41] In *Chapman*, the ECtHR held that Roma people's particular needs and views should be considered in planning regulations and decision-making.[42] Yet it found that the international emerging consensus on States' obligations to protect the identity, security and lifestyle of minorities was insufficiently clear to derive any guidance. On the other hand, while the Court was willing to apply the concept of home to caravans, bungalows and makeshift houses regardless of their lawfulness, it was very cautious not to intrude into housing rights and socio-economic policies.

Besides granting States a wide margin of appreciation in planning and housing matters, the ECtHR adopted a formal approach to the availability of suitable sites for Gypsies and Travellers.[43] It also made clear what does not fall under Article 8 of the ECHR. In fact, in *Chapman*, the Court held that such a right does not involve a right to be provided with a home. Therefore, it could not require the State to provide a number of suitable sites to the Gypsy community. Nor did this entail a right to differential treatment in land-use control, which would be discriminatory to the general population.[44] While the Court appeared aware of the potential economic implications of its interpretation for the State, it displayed a lack of awareness of the socio-economic situation of most Roma/Traveller people. The Court weighed the applicant's purported liberty to move somewhere else (notably to private sites),[45] forgetting that the freedom to move

40 UN Human Rights Committee (HRC), CCPR General Comment No 23: Article 27 (Rights of Minorities) of 8 April 1994 [1994] CCPR/C/21/Rev.1/Add.5, §7.

41 *Chapman v United Kingdom*, above n 37, §93; GC Cases of *Beard v United Kingdom*, no 24882/94, §107, ECHR 2001; *Coster v United Kingdom*, no 24876/94, §110, ECHR 2001; *Lee v United Kingdom*, no 25289/94, §98, ECHR 2001.

42 *Chapman v United Kingdom*, above n 37, §93.

43 Ibid, §111.

44 Ibid, §95–99.

45 Ibid, §97.

to private sites may be out of reach to those who cannot afford them or are rejected on the basis of entrenched prejudices.[46] A similar oversight is observable in *Wells*. In this case, domestic courts regarded the applicant's destitution and the fact that he had nowhere else to go as irrelevant to his inability to comply with an enforcement notice. The ECtHR limited itself to endorsing that rationale, while highlighting that many other persons are not able to continue residing on sites or in houses that are attractive to them.[47]

In this first stage, quite a narrow view of the Gypsy way of life received protection.[48] *Chapman* and other judgments issued since 2001 have attached little weight to the cultural commitments of the applicants, presenting these as mere preferences or wishes.[49] They also reduced the protection given to the Gypsy way of life to encompass only the occupation of caravans and the accommodation of nomadism. Although the Court acknowledged that many Roma no longer live a nomadic life,[50] it noted that the applicants appeared not to be pursuing an itinerant life anymore, which meant that the case was not about 'the traditional itinerant Gypsy lifestyle'.[51] In the British context, Poulter observes that defining Travellers by their nomadism or by folkloric expectations of their behaviour is mostly a legal creation.[52] In this way, 'the state has retained the power to control their use of the land, differentiate their authentication and respond to the prejudices of the majority population'.[53] Nomadism, in fact, does not adequately reflect the lived experience of many Roma and Travellers, nor is its protection instrumental to achieving justice. Protecting a Gypsy lifestyle only if it is nomadic promotes exclusion and exposes Gypsies and Travellers to greater socio-economic disadvantage, as itinerancy confines them to a life that is

---

46 Ibid, joint dissenting opinion of judges Pastor Ridruejo, Bonello, Tulkens, Strážnická, Lorenzen, Fischbach and Casadevall, §6.

47 *Wells v United Kingdom*, no 37794/05, §10, ECHR 2007.

48 On related criticism, see e.g. J Ringelheim, 'Chapman Redux: The European Court of Human Rights and Roma Traditional Lifestyle' in E Brems (ed), *Diversity and European Human Rights: Rewriting Judgments of the ECHR*, Cambridge University Press, Cambridge 2012, pp 431–434.

49 *Chapman v United Kingdom*, above n 37, §113; *Beard v United Kingdom*, above n 41, §125; *Coster v United Kingdom*, above n 41, §126; *Lee v United Kingdom*, above n 41, §114; *Wells v United Kingdom*, above n 47, p 10.

50 See e.g. *Chapman v United Kingdom*, above n 37, §73; *Beard v United Kingdom*, above n 41, §84; *Coster v United Kingdom*, above n 41, §87.

51 *Chapman v United Kingdom*, above n 37, §105; *Beard v United Kingdom*, above n 41, §116; *Coster v United Kingdom*, above n 41, §119; *Lee v United Kingdom*, above n 41, §107; *Harrison v United Kingdom*, no 32263/96, p 12, ECHR 2001. On the importance for human rights bodies to engage with cultural or minority norms, see V David and J Fraser; 'A Legal Pluralist Approach to the Use of Cultural Perspectives in the Implementation and Adjudication of Human Rights Norms' (2017) 23 *Buffalo Human Rights Law Review* 75–118.

52 See S Poulter, above n 4, p 541; R Home, 'Gypsies and Travellers in the United Kingdom' (2009) 20(3) *Stellenbosch Law Review* 538.

53 Ibid, S Poulter, p 541.

no longer economically viable, limiting their options to precarious and insecure occupations.[54]

Fortunately, the Court has gradually accounted for the ensuing problems of a legal emphasis on nomadism. In *Connors*, for instance, it pointed out that while many Gypsies remained nomadic merely in spirit, the domestic law continued to regard nomadism as the raison d'être of special regulations that allowed summary evictions from official sites.[55] In the Court's assessment, the UK had created great obstacles to pursuing an itinerant lifestyle while also excluding those living a settled life from procedural protection. In subsequent case law, a settled Traveller/Roma lifestyle marked, for example, by community life with strong family and social ties also received protection under Article 8.[56] However, in the meantime, the Court, when deciding on the admissibility of a case, took the problematic view that a Traveller cultural identity is an inner trait one is born with.[57] In so doing, it not only denied the socially constructed character of all identities and group boundaries, but it also conveyed a preference for 'inner' over 'chosen' traits, which favours assimilation over accommodation.

3.2. INTEGRATING THE 'HOME' DIMENSION OF ARTICLE 8 AND OTHER SOCIAL RIGHTS GUARANTEES

Following *Connors*, respect for the home began to be translated into procedural safeguards against eviction. The Court also attached considerable weight to the fact that the applicant and his family were rendered homeless.[58] The case concerned the application of a summary eviction procedure justified by the State on the ground that accommodating Roma and Travellers' needs (consistent with their nomadic lifestyle) required the authorities to be flexible in the management of site provision. As a result, the applicant was deprived of guarantees enjoyed by tenants living in conventional housing and other mobile homes. Thus, in this case, a measure allegedly aimed at recognising the cultural specificity of Roma and Travellers hindered their socio-economic security.

Adopting a procedural perspective, in *Connors* the ECtHR carried out a more comprehensive and less formalistic examination of the domestic legal

---

54 The Traveller Movement, *A Place to Call Home: Ethnicity, Culture and Planning for Traveller Sites*, The Traveller Movement, London 2014, pp 3–4, 8.

55 *Connors v United Kingdom*, above n 38, §93.

56 *Yordanova v Bulgaria*, above n 33, §105, 121, 131; *Winterstein v France*, above n 33, §71.

57 *Horie v United Kingdom*, above n 28, §§28–29. For a critical view of the decision adopted in this case, see also the post by L Peroni and A Timmer, 'Gypsy Way of Life "by Birth" or "by Choice"', *Strasbourg Observers*, http://strasbourgobservers.com/category/cases/horie-v-uk (accessed 6 April 2017).

58 *Connors v United Kingdom*, above n 38, §85.

framework. For instance, it closely examined whether the summary eviction really accomplished its purported aims. Furthermore, it addressed the policies in place. It took into account, inter alia, that 70% of local authorities did not have any written Gypsy/Traveller accommodation policy, that there was almost no increase in the number of local authorities' pitches and that no special allowances were made for Gypsies in the planning criteria applied by authorities deciding on the stationing of caravans on private sites.[59] *Buckland*, a case similar to *Connors*, was also decided on procedural grounds.[60]

Later, in *Yordanova* and *Winterstein*, procedural safeguards were expanded and the right to respect for one's home became closer to the right to housing. These cases, unlike previous ones, concerned the eviction of mostly settled Roma and Traveller communities which had resided for decades in de facto tolerated settlements in Bulgaria and France respectively. In *Yordanova*, most people lived in single-storey houses, while in *Winterstein*, the majority occupied caravans and mobile homes. In these judgments, the Court held that any person facing the risk of losing his or her home has the right to have the reasonableness and proportionality of the measure reviewed by an independent tribunal. This includes giving adequate reasons to the relevant arguments raised in connection with the eviction.[61] In addition, proportionality review requires an evaluation of alternative, less restrictive measures and a consideration of the risk of homelessness.[62] Third, the socially disadvantaged position of the applicants' groups and their specific needs also have to be considered in the assessment of proportionality, as well as in devising solutions to their unlawful settlement and, if removal were necessary, in deciding on its timing, modalities and, if possible, arrangements for alternative shelter.[63] It is interesting to observe that the aforementioned four cases where socio-economic interests were more visibly incorporated into the analysis were also cases where the legal discourse on a Gypsy lifestyle appeared more tenuous.

On a more substantive note, in *Yordanova* the ECtHR also tempered its previous exclusion of a duty to provide housing from the scope of Article 8, deciding that such an obligation towards particularly vulnerable individuals could indeed flow from it.[64] In *Winterstein* the Court not only emphasised the duty of the State to consider the applicants' needs and lifestyles in making

---

59 Ibid, §85.

60 *Buckland v United Kingdom*, no 40060/08, §§68–70, ECHR 2012.

61 *Yordanova v Bulgaria*, above n 33, §118; *Winterstein v France*, above n 33, §§83–84.

62 Ibid, *Yordanova v Bulgaria*, §§124–126. See also A Remiche, '*Yordanova and Others v Bulgaria*: The Influence of the Social Right to Adequate Housing on the Interpretation of the Civil Right to Respect for One's Home' (2012) 12(4) *Human Rights Law Review* 798; ibid, *Winterstein v France*, §87.

63 Ibid, *Yordanova v Bulgaria*, §132; ibid, *Winterstein v France*, §88.

64 Ibid, *Yordanova v Bulgaria*, §130.

arrangements for alternative shelter (e.g. family plots instead of conventional housing),[65] but also affirmed the need to provide alternative housing in cases of forced eviction of Roma and Travellers.[66] The socio-economic permeation of Article 8 thus resulted in stronger protection of tenure and this allowed more responsiveness towards Roma and Travellers. This may explain the view, advanced by Salomon, that sometimes civil/political rights are framed as socio-economic rights and, as socio-economic rights, they are interpreted as minority rights.[67]

It is relevant to bear in mind that cases like those discussed thus far often pose the possibility of appealing to different normative sources, including non-official ones. In this respect, it is notable how in *Yordanova* and *Winterstein*, the Court's interpretation not only takes heed of an ample set of domestic regulations and policies, but also appears to be influenced by international sources other than the ECHR.[68] An important driver for this is that the applicants' claims involved social rights issues not provided for by the Convention. The Court thus referred to, for example, the European Social Charter, Resolutions and Recommendations of the Committee of Ministers and the Parliamentary Assembly of the Council of Europe. It also considered decisions from the European Committee of Social Rights (ECSR) and General Comments of the UN Committee on Economic, Social and Cultural Rights (UN CommESCR).[69] These sources provide specific standards on the right to housing and, particularly, on forced eviction. These include consultation with the community or individual concerned, reasonable notice, provision of information, a guarantee that the eviction will be carried out in a reasonable manner and alternative housing measures. This might explain the Court's emphasis, in both cases, on procedural guarantees for securing respect for the home.

65 *Winterstein v France*, above n 33, §§90–94.

66 Ibid, §87.

67 M Salomon, 'Socio-economic Rights as Minority Rights' in M Weller (ed), *Universal Minority Rights*, Oxford University Press, Oxford 2007, p 433.

68 For an analysis of Roma, Travellers and indigenous cases from the perspective of legal pluralism, see V David and J Fraser, above n 51, pp 99–118. On the Court's practice of cross-referencing, see D Staes, 'When the European Court Refers to External Instruments: Mapping and Justifications', doctoral thesis, April 2017, defended at the Université libre de Bruxelles and the Université Saint-Louis as part of the Human Rights Integration project.

69 In *Yordanova*, the Court listed these instruments and decisions as 'relevant international material' (§§73–83), whereas in *Winterstein*, it included them in its analysis on the merits (§87). Some of the specific sources referenced in these judgments are: Committee of Ministers of the Council of Europe, Recommendation 2005 on improving the housing conditions of Roma and Recommendation 2008 on policies for Roma and/or Travellers in Europe; the Committee on Economic, Social and Cultural Rights, General Comment No 7 concerning forced evictions and the right to adequate housing under the International Covenant on Economic, Social and Cultural Rights, E/1998/22, 20 May 1997; and *European Roma Rights Centre v Bulgaria*, no 31/2005, ECSR 2006.

As for socio-economic rights within the ECHR, it is interesting to note that the right to education (Article 2, Protocol 1) has been invoked in Roma and Traveller cases dealing with planning and housing matters. However, this claim has not attracted the ECtHR's attention. Some applicants have claimed its violation to the detriment of their children whose school attendance gets disrupted every time they are forced to move. Nonetheless, the Court has barely reacted to this, as it finds such claims to be insufficiently substantiated.[70] The right to property has likewise had little impact. Applicants have unsuccessfully alleged violation of this in relation to their lands, homes and belongings, particularly for the losses and damages resulting from eviction. This issue is not a minor one, considering the harm experienced by those who lose the very few possessions they have and their major difficulties in acquiring material goods. The European Roma Rights Centre (ERRC) has also used the right to property as a vehicle to bring in the existing human rights standards on forced eviction.[71] Yet, as explained above, this has taken place mainly through the right to respect for the home. In any event, the wide margin of appreciation enjoyed by States with regard to the right to property makes this a rather constrained tool for advancing the interests of Roma and Travellers.

3.3. INTEGRATING EQUALITY AND DIFFERENCE?

The conceptual and normative exploration conducted above shows that equality and non-discrimination are potentially useful avenues to bridge identity-based and socio-economic concerns. As such, it is important to inquire what place equality and non-discrimination have in this case law. There is a clear contrast between the view of Roma and Travellers, on the one hand, and that of the Court, on the other, with respect to the relevance of this right to deal with these cases. While the former have continually claimed a violation of Article 14 of the ECHR, the Court has mostly found no further issue to examine under this provision once it has decided on Article 8.[72] It has thus missed the opportunity to address the applicants' complaints of cultural and economic disadvantage as a matter of equality. Nonetheless, it has addressed equality issues under Article 8. In doing so, it has transitioned from a very formalistic reading of equality,

---

70 *Coster v United Kingdom*, above n 41, §137; *Lee v United Kingdom*, above n 41, §125; *Harrison v United Kingdom*, above n 51, §2, p 14, ECHR 2008; *Clark and others v United Kingdom*, no 28575/95, §3, p 13, ECHR 2001.

71 European Roma Rights Center, Written Comments in the case of *Winterstein and others v France*, submitted on 13 June 2007, p 3 (§IV).

72 This has been the case even when the allegation was one of direct rather than indirect discrimination. See *Harrison v United Kingdom*, above n 51, pp 9–10, 14–15.

which precluded differential treatment in land-use regulations,[73] to a more substantive approach requiring States to correct factual inequalities.[74] However, all in all, Article 14's framework remains under-utilised by the Court in these cases.[75]

Somewhat similarly to this jurisprudence on Roma and Travellers, indigenous cases before the IACtHR also reveal the connection between cultural and economic rights assertions. In this context, legal arguments on indigenous cultural identity have been particularly successful and more closely linked to economic rights to land and resources. The following section explores how the IACtHR integrates both areas of concern and whether challenges like those discussed above nonetheless arise in indigenous land cases.

4. INTEGRATING THE CULTURAL IDENTITY AND SOCIO-ECONOMIC INTERESTS OF INDIGENOUS AND TRIBAL PEOPLES BEFORE THE IACTHR

Long-standing demands arising from a history of coercive land destitution and discrimination against indigenous peoples in the Americas have resulted in several cases before the IACtHR. Most cases concern collective rights claims over land and natural resources in the context of extractive or development projects and displacement of indigenous communities, resulting in harsh living conditions.

The entry point for litigating these claims is the right to property (Article 21 of the American Convention on Human Rights – hereinafter, ACHR) which became the normative umbrella under which the IACtHR addresses nearly all rights violations affecting indigenous people.

It is well known that when dealing with these cases and despite limitations in the treaty wording, the IACtHR has recognised indigenous and tribal peoples' right to communal property over their ancestral lands and natural resources.[76]

---

73 *Chapman v United Kingdom*, above n 37, §§95–99.

74 *Yordanova v Bulgaria*, above n 33, §129. Some view *Connors* as conveying the message that ensuring equality for certain groups may require differential treatment (e.g. C O'Cinneide, 'The Right to Equality: A Substantive Legal Norm or Vacuous Rhetoric?' (2008) 1(1) *UCL Human Rights Review*, 92; and R Sandland, above n 5). But there the Court showed its comfort with the fact that the applicant, unlike Chapman, did not claim any exemptions from general laws, but wanted the same tenancy protection afforded to the majority population (§86).

75 This contrasts with the analysis undertaken in cases concerning the educational segregation of Roma children, which has led to findings of indirect discrimination. See e.g. *DH and others v Czech Republic*, no 57325/00, ECHR 2007; *Oršuš and others v Croatia*, no 15766/03, ECHR 2010.

76 The judgment that inaugurated this jurisprudence is *Mayagna (Sumo) Awas Tingni Community v Nicaragua* (hereinafter *Awas Tigni v Nicaragua*), 31 August 2001, IACHR Series C no 79. The application of this jurisprudence to tribal (non-indigenous, strictly speaking) peoples started with *Moiwana Community v Suriname*, 15 June 2005, IACHR Series C no 124.

The sub-sections below first explore how the content of the right to property has been enlarged in a way that makes it inclusive of collective claims. Then it is discussed how this collective reading is constructed around the recognition of an indigenous cultural identity and the exclusionary risks that come with this. In addition, this section examines the normative frameworks used by the Court to integrate socio-economic rights and disadvantages. Like the previous section, this section also underscores the risks of over-emphasising the cultural specificity of people whose rights violations also have economic and structural roots.

4.1. ENLARGING THE NOTION OF PROPERTY AND THE LIST OF RELEVANT NORMS

Undoubtedly, the fact that collective forms of ownership are considered property under Article 21 of the ACHR is a notable stance.[77] Collective property based on customary tenure or on the use of the land does not conform to our classic understanding of property.[78] Yet, the IACtHR does not accept that this could be the only way to conceive of property, as it explained in *Sawhoyamaxa*. This case concerned an indigenous community who claimed ownership of lands which had been transferred to private hands and who had endured appalling living conditions while domestic proceedings were pending. The Court held:

> disregard for specific versions of use and enjoyment of property, springing from the culture, uses, customs, and beliefs of each people, would be tantamount to holding that there is only one way of using and disposing of property, which, in turn, would render protection under Article 21 of the Convention illusory for millions of persons.[79]

In reconstructing the right to property, the IACtHR adopted an evolutionary interpretation of the ACHR that takes heed of current circumstances and recent developments in international law. It also applied a 'pro-personae' interpretation according to which the Convention provisions should be read in the way that

---

77 This has the practical advantage of protecting communities whose collective land ownership has not been recognised by domestic law. The Court had to confront this question in the cases against Suriname.

78 In this vein, see L Peroni, 'Challenging Culturally Dominant Conceptions in Human Rights Law: The Cases of Property and Family' (2010) 4 *Human Rights and International Legal Discourse* 244.

79 *Sawhoyamaxa Indigenous Community v Paraguay* (hereinafter *Sawhoyamaxa v Paraguay*), 29 March 2006, §120, IACHR, Series C no 146; *Kichwa Indigenous People of Sarayaku v Ecuador* (hereinafter *Sarayaku v Ecuador*), 27 June 2012, §161, IACHR Series C no 245; *Kuna Indigenous People of Madungandí and the Emberá Indigenous People of Bayano and Their Members v Panama* (hereinafter *Kuna and the Emberá v Panama*), 14 October 2014, §111, IACHR Series C no 284.

is most protective of human rights.[80] Article 31 of the Vienna Convention on the Law of Treaties and Article 29 of the ACHR are the primary tenets of the Court's creative interpretation.[81] The Court has, within this framework, integrated international norms outside the Inter-American context. It has notably relied on the International Labour Organization's Convention No 169 concerning Indigenous and Tribal Peoples in Independent Countries and, where this has not been ratified, it has turned to international general instruments and to indigenous/tribal customary norms.[82] It has also referred to domestic laws and indigenous customs. Expert evidence has been material in recognising such laws and cultural practices.[83] On this basis, the Court has elaborated a set of substantive rights and procedural guarantees. These include, recognition of indigenous people's land possession flowing from their use and customs as equivalent to an official ownership title;[84] restitution of their ancestral lands or others of equal extension and quality;[85] legal certainty over their tenure;[86] a right to be consulted on matters that may affect them;[87] and a limited recognition of the largely demanded right to free, prior and informed consent.[88]

4.2. THE PROTECTION OF INDIGENOUS CULTURAL IDENTITY AND ITS EXCLUSIONARY RISKS

It is important to observe that at the core of the above interpretation of Article 21 of the ACHR lies the protection of indigenous peoples' cultural identity and way of life. According to the IACtHR:

> the culture of the members of indigenous communities reflects a particular way of life, of being, seeing and acting in the world, the starting point of which is their close

80 See e.g. *Yakye Axa Indigenous Community v Paraguay* (hereinafter *Yakye Axa v Paraguay*), 17 June 2005, §125–30, IACHR Series C no 125.

81 The relevant parts of the provision read: 'No provision of this Convention shall be interpreted as: … (b) restricting the enjoyment or exercise of any right or freedom recognized by virtue of the laws of any State Party or by virtue of another convention to which one of the said states is a party … (d) excluding or limiting the effect that the American Declaration of the Rights and Duties of Man and other international acts of the same nature may have.'

82 See e.g. *Saramaka People v Suriname*, 28 November 2007, §130; *Moiwana Community v Suriname*, 15 June 2005, IACHR Series C no 124, §131.

83 See e.g. *Xákmok Kásek Indigenous Community v Paraguay* (hereinafter *Xákmok Kásek v Paraguay*), 24 June 2010, §§103–106, IACHR Series C no 214. See also, *Sarayaku v Ecuador*, above n 79, §§154–155.

84 *Kuna and the Emberá v Paraguay*, above n 79, §§121–122.

85 *Yakye Axa v Paraguay*, above n 80, §§138–149; *Sawhoyamaxa v Paraguay*, above n 79, §127–130.

86 *Awas Tigni v Nicaragua*, above n 76, §§153, 164; *Xákmok Kásek v Paraguay*, above n 83, §§109–121.

87 *Saramaka People v Suriname*, above n 82, §133, IACHR Series C no 172; *Sarayaku v Ecuador*, above n 79, §§159 ff.

88 Ibid, *Saramaka People v Suriname*, §§134–137. The Court even held that Article 21 entails the right of members of indigenous and tribal communities to freely determine and enjoy their own social, cultural and economic development (*Saramaka People v Suriname*, §95).

> relation with their traditional lands and natural resources, not only because they are their main means of survival, but also because they form part of their worldview, of their religiousness, and consequently, of their cultural identity.[89]

Two observations are in order here. First, the ACHR does not contain a right to cultural identity or integrity, as domestic laws of several Latin American States do. However, this did not stop the IACtHR from recognising a (collective) right to cultural identity of indigenous communities.[90] The Court first considered this right in *Yakye Axa*, where it held that such a right was affected whenever States disregarded indigenous land rights. It also held that preserving cultural identities in a democratic and pluralist society might justify restrictions on individuals' private property.[91] In subsequent cases such as *Xákmok Kásek*, the Court addressed the injury caused to the applicants' cultural identity, although it did not use the term 'right'.[92] The collective right to cultural identity was further elaborated in *Sarayaku*. Invoking other international treaties, as well as regional and international bodies which recognise a right to cultural identity of indigenous and minorities, the Court qualified this right as a fundamental one requiring the consultation of indigenous people (in accordance with their forms of organisation) about any matter that could affect them.[93] The Court also connected the harm caused by the oil company on the community's land and resources to the right to cultural identity. Interestingly, it did so by focusing on the sacred character of the sites affected and on the damage to the spiritual and ritual life of the community.[94]

This brings us to the second observation. While the IACtHR acknowledges the importance of land and its resources for economic subsistence, it has actually tended to over-emphasise the symbolic/spiritual content of the indigenous cultural identity and way of life.[95] This is reflected in several passages of the Court's reasoning, particularly when it characterises the ties between indigenous/ tribal peoples and their ancestral territories. In so doing, it has referred to

---

89 *Yakye Axa v Paraguay*, above n 80, §135; *Sawhoyamaxa v Paraguay*, above n 79, §118, *Xákmok Kásek v Paraguay*, above n 83, §261.

90 *Sarayaku v Ecuador*, above n 79, §213, 217, 220.

91 *Yakye Axa v Paraguay*, above n 80, §§146–147.

92 *Xákmok Kásek v Paraguay*, above n 83, §§174–182. Notably, the Court considered a merely 'productive' conception of the land insufficient when dealing with conflicts between the rights of indigenous people and those of the private owners of the claimed land.

93 *Sarayaku v Ecuador*, above n 79, §217. References included international case law as well as instruments such as the United Nations Declaration on the Rights of Indigenous Peoples, adopted 2 October 2007 [2007] A/RES/61/295 and the International Labour Organization (ILO), Indigenous and Tribal Peoples Convention, adopted 27 June 1989 [1989] C169.

94 Ibid, *Sarayaku v Ecuador*, §§218–220.

95 See e.g. *Saramaka People v Suriname*, above n 82, §82: 'Land is more than merely a source of subsistence for them; it is also a necessary source for the continuation of the life and cultural identity of the Saramaka people.'

'traditional uses and customs' with examples that include: ceremonial activities, languages, arts and rituals, practices in connection with nature, customary law, dresses, seasonal or nomadic hunting, fishing or gathering and use of natural resources associated with their customs or other elements characteristic of their culture.[96] This depiction seems to restrict indigenous cultural identity, which is problematic not only because of the risks of essentialism or stereotyping, but also because the depiction poses difficulties in adequately integrating the socio-economic interests of the communities concerned.

In fact, some scholars have already noted that the centrality accorded to such a static view of indigenous cultural identity has serious socio-economic implications.[97] It might, for instance, hamper the ability of the communities concerned to benefit from non-traditional practices or techniques for managing or exploiting their natural resources.[98] Similarly, three special safeguards against the restriction of indigenous people's collective property that were elaborated by the Court in *Saramaka* – namely: (1) the community's effective participation; (2) independent environmental and social impact assessment; and (3) reasonable benefit sharing – appear to apply only to resources 'traditionally' used by the community which are vital to their survival and way of life.[99] Antkowiak criticises the Court for doing so and regrets that the subsequent case of *Sarayaku* also gave rise to ambiguity over the requirement to share economic benefits.[100]

A final exclusionary risk to note here is that although the inclusion of communal property within the scope of Article 21 has the potential to address the rights of other rural populations affected by dispossession, discrimination and insecurity in land tenure, the primacy of the cultural identity discourse makes it more difficult to extend indigenous-like protection to other land users. Think, for instance, of peasants, pastoralists and landless communities in the Americas.[101] The IACtHR has already been expanding the corpus of indigenous rights to other beneficiaries. In *Saramaka* and *Operation Genesis*, for example, afro-descendant rural communities were regarded as 'tribal' people and were

---

96 *Yakye Axa v Paraguay*, above n 80, §154; *Sarayaku v Ecuador*, above n 79, §148.

97 TM Antkowiak, 'Rights, Resources, and Rhetoric: Indigenous Peoples and the Inter-American Court' (2013) 35(1) *University of Pennsylvania Journal of International Law* 161; AE Dulitzky, 'Cuando los afrodescendientes se transformaron en "pueblos tribales"' (2010) 41 *Revista El Otro Derecho* 23–26. See also RA Falk, 'The Rights of Peoples (in Particular Indigenous Peoples)' in J Crawford (ed), *The Rights of Peoples*, Clarendon Press, Oxford 1988.

98 Ibid, AE Dulitzky, p 25.

99 TM Antkowiak, above n 97, p 167; *Saramaka People v Suriname*, above n 82, §155.

100 Ibid, TM Antkowiak, p 170.

101 The former UN Special Rapporteur for the right to food, for instance, has addressed this question and called to extend the protection to at least certain traditional communities that entertain a similar communal relationship with their ancestral lands. UN, Report of the Special Rapporteur on the Right to Food, 11 August 2010 [2010] Doc A/65/281, §13, 26.

granted rights accordingly on the basis of affirming their indigenous-like cultural identity.[102] However, the jurisprudence of the Court does not provide a clear answer as to how land users whose socio-economic rights claims do not fit the cultural script discussed above may usefully benefit from Article 21 of the ACHR.

4.3. REINFORCING THE INTEGRATION OF THE SOCIO-ECONOMIC DIMENSIONS OF INDIGENOUS CASES: THE RIGHT TO A DIGNIFIED LIFE

There are, however, indigenous land cases in which the IACtHR has adopted a normative approach, whereby cultural identity and economic concerns seem more integrated. This has been particularly so in cases where communities were deprived of access to their means of survival, falling into extreme destitution. In *Yakye Axa*, the indigenous community lived in extreme destitution at the side of a highway while they awaited the resolution of their land claims. Besides the right to property, the Court addressed the case under the right to a dignified life (Article 4 of the ACHR).[103] This right binds States to generate 'minimum living conditions that are compatible with the dignity of the human person … [avoiding] creating conditions that hinder or impede it'.[104] Positive and concrete measures are required to fulfil this obligation, giving priority to those most vulnerable and at risk. Within this framework, the Court brought together socio-economic rights considerations (it looked at the lack of, for example, education, health, housing, water and sanitation) and indigenous worldviews, including their close relationship with the land.[105] The Court implied the unsuitability of the alternatives for relocation offered by the State and concluded that it had failed to undertake measures to improve the condition which prevented the members of the community from having a decent life.[106] The Court returned to the dignified life analysis in similar cases against Paraguay. In *Sawhoyamaxa*,

102 *Saramaka People v Suriname*, above n 82, §80; *Afro-descendant Communities Displaced from the Cacarica River Basin (Operation Genesis) v Colombia* (hereinafter *Operation Genesis v Colombia*), 20 November 2013, §§346–347, IACHR Series C no 270.

103 Article 4 of the ACHR does not mention dignity. The relevant paragraph reads: 'Every person has the right to have his life respected. This right shall be protected by law and, in general, from the moment of conception. No one shall be arbitrarily deprived of his life.'

104 *Yakye Axa v Paraguay*, above n 80, §162.

105 Ibid, §163. The Court noted that 'detriment to the right to health, and closely tied to this, detriment to the right to food and access to clean water, have a major impact on the right to a decent existence and basic conditions to exercise other human rights, such as the right to education or the right to cultural identity.' (§167).

106 *Yakye Axa v Paraguay*, above n 80, §§170–176.

the analysis was very close to that in *Yakye Axa*,[107] and in *Xákmok Kásek*, the Court even provided a detailed account of minimum standards regarding water, food, health and education.[108] The community's destitution was again assessed in connection with their cultural life, for the lack of access to their traditional lands had 'led them to depend almost exclusively on State actions and be forced to live not only in a way that is different from their cultural patterns, but in squalor'.[109] The IACtHR also referred to the UN CommESCR's view on how poverty restricts the ability of individuals and groups to access and contribute to cultural life and enjoy their own culture.[110]

When compared with the property framework, it has been argued that the right to a dignified life has the advantage of being normatively stronger and holding potential beyond a minimalistic focus on cultural and physical survival.[111] Moreover, such interpretation might be closer to the political and economic autonomy vindications made under the so far resisted right to self-determination.[112] Nonetheless, the right to property remains the dominant paradigm in indigenous cases, while the dignified life framework has been confined to cases where the destitute living conditions of the community members threaten their physical survival.

Finally, it is important to mention a road that, at the time of writing, has not yet been taken by the IACtHR: Article 26 of the ACHR on the progressive development of economic, social and cultural rights. After years of controversy, in 2009 the Court issued the first judgment (not related to indigenous people) affirming its contentious jurisdiction over Article 26, which would translate into the justiciability of socio-economic rights.[113] In the aforementioned case of *Sarayaku* (2012), the applicants alleged a violation of this provision, but the Court decided not to rule on that.[114] Arguments for and against the adjudication

---

107 *Sawhoyamaxa v Paraguay*, above n 79, §§159–178.

108 *Xákmok Kásek v Paraguay*, above n 83, §§194–213.

109 Ibid, §215.

110 Ibid, §216; UN Committee on Economic, Social and Cultural Rights (CESCR), General Comment no 21, Right of everyone to take part in cultural life (Article 15, para 1(a) of the Covenant on Economic, Social and Cultural Rights), adopted 21 December 2009 [2009] E/C.12/GC/21, §38.

111 TM Antkowiak, above n 97, pp 180–185.

112 Ibid. On the international resistance to the economic dimension of the right to self-determination, see S Smis, D Cambou and G Ngende, 'The Question of Land Grab in Africa and the Indigenous Peoples' Right to Traditional Lands, Territories and Resources' (2013) 35 *Loyola of Los Angeles International and Comparative Law Review* 514; A Farmer, 'Toward a Meaningful Rebirth of Economic Self-Determination: Human Rights Realization in Resources-Rich Countries' (2007) 39 *NYU Journal of International Law and Politics* 417.

113 *Acevedo Buendía et al ('Discharged and Retired Employees of the Comptroller') v Peru*, 1 June 2009, §§19, 92–106, IACHR Series C no 198.

114 *Sarayaku v Ecuador*, above n 79, §230.

of Article 26 seem to still divide the Court.[115] Thus, it is unclear whether the Court will continue to tackle socio-economic demands through civil/political rights or if it will finally opt for their direct enforceability.[116] The uncertainty around how to deal with socio-economic rights may also curtail the Court's ability to adopt more integrated approaches to the cultural and economic claims of indigenous, tribal and other individual and groups.

4.4. INTEGRATING EQUALITY AND DIFFERENCE?

In the indigenous cases reviewed above, claims to equality and non-discrimination do not seem to have featured strongly in the Court's judgments, nor in the applicants' or the Commission's legal arguments.[117] This may come as a surprise if looked at from normative and practical perspectives. From a normative viewpoint, the IACtHR has been quite progressive in embracing a substantive or 'structural' conception of equality and non-discrimination,[118] which seems well suited to addressing the plight of indigenous people in a comprehensive way. From a practical perspective, it is hard to decouple land and cultural struggles of indigenous, tribal and afro-descendant communities from their history of racial/ethnic discrimination. The Court has actually stated that special measures of protection are required to ensure the equal and effective enjoyment of indigenous and tribal peoples' rights. It has also rejected the State argument that legislation providing 'special' rights for indigenous and tribal groups raises discrimination issues for the rest of the population.[119]

---

115 See e.g. the Concurring Opinions of Judges Alberto Pérez Pérez, Humberto Antonio Sierra Porto and Ferrer Mac-Gregor Poisot in *Gonzales Lluy et al v Ecuador*, 1 September 2015, IACHR Series C no 298.

116 After the present work had been written, the IACtHR issued a judgment in which it explicitly declared the violation of Article 26 ACHR, which implies its direct enforceability. See *Lagos del Campo v. Perú*, 31 August 2017, §§153–154 and 163. On the justiciability of Article 26 and for transcending the view of differentiated standards of review, see T Melish, 'The Inter-American Court of Human Rights: Beyond Progressivity' in M Langford (ed), *Social Rights Jurisprudence: Emerging Trends in Comparative and International Law*, Cambridge University Press, Cambridge 2008, pp 24–29, 61–65.

117 Article 1.1 of the ACHR contains the obligation to respect and ensure the convention rights without discrimination. Article 24 of the ACHR enshrines the principle of equality under the law.

118 See e.g. V David, 'The Inter-American Concept of Structural Equality and Discrimination', (2017) 2(2) *Anti-Discrimination Law Review* 12; V Abramovich, 'From Massive Violations to Structural Patterns: New Approaches and Classic Tensions in the Inter-American Human Rights System' (2009) 6(11) *Sur – International Journal of Human Rights* 17.

119 *Saramaka People v Suriname*, above n 82, §§99–103.

The IACtHR has explicitly connected the equality and non-discrimination provisions enshrined in Articles 1.1 and 24 of the ACHR to the plight of indigenous peoples by taking 'into account the specific characteristics that differentiate the members of the indigenous peoples from the general population and that constitute their cultural identity'.[120] Yet only in *Xákmok Kásek* did the Court find that the extreme institutional, socio-economic and cultural deprivation experienced by the community amounted to de facto discrimination.[121] No discrimination ground was specified. Later, however, this approach appeared to be in retreat. In 2014, in a style reminiscent of its European counterpart, the IACtHR declined a pronouncement on an alleged violation of the right to equality under the law (Article 24 of the ACHR) and referred to its findings under the right to property and judicial protection.[122]

The two lines of case law discussed thus far suggest that the protection of cultural identities and ways of life has successfully enhanced the rights of Roma, Travellers, indigenous people and afro-descendant rural people. Nevertheless, this 'culturalisation' of rights has not come without problems.[123] Human rights courts have tended to over-emphasise the applicants' cultural identity while endorsing an essentialist view of it. This has fostered fragmentary accounts and normative responses. Notably, only a narrow set of practices may receive protection (e.g. hunting, farming and travelling); some people may be excluded from protection (e.g. peasants, pastoralists and 'New Travellers'); and, as the interplay between the cultural and the socio-economic gets obscured, so does the way to redress the problem. For instance, the more Travellers become settled, the more they need security in land tenure, which they will not get if legal frameworks insist on nomadism. Meanwhile, a nomadic life tends to exacerbate socio-economic disadvantage, which is a significant reason why Travellers settle. Since it may be neither feasible nor desirable to remove the cultural identity aspect from human rights norms, some correctives may be needed to approach these issues more holistically. It is submitted that taking an integrated view of relevant norms, applying a substantive or structural conception of equality, using a perspective of intersectionality and integrating insights from socio-economic rights and participatory mechanisms may all be particularly helpful in this regard. The next section turns to these tools, which have already been used to some extent by the ECtHR and the IACtHR.

---

120 *Yakye Axa v Paraguay*, above n 80, §63; *Sawhoyamaxa v Paraguay*, above n 79, §83.

121 *Xákmok Kásek v Paraguay*, above n 83, §§273–275.

122 *Kuna and the Emberá v Paraguay*, above n 79, §§203–204. Previously, in the *Operation Genesis* case, the Court dismissed the examination of the equality and non-discrimination claims made by the applicants and the Commission: *Operation Genesis v Colombia*, above n 102, §§307–312, 337.

123 In this vein, see also K Engle, *The Elusive Promise of Indigenous Development: Rights, Culture, Strategy*, Duke University Press, Durham, NC 2010, pp 13–14, 133 ff.

5. OPPORTUNITIES AND LEGAL TOOLS FOR INTEGRATION

One mechanism that has aided integration is the dynamic interpretation of convention norms, which is discernible in various judgments. The regional courts, seeking to update the respective human rights conventions to take account of the current circumstances, relied to various extents on several normative sources: international, regional, national law and even non-State laws. By resorting to a vast set of norms, the courts gave cultural significance to legal concepts (e.g. property, home and family life), recognised a right to cultural identity or to live in accordance to one's own cultural identity and applied differentiated standards in view of people's minority status, vulnerability or specifically protected condition. In addition, the consideration of other conventional norms led the courts to introduce some socio-economic guarantees. For example, safeguards against eviction were recognised within the scope of the right to respect for the home, and access to food and water (among other things) was protected under the right to life. This approach has served to reaffirm the indivisibility and interdependence of all human rights. Such a comprehensive normative outlook – an 'integrated perspective to human rights'[124] – thus appears useful in terms of addressing the experience of people who are at the crossroads of different social positions and rights regimes.[125] Importantly, the cases reviewed also suggest that normative integration, as a process for interpretation and application of convention norms, facilitates the handling of complex demands without necessarily leading to uniform normative outcomes.[126]

Integrating dimensions of socio-economic rights into convention rights generally regarded as civil and political merits separate consideration. As seen earlier, the plight of Roma, Travellers and indigenous applicants often has to do with socio-economic security. Socio-economic rights may assist not only in the redistribution realm, but also in combating cultural prejudice. Also, if properly tailored to the actual experiences of people, socio-economic rights may respond to needs arising from cultural change. Yet judges may find it difficult to give effect to the indivisibility and inter-dependence of rights without exceeding their mandate. As such, it might be worthwhile to explore alternatives. One possibility is the use of standards of review similar to those applicable to socio-economic

124 E Brems, above n 1, 451–56.

125 Ibid, pp 465–467.

126 On the idea that integration may be seen as opposing pluralism, see B Oomen, 'The Application of Socio-legal Theories of Legal Pluralism to Understanding the Implementation and Integration of Human Rights Law' (2014) 4 *European Journal of Human Rights* 484. On the argument that integration does not mean uniformisation, see E Brems, above n 1, p 469.

rights. Of the standards used to operationalise the progressive realisation norm which governs social rights, that of reasonableness holds particular potential for the present discussion.[127] In fact, one advantage of reasonableness is that it may actually facilitate the examination of the policies in place and thus the underlying institutional arrangements leading to violations. To determine whether States have discharged their obligations, the standard of reasonableness scrutinises whether deliberate, concrete and non-discriminatory measures were adopted, as well as whether the disadvantaged position of certain groups was taken into account and situations of greater risk were prioritised.[128] Interestingly, the case law considered in this chapter suggests that the regional courts have already applied elements of review that resonate with these criteria.

Consider, for instance, the IACtHR's dignified life framework, whereby the Court examined the steps taken by the State and the levels of satisfaction of socio-economic rights in light of both cultural demands and the risks faced by the members of the indigenous communities concerned. In the case of the ECtHR, the procedural safeguards required by the right to respect for the home in the cases outlined above provide another example. The ECtHR's inquiry in such cases evokes the reasonableness review, with its evaluation of the adequacy, flexibility and aims of laws and policies, including related decision-making processes. That is why the reasonableness review has been identified with a so-called 'proceduralisation' of socio-economic rights. Although such proceduralisation has been strongly criticised for emptying socio-economic rights of any substantial/material content,[129] it should be recalled that for a court facing institutional limitations on adjudicating those rights, a procedural approach may constitute a step forward.

Admittedly, one anticipated objection to the contentions advanced here is that resorting to social rights-like review might introduce weaker standards

---

127 Since within human rights law the standard of progressive realisation is unique to ESC rights, the doctrine has elaborated specific criteria for their judicial review. The most widely known are the standards of 'reasonableness' and the 'minimum core'. For an overview of 'reasonableness', see the references below in n 129. For a discussion on 'minimum core', see e.g. KG Young; 'The Minimum Core of Economic and Social Rights: A Concept in Search of Content' (2008) 33 *Yale Journal of International Law* 113.

128 See e.g. UN General Assembly, Optional Protocol to the International Covenant on Economic, Social and Cultural Rights, adopted 5 March 2009 [2009] A/RES/63/117, Article 8(4)(b)(f); B Porter, 'The Reasonableness of Art. 8(4): Adjudicating from the Margins' (2009) 27(1) *Nordic Journal of Human Rights* 39; S Liebenberg, 'Enforcing Positive Socio-economic Rights Claims: The South African Model of Reasonableness Review' in J Squires, M Langford and B Thiele (eds), above n 23, pp 73–88.

129 See e.g. D Bilchitz, 'Towards a Reasonable Approach to the Minimum Core: Laying the Foundations for Future Socioeconomic Rights Jurisprudence' (2003) 19 *South African Journal of Human Rights* 10; M Pieterse, 'Eating Socioeconomic Rights: The Usefulness of Rights Talk in Alleviating Social Hardship Revisited' (2007) 29 *Human Rights Quarterly* 808.

than those applicable to civil and political rights.[130] However, the fear appears misplaced. All human rights need time and the adoption of adequate measures to be fully realised. Hence, as argued by Brems, progressive realisation can be used to accommodate not only socio-economic diversity, but also cultural diversity.[131]

A third aspect to note is that the regional courts relied infrequently on substantive equality and non-discrimination provisions to solve the cases at hand, which is unfortunate. The advantage of substantive equality is that it enables the adjudicator to pinpoint the underlying structural inequalities. It acknowledges that certain cultural patterns institutionalise not only cultural subordination but also socio-economic and political disadvantage, while the latter in turn reinforces cultural domination. From this perspective, the courts do not need to define and protect any particular lifestyle or cultural content. It is enough to note the cultural injustice – that planning, housing and land regulations were all made in the absence of any consideration of Roma, Travellers and indigenous peoples. In other words, impermissible cultural interferences could also be determined by asking whether devaluation of the cultural identity or practice stems from social devaluation of the group itself.[132] Human rights courts could operationalise substantive equality either by further scrutinising de facto and indirect discrimination, including on grounds of socio-economic disadvantage, as well as by requiring States to adopt positive measures to ensure effective equality. Of course, this could require more creativity and flexibility from judges, many of whom may still be attached to a formal equality paradigm.[133]

Another valuable device is intersectionality. The idea of 'intersectionality', coined within critical race theory and feminism,[134] has gradually been introduced in international law.[135] The concept recognises that oppressive experiences

---

130 The reason for this lies in the progressive realisation criterion governing economic, social and cultural rights. See UN General Assembly, International Covenant on Economic, Social and Cultural Rights, adopted 16 December 1966, Article 2(1); UN General Assembly, Convention on the Rights of the Child, 20 November 1989 [1989], Article 4.

131 E Brems, 'Human Rights: Minimum and Maximum Perspectives' (2009) 9(3) *Human Rights Law Review* 366.

132 In this vein, see RR Banks, 'Class and Culture: Indeterminacy of Non-discrimination' (2009) 5(1) *Stanford Journal of Civil Rights & Civil Liberties* 7.

133 C O'Cinneide, above n 74, p 99; S Besson, 'Evolutions in Non-discrimination Law within the ECHR and the ESC Systems: It Takes Two to Tango in the Council of Europe' (2012) 60(1) *American Journal of Comparative Law* 173.

134 K Crenshaw, 'Demarginalizing the Intersection of Race and Sex: A Black Feminist Critique of Antidiscrimination Doctrine, Feminist Theory and Antiracist Politics' (1989) *University of Chicago Legal Forum* 139; K Crenshaw, 'Mapping the Margins: Intersectionality, Identity Politics and Violence against Women of Color' (1991) 43(6) *Stanford Law Review* 1241.

135 Notably, the Convention on the Rights of Persons with Disabilities expressly recognises the intersectional discrimination experienced by these persons, including on grounds such as 'social origin', 'property' and 'other status'. UN General Assembly, Convention on the Rights

are not compartmentalised; instead, they are compounded because multiple identities relating to specific contexts cut across a person's life. Rather than adding layers of discrimination, such an approach facilitates the identification of the unique types of violations which occur at the intersections of various systems of oppression.[136] In the cases reviewed here, such a perspective would enable human rights courts to take account of how socio-economic, cultural and racial inequalities structure regulations and practices over land, planning, housing and property, as well as how they impact differently on women, children and other individuals belonging to culturally defined communities. From this perspective, the applicants' hardship resulting from poverty in cases such as *Chapman* and *Wells*, for example, would have not been overlooked. In the judicial sphere, intersectionality is commonly applied through the right to equality and non-discrimination, but it could also be used in the proportionality analysis conducted under other provisions.[137] At a more general level, intersectionality illuminates the relevance of specialised human rights standards that are more tailored to the concrete experience of the rights holders.

Finally, the IACtHR's jurisprudence on indigenous rights underscores the potential of legal tools to foster people's participation. The Court has required States to conduct, at a minimum, informed consultation processes and, at best, to obtain the free prior consent of indigenous communities on matters affecting their socio-economic, cultural and political life. By requiring States to undertake a process of dialogue, the Court opens up a path to bridge the abstract civil/political convention rights with the particular economic needs and cultural views of indigenous peoples. Participation can actually mitigate the law's tendency to reify cultural identity claims, as those belonging to the cultural group in question will be able to define and contest what is regarded as their culture. Importantly, a procedural tool for a dialogical construction of rights does not need to be confined to indigenous people. On the contrary, its use could be justified whenever the rights of otherwise unheard communities are threatened by regulations or decisions that overlook their specific needs and identities. Sandra Liebenberg, for instance, explains how a 'meaningful engagement' strategy has been used by the South African Constitutional Court in cases of

of Persons with Disabilities, adopted 24 January 2007 [2007] A/RES/61/106, preamble. See also UN Committee on Economic, Social and Cultural Rights (CESCR), General Comment No 20, Non-discrimination in economic, social and cultural rights (art. 2, para. 2, of the International Covenant on Economic, Social and Cultural Rights), 2 July 2009 [2009] E/C.12/GC/20, §§17, 27.

136 See e.g. C Mackinnon, 'Intersectionality as a Method: A Note' (2013) 38(4) *Signs* 1019, 2023–24; JE Bond, 'International Intersectionality: A Theoretical and Pragmatic Exploration of Women's International Human Rights Violations' (2003) 52 *Emory Law Journal* 157.

137 One possibility to do so is to enlarge the array of human experiences that are taken as a point of reference in the interpretation of substantive provisions. Moreover, intersectionality could also be promoted through the flexible notion of vulnerability.

eviction of impoverished communities.[138] Furthermore, as discussed earlier, international bodies monitoring socio-economic rights, whose instruments and decisions have been referred to by the ECtHR and the IACtHR, have also endorsed consultation as a prerequisite for authorising evictions.

In the latest judgments concerning the eviction of Roma and Traveller communities, the ECtHR has required authorities to consider their particular situation and vulnerability when devising solutions and modalities to carry out evictions. While this still falls short of demanding participation of the communities in decision-making processes, it might provide an incipient basis to move in that direction. The ECtHR should then continue down this road and promote the use of dialogical/participatory mechanisms. The Court might endorse a sort of consultation-like requirement or weigh up in its proportionality analysis the extent to which State authorities have attempted to engage in dialogue. In *Winterstein v France*, for instance, State authorities deliberately refused the applicants' request to enter into mediation and participate in a study concerning their situation.[139] In any case, to really explore the potential of dialogical processes, the courts should dictate the normative parameters within which these take place.[140]

The suggestions made thus far do not attempt to be exhaustive. Certainly, other legal tools and concepts might assist judges in addressing rights claims involving cultural and socio-economic hardship without losing sight of their inter-play. Exploring avenues that promote an integrated view of rights is worthwhile not only for ethno-cultural minorities, but also for many other individuals and groups who experience violations across different types of harms, rights and identities.

6. CONCLUSION

The case law discussed above reveals how challenging it is for human rights courts to adjudicate on allegations of violations whereby discrimination and cultural subordination structure socio-economic institutions and vice versa. The difficulties are apparent in, for instance, the tendency to prioritise the identification of protected cultural identities while overlooking the interlocked axes of inequality and socio-economic disadvantages. Conversely, as happened with the first Roma and Traveller cases, it is also problematic when judges reduce

138 S Liebenberg, 'Engaging the Paradoxes of the Universal and Particular in Human Rights Adjudication: The Possibilities and Pitfalls of "Meaningful Engagement"' (2012) 12 *African Human Rights Law Journal* 1.

139 *Winterstein v France*, above n 33, §29.

140 S Liebenberg, above n 138, p 20.

their plights to an issue of material resources only. None of these approaches is satisfactory, which is why the previous sections have examined the extent to which the regional courts have (not) found ways to integrate into their normative responses the cultural and economic needs arising from the applicants' lived experience. In view of this, this chapter has also attempted to shed light on the legal techniques which may open up avenues to better undertake that challenge.

THE USE OF EXTERNAL INSTRUMENTS BY THE EUROPEAN COURT OF HUMAN RIGHTS

(Missed) Opportunities for the Rights of Persons with Disabilities

Dorothea Staes and Joseph Damamme*

---

* This research has been funded by the Interuniversity Attraction Poles Programme initiated by the Belgian Science Policy Office, more specifically the IAP, 'The Global Challenge of Human Rights Integration: Towards a Users' Perspective' (www.hrintegration.be). We are grateful to Professor Isabelle Hachez, Dr Gauthier de Béco, Constantin Cojocariu, Alan Cusack and Rodolphe Genissel for their helpful comments on an earlier draft of this chapter. The authors would also like to thank Ana-Maria Corrêa and Rebecca Moffat for their proofreading work and suggestions. Dr Dorothea Staes is an affiliated researcher at the Université libre de Bruxelles Centre Perelman de Philosophie du Droit (http://www.philodroit.be/?lang=en). Email: thea.staes@hotmail.com. Joseph Damamme is a PhD candidate at the Université libre de Bruxelles (Center of European Law) and involved in the Equality Law Clinic (http://www.philodroit.be/-ELC-?lang=en). He acted as an advisor to counsel (Constantin Cojocariu) in ECtHR, Gherghina v Romania, a case that will be discussed further in this chapter. Email: jdamamme@ulb.ac.be.

1. INTRODUCTION

The European Court of Human Rights (ECtHR), located in Strasbourg, decides on violations of the European Convention on Human Rights (ECHR) and its Protocols – its primary sources.[1] These instruments focus on the protection of all human beings and do not address particular categories, such as persons with disabilities. This does not hinder the ECtHR in developing case law on the rights of persons with disabilities, based, for instance, on the prohibition of discrimination (Article 14 of the ECHR),[2] the prohibition of torture or inhuman or degrading treatment (Article 3 of the ECHR),[3] the right to liberty and security (Article 5 of the ECHR)[4] or the right to respect for private life and family life (Article 8 of the ECHR).[5]

To ensure the protection of persons with disabilities in the Strasbourg context, the ECtHR adopts a global perspective lens and includes references to what we call the external normative context. This context covers instruments other than the Court's primary sources (the ECHR and its Protocols),[6] such as the United Nations Convention on the Rights of Persons with Disabilities (UNCRPD),[7]

---

1 Article 32 of the ECHR provides that the ECtHR has jurisdiction to consider matters that concern the interpretation and application of the ECHR and its Protocols.

2 This article protects persons with a disability from discrimination in the enjoyment of rights covered by other articles of the ECHR, such as the right to private and family life (Article 8 of the ECHR). See, for example, *Glor v Switzerland*, no 13444/04, ECHR 2009 (the Court decided in this case that Article 14 of the ECHR covers 'disability').

3 See, for example, *M.S. v Croatia (No 2)*, no 75450/12, ECHR 2015.

4 Ibid.

5 See, for example, *Ivinović v Croatia*, no 13006/13, ECHR 2014; *McDonald v United Kingdom*, no 4241/12, ECHR 2014; *Glor v Switzerland*, above n 2.

6 Instruments attached to the Court's internal (institutional) context, such as the *travaux préparatoires*, previous case law of the ECtHR and the Rules of the Court also fall outside this context.

7 Convention on the Rights of Persons with Disabilities, adopted on 24 January 2007, G.A. Res. 61/106, UN Doc A/RES/61/106 (entered into force on 3 May 2008).

documents of the monitoring body the UN Committee on the Rights of Persons with Disabilities (hereinafter the UNCRPD Committee), instruments of the Council of Europe (CoE) concerning disabled persons such as Recommendations of the Committee of Ministers or the Parliamentary Assembly, judgments of national supreme courts on disability and recommendations of the International Labour Organization (ILO).

This referencing practice is not explicitly authorised by the ECHR, but on some occasions, the Court has found a legal justification in the rule on treaty interpretation enshrined in Article 31, paragraph 3(c) of the Vienna Convention on the Law of Treaties (VCLT).[8] The latter provision states that 'there shall be taken into account, together with the context: (c) any relevant rules of international law applicable in the relations between the parties'.[9] As the Court noted, the ECHR 'cannot be interpreted in a vacuum'.[10]

External referencing in the Strasbourg Court's decision-making is not without its critics. The phenomenon – together with the legitimacy concerns that it brings – has been covered by several academic contributions.[11] This chapter does not give a general overview of arguments in favour or against the referencing practice, but touches upon the (optimisation of) opportunities and

8 For a key case in this respect, which equally gives an overview of other Strasbourg cases referring to external instruments and which attempts to explain and justify the external referencing practice, see ECtHR, *Demir and Baykara v Turkey*, no 34503/97, ECHR 2008. For a comprehensive overview of references in recent Strasbourg Grand Chamber cases, see D Staes, 'When the European Court Refers to External Instruments. Mapping and Justifications', doctoral thesis under the supervision of I Rorive and S Van Drooghenbroeck, defended at the Université Saint-Louis on 26 June 2017.

9 In the *Demir and Baykara* case, the Court explained external referencing practice by referring to Articles 31–33 of the VCLT, see *Demir and Baykara v Turkey*, above n 8. The Court used Article 31, paragraph 3(c) of the VCLT to stress that the provisions of the Convention are not considered 'as the sole framework of reference for the interpretation of the rights and freedoms enshrined therein', but that account must be taken of 'any relevant rules and principles of international law applicable in relations between the Contracting Parties' (ibid, §67).

10 See, *inter alia*, ECtHR, *Golder v United Kingdom*, no 4451/70, §29, ECHR 1975; and *Al-Adsani v United Kingdom*, no 35763/97, §55, ECHR 2011.

11 See, inter alia, F Vanneste, *General International Law before Human Rights Courts: Assessing the Specialty Claims of International Human Rights Law*, Intersentia, Antwerp 2010, p 625; F Tulkens, S Van Drooghenbroeck and F Krenc, 'Le soft law et la Cour européenne des Droits de l'Homme: questions de légitimité et de méthode' (2012) 91 *Revue trimestrielle des droits de l'homme* 381, 434; M Forowicz, *The Reception of International Law in the European Court of Human Rights*, Oxford University Press, Oxford 2010, p 456; D Staes, 'The Use of Documents Other Than the European Convention on Human Rights and its Protocols in Cases before the European Court of Human Rights: Reflections from and upon a Users' Perspective' (2014) 2 *Human Rights & International Legal Discourse* 186; T Barkhuysen and ML van Emmerik, 'Ongebonden Binding: Verwijzing naar Soft Law Standaarden in Uitspraken van het EHRM' (2010) 35 *Nederlands Juristen Comité voor de Mensenrechten (NJCM) Bulletin* 827; G Gonzalez, 'Les sources internationales dans la jurisprudence de la Cour européenne des Droits de l'Homme' (2007) 7 *Cahiers de l'Institut de Droit Européen des droits de l'Homme de l'Université de Montpellier* 307.

concerns of external referencing in relation to human rights integration and the protection of persons with disabilities.

Section 1 of this chapter discusses the Strasbourg Court's comprehensive approach to external instruments relevant to the protection of the rights of persons with disabilities. Such an approach yields opportunities for human rights integration, both from a bottom-up and a top-down understanding. A top-down view on integration draws attention to tendencies of convergence or divergence between diverse normative instruments. A bottom-up view includes a human rights users' perspective,[12] paying attention to the particular situation of persons with disabilities and to all relevant aspects of their rights and experiences.[13] Both these views are discussed in section 2. On the one hand, the Strasbourg Court's referencing practice contributes to integrative tendencies in the domain of the protection of persons with disabilities; on the other hand, some cases demonstrate that the Court has not exploited the integrative opportunities fully.

Although the Strasbourg cases discussed here refer to numerous external instruments, this chapter pays particular attention to the UNCRPD. The reason for this choice lies in the success of this instrument, both at a European and a global level.[14] The UNCRPD was the first human rights treaty to allow ratification by an organisation of regional integration[15] and has been ratified by the European Union (EU).[16] It represents an important paradigm shift in respect of the protection of persons with disabilities, recognising that persons with disabilities should not be seen merely as recipients of charity or medical attention, but as holders of rights who have inherent human dignity worthy of protection equal to that of other human beings.[17]

---

12 On a users' approach, see E Desmet, 'Analysing Users' Trajectories in Human Rights: A Conceptual Exploration and Research Agenda' (2014) 2 *Human Rights & International Legal Discourse* 121.

13 For a contribution addressing an integrative approach to human rights (mainly from within what we call a bottom-up perspective), see E Brems, 'Should Pluriform Human Rights Become One? Exploring the Benefits of Human Rights Integration' (2014) 4 *European Journal of Human Rights* 447.

14 On 4 June 2018, the instrument had been widely ratified (by 177 States), https://www.un.org/development/desa/disabilities/convention-on-the-rights-of-persons-with-disabilities.html (accessed 4 June 2018). All EU Member States have ratified it. With regards to the CoE Member States, all have ratified except for Liechtenstein.

15 UNCRPD, Article 44.

16 Decision 2010/48/EC of the Council concerning the conclusion, by the European Community (now European Union), of the United Nations Convention on the Rights of Persons with Disabilities [2010] OJ L23/35.

17 Such a paradigm shift from a medical to a rights-based approach to disability might have significant implications for more traditional legal frameworks such as domestic legal frameworks challenged before the ECtHR. The use of the UNCRPD by the ECtHR has attracted considerable attention in legal doctrine (e.g. E Flynn and A Arstein-Kerslake, 'The Support Model of Legal Capacity: Fact, Fiction and Fantasy?' (2014) 31 *Berkeley*

2. THE COURT'S COMPREHENSIVE APPROACH TO EXTERNAL INSTRUMENTS

A few examples of ECtHR cases on the rights of persons with disabilities are sufficient to support the argument that the Court has a comprehensive view on the external normative setting and, accordingly, relies on a wide diversity of normative instruments for interpretative purposes.[18]

A first example is the case of *Glor v Switzerland*[19] of 30 April 2009, in which the Strasbourg Court included 'disability' in the list of discrimination grounds under Article 14 of the ECHR.[20]

This was in line with the UNCRPD[21] and the Council of Europe Parliamentary Assembly Recommendation of 2003 on full social inclusion of persons with disabilities.[22] The Court used these external instruments to hold that there is 'a European and a worldwide consensus on the need to protect people with disabilities from discriminatory treatment'.[23] The Court's view was also in accordance with EU law, which requires EU Member States to prohibit discrimination based on disability.[24]

Journal of International Law 124) and by civil society (see e.g. OPEN SOCIETY FOUNDATIONS, 'Community, Not Confinement, The Role of the European Union in Promoting and Protecting the Right of People with Disabilities to Live in the Community' (2015), drafted by Dr Israel Butler, https://www.opensocietyfoundations.org/sites/default/files/community-not-confinement-20151014.pdf (accessed 30 June 2017)), and within institutional circles (see e.g. EU AGENCY FOR FUNDAMENTAL RIGHTS, 'Involuntary Placement and Involuntary Treatment of Persons with Mental Health Problems' (2012), http://fra.europa.eu/sites/default/files/involuntary-placement-and-involuntary-treatment-of-persons-with-mental-health-problems_en.pdf. (accessed 30 June 2017)). These contributions often pay attention to how the UNCRPD may 'influence' the ECtHR in interpreting the ECHR and how it can be used as an 'aid' for this purpose.

18 This observation also follows from *Demir and Baykara v Turkey*, above n 8, §§65 et seq. In this case, the Court explicitly mentioned that external referencing practice encompasses a diversity of instruments.

19 *Glor v Switzerland*, above n 2, §80. This case dealt with the obligation of a person unfit for military service to pay exemption tax and with the distinction that had been made on the basis of the seriousness of the disability.

20 This finding is in line with precedents where the Court had already found this list to be non-exhaustive. In the *Glor* case (§80), the Court referred to *Stec and others v United Kingdom*, where it was stated that 'sex' falls 'within the non-exhaustive list of prohibited grounds of discrimination in Article 14' (although 'sex' is explicitly mentioned in this provision). *Stec and others v United Kingdom*, no 65731/01, §50, ECHR 2006.

21 The facts of the case date from before the entry into force of this instrument (3 May 2008).

22 Rec.1592(2003).

23 *Glor v Switzerland*, above n 2, §53.

24 See Council Directive 2000/78/EC of 27 November 2000 establishing a general framework for equal treatment in employment and occupation [2000] OJ L303, 2 December 2000, pp 16–22) adopted on the basis of Article 19, §1 of the Treaty on the Functioning of the European Union (TFEU), which is the provision conferring the competence to take appropriate action to combat discrimination based on disability.

A further example is the Grand Chamber case of *Stanev v Bulgaria* of 17 January 2012. According to the ECtHR, this case concerned the lack of direct access to court for a disabled person seeking restoration of his legal capacity and a violation of Article 6 of the ECHR (right to a fair trial and access to court). Based on a comparison of national legal systems, the Court noted 'a trend at [the] European level towards granting legally incapacitated persons direct access to the courts to seek restoration of their capacity'.[25] The Court also stated that it 'is obliged to note the growing importance which international instruments for the protection of people with mental disorders are now attaching to granting them as much legal autonomy as possible' and it referred in this connection to the UNCRPD and a Recommendation of the Council of Europe Committee of Ministers of 1999 concerning the legal protection of incapable adults.[26]

Another example is the case of *M.S. v Croatia (No 2)* of 19 February 2015. This case concerned a woman's involuntary confinement in a psychiatric hospital for one month, where she was also tied to a bed in an isolation room for a night. She alleged ill-treatment and the lack of an effective investigation, in violation of Article 3 of the ECHR on the prohibition of torture and inhuman or degrading treatment or punishment. She also complained of having been unlawfully and unjustifiably detained and of the absence of adequate procedural safeguards in this respect, said to be in violation of Article 5 of the ECHR on the right to liberty and security.

The Court concluded the *M.S.* case by finding a violation of both articles invoked. With regard to the violation of Article 3 of the ECHR, it drew attention to 'the developments in contemporary legal standards' on coercive and non-consensual measures against mentally ill persons to argue that those measures should be of last resort.[27] The Court also cited a Report of the Special Rapporteur on Torture of 2013 and a recommendation of the CoE Committee of Ministers concerning the protection of the human rights and dignity of persons with mental disorders.[28] In addition, it stated that: 'It must be shown that the coercive measure at issue was not prolonged beyond the period which was strictly necessary for that purpose.' The latter position was built, inter alia, on the UN Principles for the Protection of Persons with Mental Illness and for the Improvement of Mental Health Care of 1991 (hereafter 'MI Principles'), a report of the European Committee for the Prevention of Torture and Inhuman or Degrading Treatment or Punishment (CPT) and the earlier-mentioned CoE Recommendation.[29] The ECtHR held that the use of physical constraint against

25 *Stanev v Bulgaria*, no 36760/06, §243, ECHR 2012.
26 Ibid, §§244–245.
27 *M.S. v Croatia (No 2)*, above n 3, §104.
28 See ibid. The Court also referred to national law and prior Strasbourg case law.
29 Ibid, §105.

the applicant, who had not consented to her admission to the hospital, violated the relevant international standards.[30] It also found a violation of Article 5 of the ECHR by noting that 'an effective legal representation of persons with disabilities requires an enhanced duty of supervision of their legal representatives by the competent domestic courts'. The Court supported this statement by the MI Principles.[31] In addition, the ECtHR stressed the applicant's need for effective access to justice and for direct engagement in a discussion of her situation, referring, inter alia, to Article 13 of the UNCRDP, which recognises effective access to justice for persons with disabilities on an equal basis with others.[32]

From these examples, it is clear that the Court has a comprehensive approach to the external normative context and refers to a wide diversity of instruments without any clear distinction as to their origin, scope or legal status.[33] In the abovementioned cases, the ECtHR cited instruments from other kinds of organisations (politically representative or not)[34] and from other courts,[35] as well as instruments of various scopes[36] including those addressing human rights other than civil and political rights.[37] In addition, the Court did not only take account of '(hard) legal sources' but also referred to instruments that are 'soft by nature'[38] or that are 'soft' because they were not ratified by

---

30 Ibid, §108.

31 Ibid, §154.

32 Ibid, §§157 and 159.

33 See also E Brems, above n 13, 448–450. A comprehensive approach is not per se integrative (see below), but an integrative approach, to use the words of Brems, requires a 'comprehensive approach to the sources of human rights law'. Brems adds that an integrated view requires, inter alia, 'taking into account all human rights provisions that are relevant in a particular situation and hence a maximum widening of the range of human rights sources that are on the table'. E Brems, above n 13, 452.

34 Examples of such references (taken from the abovementioned cases) include references to instruments of the UN and the CoE. Note that the ECtHR explicitly acknowledged that it refers to bodies that have no function to represent the States parties; see *Demir and Baykara v Turkey*, above n 8, §71.

35 See, for instance, *I.B. v Greece*, no 552/10, §§36–38, ECHR 2013, which includes a reference to a judgment of the South African Constitutional Court: *Hoffmann v South African Airways*.

36 References to the UNCRPD illustrate reliance on an instrument of a universal scope with a categorical focus on persons with disabilities. References to CoE instruments provide examples of importing instruments with a regional scope, focusing on various aspects ratione materiae (such as the CoE Parliamentary Assembly Recommendation of 2003 cited in *Glor v Switzerland*, above n 2 and Rec(2004)10 of the CoE Committee of Ministers cited in *M.S. v Croatia (No 2)*, above n 3).

37 See, for example, the reference to the UN Committee on Economic, Social and Cultural Rights in ECtHR, *I.B. v Greece*, above n 35, §84.

38 Instruments that are 'soft by nature' include instruments that never intended to establish binding provisions. For examples, see the references in *M.S. v Croatia (No 2)* to the UN Principles for the Protection of Persons with Mental Illness and for the Improvement of Mental Health Care of 1991, to a report of the European Committee for the Prevention of Torture and Inhuman of Degrading Treatment or Punishment (CPT) and to recommendations of the CoE.

the respondent State (and/or by other Member States).[39] Indeed, in *Demir and Baykara* the Court announced that when it searches for 'common ground among the norms of international law', 'it has never distinguished between sources of law according to whether or not they have been signed or ratified by the respondent State'[40] and that 'it is not necessary for the respondent State to have ratified the entire collection of instruments that are applicable in respect of the precise subject matter of the case concerned'.[41]

3. EXTERNAL REFERENCING FROM AN INTEGRATIVE PERSPECTIVE: MISSED OPPORTUNITIES

3.1. TOP-DOWN: CONVERGENCE OR DIVERGENCE?

3.1.1. Convergence

The abovementioned Strasbourg cases (*Glor*, *Stanev* and *M.S. (No 2)*) offer examples where the Court referred to external instruments in the 'law section'[42] of the judgment to interpret the ECHR in cases concerning persons with disabilities. On some occasions, the ECtHR cited external instruments to establish a consensus, a trend or a development (on a European or a worldwide scale). On other occasions, the ECtHR, without explicitly mentioning a consensus or a trend, invoked external instruments in support of its position. Although the Court did not make this plain in so many words, this illustrates a tendency to keep up with present-day developments and evolutions in the normative setting. The Court seems to strive for convergence.

This shows that some external instruments exercise a normative effect on the Court's reasoning.[43] They offer a persuasive support to the Court's arguments.[44]

39 For example, in the case of *Glor v Switzerand* (above n 2), the Court used the UNCRPD which had not yet entered into force and at a time Switzerland had not even signed it (it signed and ratified it long after the facts of the case occurred, namely on 15 April 2014). For other examples of cases using non-binding instruments, see *Demir and Baykara v Turkey*, above n 8, §§62, 76, 103 and 149.

40 Ibid, §78.

41 Ibid, §§85–86.

42 The Strasbourg Court generally divides its judgments into two parts: one concerning the 'facts' and the other concerning the 'law'. It is under the latter part that the Court develops its legal reasoning. In this chapter, we refer to both different parts as the 'facts' section and the 'law' section.

43 I Hachez, 'Balises conceptuelles autour des notions de "source du droit", "force normative" et "soft law"' (2010) 65 *Revue interdisciplinaire d'études juridiques* 1, 17–20. Thibierge issued a collective work on the notion of 'normative force'; see C Thibierge et al., *La force normative. Naissance d'un concept*, Bruylant, LGDJ, Brussels 2009, p 891.

44 On 'persuasive authority', see P Glenn, 'Persuasive Authority' (1987) 32 *McGill Law Journal* 263; and F Schauer, 'Authority and Authorities' (2008) 94 *Virginia Law Review* 1931.

At the same time, their use narrows the gap between the ECHR and other rules and standards within the normative context. At the level of the legal architecture, this leads to a harmonisation process. From a top-down perspective, the references thus reflect a coordinative integrative approach, in the sense of stimulating the integration of diverse instruments into a more coherent whole.[45] Such a rapprochement softens concerns that are often associated with the 'fragmentation' of international law, to the benefit of legal certainty.[46]

3.1.2. Divergence

In some cases, the ECtHR does not cite external instruments or refers to them in a dismissive manner, meaning that it considers them in contrast to the ECHR.[47] Dismissive references demonstrate that a comprehensive approach to the external normative context does not necessarily imply a coordinative approach, but might maintain (or even increase) divergences to the detriment of harmonisation.

While external instruments can be contrasted with the ECHR for argumentation purposes, it results in a lack of clarity when the ECtHR simply ignores them. For instance, it happens that the Court cites an external instrument under the 'facts section' of the case, but does not take it into account in the 'law section'. This confusing phenomenon can be illustrated by two Strasbourg

---

See also J Allard and L van den Eynde, 'Le Dialogue des Juges comme Source de Droit: Arguments entre Idéalisation et Scepticisme' in I Hachez, Y Cartuyvels, H Dumont, P Gérard, F Ost and M van de Kerchove (eds), *Les Sources du Droit revisitées. Volume 3: Normativités concurrentes*, Publications de l'Université Saint-Louis, Brussels 2013, p 287.

45 The 'coordinative model' reflects one of the models of integration. For an overview of three theoretical models of human rights integration ('hierarchy', 'coordination' and 'conflict') inspired by global law theories, see M Baumgärtel, D Staes and FJ Mena Parras, 'Hierarchy, Coordination or Conflict? Global Law Theories and the Question of Human Rights Integration' (2014) 3 *European Journal of Human Rights* 326.

46 Concerns associated with fragmentation are the presence of incoherent, overlapping or contradictory standards, case law and institutional competences. See the Study Group of the International Law Commission, 'Fragmentation of International Law: Difficulties Arising from the Diversification and Expansion of International Law', report finalised by Martti Koskenniemi, UN Doc A/CN.4/L.682 (13 April 2006).

47 Cf. M Rosenfeld, 'Constitutional Migration and the Bounds of Comparative Analysis' (2001) 58 *NYU Annual Survey of American Law* 70. On 'dismissive uses', see D Staes, above n 8, Part II, Chapter 3, §1. Sometimes, the Court even builds its conclusions on a reading of a source that clearly runs afoul of the rationale of this source. See in this respect *R.P. v United Kingdom*, no 38245/08, ECHR 2012; and the comment by L Series, 'Legal Capacity and Participation in Litigation: Recent Developments in the European Court of Human Rights' in L Waddington, G Quinn and E Flynn (eds), *European Yearbook of Disability Law*, Volume 5, Intersentia, 2014, 542, pp 123–124. Here, the ECtHR endorsed the role of litigation guardians as substituted decision-makers for persons deprived of capacity to litigate, which has been clearly rejected by the UNCRPD Committee.

cases, one dealing with deprivation of legal capacity (*Ivinović v Croatia*)[48] and the other with deprivation of liberty (*M.S. v Croatia (No 2)*).[49] In these cases, the Strasbourg Court, although it cites Article 12 of the UNCRPD (on equal recognition before the law) and Article 14 of the UNCRPD (on deprivation of liberty), ignores some major aspects of these provisions.

3.1.2.1. Missed Opportunities with Regard to Legal Capacity

The case of *Ivinović v Croatia* is one of a long series of cases brought to the Court concerning the deprivation of legal capacity.[50] Deprivation of legal capacity means, first, deprivation of the right to be recognised as a person before the law and to be a holder of rights, and, second, the right to be a 'legal agent' whose decisions are respected and validated by the law.[51] *Ivinović v Croatia* illustrates that the deprivation of one's legal capacity is a particularly disadvantageous measure as it hinders or makes impossible the exercise of other rights. In casu, the deprivation of legal capacity prevented the applicant from accessing her money and other assets and restricted her from making decisions about her medical treatment. The case further illustrates that deprivation of legal capacity primarily impacts persons with (certain) disabilities.[52] Indeed, as the Croatian authorities admitted before the ECtHR, the decision to deprive Mrs Ivinović of her legal capacity was based on her 'illness'[53] and the fact that she had incurred significant debts. Depriving an individual of legal capacity on those accumulated grounds (illness and financial position) reflects what is often called 'the outcome approach',[54] which is based on the idea that a person

---

48 *Ivinović v Croatia*, above n 5.

49 *M.S. v Croatia (No 2)*, above n 3.

50 For other cases on this issue, see ECtHR, *Alajos and Kiss v Hungary*, no 38832/06, ECHR 2010; *Lashin v Russia*, no 33117/02, ECHR 2013.

51 This understanding of 'legal capacity' is endorsed by the Office of the United Nations High Commissioner of Human Rights (see Office of the United Nations High Commissioner of Human Rights, 'Legal Capacity', Background Conference Document for the Sixth Session of the Ad Hoc Committee on a Comprehensive and Integral International Convention on Protection and Promotion of the Rights and Dignity of Persons with Disabilities, 1–12 August 2005) and by several scholars (see, inter alia, E Flynn and A Arstein-Kerslake, above n 17, 124, with further references; A Dhanda, 'Legal Capacity in the Disability Rights Convention: Stranglehold of the Past or Lodestar for the Future?' (2007) 34 *Syracuse Journal of International Law and Commerce* 429).

52 E Flynn and A Arstein-Kerslake, above n 17, 125, saying that this particularly holds true for persons diagnosed with cognitive disabilities.

53 See *Ivinović v Croatia*, above n 5, §§15 and 33.

54 See, on this approach, Centre for Disability Law and Policy at NUI Galway, 'Submission on Legal Capacity', prepared for the Oireachtas Committee on Justice (2011) Defence & Equality, 10, http://www.nuigalway.ie/cdlp/documents/cdlp_submission_on_legal_capacity_the_oireachtas_committee_on_justice_defence_and_equality_.pdf (accessed 30 June 2017); A Dhanda, above n 51, 431–432.

should 'lose the right to continue to make decisions'[55] when he or she makes poor ones. Typically, as was the case for Mrs Ivinović, the persons concerned are brought under guardianship, trusteeship or similar mechanisms and their legal capacity is exercised by a third party without their consent.

While the ECtHR in *Ivinović* found a violation of Article 8 of the ECHR (the right to private life and family life) by building its reasoning on the procedural shortcomings in respect of the deprivation of the applicant's legal capacity,[56] it ignored the principles flowing from Article 12 of the UNCRPD, a provision which is mentioned under the 'facts section' of the judgment.[57] Article 12 of the UNCRPD operates as a fundamental safeguard against unjust acts leading to a deprivation of legal capacity and it expressly affirms that 'persons with disabilities enjoy legal capacity on an equal basis with others in all aspects of life'. The 'outcome approach', as adopted by the national authorities, runs counter to Article 12 of the UNCRPD as this approach 'sets the decision-making bar higher for persons with disabilities',[58] while other persons' 'right to gain experience and to make mistakes is taken for granted'.[59] Article 12 of the UNCRPD does not ignore that some persons may have decision-making deficiencies. However, the provision requires States to take appropriate measures for persons with decision-making deficits 'to provide access … to the support they may require in exercising their legal capacity'. As made clear by the UNCRPD Committee in various reports on States parties, Article 12 of the UNCRPD calls for replacing the substitution of the person through guardianship-like mechanisms by supported decision-making mechanisms.[60] In a General Comment on Article 12 of the UNCRPD, adopted before the *Ivinović* judgment was delivered, the same Committee identified several forms of 'support', such as assistance for certain types of decisions, peer support, advocacy or assistance with communication.[61] In any case, the support mechanism is

---

55 G Quinn, 'Personhood & Legal Capacity Perspectives on the Paradigm Shift of Article 12 CRPD', *HDOP Conference Harvard Law School*, 20 February 2010, http://www.nuigalway.ie/cdlp/staff/gerard_quinn.html (accessed 30 June 2017).

56 See *Ivinović v Croatia*, above n 5, §46: 'national courts, in depriving partially the applicant of her legal capacity, did not follow a procedure which could be said to be in conformity with the guarantees under Article 8 of the Convention'. See for the same remark V David, '*Ivinović v Croatia*: Legal Capacity and the (Missing) Call for Supportive Decision-Making', 23 October 2014, http://strasbourgobservers.com/2014/10/23/ivinovic-v-croatia-legal-capacity-and-the-missing-call-for-supportive-decision-making (accessed 30 June 2017).

57 *Ivinović v Croatia*, above n 5, §21.

58 G Quinn, above n 55.

59 Centre for Disability Law and Policy at NUI Galway, above n 54, 25.

60 See e.g. CRPD Committee, Consideration of reports submitted by States parties under Article 35 of the Convention, Concluding observations of the Committee on the Rights of Persons with Disabilities on Tunisia, Fifth Session, 11–15 April 2011, CRPD/C/TUN/CO/1.

61 UN Committee on the Rights of Persons with Disabilities, 'General Comment No. 1 on Article 12: Equal recognition before the law', 11 April 2014, §17. Note that several scholars

meant to facilitate the exercise of legal capacity and not to supplant the person in need of assistance.[62]

Ivinović represents a missed opportunity with regard to both the abolition of the 'outcome approach', which justifies deprivation of legal capacity based on a disability, and the shift from substituted to supported decision-making.[63] While the ECtHR cited Article 12 of the UNCRPD under the 'facts section' of the case, it did not take this provision genuinely into account when interpreting Article 8 of the ECHR. Indeed, the ECtHR did not call into question the link between disability and deprivation of legal capacity. Hence, to the detriment of convergence between the ECHR and the UNCRPD, the Court's judgment focused only on procedural shortcomings and not on concerns inherent to the 'outcome approach'. Furthermore, no attention was paid to replacing substituted decision-making with supported decision-making, despite the fact that the third-party interveners specifically referred to the findings of the UNCRPD Committee in this respect.[64] The ECtHR thereby left unchallenged measures which, in our understanding, run counter to Article 12 of the UNCRPD. This is particularly regrettable, since the case of *Ivinović* – due to the reference to and thus the Court's awareness of Article 12 of the UNCRPD – could have been an excellent opportunity to tackle such measures.

3.1.2.2. Missed Opportunities with Regard to Deprivation of Liberty

Another missed opportunity for integrating principles of the UNCRPD touches upon the deprivation of liberty of persons diagnosed to have intellectual or psychosocial impairments (or other labels such as 'mental disorder'). In *M.S. v Croatia (No 2)*, the applicant, who initially visited a doctor because of persistent back pain, was sent to a hospital emergency service where she was

---

have identified concrete examples of supported decision-making measures established by some States or States regions. See, inter alia, Centre for Disability Law and Policy at NUI Galway, above n 54, 37–38; M Bach and L Kerzner, *A New Paradigm for Protecting Autonomy and the Right to Legal Capacity: Advancing Substantive Equality for Persons with Disabilities through Law, Policy and Practice, Commissioned by the Law Commission of Ontario*, October 2010, https://www.lco-cdo.org/wp-content/uploads/2010/11/disabilities-commissioned-paper-bach-kerzner.pdf (accessed 30 June 2017); P Gooding, 'Supported Decision-Making: A Rights-Based Disability Concept and its Implications for Mental Health Law' (2012) 20 *Psychiatry, Psychology and Law* 431.

62 In some cases, less restrictive support mechanisms may fail. It is only then that substituted decision-making mechanisms may be accepted (as a last resort measure) through 'Co-Decision-Making' and 'Facilitated Decision-Making'. For detailed information on these mechanisms, see Centre for Disability Law and Policy at NUI Galway, above n 54, 35–36.

63 See also V David, above n 56.

64 *Ivinović v Croatia*, above n 5, §34, ECHR 2014. See the third party submission of PERSON Project and Mental Health Europe (2013), http://www.nuigalway.ie/cdlp/documents/2013%2007%2005%20Ivinovic%20v%20Croatia.pdf (accessed 30 June 2017).

involuntarily hospitalised after being diagnosed by a psychiatrist as having 'acute psychotic disorder, systemic delusional disorder and delusional dysmorphic disorder'.[65] Among other questions, the Court was asked whether the involuntary admission to the psychiatric hospital (where she was confined for one month) amounted to a violation of Article 5(1)(e) of the ECHR. This provision allows the 'lawful detention of persons … of "unsound mind"'.

According to the well-established ECtHR case law,[66] there are three criteria which must be met in order for the deprivation of liberty of persons of 'unsound mind' to be legal (known as the 'Winterwerp criteria'): (i) the concerned individual must be reasonably shown by an objective medical expert to be of unsound mind; (ii) the mental disorder must be of a kind or degree warranting compulsory confinement; and (iii) the validity of continued confinement depends on the persistence of such a disorder.[67] With respect to persons of 'unsound mind', the deprivation of liberty can take various forms, such as involuntary admission in a psychiatric hospital (as was the case in *M.S. v Croatia (No 2)*) or placement in a social care institution for people with mental disorders (often referred to as 'long-term institutionalisation').[68] It is important to note that the deprivation of liberty is not based on any conviction for a criminal offence.[69] Rather, States tend to rely on other justifications such as the need for 'health care' (as in *M.S. v Croatia (No 2)*) or 'perceived dangerousness', as we will discuss further below.[70]

The approach followed under Article 5(1)(e) of the ECHR is challenged by Article 14 of the UNCRPD, which is quoted under 'Relevant international material' in the 'facts section' of *M.S. v Croatia (No 2)*.[71] Fennell and Khaliq went as far as to assert that the ECHR and the UNCRPD provisions are based on 'opposite premises'.[72] On the one hand, Article 14 of the UNCRPD states

---

65 *M.S. v Croatia (No 2)*, above n 3, §13.

66 *Winterwerp v The Netherlands*, no 6301/73, ECHR 1979.

67 These criteria are recalled in *M.S. v Croatia (No 2)*, above n 3, §143.

68 Based on an understanding of 'institution' shared by the CoE, the UN and civil society organisations, the Open Society Foundations defines the term as 'long-stay residential facilities that segregate and confine people with mental, intellectual, and physical disabilities' that are 'characterized by a regimented culture'; see Open Society Foundations, above n 17, 17.

69 L Gostin and L Gable, 'The Human Rights of Persons with Mental Disabilities: A Global Perspective on the Application of Human Rights Principles to Mental Health' (2004) 63 *Maryland Law Review* 20, 63.

70 See, for example, *Hutchinson Reid v United Kingdom*, no 50272/99, §52, ECHR 2003: 'confinement may be necessary not only where a person needs therapy, medication or other clinical treatment to cure or alleviate his condition, but also where the person needs control and supervision to prevent him, for example, causing harm to himself or other persons'.

71 Ibid, §46.

72 P Fennell and U Khaliq, 'Conflicting or Complementary Obligations? The UN Disability Rights Convention, the European Convention on Human Rights and English Law' (2011) 6 *European Human Rights Law Review* 662, 674 et seq.

that 'the existence of a disability shall in no case justify a deprivation of liberty', which has been qualified by the UNCRPD Committee as a non-discrimination provision.[73] The prohibition of deprivation of liberty based on disability encompasses a prohibition of detention on the basis of 'impairment'.[74] On the other hand, Article 5(1)(e) of the ECHR authorises a deprivation of liberty of persons of 'unsound mind', which amounts to allowing deprivation of liberty based on impairment.[75] While the concept of 'unsound mind' has not been defined by the ECtHR,[76] it associated 'unsound mind' with mental disorder and it has considered various mental illnesses, such as paranoid schizophrenia[77] or psychotic disorder, to fall within this category.[78] The approach under Article 5(1)(e) of the ECHR, contrary to Article 14 of the UNCRPD, thus allows detention based on the diagnosis of a particular impairment. Admittedly, the ECtHR requires that the mental disorder must be of a kind or degree warranting compulsory confinement (meaning serious mental disorders). Still, the Court's approach is based on the diagnosis of an impairment, which is intrinsically discriminatory. This clearly contrasts with the approach under Article 14 of the UNCRPD.

Interestingly, in *M.S. v Croatia (No 2)*, the Court referred (in the 'facts section') to the UNCRPD Committee's concluding observations under Article 14 of the UNCRPD,[79] where the Committee, addressing Austrian legislation, found that 'the legislation was in conflict with Article 14 of the Convention [UNCRPD] because it allows a person to be deprived of liberty

---

73 See e.g. CRPD/C/AUT/CO/1, 13 September 2013, §§29–30; CRPD/C/CZE/CO/1, 15 May 2015, §§26–28 and UNCRPD Committee guidelines on Article 14 of the Convention on the Rights of Persons with Disabilities, The right to liberty and security of persons with disabilities, adopted during the Committee's 14th session, September 2015, available at: http://www.ohchr.org/EN/HRBodies/CRPD/Pages/CRPDIndex.aspx (accessed 1 July 2017) (hereinafter 'UNCRPD Guidelines').

74 Broadly defined as 'a physical, psycho-social, intellectual or sensory personal condition'; see UNCRDP Guidelines §6, note 1.

75 See in the same direction, P Fennell and U Khaliq, above n 72, 665.

76 The Court held in several cases that the term 'persons of unsound mind' 'does not lend itself to precise definition since its meaning is continually evolving as research in psychiatry progresses'; see e.g. *Winterwerp v The Netherlands*, above n 66, §37; and *Rakevich v Russia*, no 58973/00, §26, ECHR 2003.

77 *DD v Lithuania*, no 13469/06, ECHR 2012.

78 Ibid, §§62–63.

79 As far as we could ascertain, this is the first time that the ECtHR referred to the UNCRPD Committee practice in the part of the judgment not devoted to parties or third-party argumentation (finding based on a search in the 'Hudoc' database with the keyword 'Committee on the Rights of Persons with Disabilities' in the field 'Text'). For subsequent references to this Committee practice in the 'international relevant materials' section, see *Guberina v Croatia*, no 23682/13, ECHR 2016; and *A.-M.V. v Finland*, no 53251/13, ECHR 2017. For references to UNCRPD practice in the part of the judgment devoted to third-party interveners' argumentations, see *Mihailovs v Latvia*, no 35939/10, ECHR 2013. For similar references in a concurring or dissenting opinion, see *Kuttner v Austria*, no 7997/08, ECHR 2015.

on the basis of actual or perceived disability'.[80] However, no further use of the UNCRPD Committee findings was made in the ECtHR's legal reasoning (under the 'law section'). The Court found a violation of the ECHR by confining the ruling to procedural shortcomings; it highlighted that when the applicant challenged her involuntary internment, she did not have the opportunity to be heard before a court.[81] The ECtHR held that the 'procedural failures obviate the need for the court to examine whether national authorities met the substantive requirement for the applicant's involuntary hospitalization by proving that her mental condition had necessitated the deprivation of her liberty'.[82] Thus, while the Court focused on procedural shortcomings, it avoided a substantive examination of Article 5(1)(e) in the light of Article 14 of the UNCRPD, which might call into question the allowance of a deprivation of liberty on the grounds of a mental disorder. On the contrary, by stating that there was no need to prove that the mental condition had necessitated the deprivation of her liberty, the ECtHR suggested that a mental condition may justify the deprivation of liberty. It thereby stayed close to the text of Article 5 of the ECHR referring to 'unsound mind'.

The lack of a substantial examination reflects a missed opportunity to recognise the discriminatory nature of deprivation of liberty on the basis of the diagnosis of an impairment. In a separate opinion in the case of *Kuttner v Austria*,[83] delivered some months after the *M.S. v Croatia (No 2)* judgment, Judge Pinto de Albuquerque took the opportunity to recognise the discriminatory nature of 'disability-based arrest, detention or imprisonment' and stated that these forms of deprivation of liberty are 'in breach of Article 14, §1 (b) of the UNCRPD'. Interestingly, the judge strongly relied on the UNCRPD's practice to support his statement. As far as we know, this has been the clearest statement made by a judge of the ECtHR linking the prohibition of discrimination to the deprivation of liberty based on disability. While Judge Pinto de Albuquerque stressed the discriminatory nature under Article 14 of the UNCRPD, one might argue that the same reasoning should be attached to Article 14 of the ECHR (prohibition of discrimination).

Creating more convergence between the ECHR and the UNCRPD with respect to the issue of deprivation of liberty of persons with disabilities would nonetheless be a difficult and complex undertaking.

---

80 *M.S. v Croatia (No 2)*, above n 3, §48, quoting the CRPD Committee Concluding observations on the initial report of Austria CRPD/C/AUT/1 (2–13 September 2013).

81 See *M.S. v Croatia (No 2)*, above n 3, §§157–159. In this respect, the Court made explicit reference to Article 13 of the UNCRPD, which obliges States parties to ensure access to justice for persons with disabilities.

82 Ibid, §161.

83 Partly concurring and partly dissenting opinion of Judge Pinto de Albuquerque in *Kuttner v Austria*, above n 79. The case as decided by the majority was strictly focused on the procedural safeguards in relation to the deprivation of liberty.

First, as might be clear by now, there is a different approach under the ECHR and the UNCRPD. Admittedly, this is not necessarily a problem. The UNCRPD offers greater protection to persons with a disability, which is allowed under and respected by the 'human rights safeguard' enshrined in Article 53 of the Convention.[84] However, if the Court were willing to integrate the UN approach and adapt to the higher standard that it offers, this would run counter to the wording of Article 5(1)(e) of the ECHR, allowing deprivation of liberty of persons of 'unsound mind'. Would the Court, inspired by the UNCRPD, ever be willing and allowed to interpret away the text of the Convention? This is challenging from an international law perspective, particularly because not all the CoE Member States have ratified the UNCRPD. Nonetheless, previous Strasbourg case law shows that such an option is not entirely unimaginable.[85]

Second, even when deprivation of liberty on the basis of disability is considered to interfere with the prohibition on discrimination, it is possible that it is still justified under other articles of the Convention, such as Article 2 on the right to life. Indeed, it is important to bear in mind that some impairment might be perceived as dangerous to the concerned individual (e.g. the most extreme situation being the risk of committing suicide) or to others (e.g. risk of

84 Article 53 of the ECHR provides that: 'Nothing in this Convention shall be construed as limiting or derogating from any of the human rights and fundamental freedoms which may be ensured under the laws of any High Contracting Party or under any other agreement to which it is a party.' This article implies that national authorities, for instance by ratifying another treaty, are allowed to offer higher protection standards. It offers a human rights safeguard, which prevents conflicts between human rights provisions and interpretations. See G Rosoux, *Vers une 'dématerialisation' des droits fondamentaux? Convergence des droits fondamentaux dans une protection fragmentée, à la lumière du raisonnement du juge constitutionnel belge*, Bruylant, Brussels 2015, pp 516 et seq. Some authors argue that the Court could apply Article 53 of the ECHR to evolve its case law when (ratified) external instruments offer higher protection standards. See E Brems, above n 13, 465–466; D Staes, above n 8, 257–278. Authors like Fennell and Khaliq stress that the priority rule – as enshrined in Article 53 of the ECHR – only applies when an external instrument is ratified by all the Member States of the ECHR, which is not the case with regard to the UNCRPD. See P Fennell and U Khaliq, above n 72, 670 et seq.

85 Remember that in *Schalk and Kopf v Austria*, the Strasbourg Court, when interpreting Article 13 of the ECHR providing that '*Men and women* of marriageable age have the right to marry and to found a family, according to the national laws governing the exercise of this right (emphasis added)', says: 'Regard being had to Article 9 of the Charter (of fundamental rights of the EU), therefore, the Court would no longer consider that the right to marry enshrined in Article 12 must in all circumstances be limited to marriage between *two persons of the opposite sex*. Consequently, it cannot be said that Article 12 is inapplicable to the applicants' complaint. However, as matters stand, the question whether or not to allow same-sex marriage is left to regulation by the national law of the Contracting State' (emphasis added) (*Schalk and Kopf v Austria*, no 30141/04, §61, ECHR 2010). Thanks to Constantin Cojocariu for drawing our attention to this case.

sexual offences or murder).[86] Both 'health care' and 'perceived dangerousness' might be considered as 'legitimate aims' justifying a difference in treatment under Article 14 of the ECHR. However, as long as the measure remains linked to the existence of a disability, there would be a 'divergence' between the ECHR and the UNCRPD, especially because the UNCRPD Committee says that Article 14 of the UNCRPD prohibits a deprivation of liberty based solely on a disability, but also based on the combination between a disability and 'health care' or 'perceived dangerousness'.[87] The UNCRPD Committee's rationale runs counter to that of the ECtHR, which tends to give discretion to clinical judgement made by psychiatrists on whether an individual poses a particular threat to himself or herself or others.[88]

We conclude by recalling that in the normative context, there is a 'cacophony'[89] of instruments concerning persons with disabilities. The interpretation of the ECHR is influenced by references to the practice of other institutions on the protection of persons with disabilities, which reduces the isolation in which normative instruments operate and leads to more convergence. However, this tendency is not consistently observed within the Court's decision-making process. Sometimes the Court does not (fully) integrate external instruments and divergences persist or are created. After these observations, which focus on the impact of external references on the relationship between different instruments, we will now look at the issue through the lens of the human rights user – in casu, the person with a disability.

---

86 Some authors noticed that deprivation of liberty could be necessitated (and not only allowed) in order to protect the right to life (either to prevent the concerned individual from committing suicide or doing harm to others) enshrined in Article 2 of the ECHR. See P Fennell and U Khaliq, above n 72, 666.

87 See CRPD Committee,'Guidelines on article 14 of the Convention on the Rights of Persons with Disabilities, The right to liberty and security of persons with disabilities', adopted during the Committee's 14th session, held in September 2015, §13. See, for the same position, Office of the High Commissioner of Human Rights and the Secretary General, 'Thematic Study on Enhancing Awareness and Understanding of the Convention on the Rights of Persons with Disabilities', UN Doc A/HRC/10/48 (26 January 2009), §48. First, the need of therapy, medication or other clinical treatment to cure or alleviate the condition of the concerned individual has been clearly rejected by the UNCRPD Committee as a ground for deprivation of liberty, which stated that 'involuntary commitment in mental health facilities carries with it the denial of the person's legal capacity to decide about care, treatment, and admission to a hospital or institution, and therefore violates article 12 in conjunction with article 14' (CRPD Guidelines, §15). The Committee also rejected the involuntary detention of persons with disabilities based on risk or dangerousness 'tied to impairment or health diagnosis' (ibid, §§13–15). While the Committee recalled that 'all persons, including those with disabilities, have a duty to do no harm', it stressed that 'decisions about medical and psychiatric treatment must be based on the free and informed consent of the person concerned and respect the person's autonomy, will and preferences' (ibid, §15).

88 P Fennell and U Khaliq, above n 72, 674.

89 A notion taken from E Brems, above n 13, 451.

3.2. BOTTOM-UP: AN INTEGRATED VIEW ON DISABLED PERSONS?

The following section starts from a bottom-up view on integration. More particularly, it focuses on how external references might serve to promote an integrative view of rights holders (in casu, persons with disabilities) from within a user-centric approach.[90] An integrative perspective takes all (aspects of) relevant human rights norms and claims into account simultaneously.[91] It ensures due respect to the identity and lived experience of persons with a disability.[92] An integrative approach, inter alia, takes account of the particular situation, needs and characteristics of disabled persons, higher standards of protection and rights holders' procedural satisfaction.[93] This section elaborates on the latter issues using examples of Strasbourg cases to both illustrate an integrative approach and demonstrate missed opportunities in this respect.[94]

3.2.1. *Taking Account of the Specific Situation, Needs and Characteristics of Disabled Persons*

An integrative view on persons with disabilities requires a full consideration of the particular situation and multifaceted identity and experiences of disabled persons.[95] The method of interpretation should therefore consider instruments which specifically deal with disabled persons, with the precise circumstances that these persons may face (such as employment relations, detention because of mental illness and so on) or with the social, economic and cultural aspects of their situation.

---

90 For more information on a users' approach, see E Desmet, above n 12, 111–120.

91 E Brems, above n 13, 456 and 458, considering the referencing to external instruments to be the expression of an integrated view on the part of the judges. According to Brems, the principles of universality, indivisibility and inter-dependence plead in favour of such an integrated approach. See ibid, 454.

92 Brems interestingly says the following about human rights integration in the light of doing justice to the lived experience: 'Another consideration from the viewpoint of rights holders is that an integrated human rights perspective may do better justice to the lived experience of those who undergo human rights violations. This is because an integrated approach allows dealing with the issue as a whole, instead of artificially lifting out one aspect or cutting the matter up in several issues to be evaluated separately. This plays out in at least three dimensions: the integration of the general and the specific (a), intersectionality (b) and indivisibility/interdependence (c).' See ibid, 465. These three dimensions have inspired this chapter.

93 Also, Brems considers human rights integration from the perspective of the rights holders, which, in her view, includes giving priority to the highest protection and doing justice to the lived experiences; see ibid, 464 et seq.

94 Brems alludes to missed opportunities too. She stresses that the development of an integrated view on the rights holders is far from complete and that therefore the total experience of the rights holders is still often ignored in Strasbourg cases. See ibid, 454 and 468 et seq.

95 Ibid, 452 and 455.

3.2.1.1. Specialised Human Rights Instruments

Brems draws attention to the importance of considering rights holders' 'different specific characteristics that have been recognized as relevant by international human rights law and that therefore affect their human rights claims' and stresses that an 'integrated human rights perspective requires attention to such differences, in particular by making appropriate reference to specialised human rights provisions that may be relevant for only some of the affected persons'.[96] An example of a case referring to specialised human rights instruments which reflect a particular field of expertise is *M.S. v Croatia (No 2)*. In this case, the Court cited instruments addressing persons with a disability, or more precisely, persons suffering from mental illness.[97] The Court thereby refined its perspective so as to take account of the particular kind of disability from which the person suffers and the particular concerns and needs this disability brings. However, as stressed above, the ECtHR also missed opportunities in the *M.S.* case by not fully capturing some substantive approaches of the specialised UNCRPD and its monitoring Committee.[98]

Considering more specific instruments can also help to identify States' precise obligations towards persons with disabilities. For instance, an integrative approach, which requires a comprehensive assessment of the problems persons with disabilities typically face, might encourage a State to avoid and prevent stereotyping.[99] Here, the Court could make use of the UNCRPD, an instrument containing a specific provision on the issue of stereotyping.[100] The 'social model of disability'[101] is particularly relevant in this context as it recognises that disability can be the result of socially created barriers, such as negative reactions (e.g. in the form of stereotypes) to a specific impairment.[102]

---

96 Ibid, 460–461 and 465.

97 See, for instance, the reference to the UNCRPD (§157) and to the MI Principles (§105 and 154) in *M.S. v Croatia (No 2)*, above n 3.

98 Ibid, §47.

99 In relation to the fight against discrimination against women, the Court argued the importance of combating stereotypes with reference to the UN Convention on the Elimination of All Forms of Discrimination against Women; see ECtHR, *Konstantin Markin v Russia*, no 30078/06, 22 March 2012, §§49 and 140.

100 Article 8, §1(b) of the UNCRPD provides that 'State Parties undertake to adopt immediate, effective and appropriate measures ... to combat stereotypes, prejudices and harmful practices relating to persons with disabilities, including those based on sex and age, in all areas of life'.

101 On the development of this model, see, *inter alia*, M Oliver, *Understanding Disability: From Theory to Practice*, St. Martin's Press, New York 1996, pp 31–32.

102 See, inter alia, C Barnes, 'The Social Model of Disability: A Sociological Phenomenon Ignored by Sociologists' in T Shakespeare (ed), *The Disability Reader: Social Science Perspectives*, Continuum, London 1998, pp 65–78; M Crossley, 'The Disability Kaleidoscope' (1999) *74 Notre Dame Law Review* 621–716 (especially at 633); and L Waddington, 'Saying All the Right Things and Still Getting it Wrong: The Court of Justice's Definition of Disability and Non-discrimination Law' (2015) 22 *Maastricht Journal of European and Comparative Law* 576, 587.

The ECtHR seemed to embrace the social model in *Kiyutin v Russia*.[103] This case dealt with the refusal of Russian authorities to grant a residence permit because of an HIV-positive status. In its arguments, the Court referred to instruments which aim to combat the negative stereotyping of persons with HIV (for instance, the UN Declaration of Commitment on HIV/AIDS).[104] These external instruments supported the Court's finding that persons with HIV 'are a vulnerable group with a history of prejudice and stigmatisation and that the State should be afforded only a narrow margin of appreciation in choosing measures that single out this group for differential treatment on the basis of their HIV status'.[105]

I.B v Greece, which concerned the dismissal of a person with HIV, is another welcome development regarding a State's obligation to combat stereotypes. Indeed, the Court held in this case that persons with HIV 'have to face up to a whole host of problems … and above all to sometimes deeply rooted prejudices even among the most highly educated people'.[106] At the same time, the case missed the opportunity to use external instruments to promote 'reasonable accommodation'.[107] The latter concept requires positive steps by means of modification or adjustment of a particular rule or measure to accommodate the impairment. The rationale of this concept is that failure to accommodate can result in denying an individual equal opportunity.[108] The issue of 'reasonable accommodation' was not raised in *I.B. v Greece*.[109] Nonetheless, the case would have been a good opportunity for third parties to raise the issue and inspire the Court to recognise, as the UNCRPD does, that persons with disabilities have the right to reasonable accommodation, even in their relations with private employers.[110]

The opportunity to integrate the concept of reasonable accommodation into the interpretation of the ECHR was embraced in the context of education in

---

103 ECtHR, *Kiyutin v Russia*, no 2700/10, ECHR 2011.

104 United Nations, General Assembly, Declaration of Commitment on HIV/AIDS, 27 June 2001, A/RES/S-26/2. See *Kiyutin v Russia*, above n 103, §64.

105 Ibid.

106 *I.B. v Greece*, above n 35, §80. See also A Timmer, 'HIV-Based Employment Discrimination: The ECtHR Takes a Strong Stance in *I.B. v Greece*', 21 October 2013, https://strasbourgobservers.com/2013/10/21/hiv-based-employment-discrimination-the-ecthr-takes-a-strong-stance-in-i-b-v-greece (accessed 30 June 2017).

107 See UNCRPD, Article 2. See also A Timmer, above n 106.

108 L Waddington, 'Reasonable Accommodation: Time to Extend the Duty to Accommodate beyond Disability?' (2011) 36 *NTM/NJCM-Bulletin* 186, 187.

109 However, see the reference to a judgment delivered by the Supreme Court of South Africa dealing with this concept and imported in the 'facts' section of judgment in *I.B. v Greece*, above n 35, §§36–38.

110 For a UNCRPD Committee communication where the UNCRPD was applied (here, Article 9 on accessibility) in a case originating in a dispute between two private parties (a bank and some of the bank clients), see UNCRPD, *Nyusti and Takács v Hungary*, Communication no 1/2010, Views adopted on 16 April 2013.

Çam v Turkey.[111] In this case, the applicant, who is blind, challenged a music academy's refusal to enrol her under Article 14 of the ECHR (prohibition of discrimination) in conjunction with Article 2 of Protocol No 1 of the ECHR (the right to education). The Court argued that the applicant's blindness was the sole reason for refusing her enrolment and that Turkey's justification for this – that the music academy lacked appropriate infrastructures to admit students with disabilities – was not acceptable.[112] The Court supported its arguments with references to external instruments, including the UNCRPD, which provide a duty of 'reasonable accommodation'.[113] The essence of this concept is to oblige the duty bearer to undertake the necessary and appropriate modifications and adjustments. Therefore, Member States cannot simply rely on the lack of adaptation of their educational facilities to justify a refusal to enrol students with disabilities; on the contrary, they are bound to make the necessary changes. The reference to the UNCRPD enriched the content of Article 14 ECHR as the UN instrument states that 'discrimination on grounds of disability also covers refusal to make reasonable accommodation'.[114] As far as we can ascertain, this finding had never been expressed so clearly by the Strasbourg Court.

3.2.1.2. Integration of Rights of the 'Second Generation'

Another judicial technique that does justice to the specific circumstances and the lived experience of disabled persons is using external instruments which protect social, economic and cultural rights. An integrative view on persons with disabilities encourages such references as they might stimulate a comprehensive assessment of the rights holders' situation. The idea of the indivisibility and interdependence of all categories of human rights underlies such an integrative (or inter-dependent)[115] approach.[116]

---

111 *Çam v Turkey*, no 51500/08, ECHR 2016.

112 Ibid, §63.

113 In this vein, it refers to Article 2 of the UNCRPD, which defines the concept as follows: 'necessary and appropriate modification and adjustments not imposing a disproportionate or undue burden, where needed in a particular case, to ensure to persons with disabilities the enjoyment or exercise on an equal basis with others of all human rights and fundamental freedoms'. See ibid, §65.

114 Ibid, §67.

115 The ECHR and its Protocols, with some exceptions, mainly focus on civil and political rights. An important Strasbourg case integrating the interpretation of civil and political rights with the interpretation of economic, social and cultural rights is *Sidabras and Dziautas v Lithuania*, nos 55480/00 and 59330/00, ECHR 2004. For a summary of this case, see V Mantouvalou, 'Work and Private Life: *Sidabras and Dziautas v Lithuania*' (2005) 30 *European Law Review* 573. An integrative approach in a sense of integrating different generations of human rights is sometimes addressed by the notion of 'interdependent approach'. See S Alemahu Yeshanew, *The Justiciability of Economic, Social and Cultural Rights in the African Regional Human Rights System. Theory, Practice and Prospect*, Intersentia, Cambridge 2013, pp 299–321.

116 The categorisation of these rights in 'generations' is in itself controversial as it alludes to economic, social and cultural rights having a 'secondary' status (see ibid,

The case of *I.B. v Greece* on the protection of an HIV-positive employee against dismissal offers an example in this respect.[117] *I.B. v Greece* was inspired by instruments generally associated with 'second generation' rights, notably the General Comment of the UN Committee on Economic, Social and Cultural Rights (which states that the prohibition of discrimination includes health status, in particular HIV status)[118] and ILO Recommendation No 200 Concerning HIV and AIDS and the World of Work. These all touch upon 'health' and 'work' and were relied upon to conclude that provisions governing non-discrimination also grant protection to HIV-infected persons, including a prohibition on discrimination in employment. The case of *I.B. v Greece* implicitly demonstrated how including non-discrimination as an element of social and economic rights enhances the justiciability of such rights.[119]

The case of *Gherghina v Romania* represents a missed opportunity to explicitly include provisions touching upon socio-economic aspects of rights of persons with disabilities. This case concerned the physical inaccessibility of a university for a student in a wheelchair. The student argued that he was discriminated against in the exercise of his right to education under Article 14 of the ECHR in conjunction with Article 2 of Protocol No 1 of the ECHR. The ECtHR found the case inadmissible because of a failure to exhaust national remedies. In order to explain the absence of national case law on the accessibility of public buildings, it stressed that the 'evolutions under international law' were only 'recent'. Article 24 of the UNCRPD, which proclaims a right to inclusive education, was not taken into consideration.[120]

3.2.2. *Taking Account of Higher Protection Standards*

From the perspective of persons with disabilities, it is beneficial that the ECtHR takes account of and gives priority to external instruments when these

---

S Alemahu Yeshanew, pp 300–301). The principles of indivisibility, inter-dependence and inter-relatedness of human rights call for a unified understanding of rights (ibid, p 302). See also E Brems, above n 15, 466 et seq; and, in the specific context of the rights of persons with disabilities, see A Dhanda, above n 51, 456–457.

117 One could find it doubtful that disability encompasses HIV. However, HIV has been recognised as a disability in several jurisdictions. See e.g. the US Supreme Court (under the Americans with Disabilities Act, 1990), US Supreme Court, *Bragdon v Abbott*, 524 US 624 (1998). In addition, in *I.B. v Greece*, the ECtHR noted that decisions of domestic courts and other bodies for human rights protection (also at a domestic level) show that they grant protection against the dismissal of HIV-positive persons through the prohibition imposed on grounds of discrimination, such as disability (also mentioning health); see ECtHR, *I.B. v Greece*, above n 35, §§39–47 (concluding that conditions such as HIV infection falls within the term 'other status' in the text of Article 14 of the ECHR 'either as a form of disability or in the same way as a disability', ibid, §73).

118 Ibid, §35.

119 On the issue of attaching socio-economic rights to anti-discrimination rights: see S Alemahu Yeshanew, above n 115, 306 et seq.

120 UNCRDP, Article 24.

instruments offer a higher protection standard as compared to the ECHR. If the Court adapts its level of protection, it encourages a 'race to the top' in protecting the rights of persons with disabilities, as well as promoting equal protection across legal systems.[121] The principles of universality of human rights or the observance of an ius gentium[122] could be mobilised to argue in favour of such an approach.[123] Rather innovatively, it may also be argued that the 'human rights safeguard' of Article 53 of the ECHR obliges the ECtHR to change its case law by aligning it with ratified external instruments which offer higher protection standards.[124] Although the ECtHR does not follow this argumentation, it reflects the way forward if an integrated approach is to be achieved.[125]

We mentioned earlier that external referencing might enhance convergence between various instruments. However, such a rapprochement does not necessarily raise the Strasbourg Court's level of protection, as the European or international trend might offer standards below what is sought by the applicant. Thus, from the perspective of persons with disabilities, harmonisation is not the most advantageous path to follow per se.[126]

In the recent case of *Gherghina v Romania*, we find evidence of the Strasbourg Court relying on international law to trivialise concerns about the national remedies available to persons with disabilities regarding securing universal access to buildings open to the public. On the requirement to exhaust national remedies, the applicant argued that the absence of national case law on the issue was due to a lack of foreseeability and clarity in domestic law. In response to this allegation, the Court admitted that the domestic proceedings were seldom used, but instead of examining in concreto why this was the case (as the applicant argued, perhaps the national law was not clear enough), it justified the situation by saying that the protection of the rights of persons with disabilities in national law – alongside developments in international law – was relatively recent.[127]

---

121 Brems draws attention to how an integrated approach to human rights law can avoid a 'race-to-the-bottom' from a human rights duty bearer's perspective; see E Brems, above n 13, 462–463.

122 Waldron speaks of an *ius gentium* requiring approaching 'all peoples as members of a single community' and including a legitimate concern 'about inconsistencies and disparities in the administration of fundamental rights'. J Waldron, *Partly Laws Common to All Mankind: Foreign Law in American Courts*, Yale University Press, New Haven 2012, p 133, quoted by L van den Eynde, 'Interpreting Rights Collectively: Comparative Arguments in Public Interest Litigants' Briefs on Fundamental Rights Issues', doctoral thesis under the supervision of J Allard and E Bribosia, defended in November 2015 at the Université libre de Bruxelles.

123 Also, Brems mentions the relevance of the principle of universality in this respect; see E Brems, above n 13, 454.

124 Brems made this innovative proposal, which is so far not followed by the Court; ibid, 465–466. The argument is developed more elaborately in D Staes, above n 8, 257–278.

125 E Brems, above n 13, 465–466. On this argument, see also above n 84.

126 The interests of rights holders might thus sometimes be best served by not introducing external instruments or by creating opposition between them. As such, the phenomenon of fragmentation is not always a concern from a rights holder's point of view.

127 *Gherghina v Romania*, no 42219/07, §100, ECHR 2015.

Notably, the Court did not even explicitly mention the UNCRPD as a relevant instrument, referring only generally to 'international law and practice'.[128] We cannot shake off the impression that the Court here (mis)used the developments in international law as a kind of 'excuse' or 'justification' for the State's inertia in offering satisfactory domestic proceedings for disabled persons who lack access to public buildings. Thus, in this admissibility decision, the Court seems to justify the infrequent use of domestic proceedings by a lack of action at the international level. Here, the use of international law contributes to a so-called 'race to the bottom'. The third parties to the case of *Ghergina* envisioned a different conclusion in their reference to international law, arguing that in the light of recent developments in international law, 'the national authorities could no longer avoid the issue or delay honouring their obligation to progressively ensure the accessibility of buildings for public use'.[129] On a different note, the case of *Çam v Turkey* illustrates that the UNCRPD can be a powerful tool for the inclusion of students with disabilities once the high bar of exhausting domestic remedies is met.[130]

3.2.3. *Integration of Procedural Interests*

Besides taking account of the specific needs of disabled persons and integrating higher protection standards, external referencing also has the ability to serve

128 Ibid.

129 Ibid, §82 (referring to third-party comments submitted by the International Disability Alliance, the European Disability Forum and the Romanian National Disability Council).

130 In a similar vein, in the field of tax law, see *Guberina v Croatia*, above n 79, where the Strasbourg Court found a violation of Article 1 of Protocol 1 to the ECHR (the right to property) in conjunction with Article 14 of the Convention. The applicant in this case was a father whose son is a wheelchair user. Relying on a provision granting a tax exemption to individuals buying a flat or a house in order to solve their 'housing needs', he requested the benefit to support the transfer from their inaccessible flat to an accessible one. The domestic authorities refused to grant the tax exemption, stating that the first property satisfied 'all housing needs in terms of hygiene and technical requirements as well as the basic infrastructure' (§12). According to the Court, the family's specific needs arising out of the child's disability were not taken into account. Two main findings emerge from the ECtHR's judgment. First, the Court held that the alleged discriminatory treatment of an applicant having close personal links and providing care to an individual having a disability is a form of disability-based discrimination covered by Article 14 of the ECHR. This captures a situation often referred to as 'discrimination by association'. This finding is in line with case law of the Court of Justice of the EU (*S. Coleman v Attridge Law and Steve Law*, C-303/06, 17 July 2008), to which the Strasbourg Court referred in the 'facts section' (at §41) and in the 'law section' (at §77). Second, the Court found that the authorities, when applying the domestic legislation, had not sufficiently taken account of the principles enshrined in the ratified UNCRPD (notably 'reasonable accommodation'). For comments on this case, see E Bribosia and I Rorive, 'Equality and Non-discrimination' (2017) 2 *European Journal of Human Rights* 191, 197–198; and C Cojocariu, 'Guberina and Gherghina: The Two Sides of the Court's Disability Jurisprudence', 17 May 2016, https://strasbourgobservers.com/2016/05/17/guberina-and-gherghina-the-two-sides-of-the-courts-disability-jurisprudence (accessed 30 June 2017).

the procedural interests of persons with disabilities and of rights holders more generally. This is true, first, because persons with disabilities or organisations defending their rights might use external instruments to build their case and, second, because the Court might increase the argumentative quality of its judgments by using external references.

3.2.3.1. The Strategic Use of External Instruments by Third Parties

It is difficult to assess the extent to which the use of external instruments by a third party influences the ECtHR. In any case, the judges are the ones ultimately deciding whether to make use of them in their legal reasoning.[131] Nevertheless, it is not unlikely that the citation of external instruments by third parties stimulates the Court's referencing practice: the judges might 'filter' the instruments referenced by third parties in the first place.[132] Third parties referring to external instruments and the influence this might have on the Court's reasoning – which is in fact more an assumption than a firm research result – may be a way to integrate third parties' interests into the procedure. Indeed, external instruments can offer them influential 'tools' for strategic litigation purposes, enhancing their participation in the Court's decision-making process. Bearing in mind that, compared to judges, third parties often have more time and resources to research the relevance of external instruments, their 'power' in this respect 'might become' particularly noteworthy.[133]

---

131 In accordance with the legal maxim *da mihi factum, dabo tibi jus*, they are not obliged to import the external instruments used by (third) parties. It is the independent responsibility of the judges to develop a legal reasoning and to give a legal qualification to the facts, without being bound by what is pleaded by the (third) parties (or what is brought to them by the Court's Research Division). See F Tulkens, S Van Drooghenbroeck and F Krenc, above n 11, 470 et seq; L van den Eynde, 'Iura novit curia ...? Une aide externe pour l'interprétation du droit peut néanmoins être bienvenue. La présentation d'arguments de droit comparé au juge par les amicus curiae' (2017) 1 *Administration Publique* 69.

132 Based on the observations of, *inter alia*, H Senden, *Interpretation of Fundamental Rights in a Multilevel Legal System: An Analysis of the European Court of Human Rights and the Court of Justice of the European Union*, Intersentia, Cambridge 2011, pp 135 and 261; JF Flauss, 'La Présence de la Jurisprudence de la Cour Suprême des Etats-Unis d'Amérique dans le Contentieux européen des Droits de l'Homme' (2005) 62 *Revue trimestrielle des droits de l'homme* 313, 317; F Tulkens, S Van Drooghenbroeck and F Krenc, above n 11, 470 et seq; E Voeten, 'Borrowing and Nonborrowing among International Courts' (2010) 39 *Journal of Legal Studies* 547; L van den Eynde, above n 122. The use of external instruments in the reports of the Research Division also seems likely to influence the Court. The Research Division is, inter alia, in charge of studying questions of comparative and international law and has been expanded because of the increasing need to consider non-ECHR material. See M Forowicz, above n 11, p 401. It is thus likely that referencing practice has been intensified under the Research Division's auspices. See ibid; and H Senden, above n 132, pp 135 and 261.

133 See JF Flauss, above n 132, 317. See also F Tulkens, S Van Drooghenbroeck and F Krenc, above n 11, 473.

They might thus find opportunities in the normative diversity to support the argument of their cases, influence judicial interpretation and pursue their strategic agendas.

In *M.S. v Croatia (No 2)*, for example, the third parties used some external provisions (in casu Article 13 of the UNCRPD) which later appeared in the Court's legal reasoning.[134] However, this is not a constant practice. It also happens that third parties make reference to several instruments to which the Court does not respond. In *M.S v Croatia (No 2)*, for example, the Court did not consider the third party's comment that a deprivation of liberty based on 'the existence of a disability' was relevant under the prohibition of discrimination enshrined in Article 14 of the ECHR.[135] This was in fact an invitation by the third party to consider the interpretation of Article 5(1)(e) of the ECHR (allowing the deprivation of liberty of persons of 'unsound mind') in light of Article 14 of the UNCRPD and Article 14 of the ECHR, but the Court did not respond to the argument. We notice a similar phenomenon in the case of *Ivinović v Croatia*. Here, while the third parties referred to the UNCRPD to argue for the need to replace substituted decision-making with supported decision-making in the exercise of a person's legal capacity, the Court did not include a 'supportive' approach to legal capacity.[136]

3.2.3.2. External Referencing Enhancing the Quality of Argumentation

The use of external instruments might increase the quality of the ECtHR's argumentation, which enhances the Court's persuasiveness and credibility. External instruments can fulfil various functions within legal reasoning. They might help the search for consensus or trends, contribute to shape a notion or a difficult argument, etc. At a practical level, external instruments add value because of the concrete argumentative tools they can offer.[137] As demonstrated by several examples above (such as *Glor v Switzerland*,

---

134 *M.S. v Croatia (No 2)*, above n 3, §135. Note that not all third parties are supportive to the applicant's interests. Governments and conservative NGOs might equally use external instruments in their third-party submissions to prevent a further development of human rights on a certain issue.

135 Third Party Submission of the Centre for Disability Law and Policy at NUI Galway and the SHINE in ECtHR, *M.S. v Croatia (No 2)*, above n 3, lodged on 9 November 2012 and communicated on 6 May 2013, §19. We thank Dr Flynn of the Centre for Disability Law and Policy for sending us this submission.

136 *Ivinović v Croatia*, above n 5, §34.

137 J Allard, 'Le Dialogue des Juges à la Cour européenne des Droits de l'Homme et à la Cour Suprême des Etats-Unis: Constats et Perspectives philosophiques' in J Allard, G Haarscher, L Hennebel and G Lewkowicz (eds), *Juger les Droits de l'Homme. Europe et Etats-Unis Face à Face*, Bruylant, Brussels 2008; I Rorive, E Bribosia and L van den Eynde, 'Same-Sex Marriage: Building an Argument before the European Court of Human Rights in Light of the US Experience' (2014) 32 *Berkeley Journal of International Law* 1.

M.S. v Croatia (No 2) and *Stanev v Bulgaria*), they show what was done or decided in other and often more specialised normative systems. External referencing can, accordingly, make new interpretations richer and more authoritative and convincing (even when the applicant loses his or her case).[138] Of course, the latter statement is only true if the use of external instruments by the ECtHR is accompanied by a convincing methodology, which is not always the case. The ECtHR is not very clear about the selection, the function and the position of external instruments. Unsurprisingly, the Strasbourg Court has been criticised for 'cherry-picking', alluding to an incoherent and unclear method of 'picking and choosing' external instruments in opportunistic ways. Concerns also address the inadequate legal justification for the referencing practice, especially when the instruments used for guidance have not been ratified by the respondent State in question.[139]

We also notice confusing methodological practices in certain decisions on the protection of persons with disabilities. For instance, in some cases, the Court quoted the content of an external instruments such as the UNCRPD in the 'facts section', but did not subsequently use it in the legal reasoning under the 'law section'. In addition, the Court sometimes referred to instruments with a diverging rationale, like in *Ivinović v Croatia*. In this case, when mentioning the relevant law (under the 'facts section'), the Court cited Article 12 of the UNCRPD on the one hand (rejecting a deprivation of legal capacity on account of disability) and the CoE principles concerning the legal protection of incapable adults on the other hand (allowing such a deprivation), without specifying which approach should prevail.[140]

In conclusion, we note that external referencing initiated by third parties has the potential – in disability cases and more generally – to stimulate their procedural participation, which reflects one of the standards of process legitimacy.[141] In addition, external referencing has the potential to strengthen the quality of the

---

138 Inspired by C McCrudden, 'A Common Law of Human Rights?: Transnational Judicial Conversations on Constitutional Rights' (2000) 20 *Oxford Journal of Legal Studies* 499, 514 and 527; F Tulkens, S Van Drooghenbroeck and F Krenc, above n 11, 483; AML Coccu Ortu, 'La comparaison en tant que méthode de détermination du standard de protection des droits dans le système CEDH' 2011 (4) *Rivista Telematica Giuridica dell'AIC* 1, 5 and 29.

139 On concerns of 'cherry-picking' and unsatisfactory justifications, see J Allard, above n 137, 133 et seq; C. McCrudden, above n 138, 507; F Tulkens, S Van Drooghenbroeck and F KRENC, above n 11, 464; J Gerards, 'Rechtsvinding door het Europees Hof voor de Rechten van de Mens' (2006) 31 *NJCM Bulletin* 93, 120; T Barkhuysen and ML van Emmerik, above n 11, 834; AML Coccu Ortu, above n 138, 13.

140 See *Ivinović v Croatia*, above n 5, §§21 and 22. In this regard, David notes that the CoE instrument reflects an outdated approach to rights of persons with disabilities, in contrast with the UNCRPD; see V David, above n 56.

141 Y Shany, *Assessing the Effectiveness of International Courts*, Oxford University Press, Oxford 2014, p 265. Both 'formal participation' (parties must be offered the opportunity to present their story and arguments) and 'substantive participation' (the contributions of the parties must be truly considered) are of importance. See E Brems and L Lavrysen,

ECtHR's decision-making, rendering arguments more specific and acceptable. Both observations are beneficial for procedural justice and thus for the parties' satisfaction with the legal process.[142] However, to optimise the potential of external referencing, the transparency and consistency of the referencing method should be enhanced.[143]

4. CONCLUSION

The Strasbourg Court refers more and more frequently to various external instruments as an aid for the interpretation and application of the ECHR and its Protocols. This chapter has examined such practice in cases relating to the rights of persons with disabilities, an area consisting of diverse protection instruments developed under various institutions and systems. The idea of 'human rights integration' has been the red line guiding the examination. For this reason, we started from the idea that using external instruments to interpret the ECHR and its Protocols has the potential to promote an integrated approach – from both a top-down and a bottom-up understanding – towards the rights of persons with disabilities.

First, from a top-down view on the human rights architecture, we notice that the referencing practice stimulates the rapprochement of various instruments on the rights of disabled persons, enhancing the peaceful and harmonious coexistence of the relevant norms. Second, a bottom-up perspective shows us how external instruments might enhance an interpretation of the Convention which takes sufficient account of the experiences and identities of persons with a disability. References to specialised categorical human rights catalogues or instruments containing so-called 'second generation' rights have proven to be particularly adequate in this regard.

In addition to cases which demonstrate an integrative and coordinative human rights approach, this chapter has also presented cases where the ECtHR missed an important opportunity to enhance convergence with external instruments, not least with regard to issues of legal capacity and the deprivation

'Procedural Justice in Human Rights Adjudication: The European Court of Human Rights' (2013) 35 *Human Rights Quarterly* 176, 181.

142 Procedural justice gained popularity in legitimacy assessment and includes criteria of a procedural nature such as participation, neutrality, respect and trust. See ibid, E Brems and L Lavrysen, 176–200 (and the references therein); Y Shany, above n 141, p 137. The central idea behind procedural justice is that people instead assess legitimacy on the evaluation of the fairness of the decision-making process than on whether they can agree with the substantive content of the outcome of the decisions. See ibid, pp 139–140 and 143; E Brems and L Lavrysen, above n 141, 182 and the references therein.

143 For suggestions on enhancing the method of external references, see D Staes, above n 8.

of liberty of persons with disabilities. Such examples do not correspond to an integrative view on the normative context, which requires the ECtHR to pay attention to external instruments, treating them consciously and allowing them to make the interpretation of the ECHR more precise, specialised and up to date. The practice of referencing has the potential to strengthen the Court's arguments and the persuasiveness of its reasoning, under the condition that the methodology behind this practice is clear and does not hinder the further development of human rights. If such concerns are kept in mind, cross-fertilisation between the various instruments which protect disabled persons has a bright future.

PART III

HUMAN RIGHTS DYNAMICS IN EUROPE

THE EUROPEAN UNION IN THE INTERNATIONAL SYSTEM OF HUMAN RIGHTS PROTECTION

Solo Singer or Voice in the Choir?

Bruno De Witte*

1. INTRODUCTION

The musical metaphor in the title of this chapter echoes a publication by Olivier De Schutter some time ago, entitled 'L'Europe des droits de l'homme: un concerto à plusieurs mains'.[1] De Schutter's contribution dealt with the relations between the European Union (EU) and the Council of Europe, and especially those between the Court of Justice of the European Union (CJEU) and the European Court of Human Rights (ECtHR). His main argument was that, despite the presence of

* Bruno De Witte is Professor of European Law at Maastricht University (The Netherlands), and Part-time Professor of Law at the European University Institute, Florence. He is co-director of the Maastricht Centre for European Law. Email: bruno.dewitte@eui.eu.

1 O de Schutter, 'L'Europe des droits de l'homme: un concerto à plusieurs mains', in E Bribosia, L Scheeck and A Ubeda de Torres (eds), *L'Europe des Cours – Loyautés et résistances*, Bruylant, Brussels 2010, 259.

an element of competition between the two courts, their relationship should essentially be seen as a complementary and harmonious coexistence, similar to that of two piano players sitting side by side playing one single piece of music.

This was the dominant view in the legal literature until recently,[2] and it was supported by a number of factors, such as: the increasing direct dialogue between the members of the ECtHR and the CJEU; the fact that the Treaty of Lisbon contained the promise of a future accession of the EU to the ECHR; and the peaceful coexistence between the two organisations also at the political level, as expressed by the Memorandum of Agreement between the Council of Europe and the EU concluded in 2007, and the modus vivendi reached by the two organisations when the EU's Fundamental Rights Agency was created around the same time. The Agency was instructed, in its founding Regulation, to cooperate closely with the human rights bodies of the Council of Europe.[3]

However, many things have happened since and it would seem appropriate to reconsider this positive assessment in the light of recent developments. Although this chapter will take, as its core, the developments in the relationship between the CJEU and the ECtHR (section 2), it will also examine the attitude adopted by the Court of Justice to other international human rights instruments (section 3) and will end with an examination of the role played by the political (non-judicial) institutions of the EU within the global landscape of international human rights law (section 4).

2. THE CHANGING RELATIONSHIP BETWEEN THE TWO EUROPEAN COURTS

Two main developments in recent years have affected the relationship between the two European courts in the field of the protection of human rights: the failed accession of the EU to the ECHR; and the dominant role now played by the EU's Charter of Fundamental Rights (CFR) in the fundamental rights practice of the CJEU.

2.1. THE FAILED ACCESSION OF THE EU

The first and most spectacular development is in fact a non-development, namely the fact that the promised accession of the EU to the ECHR did not

2 See for example also T Lock, *The European Court of Justice and International Courts*, Oxford University Press, Oxford, 2015, p 168: 'The cooperation between the two courts is an example of comity in action.'

3 Council Regulation 168/2007 of 15 February 2007 establishing a European Union Agency for Fundamental Rights [2007] OJ L53/1, Article 9.

materialise, due to the reluctance expressed by the CJEU in its Opinion 2/13. It is true that the accession of the EU to the ECHR could have seemed less urgent after the Lisbon Treaty, for two main reasons: first, because the Lisbon Treaty had given binding legal status to the EU's own CFR, thereby boosting the visibility and quality of fundamental rights protection in the EU legal order, compared to the previous situation where such protection was mainly based on unwritten general principles of EU law; and, second, because the position of the ECHR *within the EU legal order* had markedly improved due to the Lisbon Treaty. Article 6(3) TEU now clearly states that Convention rights *shall constitute* general principles of EU law rather than being a mere source of inspiration for those principles (as the CJEU traditionally put it) and, furthermore, Article 52(3) of the EU CFR contains a remarkable clause stating that Charter rights that correspond to Convention rights (and many of them do) shall have the same meaning and scope as those Convention rights – thereby in fact aiming at transposing a large amount of Strasbourg jurisprudence into the EU legal order. Nevertheless, despite those changes in the EU legal order which seemed to make accession to the ECHR a less urgent matter, there were also several good reasons for undertaking the formal accession of the EU to the Convention, such as: the creation of an external scrutiny on the EU legal order's respect for fundamental rights in the same way as national legal orders are being scrutinised; the creation of a new remedy for individuals against EU acts interfering with their fundamental rights, especially in areas where no adequate remedies exist under EU law, as in the domain of the Common Foreign and Security Policy (CFSP); and the possibility for the EU institutions to be fully associated with cases before the Strasbourg Court having an EU law dimension rather than having to watch 'from the sidelines'.[4] The price to be paid for these improvements in fundamental rights protection would be that divergences between the CJEU and the ECtHR on the appropriate level of protection become more concrete in relation to individual cases: for example, accession would create the possibility for the ECtHR to find a breach of the Convention where the CJEU has previously held that the measure was in compliance with the EU CFR. This possibility for concrete disagreements between the two European courts, replacing their 'dialogue' at arm's length, might well have been the main unstated reason for the CJEU's severe and uncompromising rejection of the Draft Accession Agreement.

---

4 For more elaborate discussions of the reasons pleading for EU accession to the ECHR, see J Calleweart, *The Accession of the European Union to the European Convention on Human Rights*, Council of Europe, Strasbourg 2014, Chapter 1; and E Spaventa, 'A Very Fearful Court? The Protection of Fundamental Rights in the European Union after Opinion 2/13' (2015) 22 *Maastricht Journal of European and Comparative Law* 35, 37–44. But see the article published by Antonio Tizzano in 2011 in which he expressed doubts about the need for accession (note that Judge Tizzano was the rapporteur of Opinion 2/13): A Tizzano, 'Les Cours européennes et l'adhésion de l'Union à la CEDH' (2011) *Il Diritto dell'Unione Europea* 29.

This is not the place to analyse once again the arguments deployed by the CJEU in its Opinion 2/13 to deny accession, despite the painstaking negotiation of a sophisticated Accession Agreement. I have stated elsewhere, in agreement with most other commentators, why none of those arguments seems persuasive.[5] What is perhaps most striking, apart from the specific arguments, is the general tone of the Opinion. The primary concern of the CJEU, throughout its lengthy Opinion, is to protect the autonomy of the EU legal order against 'foreign' influence, whereas the concern to ensure optimal protection of human rights for European citizens is voiced nowhere. The Court emphatically does not define itself as a participant in a human rights choir, but rather as the guardian of the separateness of the EU legal order.

2.2. SELECTIVE USE OF THE CONVENTION AND ITS CASE LAW

A second development of recent years is that the CJEU, in its fundamental rights case law, has chosen to rely much more heavily on the EU's own CFR than on the European Convention of Human Rights (ECHR). The ECHR and the case law of the Strasbourg Court are still present in the case law of the CJEU, but they are used more sparingly and selectively than they were before the entry of force of the Treaty of Lisbon. The failure to *systematically* refer to the case law of the ECtHR is, of course, not problematic from the point of view of Convention law. The ECtHR has never made it a duty for national courts to expressly refer to the case law of Strasbourg when adjudicating cases involving rights protected under the Convention. Rather, the only relevant requirement, laid down in Article 13 of the Convention, is that the national legal systems should offer remedies for the alleged violation of Convention rights. It does not matter whether this happens on the basis of national constitutional rights corresponding to those of the Convention or on the basis of the directly effective provisions of the Convention itself; nor do national courts, when applying the ECHR, have to refer to the jurisprudence of the Strasbourg court. Yet, things might be different from the point of view of EU law. As already mentioned, Article 52(3) of the CFR states that when the Charter rights correspond to Convention rights, the 'meaning and scope of those rights shall be the same' as those of the Convention. Strictly speaking, the CJEU would therefore have to proceed to a double check whenever a right contained in the Convention is at stake: it should assess the EU or national measures in light of the CFR first and then move on to check whether that interpretation of the CFR also corresponds to the views adopted

[5] B De Witte and S Imamovic, 'Opinion 2/13 on Accession to the ECHR: Defending the EU Legal Order against a Foreign Human Rights Court' (2015) 40 *European Law Review* 683.

by the ECtHR about the corresponding Convention right. However, the CJEU does not do so systematically, or at least it does not always provide evidence in its judgments that it checked the case law of its counterpart in Strasbourg.

Take, for instance, the well-known *Google Spain* judgment of May 2014,[6] in which the CJEU interpreted EU data protection legislation in light of the CFR so as to create a right for individuals, in certain circumstances, to have one's personal data deleted from search engines (a right sometimes described as a 'right to be forgotten'). In this judgment, the CJEU referred to many of its own previous rulings, but did not mention a single ECtHR judgment, despite the fact that Article 8 of the ECHR undoubtedly protects data privacy and was therefore relevant to the facts of the case. This lack of reference to Strasbourg case law could seem understandable and appropriate, given that the CJEU went on to offer *more* protection to the right to privacy than the ECtHR did in similar cases. However, the question arises whether the extensive protection given to the right to privacy and data protection negatively reflects on the exercise of the right to information that, arguably, was also at stake in this dispute. The ECtHR had already ruled precisely on this question of how to balance the conflicting demands of both these human rights in the case of *Delfi v Estonia*,[7] but the CJEU chose not to refer to that case or to any other ECtHR judgment.[8] We are therefore left in the dark as to whether the CJEU did, in fact, examine the available case law from Strasbourg and felt convinced that it acted in accordance with it or whether, on the contrary, it just failed to look into the case law of the ECtHR. This cherry-picking attitude appears problematic, not so much from the Convention perspective, but rather from EU law's own perspective, since the adoption of the EU CFR was very much predicated on the view that the new Charter could offer more protection than the Convention but never less, and this view was clearly laid down in the Articles 52 and 53 of the Charter.

Indeed, the CJEU persists in treating the ECHR as an 'external' source of human rights protection. It does so, in particular, when national courts formulate preliminary questions of interpretation or validity that refer to the ECHR. In answering those preliminary questions, the CJEU either ignores the fact that they are formulated with reference to the ECHR or starts by correcting the national court. Take, for example, the *Ordre des barreaux* case of 2016.[9] The Belgian Constitutional Court had referred a question on the validity of the

---

6 CJEU, Case C-131/12, *Google Spain SL, Google Inc. v Agencia Española de Protección de Datos, Mario Costeja González*, ECLI:EU:C:2014:317.

7 *Delfi v Estonia*, no 64569/09, ECHR 2013.

8 For criticism in this point, see E Frantziou, 'Further Developments in the Right to Be Forgotten: The European Court of Justice's Judgment in Case C-1313/12' (2014) 14 *Human Rights Law Review* 761, 772–775.

9 CJEU, Case C-543/14, *Ordre des barreaux francophones et germanophones and others v Conseil des ministres*, ECLI:EU:C:2016:71.

VAT Directive 2006/112 because that directive required the Member States to terminate the VAT exemption for lawyers; the referring court wondered whether this was compatible with the right to an effective remedy and the principle of equality of arms as protected not only by Article 47 of the EU CFR, but also by Article 6 of the ECHR and Article 14 of the International Covenant on Civil and Political Rights (ICCPR). The CJEU started its ruling by stating that the ECHR 'does not constitute, as long as the European Union has not acceded to it, a legal instrument which has been formally incorporated into EU law', and the same obviously applied to the ICCPR. 'Accordingly', the Court added, 'an examination of the validity of Directive 2006/112 must be undertaken solely in the light of the fundamental rights guaranteed by the Charter.' It then analysed the question in the light of Article 47 of the EU CFR and did not consider at all Article 6 of the ECHR or the case law of the Strasbourg Court.

In other cases, the Court reformulated a national court's ECHR-based question into a Charter-based one. This can be illustrated by the *J.N.* judgment decided by the Grand Chamber in 2016.[10] J.N. had served repeated prison sentences in the Netherlands and was ordered to leave the country, but then applied for asylum. The question arose whether he could, despite this application, be detained in the Netherlands. The applicable EU asylum reception directive of 2013 lists the limited cases allowing for detention, including for reasons of 'national security and public order'. The Dutch Council of State had doubts as to the validity of that provision in light of the right to personal liberty, as protected by Article 5 of the ECHR, and confronted the CJEU with that doubt through a preliminary ruling on the validity of the Directive. The CJEU responded that the EU legislature had 'struck a fair balance' between the right to liberty and the legitimate aim of protecting security and order, and came to this conclusion on the basis of a Charter-conform interpretation of the Directive and after a lengthy discussion of the proportionality of the interference with the right to liberty. The question of validity had been asked by the Dutch court in terms of the ECHR, but the CJEU restated, as in other cases, that 'the ECHR does not constitute, as long as the European Union has not acceded to it, a legal instrument which has been formally incorporated into EU law' and therefore the examination of the validity 'must be undertaken solely in the light of the fundamental rights guaranteed by the Charter' (paragraphs 45–46). However, the CJEU did in fact operate, at the end of its judgment, a 'ECHR check' based on Article 52(3) CFR, including an examination of the relevant case law of the ECtHR (paragraphs 77–81). One may well wonder what the purpose of this ECHR check is if the examination of the validity of an EU measure 'must be undertaken solely in the light of the Charter', except if one adopts the somewhat circular

---

10 CJEU, Case C-601/15 PPU, *J.N.*, ECLI:EU:C:2016:84.

reasoning that 'in the light of the Charter' includes the examination of the ECHR case law due to the wording of Article 52(3). Yet, as we have seen, the Court sometimes accomplishes such a secondary Convention check, whereas in other cases (such as *Ordre des barreaux*), it is omitted from the judgment and one may wonder whether the Court has actually carried out the check.

Thus, when examining the case law of the CJEU over the last three or four years, one finds a wide variety of usages of the ECHR jurisprudence, from cases in which the ECHR and its case law are fully exploited and applied as if they were an integral part of the EU legal order, over cases in which the Court gives a passing nod to the Strasbourg case law, to cases in which both the Convention and its case law are entirely absent, even though they could have been mentioned.[11] There has been no case in which the CJEU flatly contradicted the views adopted by its counterpart in Strasbourg, although there have been notorious areas of divergence and tensions, most obviously as regards the question of whether the mutual trust between EU Member State authorities should be limited by fundamental rights considerations.[12]

Therefore, the impression prevails that the CJEU has chosen not to tie its hands completely and to preserve the possibility of steering its own course in the fundamental rights field, even where the Charter rights replicate those of the Convention. Although this attitude is probably not what the drafters of Article 52(3) of the CFR intended, it could be argued that this vindication of autonomy has a positive side as well: 'a system where the CJEU normally follows the case law of the ECtHR, but is not strictly bound by it, is preferable as it allows the CJEU to deviate in well-founded instances and thus trigger a dialogue with the ECtHR allowing it to review or refine its case law'.[13]

3. THE CJEU AND INTERNATIONAL HUMAN RIGHTS TREATIES OTHER THAN THE CONVENTION

In pre-CFR times, the CJEU referred only very sporadically to international human rights treaties other than the Convention, in a proportion of about one reference for every 100 references to the ECHR. Moreover, those references never played a decisive role in the Court's rulings. Invocations of other human rights treaties mainly occurred in cases in which the Convention did not provide enough 'inspiration', so that the CJEU had to refer to other sources for developing

---

11 On this typology of recent cases, see further the discussion in Jasper Krommendijk's chapter in this volume.

12 On the divergent approaches of the two courts in this matter, see, in particular, E Bribosia and A Weyembergh, 'Confiance mutuelle et droits fondamentaux: Back to the future' (2016) *Cahiers de droit européen* 469, 483–505.

13 T Lock, above n 2, p 184.

the EU's own general principles of EU law. One such example from the early days is *Defrenne v Sabena III*, where the Court, in reaching the conclusion that protection against sex discrimination was a fundamental Community right, found support in the fact that 'the same concepts are recognized by the European Social Charter of 18 November 1961 and by Convention No 111 of the International Labour Organization of 25 June 1958 concerning discrimination in respect of employment and occupation'.[14] In later cases, occasional references were made by the Court, for example, to the two UN Covenants and to the UN Convention for the Elimination of Discrimination against Women, but they were never decisive for the outcome of the case.[15] However, there have been a few cases in which, absent any relevant ECHR dimension, international instruments were given a prominent role by the CJEU. Thus, in *Laval* and *Viking Lines*, the Court identified the right to take collective action as a general principle of EC law through a 'melting pot' approach, distilling a general principle from a combination of international instruments:

> the right to take collective action, including the right to strike, is recognised both by various international instruments which the Member States have signed or cooperated in, such as the European Social Charter, signed at Turin on 18 October 1961 – to which, moreover, express reference is made in Article 136 EC – and Convention No 87 concerning Freedom of Association and Protection of the Right to Organise, adopted on 9 July 1948 by the International Labour Organization – and by instruments developed by those Member States at Community level or in the context of the European Union, such as the Community Charter of the Fundamental Social Rights of Workers adopted at the meeting of the European Council held in Strasbourg on 9 December 1989, which is also referred to in Article 136 EC, and the Charter of Fundamental Rights of the European Union proclaimed in Nice on 7 December 2000 … [T]he right to take collective action, including the right to strike, must therefore be recognised as a fundamental right which forms an integral part of the general principles of Community law.[16]

One may note that the Court here uses a mixture of binding and non-binding legal instruments (the EU CFR was, of course, not yet binding at the time of the *Viking* and *Laval* judgments), and that, moreover, some Member States

---

14 CJEU, Case 149/77, *Gabrielle Defrenne v Sabena*, ECLI:EU:C:1978:130, para 28.

15 See, for example, CJEU, Case C-73/08, *Nicolas Bressol and others v Gouvernement de la Communauté française*, ECLI:EU:C:2010:181, paras 83–88, where the Court rejected an argument drawn from the UN Covenant on Economic, Social and Cultural Rights, but without discussing the legal status of that Covenant in EU law.

16 CJEU, Case C-438/05, *Viking Line*, ECLI:EU:C:2007:772, paras 43–44; CJEU, Case C-341/05, *Laval*, ECLI:EU:C:2007:809, paras 90–91. See also, in the same vein, Case C-540/03, *European Parliament v Council* (the family reunification case), ECLI:EU:C:2006:429, paras 37–39, where the ECJ referred to the European Social Charter, the Civil Covenant and the Convention on the Rights of the Child.

(such as the UK) had not accepted to be bound by *any* of the international instruments listed by the Court. The CJEU thus uses the 'transmutation' of the international standards into general principles of EU law as a way of developing *new* legal obligations for (some) States when acting within the scope of EU law. However, no further reference was made, in *Laval* and *Viking*, to the practice of the international monitoring bodies, especially those of the ILO, when the Court went on to balance the right to take collective action against other values (in casu, the freedom of establishment and the freedom to provide services).[17]

With the attribution to the CFR, through the Lisbon Treaty, of the full force of primary EU law, the modest 'gap-filling' role of international human rights has now ceased; they are no longer needed to provide inspiration for the formulation of unwritten general principles of EU law, given that the EU now has its own written bill of rights. Still, the CFR itself does not ignore those other human rights instruments. According to its Article 53:

> Nothing in this Charter shall be interpreted as restricting or adversely affecting human rights and fundamental freedoms as recognized, in their respective fields of application, by Union law and international law and by international agreements to which the Union or all the Member States are party.

The reference in this article to 'international law', as something separate from 'international agreements', is odd, but is possibly intended to refer to the recognition of human rights norms under customary international law. The restriction to treaties to which all Member States are parties is rather strange and inappropriate. It should not be read a contrario as meaning that the EU CFR can affect the protection provided by human rights treaties that have been ratified by fewer than 28 Member States. For example, the Revised Social Charter of the Council of Europe has not been ratified by all EU Member States, but that circumstance cannot be used for arguing that the EU CFR, by not incorporating one or other of the rights of the Revised Social Charter, would modify the obligations accepted by the countries that have ratified that Revised Social Charter. Yet, this may have encouraged the CJEU in its attitude of disdaining the European Social Charter and entirely ignoring the decisions of the European Committee of Social Rights, even when those decisions involve EU-related measures, such as the austerity measures implemented in Greece. A case that illustrates this neglect is the recent judgment of the General Court in *Sotiropoulou*, in which it briefly examined the compatibility of EU-based pension cuts implemented in Greece with the social rights of the CFR, but did

17 See T Novitz, 'A Human Rights Analysis of the *Viking* and *Laval* Judgments' (2007–2008) 10 *Cambridge Yearbook of European Legal Studies* 541, 559: 'While the Court was prepared to make reference to ILO Convention No 87 when holding that the right to take collective action constituted a fundamental right, it seems that it adopted a peculiarly restrictive interpretation of that right which neglects ILO jurisprudence.'

not refer to the earlier decisions of the European Social Rights Committee in which similar pension cuts had been found in violation of the Social Charter.[18]

One international human rights treaty occupies a special place in the CJEU's case law, namely the UN Convention on the Rights of Persons with Disabilities (CRPD). This Convention was ratified by the EU (on this ratification, see further section 4 below) and has therefore become part of the EU legal order. Since the entry into force of the CRPD, the CJEU has been confronted, in a number of cases, with its significance for the EU's regime of fundamental rights protection. Briefly said, whereas the CJEU accepted that EU legislation (and national legislation implementing EU law) could and should be interpreted in conformity with the provisions of the CRPD, it has refused to use the CRPD as a standard for reviewing the validity of EU law. This was decided in a Grand Chamber judgment of March 2014 upon a reference by the Irish Equality Tribunal.[19] The applicant in the main dispute, Ms Z, had been refused maternity or adoptive leave by her employer when she became a mother through surrogacy. As the reason for her recourse to surrogacy was her inability to support a pregnancy, she claimed that the refusal constituted discrimination on (among other things) grounds of disability in the sense of EU Directive 2000/78 on equal treatment in employment. The Irish court added a specific question as to whether the UN Convention was 'capable of being relied on for the purposes of interpreting, and/or challenging the validity, of Directive 2000/78'. The CJEU answered yes to the first prong of that question, adding that EU secondary legislation, such as Directive 2000/78, must be interpreted in a matter that is consistent with the Convention (paragraph 75), although this did not result in that Directive's applicability to the case at hand. As to the second prong of the question, the Court emphatically insisted that the validity of Directive 2000/78 could not be assessed in the light of the CRPD because that Convention's provisions were not unconditional and sufficiently precise and therefore did not have direct effect in EU law (paragraph 90). The main reason for this restrictive view was that the CRPD requires its States parties to take implementing measures to achieve the objectives of the Convention. Yet, as the EU's employment discrimination directive could very well be considered as such an implementing measure, the Court could have reviewed it in terms of whether it constituted an adequate

18 General Court, Case T-531/14, *Leimonia Sotiropoulou v Council of the European Union*, ECLI:EU:T:2017:297. On the 'austerity' decisions of the European Social Rights Committee, see O de Schutter and P Dermine, 'The Two Constitutions of Europe: Integrating Social Rights in the New Economic Architecture of the Union' (2017) *Journal européen des droits de l'homme* 108, 137–140; and, in more detail, P Stangos, 'Les répercussions juridiques sur l'Union européenne des décisions du Comité européen des droits sociaux relatives aux mesures d'austérité de la Grèce' (2015) *Revue trimestrielle des droits de l'homme* 909.

19 CJEU, Case C-363/12, *Z v A Government Department and the Board of Management of a Community School*, ECLI:EU:C:2014:159.

implementation of the EU's international obligations. The least one can say is that the CJEU did not make a great effort to ensure the effective enforcement of the sole human rights treaty concluded by the EU so far.

4. NON-JUDICIAL INTERACTIONS: THE ROLE OF INTERNATIONAL HUMAN RIGHTS IN THE EXTERNAL RELATIONS OF THE EU

Human rights interactions between the EU and the outside world also, and increasingly, happen outside the judicial arena. The political institutions of the EU occasionally refer to international human rights instruments or support international human rights actors. This kind of interaction happens essentially in the context of the EU's *external* relations. One can distinguish two types of interaction: the relatively limited occasions in which the EU contributes to standard-setting (i.e. to the *formation* of international human rights law); and the more frequent occasions in which the EU institutions contribute to the effective *application* of international human rights.

4.1. THE FORMATION OF INTERNATIONAL HUMAN RIGHTS NORMS

The most obvious interconnection between the EU and the rest of the world in the field of human rights is the fact that the EU has recently become involved in human rights standard-setting at the international level. Since the EU is an unusual subject of international law, its participation in multilateral human rights conventions requires those conventions to have a clause allowing for accession not only by States but also by 'regional integration organizations' or similar expressions. The classical international human rights conventions do not have such clauses, but when new initiatives are taken, the EU is able to appear on the negotiation scene and can insist on its inclusion. Thus, the European Community helped to negotiate, and signed, the CRPD, which was adopted by the United Nations General Assembly on 13 December 2006.[20] This Convention does indeed contain a 'regional integration organizations' clause. The competence of the European Community to sign the Convention was based on Articles 13 and 95 of the EC Treaty, thus connecting the Convention to

---

20 G de Burca, 'The EU in the Negotiation of the UN Disability Convention' (2010) 35 *European Law Review* 174.

both the anti-discrimination and internal market competences.[21] The EU then ratified the CRPD without waiting for most or all of its Member States taking that step.[22] Ratification not only entails the binding effect of this Convention for the EU institutions, but also the submission by the EU to the international monitoring mechanism set in place by the Convention. The EU submitted its first report on implementation of the Convention in 2014[23] and the following year, the Committee on the Rights of Persons with Disabilities adopted its 'Concluding observations',[24] in which it listed a long series of recommendations that the EU is invited to comply with before the time of submission of its second report. This is thus a first example of a dialogue between the EU's political institutions and an international human rights treaty body.

In addition to this single example of participation in human rights treaty-making, the EU also contributes on an ongoing basis to the emergence of human rights norms through its institutional practice, which can count as 'state practice' for the emergence or modification of customary international law. Such normative activities occur within the framework of the UN Human Rights Council in particular, in which the EU actively seeks to coordinate and represent the positions of its Member States as regards current human rights issues.[25]

4.2. THE APPLICATION OF INTERNATIONAL HUMAN RIGHTS NORMS

Human rights are a true leitmotif of the EU's external relations, at least at the level of policy documents, if not always in practice. Several aspects of that

21 For a discussion of how the ratification of this human rights treaty fitted into the competences of the EU, see L Waddington, 'The European Union and the United Nations Convention on the Rights of Persons with Disabilities: A Story of Exclusive and Shared Competences' (2011) 18 *Maastricht Journal of European and Comparative Law* 431. See also D Ferri, 'The Conclusion of the UN Convention on the Rights of Persons with Disabilities by the EC/EU: A Constitutional Perspective' in L Waddington and G Quinn (eds), *European Yearbook of Disability Law*, Vol. 2, Intersentia, Antwerp 2010, 47.

22 Council Decision of 26 November 2009 concerning the conclusion, by the European Community, of the United Nations Convention on the Rights of Persons with Disabilities [2010] OJ L23/35.

23 Initial report of the EU, 5 June 2014, CRPD/C/EU/1.

24 Concluding observations by the Committee on the Rights of Persons with Disabilities, 2 October 2015, CRPD/C/EU/CO/1.

25 However, it should be noted that both the EU and its individual Member States can operate and submit or support resolutions within that body: see KE Smith, 'EU Member States at the UN: A Case of Europeanization Arrested?' (2017) 55 *Journal of Common Market Studies* 628. For an earlier assessment, see KE Smith, 'The European Union at the Human Rights Council: Speaking with One Voice But Having Little Influence' (2010) 17 *Journal of European Public Policy* 224.

external human rights policy consist in contributing to the effective application of international human rights norms. Through the use of the multiple political and legal instruments at its disposal, the EU can seek to advance the cause of the protection of human rights in the outside world. Examples of this are its enlargement policy, its trade and development relations and its funding of human rights projects. We will briefly discuss each of these in turn.

The most visible use of human rights at the political level in the EU's external policy is probably in the context of its enlargement. In the course of preparation for accession of new Member States, human rights became a central element of the elaborate political conditionality mechanism gradually set in place on the basis of the Copenhagen criteria adopted by the European Council in 1993. These continue to be a central element in relation to the current candidates for accession, as illustrated in the annual reports devoted to those countries' slow progress towards accession. The Copenhagen European Council of June 1993 famously stated that 'membership requires that the candidate country must have achieved stability of institutions guaranteeing democracy, the rule of law, human rights and respect for and protection of minorities'. Ever since then, the EU institutions have applied a human rights standard to the candidate countries that has proved to be very broad, quite demanding but vaguely defined. At the time that this human rights conditionality was adopted, the then ongoing process of ratification by Central and Eastern European countries of the ECHR was seen as an important ingredient of their approximation to the EU. Although the Copenhagen criteria refer to human rights in general terms and do not mention the ECHR in so many words, it could seem obvious that compliance with the ECHR would form the primary standard for assessment in the context of accession to the EU. It is therefore rather striking to see that the European Commission, in its Regular Reports on progress towards accession, did not use compliance with the ECHR as the primary indicator of the applicant States' human rights performance, and still does not do so with the current candidate countries. Instead, it referred to a variety of sources of human rights protection, including other Council of Europe conventions (such as the European Social Charter and the Framework Convention on National Minorities) and Organization for Security and Co-operation in Europe (OSCE) documents, while leaving open the relative importance it chooses to give to these various instruments in coming to its assessment. It did not clearly distinguish between those human rights instruments that the candidate country had ratified (and which therefore the EU would seem justified in using as a benchmark) and other human rights instruments, which the country had – often deliberately – not ratified. This absence of a clear 'legal' criterion in deciding the pertinence of the various human rights instruments shows that the Commission conceives of its accession-reporting role in political rather than quasi-judicial terms.

This can be illustrated by the Commission's progress report on Serbia for 2016.[26] Human rights are considered in two places of the report: when discussing respect for the political criteria and when discussion progress of Serbia in relation to 'Chapter 19' of the accession negotiations on the judiciary and fundamental rights. In the former part of the report, the Commission includes a 'detailed analysis of freedom of expression', but this analysis does not contain any reference to international human rights standards.[27] As for the latter part, dealing with Chapter 19, the Commission briefly mentions the number of cases decided or pending against Serbia before the ECtHR, but without elaborating on any of them individually. Over the next few pages of the report, it then examines a range of single human rights; whereas the Commission comments on the country's perceived performance, it does not reference any international human rights instruments.

The incorporation of human rights in the pre-accession context had been preceded by the formulation of a general policy of conditionality in the EU's external relations.[28] Such a general policy was solemnly affirmed in the conclusions of the Luxembourg European Council of June 1991[29] and has gradually extended ever since. The standard human rights clause, which the EU included in most of the broad international agreements concluded with third countries since the mid-1990s (but not in the agreements dealing with specific questions), states that respect for democratic principles and human rights, as laid down in the Universal Declaration of Human Rights (UDHR) or other relevant international human rights instruments, constitutes an 'essential element' of the agreement.[30] This is the basis for the EU's right to unilaterally suspend the operation of the agreement in the case of non-respect for human rights. The EU is careful not to impose extraneous human rights standards on the other countries: the 'relevant human rights treaties' are those that both the EU and its

---

26 Commission Staff Working Document, *Serbia 2016 Report*, SWD (2016) 361 of 9 November 2016.

27 Ibid, pp 19–20.

28 A rich literature on this subject developed from the late 1990s onwards. See, among others, the following book-length studies: M Bulterman, *Human Rights in the Treaty Relations of the European Community*, Intersentia, Antwerp 2001; E Fierro Sedano, *The EU's Approach to Human Rights Conditionality in Practice*, Martinus Nijhoff, The Hague 2003; L Bartels, *Human Rights Conditionality in the EU's International Agreements*, Oxford University Press, Oxford 2005. For a recent update, see F Martines, 'Human Rights Clauses in EU Agreements' in S Poli (ed), *Protecting Human Rights in the European Union's External Relations*, CLEER Papers 2016/5, 37.

29 European Council, Luxembourg, 28–29 June 1991, Conclusions of the Presidency: 'respect, promotion and safeguard of human rights is an essential part of international relations and one of the cornerstones of European co-operation as well as of relations between the Community and its Member States and other countries'.

30 For example: Article 1(1) of the Agreement establishing an Association between the European Community and its Member States, of the one part, and the Republic of Chile, of the other part [2002] OJ L352/3.

treaty partner have ratified, and by referring to the UDHR, it selects a standard which it presumes to be reflecting customary international law and therefore binding on the other States, irrespective of whether or not they have ratified the main multilateral human rights conventions. Its treaty practice, accepted by the third countries that are parties to these agreements, accordingly contributes to the reaffirmation of the UDHR as an expression of general international law. However, in its treaty relations with Eastern European countries, the EU also includes specific references to the ECHR and other regional human rights documents (the Helsinki Final Act and the Paris Charter of the OSCE).[31]

As regards external trade, references to fundamental rights have become more elaborate and ambitious in the most recent generation of trade and economic cooperation agreements, and the EU has also, unilaterally, created a system of special trade preferences for developing countries if they comply with a set of human rights and good governance obligations. This so-called 'GSP+ scheme', which was originally adopted in 2005 and revised in 2012, currently applies to ten countries, of which the largest by far, in trade terms, is Pakistan.[32] Annex 9 of the GSP Regulation lists a number of core human rights treaties (as well as other 'good governance' treaties) which the beneficiary country is expected to ratify, implement and apply in return for the trade preferences. The EU created a special monitoring system in which it relies on the reports and findings of international monitoring bodies. This 'negative conditionality' is accompanied by positive measures, namely projects on the ground that the EU supports together with the ILO in order to ensure compliance with the ILO Conventions that are included in the conditionality package.[33] One concrete instance where the EU's action under the GSP+ scheme may have helped to advance the application of a human rights instrument concerned El Salvador. After the Commission had, in 2009, opened an investigation into that country's failure to ratify ILO Convention No 87 on freedom of association, the country's constitution was amended so as to permit ratification.[34]

Human rights are also central in the EU's CFSP, that is, the non-economic branch of its external relations. The EU's activities that come under this heading are documented in an Annual Report[35] and often consist of the funding of

---

31 N Ghazaryan, 'A New Generation of Human Rights Clauses? The Case of Association Agreements in the Eastern Neighbourhood' (2015) 40 *European Law Review* 391, 398.

32 Regulation 978/2012 of the European Parliament and of the Council of 25 October 2012 applying a scheme of generalised tariff preferences [2012] OJ L303/1, Articles 9–12.

33 These various forms of interaction are mentioned in European Commission, *Report on the Generalised Scheme of Preferences Covering the Period 2016–2017*, COM(2018) 36 of 19 January 2018.

34 The example is reported by S Velluti, 'The Promotion and Integration of Human Rights in EU External Trade Relations' (2016) 32 *Utrecht Journal of International and European Law* 41, 51.

35 See, most recently, the *EU Annual Report on Human Rights and Democracy in the World in 2016.*

human rights projects across the world from the EU budget. Many of these funding activities serve to bolster the activities on the ground of national and international human rights actors or the ongoing institutional operation of such actors. Examples thereof are support for the activities of a number of UN Special Rapporteurs, support for the Indigenous Peoples' Center for Documentation, Research and Information, and support for a whole range of human rights institutions in Macedonia as part of the pre-accession process of that country.[36] Also, the EU occasionally adopts guidelines setting out the EU's policy agenda on key human rights issues.[37] Most of these guidelines contain extensive references to international and European human rights treaties, as well as to the UDHR.[38] As noted by Wouters and Hermez, by invoking those accepted international standards, 'the EU emphasizes that the Guidelines do not aim to export European values globally, but that they correspond to global human rights standards'.[39]

5. CONCLUSION

On an overall view of the legal evolution in the last decade, it is clear that the EU has become more of an international human rights actor than it used to be. This is reflected in the evolution of the founding Treaties and, in particular, in the incorporation of the EU's own CFR (which itself is heavily inspired by international human rights law) as binding primary EU law, as well as in the (not yet accomplished) constitutional duty for the EU to seek accession to the ECHR. In day-to-day practice, one can observe the frequent though irregular use by the CJEU of the ECHR and the case law of the Strasbourg Court, combined with the occasional recourse, where the facts of the case call for it, to other international human rights instruments. At the same time, the Court of Justice carefully preserves its own autonomy in steering the fundamental rights trajectory of the EU. In the activity of the political institutions of the EU, international human rights are, quite naturally, most visible in the field of external relations where the EU presents itself as an actor seeking to promote respect for human rights, although it is occasionally inconsistent in its action. It has now also become an active participant in the adoption of new

---

36 Ibid, pp 9, 32 and 42 respectively.

37 See the list of 11 Guidelines adopted until 2015 in J Wouters and M Hermez, 'EU Guidelines on Human Rights as a Foreign Policy Instrument: An Assessment', in S Poli (ed), above n 28, pp 63–64.

38 See, for example, the EU Guidelines on the promotion and protection of freedom of religion or belief, adopted on 24 June 2013, whose Annex contains a several pages-long list of universal and regional human rights norms pertaining to that freedom.

39 J Wouters and M Hermez, above n 37, p 74.

international human rights standards. The main challenge, from a legal policy perspective, will be to link the EU's own human rights norms – which have now, with the Treaty of Lisbon, become much more central to the operation of the EU – with continued attention to the development of international human rights norms outside the EU and to the monitoring activities of international bodies. The EU should refrain from moving to a splendid isolation in the human rights field; rather, its judicial and political institutions should encourage and embrace the evolution of human rights at the broader regional and universal levels.

OPINION 2/13 AS A GAME CHANGER IN THE DIALOGUE BETWEEN THE EUROPEAN COURTS?

Jasper Krommendijk*

1. INTRODUCTION

Just before Christmas 2014, the Court of Justice of the European Union (CJEU) unexpectedly put a stop to the European Union's (EU) accession to the European Convention of Human Rights (ECHR). It declared the agreement on the accession of the EU to the ECHR to be incompatible with the specific characteristics and autonomy of EU law in Opinion 2/13.[1] This Opinion reflects the increasing worries of the CJEU about the sometimes far-reaching case law of the European Court of Human Rights (ECtHR), which could hamper the effectiveness of EU law.[2] This tension has become especially visible in the Area

* Assistant Professor of EU Law, Radboud University, Nijmegen, the Netherlands. Email: J.krommendijk@jur.ru.nl. I would like to thank Leonie Huijbers, Tobias Lock and Bruno de Witte for their valuable comments on earlier versions of this chapter.

1 Opinion 2/13, ECLI:EU:C:2014:2454.

2 T Lock, 'The Future of the European Union's Accession to the European Convention on Human Rights after Opinion 2/13: Is it Still Possible and is it Still Desirable?' (2015) 2 *European Constitutional Law Review* 239, 259; X Groussot, J Hettne and GT Petursson,

for Freedom Security and Justice in cases dealing with the Dublin Regulation and the European Arrest Warrant. While the CJEU has to balance the uniformity, primacy and effectiveness of EU law, and the upholding of the system based on mutual trust and mutual recognition with fundamental rights concerns, the ECtHR's sole objective is to guarantee the latter. CJEU judges expressed their concern that the ECtHR does not always take the particularities of EU law, such as mutual trust in the context of the Dublin system, sufficiently into account, because some Strasbourg judges are not familiar with them.[3] There has also been growing uneasiness in Luxembourg with the intrusive case law of the ECtHR in relation to the preliminary reference procedure in Article 267 of the Treaty on the Functioning of the European Union (TFEU). This is because the ECtHR found violations of Article 6 ECHR in *Dhahbi* and *Schipani* for the failure of the highest Italian court to provide a statement of reasons for its refusal to request a preliminary ruling from the CJEU on the basis of Article 267 TFEU.[4] Similar frustration exists in Strasbourg vis-à-vis the CJEU and especially Opinion 2/13, which was not received warmly. Dean Spielmann, former President of the ECtHR, stated that it was 'a great disappointment' and held that the 'the onus will be on the Strasbourg Court to do what it can in cases before it to protect citizens from the negative effects of this situation'.[5] Against this background, it is not surprising that the official contacts between the CJEU and the ECtHR were only resumed in March 2016, when a delegation from the ECtHR visited

'General Principles and the Many Faces of Coherence: Between Law and Ideology in the European Union' in S de Vries, U Bernitz and S Weatherill (eds), *The EU Charter of Fundamental Rights as a Binding Instrument*, Hart Publishing, Oxford 2015, 135.

3 Interviews as discussed in J Krommendijk, 'The Use of ECtHR Case Law by the Court of Justice after Lisbon: The View of Luxembourg Insiders' (2015) 6 *Maastricht Journal of European and Comparative Law* 812, 831. However, the ECtHR has recently held in *Avotiņš* that it is 'mindful of the importance' of mutual recognition mechanisms and mutual trust, but at the same time has shown that it is willing to scrutinise EU measures based on these mechanisms in depth. *Avotiņš v Latvia*, no 17502/07, para 113, ECHR 2016; L Glas and J Krommendijk, 'From Opinion 2/13 to *Avotiņš*: Recent Developments in the Relationship between the Luxembourg and Strasbourg Court' (2017) 3 *Human Rights Law Review* 567.

4 *Dhahbi v Italy*, no. 17120/09 ECHR 2014; *Schipani v Italy*, no. 38369/09 ECHR 2015. The case law of the ECtHR on Article 267 TFEU seems to change the nature of the preliminary reference procedure from a mechanism of interjudicial cooperation to a mechanism safeguarding the individual right to a fair trial. In doing so, the ECtHR is intruding upon the 'specific characteristics and the autonomy of EU law'. However, these fears are slightly exaggerated, as argued in J Krommendijk, '"Open Sesame!" Improving Access to the CJEU by Obliging National Courts to Reason Their Refusals to Refer' (2017) 1 *European Law Review* 46.

5 ECtHR, *Annual Report* 2014, www.echr.coe.int/Documents/Annual_Report_2014_ENG.pdf, 6. Nevertheless, the ECtHR (Grand Chamber) recently upheld its *Bosphorus* doctrine, despite assertions in the literature that it might choose to drop it in the light of Opinion 2/13. See *Avotiņš v Latvia*, above n 3. For a full discussion of this judgment, see L Glas and J Krommendijk, above n 3.

the CJEU.[6] During this visit, judges of both courts talked about the two challenging issues identified above: the preliminary ruling procedure and the Dublin system in light of the ECHR.[7]

These tensions warrant the question as to whether Opinion 2/13 has led to a changing dialogue or interaction between both courts. Before Opinion 2/13, academics and scholars alike championed the practice of extensive 'cross-fertilisation' and 'parallel interpretation'.[8] By contrast, the developments sketched above seem to suggest that we might have entered a new period of increasing tensions between both courts. Opinion 2/13 could easily be interpreted as an illustration of a tendency whereby the CJEU primarily tries to come up with its own autonomous interpretation on the basis of the EU Charter of Fundamental Rights, thereby sidelining the ECHR and the case law of ECtHR.[9] This has also been the perception in Strasbourg. The 2016 report on the future of the ECHR of the Steering Committee for Human Rights referred to 'growing importance of the Charter … to the detriment of the Convention'.[10] There is also a 'corridor joke' in the CJEU that Strasbourg is almost begging the Court of Justice to cite it.[11]

But is it truly so that the CJEU has begun to cite the ECtHR less often and in different ways since Opinion 2/13? This chapter examines the case law of the CJEU after Opinion 2/13 in order to identify how the CJEU has dealt with the jurisprudence from Strasbourg and whether there has been a marked change since Opinion 2/13. It will build on earlier published work examining the interaction between both European (human rights) systems.[12]

---

6 Dean Spielmann, President of the ECtHR, held in October 2015 that official contacts had yet to resume. D Spielmann, 'Whither Judicial Dialogue', Sir Thomas More lecture, Lincoln's Inn, 12 October 2015.

7 They also had a general discussion about the recent case law of both courts. See CJEU, 'A Delegation from the European Court of Human Rights Visits the Court of Justice of the European Union', press release no 25/16, 7 March 2016, curia.europa.eu/jcms/upload/docs/application/pdf/2016-03/cp160025en.pdf.

8 FG Jacobs, 'Judicial Dialogue and the Cross-fertilization of Legal Systems: The European Court of Justice' (2003) 38 *Texas International Law Journal* 547; Joint communication from Presidents Costa and Skouris, 24 January 2011, curia.europa.eu/jcms/upload/docs/application/pdf/2011-02/cedh_cjue_english.pdf, para 1.

9 Case C-617/10, *Åkerberg Fransson*, ECLI:EU:C:2013:105, para 87. Some Advocates General have also been relatively open about the need for an autonomous interpretation; Opinion of AG Poiares Maduro in Case C-465/07, *Elgafaji*, ECLI:EU:C:2008:479, para 19–20; Opinion of AG Cruz Villalón in Case C-69/10, *Samba Diouf*, ECLI:EU:C:2011:102, para 39.

10 Steering Committee for Human Rights (CDDH), 'Report on the longer-term future of the system of the European Convention on Human Rights', CM(2015)176-add1final, 3 February 2016, para 179.

11 Interviews as discussed in J Krommendijk, above n 3, 826.

12 This chapter is partly based on earlier work with a more limited time period until June 2016 (in Dutch); J Krommendijk, 'Het Hof van Justitie van de EU en de rechtspraak van het EHRM sinds Advies 2/13. Een toenemende alleingang en autonome aanpak?' (2016) 8 *Asiel & Migrantenrecht* 356. See also L Glas and J Krommendijk, above n 3.

An earlier article focused on the way in which the case law of the ECtHR was used by CJEU judges, Advocates-General (AGs) and *référendaires* on the basis of 20 interviews with these Luxembourg insiders.[13] This chapter will reflect on these findings on the basis of a structured legal analysis of CJEU judgments in the two and a half years after Opinion 2/13.[14]

It is also not easy to answer the central research question with great certainty, given the short period of time that has lapsed since Opinion 2/13. In addition, examining from a more quantitative view whether Opinion 2/13 has resulted in a lower number of references to the ECtHR does not tell us very much, especially for such a short period of time.[15] This is also because the CJEU has no control over its case docket and the number of references to the ECtHR also depend on the number of fundamental rights-related cases that reach the CJEU in the first place. It is thus only possible to come up with some tentative observations and trends. Time will tell as to whether these trends will also result in a more solid practice.

This chapter starts with a short sketch of the legal framework as to the relevance of the ECHR and judgments of the ECtHR for the EU legal order and the CJEU (section 2). Section 3 provides a typology of different ways in which the CJEU has referred to the ECtHR or has refrained from doing so. Section 4 reflects on the main research question as to whether Opinion 2/13 has been a game changer or not and what the implications of the CJEU's case law are for the future accession of the EU to the ECHR.

2. THE LEGAL FRAMEWORK[16]

Before examining the actual practice of reliance on the case law of the ECtHR, it is important to pay attention to the legal framework governing the relevance

13 J Krommendijk, above n 3.

14 These judgments were found by searching CURIA with references to the 'European Court of Human Rights' in the period between 19 December 2014 and 19 June 2017 for the Court of Justice only, thereby excluding the General Court and the Civil Service Tribunal from the analysis. This led to 138 documents in 98 different cases, including judgments/orders or AG Opinions. All these documents were examined and AG Opinions were compared with the CJEU judgments in the respective cases.

15 Two examples of more quantitative approaches include De Búrca, who examined the period between 2009 and 2012 and found less references to the ECtHR. In addition, Eckes found more references to the ECHR (the Convention instead of the ECtHR) in the period between 2010 and 2012 than in the period between 2007 and 2009. G de Búrca, 'After the EU Charter of Fundamental Rights: The Court of Justice as a Human Rights Adjudicator' (2013) 20 *Maastricht Journal of European and Comparative Law* 168, 174–176; C Eckes, 'The Court of Justice's Participation in the Judicial Discourse: Theory and Practice' in M Cremona and A Thies (eds), *The European Court of Justice and External Relations: Constitutional Challenges*, Hart Publishing, Oxford 2014.

16 This section is for a large part based on J Krommendijk, above n 3, 814–816.

of the ECHR and the case law of the ECtHR for the EU. The EU is not yet legally bound to comply with the ECHR or the judgments of the ECtHR. In *Åkerberg Fransson* and *Kamberaj*, the CJEU determined that the ECHR 'does not constitute, as long as the European Union has not acceded to it, a legal instrument which has been formally incorporated into European Union law'.[17] The CJEU has reiterated this postulation post-Opinion 2/13 in several judgments, such as *Inuit Tapiriit Kanatami* and *J.N.*[18] The CJEU suggested in Opinion 2/13 that the ECtHR's interpretation of the ECHR is only going to be binding upon the EU after the EU's accession to the ECHR, even though there was (and still is) some discussion as to whether this is really the case.[19] In summary, at the moment, the EU is not (yet) bound by the ECHR and the ECtHR.

However, this is not the full story. As the CJEU emphasised in several cases as well, Article 6(3) of the Treaty on European Union (TEU) confirms that fundamental rights recognised by the ECHR constitute general principles of EU law.[20] In addition, it noted that Article 52(3) requires that ECHR-corresponding rights in the Charter are given the same meaning and scope as those laid down by the ECHR.[21] Yet, Article 52(3) does not refer to the case law of the ECtHR.

---

17 *Åkerberg Fransson*, above n 9, para 44; Case C-571/10, *Kamberaj*, ECLI:EU:C:2012:233, para 60.

18 Case C-398/13 P, *Inuit Tapiriit Kanatami*, ECLI:EU:C:2015:535, para 45; Case C-601/15 PPU, *J.N.*, ECLI:EU:C:2016:84, para 45.

19 Opinion 2/13, ECLI:EU:C:2014:2454, para 185. During the hearings in the context of Opinion 2/13, there was 'extensive discussion' as to whether the CJEU – after the accession of the EU to the ECHR – could refuse to recognise judgments of the ECtHR where these conflict with the constitutional identity of the EU or where they are ultra vires. See AG Kokott in Opinion 2/13, ECLI:EU:C:2014:2475, paras 167–171. The CJEU seemed to imply that such situations might indeed occur, because it held that 'it should not be possible for the ECtHR to call into question the Court's finding in relation to the scope ratione materiae of EU law' (Opinion 2/13, para 186). Note that even following accession, the CJEU is still not formally bound by the entire case law of the ECtHR, since Article 46(1) of the ECHR stipulates that judgments are binding inter partes (res judicata). In addition, judgment are declaratory in nature (AG Kokott in Opinion 2/13, paras 78 and 123). See also *Kadi I*, in which the CJEU held that UN Security Council Resolutions cannot derogate from the 'very foundations of the Community legal order' and cannot have primacy over general principles of EU law: Joined Cases 402/05 P and C-415/05 P, *Kadi*, ECLI:EU:C:2008:461 paras 304–308. ECtHR judgments are at the same time considered to have res interpretata, which means that an interpretation of the ECHR by the ECtHR that can be generalised beyond the concrete case is part of the ECHR and, as a result, is binding on State parties. A Bodnar, '*Res Interpretata*: Legal Effect of the European Court of Human Rights' Judgments for Other States Than Those Which were Party to the Proceedings' in Y Haeck and E Brems (eds), *Human Rights and Civil Liberties in the 21st Century*, Spinger, Dordrecht 2014, 223.

20 E.g. Tapiriit Kanatami and J N de Witte argued on the basis of Article 6(3) TEU that the EU is already bound by the ECHR without the accession of the EU to the ECHR. B de Witte, 'The Use of the ECHR and Convention Case Law by the European Court of Justice' in P Popelier et al (eds), *Human Rights Protection in the European Legal Order: The Interaction between the European and the National Courts*, Intersentia, Cambridge 2011, pp 17–34, 21–22.

21 Article 52(3) provides: 'In so far as this Charter contains rights which correspond to rights guaranteed by the Convention for the Protection of Human Rights and Fundamental Freedoms, the meaning and scope of those rights shall be the same as those laid down by

This was intentionally left out in order to safeguard the autonomy of the CJEU.[22] Only the Explanations to Article 52(3) make a reference to the ECtHR. The Explanations stipulate that 'the meaning and the scope of the guaranteed rights are determined not only by the text of those instruments, but also by the case law of the European Court of Human Rights'. However, the Explanations are not legally binding, but should only 'be given due regard' on the basis of Articles 52(7) of the Charter and 6(1) TEU. Nevertheless, there are some early Charter cases in which the CJEU seemed to interpret Article 52(3) more broadly and attached more legal value to the case law of the ECtHR. In *McB*, for example, the CJEU held that the Charter must 'be given the same meaning and the same scope as Article 8(1) of the ECHR, as interpreted by the case law of the European Court of Human Rights'.[23] Since Opinion 2/13, the CJEU has been more nuanced and has held that Article 52(3) merely obliges the CJEU to 'take into consideration' case law of the ECtHR when interpreting the Charter, which reflects an obligation of conduct to a greater extent.[24] Nonetheless, in some judgments, including *WebMindLicenses* and *Toma*, the CJEU followed and explicitly cited the seemingly more far-ranging *McB* reading of Article 52(3), which it framed more in terms of an obligation of result.[25]

The CJEU has become more reluctant to attach importance to the case law of the ECtHR from a formal point of view in other respects as well. Before December 2014, the CJEU already held several times that 'Article 47 of the Charter secures in EU law the protection afforded by Article 6(1) of the ECHR. It is necessary, therefore, to refer only to Article 47'.[26] The CJEU later applied this logic to other Charter provisions in *Inuit Tapiriit Kanatami II* when it held that it was appropriate for the General Court to solely examine the validity of the basic regulation on the basis of Articles 17, 7, 10 and 11 of the Charter.[27]

the said Convention. This provision shall not prevent Union law providing more extensive protection.' AG Kokott labelled Article 52(3) of the Charter a 'homogeneity clause'. Opinion of AG Kokott in Case C-109/10 P, *Solvay v Commission*, ECLI:EU:C:2011:686, para 252.

22 S Douglas-Scott, 'The Court of Justice of the European Union and the European Court of Human Rights after Lisbon' in S de Vries et al (eds), *The Protection of Fundamental Rights in the EU after Lisbon*, Hart Publishing, Oxford 2013, pp 153–179, at p 163.

23 Case C-400/10 PPU, *McB*, ECLI:EU:C:2010:582, para 53; Case C-279/09, *DEB*, ECLI:EU:C:2010:811, para 35. The CJEU determined in *Arango Jaramillo* that 'reference must be made' to the case law of the ECtHR in accordance with Article 52(3) of the Charter: Case C-334/12 RX-II, *Arango Jaramillo and others v EIB*, ECLI:EU:C:2013:134, para 43.

24 Case C-239/14, *Tall*, ECLI:EU:C:2015:824, para 54; *J.N.*, above n 18, para 44; *Inuit Tapiriit Kanatami*, above n 18, para 61.

25 Case C-205/15, *Toma*, ECLI:EU:C:2016:499, para 41; Case C-419/14, *WebMindLicenses Kft.*, ECLI:EU:C:2015:832, para 70. Note that AG Wathelet merely held in this case that 'reference should be made' to the ECtHR case law which 'could be useful'. Opinion of AG Wathelet in Case C-419/14, *WebMindLicenses Kft.*, ECLI:EU:C:2015:606, paras 110 and 113.

26 E.g. Case C-386/10 P, *Chalkor v Commission*, ECLI:EU:C:2011:815, para 51; Case C-199/11, *Otis and others*, ECLI:EU:C:2012:684, para 47; Case C-396/11, *Radu*, ECLI:EU:C:2013:39, para 32.

27 *Inuit Tapiriit Kanatami*, above n 18, para 46.

In *J.N.*, the CJEU added that the review of the validity of EU secondary law 'must be undertaken solely in the light of the fundamental rights guaranteed by the Charter'.[28] With this conclusion, the CJEU went further than its previous case law in two respects: first, by using such demanding language ('must'); and, second, by referring to the Charter in general without signalling out specific provisions. So it is no longer only Article 47 of the Charter that has a wider scope than the ECHR and that could (and must!) be interpreted autonomously, but also provisions that have the same scope and meaning as ECHR provisions.[29]

The CJEU also downplayed the relevance of Article 52(3) in *J.N.* in another way. It emphasised that consistency between the Charter and the ECHR should be sought 'without thereby adversely affecting the autonomy of Union law and … that of the Court of Justice of the European Union'. *J.N.* was the first time that the CJEU quoted this sentence from the Explanations to Article 52(3), which clearly echoes the tone of Opinion 2/13.[30] The CJEU subsequently determined that 'an EU measure must be interpreted, as far as possible, in such a way as not to affect its validity and in conformity with primary law as a whole and, in particular, with the provisions of the Charter'. *J.N.* is thus a good recent example of so-called 'Charter-centrism', which places the Charter centre stage.[31] It also reflects a wish among CJEU judges and référendaires that the importance, the autonomy and the higher level of protection of the EU's 'own catalogue' should be underlined by citing Strasbourg less often.[32]

Since *J.N.*, conflicting judgments have been rendered in which the CJEU reflected explicitly on the relationship between the Charter and the ECHR, as well as Article 52(3). Some judgments repeated several of the considerations of *J.N.* and the 'must … solely' interpret logic.[33] However, several others took a

---

28 *J.N.*, above n 18, para 46.

29 Article 47 offers more protection than Articles 13 and 6(1) of the ECHR, since Article 47(1) protects the right to an effective remedy before a court and because the right to a fair hearing in Article 47(2) is not confined to civil law disputes. For an overview of Charter articles corresponding to or with a wider scope than the ECHR, see the Explanations to the Charter (2007/C 303/02), 17–18.

30 Note that the CJEU already held in *Elgafaji* in relation to Article 15(c) of the Qualification Directive that it 'is a provision, the content of which is different from that of Article 3 of the ECHR, and the interpretation of which must, therefore, be carried out independently, although with due regard for fundamental rights, as they are guaranteed under the ECHR'. Case C-465/07, *Elgafaji*, ECLI:EU:C:2009:94, para 28.

31 K Lenaerts and JA Gutiérrez Fons, 'The Place of the Charter in the EU Constitutional Edifice' in S Peers et al (eds), *The EU Charter of Fundamental Rights: A Commentary*, Hart Publishing, Oxford 2014, pp 1559–1593, margin note 55.26; S Iglesias Sánchez, 'The Court and the Charter: The Impact of the Entry into Force of the Lisbon Treaty on the ECJ's Approach to Fundamental Rights' (2012) 49 *Common Market Law Review* 1565, 1601.

32 Interviews as discussed in J Krommendijk, above n 3, 832.

33 Case C-203/15, *Tele2 Sverige AB*, ECLI:EU:C:2016:970, paras 127–129; Case C-218/15, *Paoletti*, ECLI:EU:C:2016:748, para 22.

more ECHR-friendly approach, some of those referring to *McB* or *DEB* instead.[34] It is not entirely clear how both strands fit together, but it also seems that the *J.N.* approach is more dominant because this was a judgment of the Grand Chamber, while the others were not. In addition, the more restricted interpretation of Article 52(3), which only obliges to 'take into account' the case law of the ECtHR, is consistent with the interviews with Luxembourg insiders, who tended to exclude any formal legal binding force given to ECtHR judgments.[35]

3. A POST-OPINION 2/13 TYPOLOGY OF THE PRACTICE OF CITING STRASBOURG

Despite the formal reluctance to acknowledge the case law of the ECtHR, the CJEU has continued citing the ECtHR, even in *Inuit Tapiriit Kanatami II* and *J.N.*, in which the CJEU was particularly dismissive about the need to rely on Strasbourg.[36] This section provides an overview of CJEU judgments which referred or could have referred to the case law of the ECtHR. It will distinguish between five categories: extensive reliance on Strasbourg (section 3.1); (passing) references to the ECtHR (section 3.2); references to the ECtHR as an afterthought (section 3.3); CJEU judgments without any references to the ECtHR (section 3.4); and CJEU judgments which do not engage with (the Charter of) fundamental rights at all (section 3.5). The last two types of CJEU judgment were primarily identified on the basis of the references to the ECtHR in the judgments and opinions found in CURIA, either done by AGs, (one of) the parties and/or the referring court.[37]

As the rest of this section will show, the CJEU tends to refer to Strasbourg when this is strictly necessary, because there is a tendency to keep judgments as short as possible and there is an emphasis on solving the dispute.[38] This idea is, for example, visible in the Opinion of AG Kokott in *Inuit Tapiriit Kanatami II*, who dismissed the applicants' ECHR argument on the grounds that they failed to explain the 'additional benefit' for considering the ECHR. She implied that a reference to the ECHR would only be warranted if the ECHR imposes more stringent requirements than the Charter.[39]

---

34 *Toma*, above n 25, para 41; Case C-294/16 PPU, *JZ*, ECLI:EU:C:2016:610, paras 48–50; Case C-528/15, *Al Chodor*, ECLI:EU:C:2017:213, para 37.

35 Interviews as discussed in J Krommendijk, above n 3, 816.

36 In *Inuit Tapiriit Kanatami II*, the CJEU cited two judgments of the ECtHR to support its conclusion that future income cannot be considered possessions, 'unless it has already been earned, it is definitively payable or there are specific circumstances that can cause the person concerned to entertain a legitimate expectation of obtaining an asset'. *Inuit Tapiriit Kanatami*, above n 18, para 61. For *J.N.*, see below n 81.

37 See above n 14 for a description of the performed database search.

38 Interviews as discussed in J Krommendijk, above n 3, 825–829.

39 Case C-398/13 P, *Inuit Tapiriit Kanatami*, ECLI:EU:C:2015:190, paras 69–70.

3.1. EXTENSIVE RELIANCE ON STRASBOURG

There are several post-Opinion 2/13 judgments in which the case law of the ECtHR figures rather prominently. Two judgments, *Aranyosi* and *C.K.*, stand out in particular because the CJEU changed its approach, as set out in the introduction to this chapter, in relation to the principle of mutual trust and the protection of individuals against inhuman and degrading treatment. While in earlier judgments the CJEU seemed to prioritise the former by only accepting that fundamental rights can rebut the presumption of mutual trust 'in exceptional circumstances', it seems to have realised that mutual trust is very much dependant on the proper protection of fundamental rights.[40] In *Aranyosi*, the CJEU opted for a more fundamental rights consistent reading of the Framework Decision on the European Arrest Warrant (EAW) by concluding that the execution of an EAW must be suspended if there is a real risk of inhuman or degrading treatment for the individual concerned because of deficient detention conditions in the requesting Member States.[41] This ran counter to the heavily criticised opinion of AG Bot, who prioritised mutual trust, but did not refer to Article 52(3) and tried everything he could to stay within the confines of the EAW system and the limited grounds for non-execution.[42] On the basis of the case law of the ECtHR, the CJEU went even so far as to accept a 'positive obligation' to ensure that prison conditions are in line with fundamental rights.[43] It is one of the very few judgments in which the CJEU subscribed in such explicit terms to an important doctrine developed by the ECtHR.[44] Relying on *Aranyosi* and a considerable number of judgments of the ECtHR, the CJEU also opted for a more fundamental rights and ECHR-friendly interpretation of the Dublin III Regulation in *C.K.*[45] Just like *Aranyosi*, the CJEU again took a different stance than the AG, Tanchev, who explicitly held that the CJEU is not required to follow the approach of the ECtHR.[46] While the CJEU was only willing to admit the possibility for national courts to refuse to return an asylum seeker to the Member State in the case of 'systemic flaws' in the asylum procedure and in

40 C Rizcallah, 'The Dublin System: The ECJ Squares the Circle between Mutual Trust and Human Rights Protection', *EU Law Analysis*, 20 February 2017, http://eulawanalysis.blogspot.co.uk/2017/02/the-dublin-system-ecj-squares-circle.html.

41 Joined Cases C-404/15 and C-659/15 PPU, *Aranyosi* and *Căldăraru*, ECLI:EU:C:2016:198, paras 86–91.

42 See e.g. Fair Trials, 'AG's Bot Opinion in *Aranyosi* and *Căldăraru*: A Threat to Justice in Europe', www.fairtrials.org/wp-content/uploads/160310-Jourov%C3%A1.pdf?platform=hootsuite.

43 Ibid, para 90.

44 For an earlier precedent, see Case C-540/03, *European Parliament v Council*, ECLI:EU:C:2006:429, paras 54, 60 and 62.

45 C Rizcallah, above n 40.

46 The CJEU held that the case law of the ECtHR 'must be taken into account'. Case C-578/16 PPU, *C.K.*, ECLI:EU:C:2017:127, para 68; AG Tanchev in Case C-578/16 PPU, *C.K.*, ECLI:EU:C:2017:108, para 53.

the reception conditions in *N.S.*, it now considered the individual risks for the asylum seeker to be decisive.[47] The CJEU thus accepted 'any circumstance other than' those systemic deficiencies, including those related to the state of health of the asylum seeker. In reaching this conclusion, it relied on the judgment of the ECtHR of two months earlier in *Paposhvili*, dealing with the positive obligations of States to prevent the refoulement of severely ill persons.[48]

In *WebMindLicenses*, the CJEU was also very indebted to Strasbourg, at least in some parts of the judgment. After quoting the more Strasbourg-friendly *McB* reading of Article 52(3), the CJEU cited no less than seven ECtHR judgments to support its finding that the interception of telecommunications and seizure of emails constitutes an interference with Article 8 ECHR and consequently 'also' a limitation of the corresponding right laid down in Article 7 of the Charter.[49] In addition, it also cited five Strasbourg judgments to underline that the absence of a prior judicial authorisation to obtain certain evidence must be compensated by a strict legal framework and procedural safeguards against arbitrary interferences and/or effective ex post review.[50] Without saying that the CJEU should have foregone a reference to Strasbourg, it is unclear why the CJEU felt it necessary to rely so extensively on the ECtHR and needed to quote so many judgments. This is even more so when one compares this judgment with other judgments in which the CJEU did not make any references to the ECtHR (see section 3.4). With respect to the interception of communications, the CJEU could simply have relied on its own extensive case law in the field of data protection, such as *Digital Rights* or *Schrems*.[51] In relation to judicial authorisation, a reference to *Deutsche Bahn* (discussed below) would have seemed appropriate (or sufficient) as well.[52] In addition, the CJEU was not very

47 *N.S.* (and subsequent judgments such as *Abdullahi* and *Kaveh Puid*) were earlier criticised exactly on this point, because the CJEU came up with a (seemingly) more restrictive requirement of 'systemic flaws', which was considered to be at odds with the approach of the ECtHR in relation to Article 3 of the ECHR for whom individual circumstances alone matter. M Den Heijer, 'Case Note on *NS*' (2012) 49 *Common Market Law Review* 1735, 1747. Joined Cases C-411/10 and C-493/10, *N.S.*, ECLI:EU:C:2011:865. See, however, K Lenaerts, 'La vie après l'Avis: Exploring the Principle of Mutual (Yet Not Blind) Trust' (2017) 54 *Common Market Law Review* 805, 832.

48 *Paposhvili v Belgium*, no 41738/10, paras 174–175, ECHR 2016.

49 *WebMindLicenses Kft.*, above n 25, paras 70–72.

50 Ibid, paras 77–78.

51 However, see *Tele2 Sverige AB*, above n 33, paras 127–129; Joined Cases C-293/12 and C-594/12, *Digital Rights Ireland and others*, EU:C:2014:238; Case C-362/14, *Schrems*, ECLI:EU:C:2015:627.

52 M Fierstra, case note on Case C-419/14, *WebMindLicenses Kft.*, European Human Rights Cases 2016/107. This judgment is obviously different, since it deals with the Commission investigatory powers in the EU competition law context under Regulation 1/2003. Nonetheless, the CJEU subscribed more generally to the ECtHR approach in *Société Colas Est*. Case C-583/13 P, *Deutsche Bahn and others v Commission*, ECLI:EU:C:2015:404, paras 17–37.

consistent in its broad use of Strasbourg (see section 3.2 on the selective use of the ECtHR). With respect to the transmission of the evidence by the criminal investigation department to the tax authorities, the CJEU held that only natural persons can invoke the protection of Article 8 of the Charter. This is contrary to the Opinion of AG Wathelet, who relied on the case law of the ECtHR (and also the CJEU) that suggested that legal persons can also rely on Article 8 of the Charter and Article 8 ECHR.[53] Nor did the CJEU (and the AG) justify its approach as to the use of evidence, which was obtained in violation of EU law and the Charter. This is surprising because the CJEU is considerably more strict in terms of fundamental rights protection than the ECtHR in this field. It held, without reference to any precedent, that decisions based on wrongfully obtained evidence must simply be annulled.[54] By contrast, the ECtHR only requires such an outcome when the infringement of privacy also violates the right to a fair trial, as laid down in Article 6 ECHR.[55]

There are several other good examples of cases in which the CJEU relies relatively extensively on the ECtHR which are worth mentioning. In *Deutsche Bahn*, the CJEU reviewed the consistency of the dawn raids conducted by the European Commission in the context of the enforcement of EU competition rules, not only on the basis of the Charter but also the ECHR and the case law of the ECtHR. The CJEU, interestingly enough, did not sketch the earlier discussed legal context for this reliance through, for instance, referring to Article 52(3) of the Charter. What is even more remarkable is that the CJEU even took the ECHR and ECtHR as the starting point, since it first examined the compatibility of the CJEU's judicial review of Commission inspection decisions with Articles 8 and 6(1) ECHR, before reaching the conclusion that there was no violation of Articles 7 and 47 of the Charter.[56] Another case which runs counter to the earlier mentioned Charter-centrism is *Evonik Degussa*. The General Court primarily applied Article 8(1) ECHR instead of Article 7 of the Charter and found that the right to protection of privacy does not extend to reputational damage stemming

---

53 Contrast *WebMindLicenses Kft.*, above n 25, para 79, with the Opinion of AG Wathelet in Case C-419/14, *WebMindLicenses Kft.*, ECLI:EU:C:2015:606, paras 111–112. The CJEU referred to *Volker* as a relevant precedent, but the AG noted that subsequent judgments of the CJEU, such as *Digital Rights Ireland*, point in a different direction. Joined Cases C-92/09 and C93/09, *Volker und Markus Schecke and Eifert*, ECLI:EU:C:2010:662, paras 52–53; *Digital Rights Ireland and others*, above n 51, paras 32–37.

54 *WebMindLicenses Kft.*, above n 25, para 89. Fierstra also criticised this limited reasoning in the light of the principle of procedural autonomy, which the CJEU does not mention in this context either. M Fierstra, above n 52.

55 *Bykov v Russia*, no 4378/02, ECLI:CE:ECHR:2009:0310JUD000437802, para 89; *Rywin v Poland*, nos 6091/06, 4047/07 and 4070/07, para 72, ECHR 2016; *PG and JH v United Kingdom*, no 44787/98, para 34, ECHR 2001.

56 Case C-583/13 P, *Deutsche Bahn and others v Commission*, ECLI:EU:C:2015:404, paras 32–36 and 46–48. M Veenbrink and J Krommendijk, case note on Case C-583/13 P, *Deutsche Bahn*, European Human Rights Cases 2015/187.

from a person's own (criminal) conduct.[57] On appeal, the CJEU also relied on the ECtHR, even though it did not cite specific judgments.[58] Another noteworthy judgment that extensively discussed the ECHR, as well as the case law of the ECtHR, is *Tall*, in which the CJEU held that suspensory effect is not required for appeals against decisions not to further examine an asylum application when they do not lead to the removal of the person concerned.[59] As a matter of fact, the CJEU went much further in this respect than AG Cruz Villalon, who only mentioned the observation of the European Commission on the basis of the ECtHR that expulsion decisions must, in principle, have suspensory effects.[60] In another EAW case, *Lanigan*, the CJEU also applied the case law of the ECtHR on Article 5(1)(f) ECHR on extradition procedures in the context of surrender procedures and held that detention of the requested person is not justified when that procedure is not carried out with due diligence. The CJEU subsequently enumerated several factors reminiscent of the ECtHR case law which national courts should take into account while conducting the latter review.[61]

3.2. (PASSING) REFERENCES TO THE ECTHR

In other cases, the CJEU has made shorter references to the case law of the ECtHR. The rest of this section will distinguish between four different types of references, albeit these are by no means (mutually) exhaustive: references in sensitive cases; citations when an EU law measure or Charter provision is interpreted for the first time; seemingly superfluous references; and selective shopping in the case law of the ECtHR.

It is not surprising that references are especially made in sensitive or complex cases where a reference to another supranational court could strengthen the arguments and conclusions of the CJEU.[62] The best illustration of a post-Opinion 2/13 case in a sensitive area is *Taricco*. In this Grand Chamber judgment, the CJEU, in line with AG Kokott, expanded the obligation for Member States to prosecute VAT fraud more effectively by setting aside an Italian rule which provided for strict limitation periods. In this case, the CJEU

57 Case T-341/12, *Evonik Degussa*, ECLI:EU:T:2015:51, paras 123–126.

58 Case C-162/15 P-R, *Evonik Degussa*, ECLI:EU:C:2016:142, para 43.

59 Case C-239/14, *Tall*, ECLI:EU:C:2015:824. Compare this judgment with Case C-562/13, *Abdida*, ECLI:EU:C:2014:2453.

60 AG Cruz Villalón in Case C-239/14, *Tall*, ECLI:EU:C:2015:531, para 34.

61 C-237/15 PPU, *Lanigan*, ECLI:EU:C:2015:474, paras 59-60; *Gallardo Sanchez v Italy*, no 11620/07, ECLI:CE:ECHR:2015:0324JUD001162007, paras 41–50.

62 The landmark judgments in *Kadi I* and *N.S.* are good examples of this. Joined Cases C-402/05 P and C-415/05 P, *Kadi I*, ECLI:EU:C:2008:461; N.S., above n 47. S Iglesias Sánchez, above n 31, 1604; K Lenaerts, 'Interlocking Legal Orders in the European Union and Comparative Law' (2003) 52 *International and Comparative Law Quarterly* 873, 875.

referred to several judgments of the ECtHR in response to the observations of several interested parties that this might create tension with Article 49 of the Charter and the principle of legality. Relying on Strasbourg, the CJEU supported its conclusion that the disapplication of national law does not breach the rights of the accused.[63] It does not seem unreasonable to infer that the CJEU aimed to divert some of the anticipated criticism through its reliance on another court. This criticism was indeed voiced afterwards. *Taricco* has been criticised for lowering the level of fundamental rights protection of suspects and easily disregarding the legal traditions of Member States which attach more importance to the principle of legality and offer more protection against retroactive changes of limitation periods.[64] The heavy critique eventually spurred the Italian Constitutional Court to send another reference in which the CJEU was essentially asked to reconsider its judgment.[65] Without touching upon the question of whether this criticism is justified, the reliance on the ECtHR shows that Strasbourg could be useful in such a sensitive area as national criminal (procedural) law.[66] Other cases where a reference to the ECtHR was especially useful are *Neptune Distribution* and *CHEZ*. In *Neptune Distribution* (and later *Philip Morris*), the CJEU held that commercial information is in principle covered by the freedom of expression in Article 11 of the Charter.[67]

63 Case C-105/14, *Taricco*, ECLI:EU:C:2015:555, para 57. The CJEU also relied on the case law of the ECtHR in relation to the principle of legality in Case C-72/15, *Rosneft*, ECLI:EU:C:2017:236, paras 164–166.

64 E.g. M Lassalle, '*Taricco* Kills Two Birds with One Stone for the Sake of the PIF', *European Law Blog*, 27 October 2015, http://europeanlawblog.eu/2015/10/27/taricco-kills-two-birds-with-one-stone-for-the-sake-of-the-pif/; D Sarmiento, 'The Scope of Application of EU Law and National Criminal Law: Some Thoughts on *Taricco*', 8 September 2015, https://despiteourdifferencesblog.wordpress.com/2015/09/08/the-scope-of-application-of-eu-law-and-national-criminal-law-some-thoughts-on-taricco-c-10514/; E Billis, 'The European Court of Justice: A "Quasi-constitutional Court" in Criminal Matters?' (2016) 7 *New Journal of European Criminal Law* 20. Timmerman, however, argued that the CJEU provided an interpretation in conformity with the ECtHR, but which merely provided the minimum standard of protection and which thus consciously chose not to go beyond the level of protection under the ECHR. M Timmerman, 'Balancing Effective Criminal Sanctions with Effective Fundamental Rights Protection in Cases of VAT Fraud: *Taricco*' (2016) 3 *Common Market Law Review* 779.

65 LS Rossi, 'How Could the ECJ Escape from the *Taricco* Quagmire?', *Verfassungsblog*, 21 April 2017, https://verfassungsblog.de/how-could-the-ecj-escape-from-the-taricco-quagmire/.

66 Billis, who is of the opinion that *Taricco* is not in line with the ECtHR case law, noted that the quoted judgement of the ECtHR paradoxically underscores strict limitation periods and rejects unforeseeable rules. E Billis, above n 64, 34.

67 Nonetheless, the CJEU eventually considered the French measure which obliged Neptune Distribution to remove misleading claims about low levels of sodium in natural mineral water from packages to be justified and proportional. C-157/14, *Neptune Distribution*, ECLI:EU:C:2015:823, para 64. In *Philip Morris*, the CJEU even referred to the case law of the ECtHR without citing a particular judgment. Case C-547/14, *Philip Morris*, ECLI:EU:C:2016:325, para 147.

The CJEU in essence recognised a corporate human right to freedom of expression, a notion which is controversial and has been criticised.[68] In addition, another sensitive matter where the ECtHR has a lot of experience is discrimination against Roma.[69] In *CHEZ*, the CJEU thus referred to two judgments in relation to the concept of ethnicity and its application to the Roma community.[70]

Covaci is the best example of a judgment in which the CJEU relied on Strasbourg when it interpreted an EU law measure or Charter provision for the first time. In the first judgment about the Roadmap Directives on procedural safeguards in criminal proceedings, the CJEU made a short reference to an ECtHR judgment about the absence of necessity to provide a written translation of all items of written evidence or official documents.[71] It is, however, unclear why the CJEU made a reference to such an old Strasbourg precedent and did not rely on more recent Grand Chamber judgments of the ECtHR on this matter.[72]

In other cases, the CJEU referred to Strasbourg, but it was not always clear why this reference was needed, at least if one is convinced of the argument that the CJEU applies a Charter-centred approach. An example is *Neptune Distribution*, where the CJEU relied on the ECtHR (a second time) to support its finding that correct information about the contents of products for consumers is closely related to the protection of human health and is thus a question of general interest.[73] This support from Strasbourg seems superfluous because of the ample case law of the CJEU in which it came to a similar conclusion.[74] Nor was the CJEU doing very much with this reference in its review of the French interference in *Neptune Distribution*. Likewise, the CJEU referred to the ECtHR in *Nikolajeva* in support of its consideration that an application for registration of a trade mark constitutes a substantive interest protected under the fundamental right to property, while it could have easily based itself on its own case law.[75]

---

68 E.g. recently A Sanchez-Graells and F Marcos, '"Human Rights" Protection for Corporate Antitrust Defendants: Are We Not Going Overboard?' in P Nihoul and T Skoczny (eds), *Procedural Fairness in Competition Proceedings*, Edward Elgar, Cheltenham 2015, pp 84–107; T Isiksel, 'The Rights of Man and the Rights of the Man-Made: Corporations and Human Rights' (2016) 2 *Human Rights Quarterly* 294.

69 AG Kokott in Case C-394/11, *Belov*, ECLI:EU:C:2012:585, para 3.

70 Case C-83/14, *CHEZ Razpredelenie Bulgaria*, ECLI:EU:C:2015:480, para 46.

71 Case C-216/14, *Covaci*, ECLI:EU:C:2015:686, para 39; *Kamasinski v Austria*, no 9783/82, ECHR 1989.

72 *Hermi v Italy*, no 18114/02, ECHR 2006.

73 *Neptune Distribution*, above n 67, para 74.

74 E.g. Case C-544/10, *Deutsches Weintor*, ECLI:EU:C:2012:526, paras 50–52. This judgment was referred to four times by the CJEU.

75 Case C-280/15, *Nikolajeva*, ECLI:EU:C:2016:467, para 43; Case C-580/13, *Coty Germany*, ECLI:EU:C:2015:485. By contrast, the CJEU recognised for the first time, at least to the author's knowledge, that the rights resulting from payment to contributions to a social security scheme constitute property rights with reference to three judgments of the ECtHR. Case C-258/14, *Florescu*, ECLI:EU:C:2017:448, para 50.

One example of selective shopping in the case law of the ECtHR is the politically controversial headscarves case of *Achbita*.[76] In this judgment, the CJEU favoured the employer's wish to project an image of neutrality towards customers as part of an employer's freedom to conduct a business, as laid down in Article 16 of the Charter, over an individual's right to freedom of religion.[77] The CJEU justified the following conclusion with a selective reference to the judgment of the ECtHR in *Eweida*:

> An interpretation to the effect that the pursuit of that aim allows, within certain limits, a restriction to be imposed on the freedom of religion is moreover, borne out by the case-law of the European Court of Human Rights in relation to Article 9 of the ECHR.[78]

However, the CJEU failed to pay any attention to the fair balance test required by the ECtHR and the fact that the ECtHR was actually very strict in accepting interferences with the freedom of religion in *Eweida*. The judgment of the CJEU does not seem to fit well with the conclusion of the ECtHR, in the same paragraph as quoted in *Achbita*, in relation to the British employer's neutrality policy that 'while this aim was undoubtedly legitimate, the domestic courts accorded it too much weight'.[79]

3.3. THE ECTHR AS AN AFTERTHOUGHT

In a third category of cases, the ECtHR is not part of the considerations which led to the conclusion of the CJEU, but is only mentioned at the end of the judgment as some sort of afterthought or cross-check to support the CJEU's own conclusions. This means that the 'Strasbourg-proofness' of the CJEU's analysis is mentioned at the end as a 'by the way' note.[80] These judgments also underline the CJEU's wish to first develop its own autonomous (Charter) interpretation instead of simply relying on another court. The best illustration of this is *J.N.*, which

76 For more details, see S Ouald-Chaib and V David, 'European Court of Justice Keeps the Door to Religious Discrimination in the Private Workplace Opened: The European Court of Human Rights Could Close it', *Strasbourg Observers Blog*, 27 March 2017, https://strasbourgobservers.com/2017/03/27/european-court-of-justice-keeps-the-door-to-religious-discrimination-in-the-private-workplace-opened-the-european-court-of-human-rights-could-close-it/.

77 G Davies, '*Achbita v G4S*: Religious Equality Squeezed between Profit and Prejudice', *European Law Blog*, 6 April 2017 https://europeanlawblog.eu/2017/04/06/achbita-v-g4s-religious-equality-squeezed-between-profit-and-prejudice/.

78 Case C-157/15, *Achbita*, ECLI:EU:C:2017:203, para 39; *Eweida and others v United Kingdom*, nos 48420/10, 36516/10, 51671/10 and 59842/10, para 94, ECHR 2013.

79 Ibid, *Eweida and others*, para 94.

80 Case C-217/15, *Orsi*, ECLI:EU:C:2017:264, paras 24–25; *JZ*, above n 34, para 48; *Taricco*, above n 63, para 57; AG Wathelet in Joined Cases C-401/15 to C-403/15, *Depesme*, ECLI:EU:C:2016:430, para 58. Interviews as discussed in J Krommendijk, above n 3, 832.

dealt with the detention of asylum seekers in the context of their deportation for reasons of public order and security. The CJEU went to great lengths to examine whether detention is valid in the light of Article 6 of the Charter laying down the right to liberty, following a careful and detailed proportionality assessment in the context of Article 52(1) of the Charter.[81] The CJEU, however, had to somehow reflect upon the case law of Strasbourg, because the referring Dutch court had explicitly asked about the validity of the Reception Conditions Directive in the light of one specific judgment of the ECtHR. The CJEU did so, but only at the end as a clear afterthought: 'Finally, it must be recalled that …'[82] The approach of the CJEU can be contrasted with the Opinion of AG Sharpston, who analysed Article 5 ECHR and Article 6 of the Charter in a more combined fashion and did not solely restrict herself to an analysis of Article 5(1)(f) ECHR, but also considered the other exemptions under Article 5(1) ECHR.[83]

This marginal cross-check relates to another practice whereby the CJEU cites the ECtHR in order to argue why a certain EU practice is not contrary to the ECHR.[84] The CJEU, for example, held in the context of EU competition law that the case law of the ECtHR with respect to Article 6 ECHR – and in particular the *Menarini* judgment – does not preclude a 'penalty' from being imposed by an administrative authority (the Commission) in the first instance when such a penalty can be reviewed by a judicial body (the CJEU) that has full jurisdiction and can quash the decision of the authority.[85] The extensive reference to Strasbourg in *Deutsche Bahn* also falls into this category. The CJEU went to great lengths to argue that the system of dawn raids complies with fundamental rights.[86] It held that Article 6 ECHR is not infringed by the ex post legal and factual review by the CJEU of inspection decisions which could lead to its annulment, as a result of which the Commission is unable to use the gathered information.

---

81 *J.N.*, above n 18, paras 50–76.

82 Ibid, para 77.

83 AG Sharpston in Case C-601/15 PPU, *J.N.*, ECLI:EU:C:2016:85, paras 58, 60 and 117–125. This difference is also clear from a more quantitative point. AG Sharpston refers 54 times to the ECHR (32 times to the ECtHR) and 57 times to the Charter, while the CJEU judgments contain 21 references to the ECHR, three references to the ECtHR and 39 to the Charter. Note that doubts have been expressed as to the alleged lower level of protection offered by the CJEU. See M Rhimes, 'Freedom, Asylum Seekers, and Two Lots of European Human Rights', *UK Human Rights Blog*, 17 February 2016 https://ukhumanrightsblog.com/2016/02/17/freedom-asylum-seekers-and-two-lots-of-european-human-rights-michael-rhimes/.

84 Interviews as discussed in J Krommendijk, above n 3, 830. In *Bonda*, the CJEU also held the administrative nature of the measures provided for in the relevant Regulation 'is not called into question by an examination of the case-law of the European Court of Human Rights on the concept of "criminal proceedings" within the meaning of Article 4(1) of Protocol No 7'. Case C-489/10, *Bonda*, ECLI:EU:C:2012:319, para 36.

85 *Menarini Diagnostics v Italy*, no 43509/08, ECHR 2011; Case C-501/11 P, *Schindler*, ECLI:EU:C:2013:522, paras 35–39; Case C-510/11 P, *Kone*, ECLI:EU:C:2013:696, para 22.

86 A Steene, 'Nexans, Deutsche Bahn, and the CJEU's Refusal to Follow ECHR Case Law on Dawn Raids' (2016) 7 *Journal of European Competition Law & Practice* 1, 14.

3.4. NO REFERENCES TO THE ECTHR

There are several judgments in which the CJEU omits any reference to Strasbourg, even though this would have been possible and perhaps even appropriate. This section, first, discusses judgments in which an absence of Strasbourg is understandable; second, judgments in which a reference was possible;[87] and third, judgments where a reference would seem appropriate.

First, in some judgments, the lack of references is understandable.[88] For example, in *Léger*, the CJEU held that the permanent deferral from blood donation for men who have had sexual relations with other men may be justified only when there are no effective and less onerous alternatives in the form of detection techniques that also ensure a high level of health protection for blood recipients. There is no Strasbourg precedent on the specific point of blood bans, but even more generally it could be argued that there is no inspiration to derive from the ECtHR case law, since the ECtHR is generally considered to lag behind the CJEU in terms of protecting LGBT rights.[89] Another example is *Genc* concerning the application of the standstill clause in the EU-Turkey Association Agreement.[90] This case dealt with a Danish measure which made family reunification between a lawfully residing Turkish worker and his minor child subject to the condition that the latter had (the possibility of establishing) sufficient ties with Denmark to enable him successfully to integrate. The referring court explicitly referred to the case law of the ECtHR with respect to the right to family life in relation to the proportionality assessment. Both the CJEU and the AG did not refer to fundamental rights or the Charter, because the standstill clause offered higher protection than the ECHR.

Second, without suggesting that the CJEU should have referred to the ECtHR, a potential for invoking Strasbourg exists when the referring court explicitly refers to the case law of the ECtHR or when the AG makes references to the ECtHR.[91] The latter happened, for example, in relation to the sanctioning

---

87 For this argument in relation to the right to property, see P Oliver and C Stothers, 'Intellectual Property under the Charter: Are the Court's Scales Properly Calibrated?' (2017) 54 *Common Market Law Review* 517, 541.

88 E.g. when the CJEU could not deal with the merits of the case in appeal. Case C-176/13, *Council v Bank Mellat*, ECLI:EU:C:2016:96, paras 51–52; Case C-200/13, *Council v Bank Saderat Iran*, ECLI:EU:C:2016:284, para 49.

89 P Dunne, 'A Right to Donate Nlood? Permanent Deferrals for "Men Who Have Sex with Men" (MSM): *Léger*' (2015) 52 *Common Market Law Review* 1661, 1676.

90 Case C-561/14, *Genc*, ECLI:EU:C:2016:247.

91 See the reference of the Dutch court in Case C-453/16 PPU, *Özçelik*, ECLI:EU:C:2016:783, available at www.minbuza.nl/binaries/content/assets/ecer/ecer/import/hof_van_justitie/nieuwe_hofzaken_inclusief_verwijzingsuitspraak/2016/c-zakennummers/c-453-16-ppu-verwijzingsbs-rb-ams_redacted.pdf; Case C-108/16 PPU, *Dworzecki*, ECLI:EU:C:2016:346, para 16; See also Case C-685/15, *Online Games and others*, ECLI:EU:C:2017:452, para 40.

powers of the Commission in the context of competition law (*InnoLux*), the right to avoid self-incrimination (*HeidelbergCement*), the use of presumptions (*Anbouba*), the right to appeal (*Imtech*), the Brussels II bis Regulation and child abduction (*Bradbrooke*), the revocation of residence permits (*H.T.*), conscientious objection to military service (*Shepherd*), the disqualification of judges when they expressed provisional opinions (*Ogynyanov*), the right to a remedy against a decision to transfer an asylum seeker (*Ghezelbash*), pre-surrender detention (*Vilkas*) and the freedom of religion (*Bougnaoui*).[92] It is not always clear why the CJEU found it unnecessary to explicitly cite an ECtHR judgment in these (and other) cases. It could be that the CJEU simply agrees with the AG, but does not find it necessary to repeat the AG's analysis and citations of ECtHR.[93] Or it could be that the CJEU disagrees with the AG.

It is worthwhile discussing a judgment where a reference to the ECtHR would have been possible, but not necessarily indispensable. In *Schrems*, the CJEU declared the Commission's US Safe Harbour decision, determining that the US offers an adequate level of protection of the personal data transferred, invalid in the light of Articles 7, 8 and 47 of the Charter, dealing with respect for private and family life, the protection of personal data and the right to effective judicial protection.[94] *Schrems* can be contrasted with *WebMindLicenses*, in which the CJEU made rather extensive references to the ECtHR (see section 3.1). *Schrems* only referred to the CJEU's own precedents, including the seminal case of *Digital Rights*, where the CJEU declared the Data Retention Directive to be invalid in the light of Articles 7 and 8 of the Charter.[95] It was in this latter case that the CJEU still extensively referred to the ECtHR 'by analogy'.[96] The absence of a reference to Strasbourg in *Schrems* might, first, reflect an idea among CJEU judges that it is not necessary to constantly refer back to Strasbourg precedents or, in the words of two interviewees, to 'Adam and Eve' or 'Noah's Ark'.[97] It is generally considered sufficient to rely on the CJEU's own precedent in which the case law of the ECtHR was considered and quoted for the first time.

---

92 AG Wathelet in Case C-231/14 P, *InnoLux*, ECLI:EU:C:2015:292, para 66; AG Wahl in Case C-247/14 P, *HeidelbergCement AG*, ECLI:EU:C:2015:694, para 153; AG Bot in Cases C-605/13 P and C-630/13 P, *Anbouba*, ECLI:EU:C:2015:1, paras 51–55; AG Cruz Villalón in Case C-300/14, *Imtech*, ECLI:EU:C:2015:557, para 42; AG Jääskinen in Case C-498/14 PPU, *Bradbrooke*, ECLI:EU:C:2014:2484, paras 42 and 65; AG Sharpston in Case C-373/13, *H.T.*, ECLI:EU:C:2014:2218, paras 60 and 96; AG Sharpston in Case C-472/13, *Shepherd*, ECLI:EU:C:2014:2360, para 51; AG Bot in Case C-614/14, *Ognyanov*, ECLI:EU:C:2016:111, paras 75–91; AG Sharpston in Case C-63/13, *Ghezelbash*, ECLI:EU:C:2016:186, paras 80–83; AG Bobek in Case C-640/15, *Vilkas*, ECLI:EU:C:2016:826, paras 48–52 and 73; AG Sharpston in Case C-188/15, *Bougnaoui*, ECLI:EU:C:2016:553.

93 Interviews as discussed in J Krommendijk, above n 3, 827; K Lenaerts, above n 62, 875.

94 *Schrems*, above n 51.

95 AG Bot only referred to the ECtHR when he described the main conclusions of the CJEU in *Digital Rights Ireland*. *Schrems*, above n 51, para 193.

96 *Digital Rights Ireland and others*, above n 51, paras 47, 54 and 55.

97 Interviews as discussed in J Krommendijk, above n 3, 829–830.

This, for instance, happened in *Åkerberg Fransson*, where the CJEU referred back to *Bonda*, in which the ECtHR's *Engel* criteria determining whether a prosecution is criminal in nature played an important role.[98] *Schrems* could also be an illustration of such a natural 'dilution' of ECtHR case law.[99] Second, the absence of any engagement with the case law of the ECtHR might stem from the idea that the CJEU also expressed in *Tele 2*, that it is not necessary to examine this case law because Article 8 of the Charter has no equivalent in the ECHR.[100] It could also reflect an ever more confident stance of the CJEU, especially in areas dealing with fundamental rights where EU law is going ahead of ECHR developments, including data protection.[101]

The judgment which has perhaps led to the most criticism, because of a failure to engage with the case law of the ECtHR, is *Delvigne*. In this case, the Grand Chamber dealt with a reference for a preliminary ruling about French legislation which deprives persons convicted of serious crimes of their civic rights, including their right to vote. The omission of the ECHR and the ECtHR is especially remarkable because AG Cruz Villalón held that this case 'brings to mind immediately the case law of the European Court of Human Rights', which he extensively discussed.[102] In addition, in earlier judgments of the CJEU concerning voting for the elections of the European Parliament, the CJEU did engage with the case law of the ECtHR.[103] Pertinent ECtHR judgments include *Hirst* and *Scoppola*, where the ECtHR determined that a general, automatic and indiscriminate disenfranchisement of convicted prisoners breaches Article 3 of Protocol 1.[104] Even though Article 39 of the Charter is not mentioned as a Charter provision that corresponds to an ECHR provision, it would have seemed appropriate for the CJEU to explicitly relate to this case law, particularly in the context of the proportionality assessment.[105] This is especially true since

98 In *Bonda*, the Court of Justice adopted a material test in line with the ECtHR's *Engel* case law. *Åkerberg Fransson*, above n 9, para 35; *Bonda*, above n 84, para 37; *Engel v The Netherlands*, no 5100/71, ECLI:CE:ECHR:1976:1123JUD000510071.

99 X Groussot, J Hettne and GT Petursson, above n 2.

100 *Tele2 Sverige AB*, above n 33, para 129. This idea has been criticised on the grounds that there is equivalent case law of the ECtHR corresponding to Article 8. M White, 'The New Opinion on Data Retention: Does it Protect the Right to Privacy?', *EU Law Analysis*, 27 July 2016.

101 T Ojanen, 'Making the Essence of Fundamental Rights Real: The Court of Justice of the European Union Clarifies the Structure of Fundamental Rights under the Charter. Case Note on ECJ 6 October 2015, Case C-362/14, *Maximilillian Schrems v Data Protection Commissioner*' (2016) 2 *European Constitutional Law Review* 318, 329.

102 Opinion of AG Cruz Villalón in C-650/13, *Delvigne*, ECLI:EU:C:2015:363, para 109.

103 E.g. Case C-300/04, *Eman and Sevinger*, ECLI:EU:C:2006:545, paras 36 and 54; Case C-145/04, *Spain v United Kingdom*, ECLI:EU:C:2006:543, paras 94 and 96.

104 *Hirst v United Kingdom*, no 74025/01, §82, ECHR 2005; *Scoppola v Italy*, no 126/05, ECHR 2012.

105 H van Eijken and JW van Rossum, 'Prisoner Disenfranchisement and the Right to Vote in Election to the European Parliament: Universal Suffrage Key to Unlocking Political Citizenship?' (2016) 12 *European Constitutional Law* 114, 128; J Shaw, 'Prisoner Voting: Now a Matter of EU Law', *EU Law Analysis*, 15 October 2015.

the CJEU held that the French measure is proportionate 'in so far as it takes into account the nature and gravity of the criminal offence committed and the duration of the penalty'.[106] This conclusion is noteworthy in the light of the insufficient sketch of the factual and legal French context by the referring court. AG Cruz Villalón even noted that 'there have been few occasions where the Court has been seised of a reference for a preliminary ruling in which there is such a dearth of argument'.[107] Several observers also noted that this rather lenient analysis, giving considerable leeway to the national legislature, might not have been accepted by the ECtHR because the latter conducts a more thorough proportionality assessment.[108] Nonetheless, at the same time it does not seem to be unthinkable that the CJEU was inspired by Strasbourg and the ECtHR thus had an implicit influence, since the CJEU does not explicitly refer to everything considered.[109] First, the CJEU recognised for the first time in line with the ECtHR that the Charter provision constitutes a right of EU citizens. This is not so evident, because at first sight Article 39(2) of the Charter does not seem to include an individual right but merely lays down an obligation for States.[110] Second, the CJEU's focus on the non-blanket nature of the deprivation also echoes the case law of the ECtHR.[111]

3.5. NO REFERENCES TO (THE CHARTER OF) FUNDAMENTAL RIGHTS

There are also several cases in which the CJEU not only omits a reference to the ECHR or ECtHR, but also does not engage with the Charter of Fundamental Rights. Even though this fifth category does not strictly speaking relate to the relationship between the CJEU and the ECtHR, it is relevant to consider it.

---

106 Case C-650/13, *Delvigne*, ECLI:EU:C:2015:648, para 49. Contrast this with AG Cruz Villalón, who explicitly left the proportionality analysis for the national court. Opinion of AG Cruz Villalón in C-650/13, *Delvigne*, ECLI:EU:C:2015:363, paras 123–124.

107 Opinion of AG Cruz Villalón in C-650/13, *Delvigne*, ECLI:EU:C:2015:363, para 51.

108 H van Eijken and JW van Rossum, above n 105, 129–130; S Coutts, 'Case C-650/13 *Delvigne* – A Political Citizenship?', *European Law Blog*, 21 October 2015, https://europeanlawblog.eu/2015/10/21/case-c-65015-delvigne-a-political-citizenship/.

109 J Krommendijk, above n 3, 817. CJEU Judge Lenaerts, for example, held that the CJEU's research of ECtHR case law has often backed up a judgment of the CJEU, but 'rarely transpires directly in the reasoning'. K Lenaerts, above n 62, 873–875; G de Búrca, above n 15, 178.

110 *Delvigne*, above n 106, para 44. The ECtHR recognised this for the first time in *Mathieu-Mohin and Clerfayt v Belgium*, no 9267/81, ECHR 1987. S Platon, 'The Delvigne Judgment of the CJEU: Going Boldly … But Perhaps Not Boldly Enough', *Verfassungsblog*, 24 October 2015, https://verfassungsblog.de/the-delvigne-judgment-of-the-cjeu-going-boldly-but-perhaps-not-boldly-enough/.

111 H van Eijken and JW van Rossum, above n 105, 130; S Coutts, above n 108.

This is because this category reflects a reluctance to approach and solve cases from the perspective of fundamental rights because of the strong consciousness among CJEU judges that the Court is not a fundamental rights court.[112] CJEU judges consistently emphasise in lectures that 'the Court of Justice is not a human rights court; it is the Supreme Court of the European Union'.[113] Cases are preferably solved on the basis of secondary legislation, especially when that legislation contains a certain balance between clashing fundamental rights.[114]

In several judgments, the CJEU dodged the fundamental rights-related questions on procedural grounds and, in doing so, failed to engage or deal with the Charter on substantive grounds.[115] One example is *Willems*, which dealt with the storage and use of biometric data. The CJEU held that this fell outside the scope of Regulation No 2252/2004 on standards for security features and biometrics in passports and travel documents, which meant that the Charter is not applicable. The CJEU concluded this despite the fact that the referring Dutch court had explicitly stated in its referral that the Charter applied because Privacy Directive 95/46 was applicable. The CJEU did not engage with this argument on the Privacy Directive on the (rather questionable) grounds that 'by its questions, the referring court requests the interpretation of Regulation No 2252/2004 and only that regulation'.[116] A similar tactic was applied by the CJEU in *X and X* concerning humanitarian visas and the EU Regulation establishing the Visa Code. Even though the request for such visas was 'formally submitted' on the basis of the Visa Code and the Belgian authorities had handled the requests fully in line with the Code, the CJEU nonetheless considered that the matter fell outside the scope of the Visa Code and the Charter.[117] It justified this on the basis that the intention of the persons submitting applications for visas on humanitarian grounds was to apply for asylum immediately upon their arrival in Belgium and thus 'the purpose of the application differs from that of

---

112 The CJEU, for example, does not deal with the right to housing in relation to deficient Spanish mortgage law in several judgments, including *Gutiérrez Naranjo*, *Aziz* and *Sánchez Morcillo*. JC Benito Sánchez, 'The CJEU and Spanish Mortgage Law: Consumer Protection, Floor Clauses and Accelerated Repayment', *EU Law Analysis*, 20 February 2017. Another example given during the interviews is Case C-394/12, *Abdullahi*, ECLI:EU:C:2013:813; Interviews as discussed in J Krommendijk, above n 3, 827.

113 President Skouris during a lecture in May 2014, as quoted in L Besselink, 'The CJEU as the European "Supreme Court": Setting Aside Citizens' Rights for EU Law Supremacy', *Verfassungsblog*, 18 August 2014.

114 E.g. Joined Cases C-680/15 and C-681/15, *Asklepios Kliniken*, ECLI:EU:C:2017:317, para 27; Case C-13/16, *Rīgas satiksme*, ECLI:EU:C:2017:336. Interviews as discussed in J Krommendijk, above n 3, 827; see also in relation to intellectual property rights P Oliver and C Stothers, above n 87, 541.

115 For a pre-Opinion 2/13 case, see Case C-333/13, *Dano*, ECLI:EU:C:2014:2358, paras 89–90.

116 Case C-446/12, *Willems*, ECLI:EU:C:2015:238, para 52.

117 AG Mengozzi in Case C-638/16 PPU, *X and X*, ECLI:EU:C:2017:93, paras 32–33 and 47.

a short-term visa'.[118] The reliance on intentions rather than formal connections has been criticised.[119]

Several other post-Opinion 2/13 judgments illustrate the tendency to downplay fundamental rights as well. One interesting area where this is visible is cases dealing with the right to an effective remedy and the principle of effective judicial protection.[120] In such cases, the CJEU has also, albeit not consistently,[121] refrained from referring to or analysing the issue in the light of Article 47 of the Charter and Article 6 ECHR and the case law of the ECtHR.[122] In *Orizzonte*, for example, the CJEU ruled on an Italian court fees scheme which provides for fees that are higher in procurement cases than in ordinary administrative cases.[123] In addition, this system also enables courts to raise new (cumulative) fees for supplementary pleas which broaden the dispute. The CJEU examined this scheme in the context of the procedural autonomy of Member States and the limitations under the principle of effectiveness and equivalence. By contrast, AG Jääskinen approached the matter from the point of view of Article 47 of the Charter and also discussed a pertinent judgment of the ECtHR in relation to court fees as an obstacle to the right of access to a court.[124] Something similar happened in *Târşia*. This case dealt with the impossibility for Romanian courts to revise a final decision of a court in civil proceedings when that decision is subsequently found to be incompatible with an interpretation of EU law, while that possibility exists in relation to administrative proceedings. The Grand Chamber again approached the matter from the angle of procedural autonomy,

118 Case C-638/16 PPU, *X and X*, ECLI:EU:C:2017:173, para 47.

119 For a more extensive discussion of this (in Dutch), see J Krommendijk, Case Note on C-638/16 PPU, *X and X*, European Human Rights Cases 2017/81; M Ovádek, 'The CJEU on Humanitarian Visa: Discovering "Un-chartered" Waters of EU Law', *Verfassungsblog*, 13 March 2017, https://verfassungsblog.de/the-cjeu-on-humanitarian-visa-discovering-un-chartered-waters-of-eu-law/.

120 Case C-63/15, *Ghezelbash*, ECLI:EU:C:2016:409; Case C-155/15, *Karim*, ECLI:EU:C:2016:410. M den Heijer, 'Remedies in the Dublin Regulation: Ghezelbash and Karim' (2017) 54 *Common Market Law Review* 859, 866.

121 See recently *Toma*, above n 25, paras 41–44 and 55–56; J Krommendijk, Case Note on Case C-205/15, *Toma*, European Human Rights Cases 2016/203.

122 Safjan counted that only 16 out of the approximately 60 post-Lisbon cases dealing with effective judicial protection referred to Strasbourg case law, something which Prechal qualified as understandable because Article 47 of the Charter is a self-standing principle. M Safjan, 'A Union of Effective Judicial Protection: Addressing a Multi-level Challenge through the Lens of Article 47 CFREU', King's College London, www.kcl.ac.uk/law/research/centres/european/Speech-KINGS-COLLEGE.pdf, 9.

123 Case C-61/14, *Orizzonte Salute*, ECLI:EU:C:2015:655. J Krommendijk, 'Is There Light on the Horizon? The Distinction between "*Rewe*-Effectiveness" and the Principle of Effective Judicial Protection in Article 47 of the Charter after *Orizzonte*' (2016) 53 *Common Market Law Review* 1395.

124 *Stankov v Bulgaria*, no 68490/01, §52, ECHR 2007. AG Jääskinen in Case C-61/14, *Orizzonte Salute*, ECLI:EU:C:2015:307, para 38.

excluding any discussion of the ECHR, ECtHR or the Charter, while only referring in more general terms to the rights of the defence and the principle of legal certainty.[125] The latter is especially remarkable in this case where the referring court explicitly asked about the conformity of the Romanian rule with several Charter provisions, including Article 47. Nevertheless, AG Jääskinen discussed the case law of the ECtHR rather extensively.[126] Likewise, in *Chmieleski*, AG Wathelet discussed three judgments of the ECtHR on the proportionality of sanctions extensively, while the CJEU remained silent on these and did not even refer to the Article 49(3) of the Charter.[127]

The limited scrutiny of fundamental rights is also visible in family reunification immigration cases.[128] One example is *P and S*. In this judgment, the CJEU was critical of the relatively high amount of Dutch fines for third-country nationals who are long-term residents and who fail the civic integration examination. The CJEU held that such high fines are liable to jeopardise the achievement of the objectives pursued by Directive 2003/109 without reflecting on the case law of the ECtHR with respect to the proportionality of penalties as the AG did.[129] Another example is *K and A*, which dealt with the requirement for third-country nationals to pass a civic integration assessment.[130]

4. CONCLUDING REMARKS: OPINION 2/13 AS A GAME CHANGER?

It is beyond the scope of this chapter to reflect on the diverse approach of the CJEU from a more normative point of view. Suffice to say that an autonomous Charter-centric approach is not wholly inappropriate when EU law provides a

125 Case C-69/14, *Târşia*, ECLI:EU:C:2015:662, para 38.

126 AG Jääskinen in Case C-69/14, *Târşia*, ECLI:EU:C:2015:396, paras 40–43.

127 Case C-255/14, *Chmielewski*, ECLI:EU:C:2015:475; AG Wathelet in Case C-255/14, *Chmielewski*, ECLI:EU:C:2015:308, paras 36–64. Other cases in which the CJEU only relied on general principles of EU law instead of the Charter include Case 59/11, *Kokopelli*, ECLI:EU:C:2012:447; Case C-206/13, *Siragusa*, ECLI:EU:C:2014:126, para 34; Joined Cases C-29/13 and C-30/13, *Global Trans Lodzhistik*, ECLI:EU:C:2014:140, para 51. X Groussot, J Hettne and GT Petursson, above n 2.

128 Contrast the more recent judgments with older judgments couched in terms of fundamental rights, such as Case C-109/01, *Akrich*, ECLI:EU:C:2003:491, para 60; Case C-60/00, *Carpenter*, ECLI:EU:C:2002:434, para 42. M De Somer and MP Vink, '"Precedent" and Fundamental Rights in the CJEU's Case Law on Family Reunification Immigration' (2015) *European Integration Online Papers* 1.

129 Case C-579/13, *P and S*, ECLI:EU:C:2015:39, para 104.

130 AG Kokott did refer, albeit in a footnote, to the case law of the ECtHR in order to support the interpretation that married couples do not have an unconditional right to residence in a particular State. Case C-153/14, *K and A*, ECLI:EU:C:2015:186, para 31.

higher level of fundamental rights protection than the ECHR or the case law of the ECtHR, as in *Delvigne* and *Genc.*[131] However, what is most problematic is the diverse and conflicting approach, especially for national courts who struggle to reconcile EU law with the ECHR and the case law of the ECtHR, as is also illustrated by the request for a preliminary ruling by the Dutch court in *J.N.*[132] The typology in the previous section illustrates the diversity in the way in which the CJEU has dealt with the case law of the ECtHR. In particular, there is a discrepancy between, on the one hand, the more 'Strasbourg-friendly' judgments of *Aranyosi*, *C.K.* and *WebMindLicenses* and, on the other hand, *J.N.*, *Achbita* and *Delvigne*. These differences are nothing new and reflect earlier observations of academics and CJEU judges and référendaires that there is no uniform practice or methodology with respect to the case law of the ECtHR.[133] It is not always clear how the differences in the approach of the CJEU could be explained and what the reasons behind a (non-)citation are. It is not the purpose of this chapter to explain those differences. It is sufficient to say that some of these differences can be attributed to the composition of a Chamber and the involved judges and référendaires with different writing styles, legal backgrounds and areas of expertise.[134] In addition, the CJEU is also more compelled to refer to the ECtHR when the (intervening) parties relied on it or when the national court explicitly asked about it.[135] However, this is not necessarily always the case.[136]

The previous sections beg the question as to whether there has been a change in the way in which the CJEU has dealt with the case law of the ECtHR since Opinion 2/13. Section 2 showed that the CJEU has become more reluctant from a formal point of view to attach legal value to the ECtHR since Opinion 2/13. Yet, this has not necessarily resulted in a neglect of Strasbourg case law, as section 3 illustrated. Nor has it led to CJEU judgments that contradict the position of the ECtHR, also because CJEU judges and référendaires are (still) concerned

131 See also *Al Chodor*, above n 34.

132 Above n 18.

133 J Krommendijk, above n 3, 817; Douglas-Scott, for example, labelled the practice 'messy, unpredictable and complex', while de Búrca pointed to the 'increasingly selective' use of the Strasbourg case law and the 'detached, autonomous and potentially uninformed case law' of the Court of Justice with respect to fundamental rights. S Douglas-Scott, above n 22, 657–658 and 665; G de Búrca, above n 15, 173–174. De Witte likewise referred to the 'eclectic and unsystematic' approach. B de Witte, above n 20, 19.

134 J Krommendijk, above n 3, 825.

135 E.g. *Inuit Tapiriit Kanatami*, above n 18.

136 E.g. C-615/13 P, *Client Earth*, ECLI:EU:C:2015:489, para 29. In another case, the Council relied on the case law of the ECtHR with respect to the immunity of international organisations. Opinion of AG Bot in Case C-146/13, *Spain v Parliament and Council*, ECLI:EU:C:2014:2380, para 33 and Case C-146/13, *Spain v Parliament and Council*, ECLI:EU:C:2015:298. See also Opinion of AG Wahl in C-194/14 P, *AC-Treuhand*, ECLI:EU:C:2015:350, para 16; Case C-201/14, *Bara and others*, ECLI:EU:C:2015:638, para 46.

with preventing an open conflict with the ECtHR.[137] The current President of the CJEU, Koen Lenaerts, recently referred to the ECtHR as 'a valuable ally' from which the CJEU draws inspiration leading to a 'constructive dialogue' and 'cross-fertilization'.[138]

It is not surprising that Opinion 2/13 is not a game changer, because it is logical that the CJEU, after having delivered such a heavy blow to the ECHR system in its Opinion, exercises some caution and damage control by giving the impression that it is not hostile towards the ECtHR. This could especially be said about *Aranyosi* and *C.K.*, where the CJEU departed from Opinion 2/13 and reconciled the principle of mutual trust with fundamental rights that were fully in line with the case law of the ECtHR. Nonetheless, the CJEU increasingly relies on the Charter and its own case law. Almost all interviewees and academics noted a tendency at the CJEU to refer less often to the ECHR and the case law of the ECtHR after the entry into force of the Charter. This is a trend that had already started before Opinion 2/13 and reflects the earlier mentioned Charter-centrism idea of the EU now having its 'own catalogue' of fundamental rights.[139] Likewise, another trend which seems to have already started before Opinion 2/13, but which might have become more prominent after Opinion 2/13, is that Strasbourg is cited with less 'fanfare' and in a more modest way, without elevating the ECtHR to the level of being a prominent source of rights. The CJEU has, for example, refrained from referring to the case law of the ECtHR as 'a source of inspiration' or of being of 'special significance'.[140] Nor has it referred to the judgments of the ECtHR 'by analogy'.[141] Nor have judgments of the ECtHR been directly relied upon as if they are similar to the CJEU's own judgments.[142] The more humble role of the ECHR and the ECtHR also reflects the 'hierarchy' in Article 6 TEU, which refers to the Charter in the first paragraph, while the supplementary role of the ECHR as general principles of EU law is listed in the third paragraph.[143]

---

137 Interviews as discussed in J Krommendijk, above n 3, 820; S Morano-Foadi and S Andreadakis, 'A Report on the Protection of Fundamental Rights in Europe' (2014), dm.coe.int/CED20140017597, 43 and 47–48.

138 K Lenaerts, above n 62, 839–840.

139 Interviews as discussed in J Krommendijk, above n 3, 832; Opinion 2/13, para 170.

140 E.g. Case C-540/03, *Parliament v Council*, ECLI:EU:C:2006:429, para 35; Case C-112/00, *Schmidberger*, ECLI:EU:C:2003:333, para 71; Case C-283/05, *ASML*, ECLI:EU:C:2006:787, para 26; Opinion of AG Bot in Case C-43/12, *Commission v Parliament and Council*, ECLI:EU:C:2014:298, para 65.

141 E.g. *Digital Rights Ireland and others*, above n 51, paras 47, 54 and 55.

142 E.g. *Volker und Markus Schecke and Eifert*, above n 53, para 52. However, one (recent) exception is one of the many references to the ECtHR in *WebMindLicenses* where the CJEU referred to the ECtHR while only mentioning the relevant Charter provision, but without the relevant ECHR article. *WebMindLicenses Kft.*, above n 25, para 81.

143 J Krommendijk, above n 3, 834.

The Charter-centrism will most likely continue, since the redrafting of the agreement on the accession of the EU to the ECHR will undeniably take a long time.[144] It is increasingly questioned whether accession will ever happen, even though Jean-Claude Juncker, the President of the European Commission, held in April 2016 that accession is a political priority for the Commission. He added: 'It is also a personal commitment. We are working on a solution to that accession and we will not rest until we have found a solution.'[145] However, this was before Brexit, which has undeniably moved accession lower on the political agenda.[146] The Council of Europe Steering Committee for Human Rights, for example, held in December 2015: 'At this time, it remains to be seen when, how and if accession will be completed'.[147] The long time needed for negotiation and ratification will in any case be amply used by the CJEU to develop and bolster its own fundamental rights case law. This is also because the existence of the preliminary reference procedure also puts the ECtHR at a disadvantage, since it enables all national courts to receive guidance on fundamental rights within less than 15 months when those courts ask questions relating to the Charter. By contrast, without the entry into force of Protocol 16 to the ECHR, (the highest) national courts cannot turn to the ECtHR for Advisory Opinions and have to handle interpretational questions on their own. Because of the growing number of questions on the Charter, the CJEU will (in some cases) be forced to behave like a human rights court, even if it does not consider itself to be such a court.[148] The recent EAW judgment of the Bundesverfassungsgericht is a timely warning for the CJEU that it should not forget its tasks in relation to fundamental rights.[149] Thus, the CJEU's own self-image or reluctance to see itself as a fundamental rights court does not entirely reflect its actual practice. As a matter of fact, the CJEU has increasingly shown that it is not shying away from acting as the guardian of EU fundamental rights by issuing bold judgments in some areas of law, including data protection and privacy (*Digital Rights Ireland*, *Google Spain* and *Schrems*) or asylum (*N.S.* and *C.K.*).

The growing Charter jurisprudence of the CJEU might consequently diminish the perceived need to accede to the ECHR even more. In addition, it is not unthinkable that some EU Member States will become more wary of redrafting the accession agreement in such a way that it complies with all

---

144 Ibid, 835.

145 Assembly of the Council of Europe, ordinary session, 19 April 2016, AA16CR12.

146 The Commission's Work Programme of October 2017 nonetheless, stated that the Commission 'will continue to work towards accession'. COM(2016) 710 final.

147 Steering Committee for Human Rights, above n 10, para 177.

148 See also AG Bot in Joined Cases C-404/15 and C-659/15, PPU, *Pál Aranyosi* (C-404/15) and *Robert Căldăraru* (C-659/15 PPU), ECLI:EU:C:2016:140, para 175; D Sarmiento, 'The German Constitutional Court and the European Arrest Warrant: The Latest Twist in the Judicial Dialogue', *EU Law Analysis*, 27 January 2016.

149 Order of 15 December 2015, 2 BvR 2735.14; D Sarmiento, above n 148.

'demands' of the CJEU as laid down in Opinion 2/13. This is a monstrous exercise that would basically mean that the principle of equality of contracting parties under the ECHR should be dropped in order to preserve the specific characteristics and autonomy of EU law.[150] This would grant the EU a more favourable position under the ECHR than the other States parties, which would undoubtedly result in similar requests from other States parties to the ECHR or be used as justification for their non-compliance with the ECHR or judgments of the ECtHR. This would thus erode the ECHR regime. It remains to be seen whether EU Member States truly want to go down that bumpy road and whether they consider that the gains of an EU accession to the ECHR outweigh the risks involved. This is even more the case because the ECtHR is in practice already dealing with many EU law issues.[151]

In summary, Opinion 2/13 has to date not really been a game changer, but this might be different in several years' time when looking back in hindsight.

150 CJEU Judge Malinovský considered the accession agreement to be full of improvisation work without any precedent in international law. J Malinovský, 'L'adhésion de l'U.E. à la Convention européenne des Droits de l'Homme' (2015) *Revue générale de droit international public* 705, 739; J Polakiewicz, 'Europe's Multi-layered Human Rights Protection System: Challenges, Opportunities and Risks', *EU Law Analysis*, 13 March 2016. X Groussot, J Hettne and GT Petursson, above n 2.

151 J Polakiewicz, above n 150; L Glas and J Krommendijk, above n 3.

SHARING OF THE BURDEN OF PROOF IN CASES ON RACIAL DISCRIMINATION

Concepts, General Trends and Challenges before the ECtHR

Kristin HENRARD*

* Professor of Human Rights, with a focus on vulnerable groups, including minorities, at the Erasmus School of Law, Rotterdam, the Netherlands. Email: Henrard@law.eur.nl.

1. INTRODUCTION

When tracing convergence and divergence in international human rights law, matters of proof and, more particularly, the burden of proof, can arguably not be absent from the discussion. Indeed, there is a growing acknowledgement that the standard of proof and the allocation of the burden of proof over the parties also influence the substance of the norms concerned.[1] Furthermore, given the nature of human rights as rights inherent in being human, their actual enjoyment is essential. In the words of the European Court of Human Rights (ECtHR), rights should not merely be theoretical and illusory, but also practical and effective.[2] While there are many factors that impact this effective enjoyment of rights, judicial review and judicial protection is of crucial importance. When one's rights are not respected and one seeks redress through a court of law, questions of proof are essential. If one cannot furnish proof to the extent required by the law, one will not obtain redress and, ultimately, one cannot enjoy one's fundamental rights. Hence, it is not far-fetched to claim that the effective protection of fundamental rights hinges on the determination of the standard of proof and the allocation thereof between the parties. Furthermore, as the allocation of the burden of proof is closely intertwined with other central doctrines, such as the margin of appreciation, a better understanding of the former will also impact the latter.[3]

The general rule regarding the allocation of the burden of proof is that each party has to prove its alleged claim and the facts upon which it relies, as captured in the Latin phrase 'onus probandi incumbit actori'.[4] The problem for victims of human rights violations generally, and victims of discrimination in particular, is that they most often do not have access to the necessary evidence to support their case. These evidential difficulties in turn carry the risk of undermining the effective protection against discrimination.

A welcome means to counter this risk is the development of the special allocation of the burden of proof, or the shared burden of proof. Following the

---

1 Inter alia, T Thienel, 'The Burden and the Standard of Proof in the European Court of Human Rights' (2007) 50 *German Yearbook of International Law* 579; KM Clermont and E Sherwin, 'A Comparative View of Standards of Proof' (2002) 50 *American Journal of Comparative Law* 243–48; J Kokott, *The Burden of Proof in Comparative and International Human Rights Law*, KLI, The Hague 1998, p 1.

2 Numerous ECtHR cases contain a reference to the doctrine (principle of practical and effective rights), for example, *Stoll v Switzerland*, no 69698/01, ECHR 2007.

3 M Ambrus, 'The European Court of Human Rights and Standards of Proof: An Evidentiary Approach towards the Margin of Appreciation' in L Gruszczynski and W Werner (eds), *Deference in International Courts and Tribunals: Standard of Review and Margin of Appreciation*, Oxford Scholarship Online, Oxford 2014.

4 Latin synonyms are *affirmanti incumbit probatio* or *ei qui affirmat non ei qui negat incumbit probatio*. See, inter alia, J Kokott, above n 1, p 1; T Thienel, above n 1, 550. See below (section 2) on the influence of the standard of proof on the burden of proof.

special allocation, the applicant merely has to establish a prima facie case of discrimination, after which the defendant has to prove that no discrimination has occurred.[5] In this way, the burden of proof is divided over both parties and no longer rests predominantly on the claimant. The special allocation of the burden of proof implies two phases.[6] In the first phase, the claimant needs to 'establish, before a court or other competent authority, facts from which it may be presumed that there has been direct or indirect discrimination'.[7] Subsequently, the burden of proof shifts to the respondent who needs to prove that there has been no breach of the principle of equal treatment.[8]

In the meantime, many jurisdictions have recognised the special allocation of the burden of proof in discrimination cases. This shared burden of proof has not only been solidly enshrined in EU non-discrimination law, but can also be gleaned from the quasi-jurisprudence of several UN treaty bodies, the European Committee of Social Rights and the practice of the Advisory Committee for the Council of Europe's Framework Convention for the Protection of National Minorities.[9]

The ECtHR has a long-standing jurisprudence emphasising the importance of rights being practical and effective.[10] Not surprisingly, it has been argued that the ECtHR, 'along with other regional and global human rights protection mechanisms, has adopted the shared burden of proof generally'.[11] However, the ECtHR's jurisprudence on cases of alleged racial discrimination has often been criticised for its undue reluctance to implement the shared

5 M Ambrus, *Enforcement Mechanisms of the Racial Equality Directive and Minority Protection: Theory and Four Case Studies*, Eleven, The Hague 2010, pp 27–39; J Kokott, above n 1, pp 24–27.

6 Unlike the three phases in US and Canadian human rights litigation, where ultimately the burden of persuasion seems to rest on the claimant: Australian Human Rights and Equal Opportunity Commission, *An International Comparison of the Racial Discrimination Act 1975*, Background Paper no 1, 2008, pp 87–88. See also E Bartholet, 'Proof of Discriminatory Intent under Title VII: *United States Postal Service Board of Governors v Aikens*' (1982) 70 *California Law Review* 1201, 1210–1213, 1217; MA Mendez, 'Presumptions of Discriminatory Motive in Title VII Disparate Treatment Cases' (1980) 32 *Stanford Law Review* 1129, 1139, 1160; and more recently SW Bi, 'Race-Based Reverse Employment Discrimination Claims: A Combination of Factors to the Prima Facie Case for Caucasian Plaintiffs' (2016) 40 *Cardozo Law Review* 45.

7 Using the words of Article 8 of Council Directive 2000/43/EC of 29 June 2000 implementing the principle of equal treatment between persons irrespective of racial or ethnic origin.

8 Ibid.

9 J Kokott, above n 1, p 198; Australian Human Rights and Equal Opportunity Commission, above n 6, pp 80–83. See nn 50–51 below, where this is elaborated upon.

10 Above n 2.

11 FRA and European Court of Human Rights, *Handbook on European Non-discrimination Law*, Publications Office of the European Union, Luxembourg 2011, p 124. See also L Farkas and O O'Farraell, *Reversing the Burden of Proof: Practical Dilemmas at the European and National Level*, Publications Office of the European Union, Luxembourg 2015, p 5.

burden of proof.[12] This apparently incongruous situation invites a closer look at the relevant jurisprudence of the ECtHR, in light of conceptual and theoretical observations about the burden of proof and a noticeable trend among international courts to share the burden of proof among the parties.

This chapter starts with a clarification of the various concepts relevant to the burden of proof – particularly standards of proof, the burden of production and the burden of persuasion – to explain that in international judicial proceedings, discussions on the burden of proof mainly concern the burden of persuasion. A succinct description of the general rule of evidence is followed by a more elaborate consideration of the underlying ratio of the special allocation of the burden of proof. Next, the chapter proceeds with a discussion of the trend among international courts to adopt the shared burden of proof in cases on human rights, particularly the prohibition of discrimination. Subsequently, the analysis turns to the application of the special allocation of the burden of proof and sets out to identify the relevant factors to assess the two respective phases involved. In view of the particular expertise of the Court of Justice of the European Union (CJEU) on the special allocation of the burden of proof,[13] the third part of this chapter zooms in on the clarifications adduced by the CJEU in its case law on the Race Equality Directive (RED). In the process, the preliminary rulings in *Feryn*,[14] *Accept*[15] and *CHEZ*[16] will be discussed, highlighting both a (positive) gradual development of further guidance on the two phases of the shared burden of proof and lingering flaws or lacuna. Following this, the attention shifts to the analysis of the ECtHR's case law on the burden of proof, particularly regarding the adoption of the shared burden of proof, not only in principle but also in its application in a range of 'racial discrimination' cases. Throughout this analysis, the Court's struggle is noted with the application of the special allocation of the burden of proof in cases involving racially motivated crimes. Building on the ever-deepening judicial dialogue between the CJEU and the ECtHR,[17] the chapter concludes with an admittedly rather 'procedural' recommendation

12 See, inter alia, K Henrard, 'A Patchwork of "Successful" and "Missed" Synergies in the Jurisprudence of the ECHR' in K Henrard and R Dunbar (eds), *Synergies in Minority Protection*, Cambridge University Press, Cambridge 2009, p 329. See also M Ambrus, above n 5, p 40.

13 See the more extensive discussion below at sections 2 and 3.

14 Case C-54/07, *Centrum voor gelijkheid van kansen en voor racisme bestrijding v Firma Feryn NV*, ECLI:EU:C:2008:397 (hereinafter *Feryn*).

15 Case C-81/12, *Asociaţia Accept v Consiliul Naţional pentru Combaterea Discriminării*, ECLI:EU:C:2013:275 (hereinafter *Accept*). See below on the explanation why *Accept* is included, as it concerns Council Directive 2000/78/EC of 27 November 2000 and not Council Directive 2000/43/EC of 29 June 2000.

16 Case C-83/14, *Chez Razpredelenie Bulgaria AD v Komisia za zashtita ot diskriminatsia (Chez and another, Third Parties)*, ECLI:EU:C:2015:480 (hereinafter *CHEZ*).

17 See, inter alia, J Gerards and L Glas, 'De Verhouding tussen het EHRM en het HvJ EU na toetreding van de EU tot het EVRM' (2012) *Ars Aequi* 523–525.

for the ECtHR to follow the CJEU in gradually developing further criteria for both phases of the shared burden of proof, notwithstanding the challenges involved.

2. THE BURDEN OF PROOF: CONCEPTS AND PRACTICAL IMPORTANCE

The introduction already highlighted the crucial practical importance of questions of proof when one's rights are interfered with and one wants to obtain redress before a court of law. Questions of proof are indeed of huge practical importance and it has even been argued that what is required in terms of burden of proof 'will significantly affect the substantive meaning of the ban on … discrimination'.[18]

When discussing the burden of proof, it should be kept in mind that the burden of proof can be used in several respects, with closely related but still significantly different meanings. The standard of proof concerns the degree to which a party needs to persuade the court[19] or the 'specified measure of persuasion',[20] and this ranges from 'beyond reasonable doubt' (a very high standard), over 'clear and convincing evidence', to 'balance of probabilities' (preponderance of the evidence).[21] The allocation of the burden of proof determines how the burden of proof is divided or distributed over the parties in a case; in other words, what a party needs to prove to discharge its burden of proof. Of course, the allocation of the burden of proof is also determined by the standard of proof. Indeed, the weight of what each party has to prove also depends on the degree to which this needs to be proven.[22]

Discussing the allocation of the burden of proof is further complicated by the different types of burden of proof that are implicated and that are not always sufficiently differentiated;[23] more particularly, the burden of production on the one hand and the burden of persuasion on the other. The burden of production refers to the burden to produce or to put forward (sufficient) evidence to support one's application, and this burden shifts back and forth between the parties.[24] This burden of production is essential in adversarial trials in which the court

18 E Bartholet, above n 6, p 1202. See also J Kokott, above n 1, pp 20–21 and 83, where she highlights how substantive questions influence the burden of proof, while the burden of proof is decisive for the effective protection of the rights concerned.

19 KM Clermont and E Sherwin, above n 1, pp 243–244.

20 J Kokott, above n 1, p 1.

21 See, inter alia, KM Clermont and E Sherwin, above n 1.

22 J Kokott, above n 1, p 5.

23 Ibid, p 2.

24 M Ambrus, above n 5, pp 26–27.

only knows what the parties prove before it.[25] In international judicial proceedings, the principle of the free admission and assessment of evidence applies and the courts can examine all materials before it, whether these originate from the parties or other sources.[26] Admittedly, the applicant needs to produce sufficient proof to pass the admissibility stage, but before international courts, the argumentation focuses on the determination of which party has the burden of persuasion (to what standard of proof).[27] The burden of persuasion determines who bears the risk of non-persuasion: the party with the burden of persuasion will lose the case when he or she fails to persuade the court of his or her assertions.[28]

Following the general rules of proof, the entire burden of proof rests on the claimant,[29] in the sense that the claimant carries not only the initial burden of production but also the (ultimate) burden of persuasion.[30] However, it has long been recognised that these general rules of proof are difficult to fulfil by victims of human rights violations, and of discrimination in particular, since the evidence is generally in the hands of the perpetrator/defendant.[31] The acknowledgement of these difficulties led over time[32] to the emergence of the special allocation of the burden of proof or the shared burden of proof. This 'system' aims to reduce the burden of proof for the victim, making it possible for the victim to satisfy their burden of proof without burdening the defendant disproportionately.[33]

The special allocation of the burden of proof distinguishes two phases applicable to discrimination law: a first phase in which a presumption of discrimination is established by the claimant; and a second phase in which the respondent can rebut this presumption.[34] Considering that first the claimant needs to persuade the court that a prima facie case is established,[35] and subsequently that the defendant needs to persuade the court that no discrimination took place, one can argue that for each phase the burden of persuasion rests on a different party.

The initial burden of production rests on the claimant, who needs to produce evidence of facts that raise a presumption of discrimination. This indeed

25 CF Amarsinghe, *Evidence in International Litigation*, Brill, Leiden 2005, pp 37–41.
26 Ibid.
27 T Thienel, above n 1, 551–553, 587.
28 J Kokott, above n 1, p 2.
29 Ibid, p 11; K Monaghan, *Equality Law*, Oxford University Press, Oxford 2007, p 563.
30 M Ambrus, above n 5, pp 27–28.
31 Ibid, p 31; E Ellis, *EU Non-discrimination Law*, Oxford University Press, Oxford 2005, p 95.
32 See below section 3 for a discussion of the emergence of a trend to adopt the special allocation of the burden of proof in discrimination cases.
33 See, inter alia, L Farkas and O O'Farrell, above n 11, pp 5–6.
34 See Australian Human Rights and Equal Opportunity Commission, above n 6.
35 See also L Farkas and O O'Farrell, above n 11, p 6, where they emphasise that plaintiffs are [not] exempt from convincing the court that they have a case.

amounts to a considerable reduction of the claimant's burden of proof, since their burden is reduced to establishing merely a presumption. When the claimant persuades the court to find a prima facie case, the burden of proof shifts to the respondent who needs to rebut the presumption.[36] The respondent then needs to persuade the court that no discrimination took place. The respondent can rebut this presumption in two ways: either by negation or by justification.[37] The respondent can first of all try to negate the presumption, by negating the 'harm' or – more often – the causal relationship between the harm and the protected ground. Second, justification acknowledges the causal link, but offers a justification for the harm (causally related to the protected ground). If the respondent cannot persuade the court of the validity of his or her rebuttal, then the court finds discrimination and the claimant wins. In other words, while the burden of production still shifts between parties,[38] the burden of persuasion no longer rests exclusively on the claimant, and ultimately it is the respondent who bears the burden of non-persuasion.

The shared burden of proof thus reduces the burden of proof for the alleged victim and makes it less improbable that a finding of violation will ensue (accompanied by suitable remedies). In order to ensure that the defendant is not saddled with a disproportionate burden of proof, two things are important. First of all, the claimant needs to put forward sufficient indications of discrimination to establish a prima facie case and, second, rebutting the presumption should also not be impossible or excessively difficult.

Obviously, the actual respective burden of proof of both parties depends crucially on the requirements for a prima facie case on the one hand and the subsequent rebuttal of the presumption of discrimination thus established on the other. These respective requirements determine the exact dividing line of the burdens of proof of the parties. As these determinations will depend on all the relevant circumstances, these will be determined on a case-by-case basis. Nevertheless, over time, particular criteria and relevant factors will emerge from the judicial practice.

In this respect, the phenomenon of (transnational) judicial dialogue should not be under-estimated. As has been noted by Anne Marie Slaughter (and many others since her), a process of judicial dialogue can be denoted between

36 See also T Thinel, above n 2, pp 551–552.

37 M Ambrus, M Busstra and K Henrard, 'The Racial Equality Directive and Effective Protection against Discrimination: Mismatches between the Substantive Law and its Application' (2010) 3 *Erasmus Law Review* 177–178. For an extensive discussion see M Ambrus, above n 5, pp 42–54.

38 During the first phase, the initial burden of production is on the claimant, but already here the respondent can try to influence the court as well, namely not to find a prima facie case. In particular, arguments and proof pertaining to the negation of the causal link between harm and protected ground seem fruitful here. 'Justification' arguments would only be suitable once a prima facie case is established, hence in phase 2.

international and national courts in many different constellations,[39] implying that these courts have regard for one another's jurisprudence, thus triggering cross-fertilisation and (a measure of) convergence.

3. A TREND TOWARDS THE ADOPTION OF A SHARED BURDEN OF PROOF IN CASES ON DISCRIMINATION?

By 2011, it was already noted that regional and global human rights protection mechanisms have adopted the shared burden of proof generally in relation to proving claims of human rights violations,[40] and this is certainly visible in discrimination cases. The process of transnational judicial dialogue and the related cross-fertilisation between the respective lines of jurisprudence of international courts undoubtedly contributes to and solidifies this trend. The burden of proof and, more particularly the allocation thereof, has not only received ample and ongoing attention in US law and academic literature, especially in relation to the 1964 Civil Rights Act;[41] the shared burden of proof has also become a steady feature of the jurisprudence among United Nations (UN) treaty bodies,[42] not in the least the Human Rights Committee of the International Covenant on Civil and Political Rights[43] and the Committee on the Elimination of All Forms of Racial Discrimination.[44]

In Europe, the CJEU took the lead in adopting the shared burden of proof and established a steady line of jurisprudence ever since the *Danfoss* case,[45]

39 A-M Slaughter, 'A Typology of Transjudicial Communication' (1999) 29 *University of Richmond Law Review* 99. See also A-M Slaughter, 'A Global Community of Courts' (2003) 44 *Harvard International Law Journal* 191; O Frishman, 'Transnational Judicial Dialogue as an Organisational Field' (2013) 9 *European Law Journal* 739.

40 FRA and European Court of Human Rights, above n 11, p 124. Compare this with the assessment of J Kokott (above n 1, pp 198–199) in 1998, where she notes that international courts use shifts in the allocation of the burden of proof only in exceptional cases, also due to the tendency to apply a relatively high standard of proof.

41 See above, n 6.

42 See, inter alia, OMTC, *Seeking Remedies for Torture Victims: A Handbook on the Individual Complaints Procedures of the UN Treaty Bodies*, OMTC handbook series, OMTC Geneva 2006, pp 84, 218–219; UN, *Individual Complaint Procedures under the United Nations Human Rights Treaties*, Fact Sheet No 7 Rev 2, http://www.ohchr.org/Documents/Publications/FactSheet7Rev.2.pdf.

43 See also J Kokott, above n 1, p 198.

44 The Committee has urged states to 'envisage regulating the burden of proof in civil proceedings involving racial discrimination so that once an alleged victim has established a prima facie case that he or she has been a victim of such a discrimination, it shall be for the respondent to provide evidence of an objective and reasonable justification for differential treatment': Concluding Observations of CERD/C: Australia, UN Doc CERD/C/AUS/CO/14 (14 April 2005), p 15.

45 Case C-109/88, *Handels- og Kontorfunktionærernes Forbund i Danmark v Dansk Arbejdsgiverforening*, ECLI:EU:C:1989:383 (hereinafter *Danfoss*).

where it held that 'if the system of pay is totally lacking in transparency and statistical evidence reveals a difference in pay between male and female workers, the burden of proof shifts to the employer to account for the pay difference by factors unrelated to sex'. Indeed, it was the CJEU that introduced the shared burden of proof in EU non-discrimination law and that has gradually clarified what is needed in the two phases.[46] A provision prescribing the shared burden of proof was subsequently enshrined in the Burden of Proof Directive,[47] which focused on discrimination on the basis of sex and was confirmed in all subsequent non-discrimination directives, thus also expanding it to additional protected grounds like race.

In the meantime, several other European human rights courts have adopted the shared burden of proof in their non-discrimination jurisprudence, often with explicit reference to EU law, both directives and CJEU case law. The case law of the ECtHR[48] was already referred to in the introduction and will be further analysed below. Here, the non-discrimination case law of two other prominent European international (human rights) courts will be briefly discussed. First of all, the European Committee of Social Rights in its collective complaints procedure is often confronted with complaints about discrimination and has transferred this to strong guidance in its review of the periodic state reporting on the non-discrimination provision of the European Social Charter as well. The Committee has developed a steady line of jurisprudence insisting that states that have ratified the European Social Charter must provide in their domestic law for the sharing of the burden of proof in discrimination cases. The language used by the Committee furthermore reflects the language used in the EU Burden of Proof Directive, thus demonstrating the influence of (developments in) EU law in this matter.[49]

Similarly, since the effective protection against discrimination on the basis of ethnic origin is generally considered to be especially relevant for minorities, it should come as no surprise that the Advisory Committee, the committee carrying out the bulk of the monitoring of the Council of Europe's Framework Convention for the Protection of National Minorities (FCNM), has also embraced the shared burden of proof in its monitoring of periodic state reports in relation to the equality provision of the FCNM. In line with the Advisory Committee's focus on ways in which rights of minorities can be protected

---

46 See, inter alia, Case C-127/92, *Enderby v Frenchay Health Authority*, ECLI:EU:C:1993:859; Case C-167/97, *R v Secretary of State for Employment ex parte Seymour Smith and Perez*, ECLI:EU:C:1999:60. See below on the *Feryn*, *Accept* and *CHEZ* cases.

47 Council Directive 97/80/EC on the burden of proof in cases of discrimination based on sex [1997] OJ L14/6, 15 December 1997.

48 See also L Farkas and O O'Farrell, above n 11, p 5.

49 See, inter alia, Council of Europe, *The Protection of Fundamental Social Rights in Europe through the European Social Charter*, Council of Europe, 2001, p 63. See also European

effectively, it strongly recommends sharing of the burden of proof in relation to complaints about discrimination.[50] In this respect, it has also referred to the positive impact of the adoption of national legislation transposing the RED.[51]

4. THE SPECIAL ALLOCATION OF THE BURDEN OF PROOF: FROM PRINCIPLE TO APPLICATION (CRITERIA)

It was already highlighted that (further) case law is needed to flesh out the requirements for the two phases of the shared burden of proof. Indeed, through case law and the application of the shared burden of proof, further parameters will emerge regarding what is required to establish a '*prima facie* case' and what would satisfy the respondent's burden of proof to rebut the presumption.[52]

While there is not yet a crystallised understanding of what would amount to a presumption of discrimination, there clearly needs to be some relation to the essential elements of the concept of discrimination.[53] When considering definitions of discrimination, certain common elements emerge, more particularly a harm (less favourable treatment or disadvantage), including an element of comparison, and a causal relationship between that harm and the protected ground.[54] The respective elements of discrimination are of course entangled to a significant extent, but the element which is most difficult to prove – and for which recourse to presumptions is most needed – is the causal relationship between the harm and the protected ground.[55] Interestingly, it has been noted that 'the relevant provisions of European law are not crystal clear about the burden on parties to establish causation'.[56] Nevertheless, it can be argued that claimants no longer have to demonstrate a clear causal link between the protected ground and the harm, but can suffice with 'establishing facts that point to a probable causal link'.[57] Obviously, this leaves the question what would be required to establish a probable causal link.

Committee of Social Rights, Conclusions 2016, Council of Europe, 2017, inter alia pp 17, 40, 48, 52.

50 See, inter alia, ACFC/OP/III(2011)008, para 41; ACFC/OP/IV(2014), para 25; ACFC/OP/III(2010)001, para 44.

51 See, inter alia, ACFC/OP/III(2011)008, para 41; ACFC/OP/IV(2014)001, para 25; ACFC/OP/III(2011)004, para 35; ACFC/OP/III(2010)003, para 41; ACFC/OP/II(2013)001, para 32.

52 See, inter alia, Australian Human Rights and Equal Opportunity Commission, above n 6, p 81.

53 M Ambrus, above n 5, pp 23–24. See also M Ambrus, M Busstra and K Henrard, above n 37, p 176.

54 See also L Farkas and O O'Farrell, above n 11, pp 7, 53.

55 Australian Human Rights and Equal Opportunity Commission, above n 6, p 79.

56 L Farkas and O O'Farrell, above n 11, p 7.

57 Ibid.

Criteria that recur in literature and case law on the shared burden of proof include the seriousness of the allegation (the more serious, the higher the burden of proof to establish a prima facie case) and the seriousness of the consequences (of finding a prohibited discrimination, a criminal sanction being considered particularly heavy).[58] It has also been argued that the weight of the burden of proof for the respondent depends on the strength of the prima facie case (and the proof adduced to establish this).[59] As is also obvious in US law, the shared burden of proof is mostly applied in civil law (including employment law) cases. Sharing the burden of proof is indeed less straightforward in criminal law cases, not least in the light of basic principles of criminal law, such as the presumption of innocence, and the high standard of proof required, which are clearly not in favour of presumptions that would entail criminal responsibility.

4.1. THE CJEU AND SHARING OF THE BURDEN OF PROOF IN RACIAL DISCRIMINATION CASES: GENERAL CONSIDERATIONS

The CJEU is undoubtedly the international court with the most extensive and elaborate jurisprudence on the shared burden of proof in discrimination cases. Nevertheless, as the close analysis of the judgments below will demonstrate, questions still arise before the CJEU on what the two phases exactly entail.[60] In other words, in the CJEU jurisprudence there is also ample scope for further clarifications on the burden of proof.

While the majority of its non-discrimination jurisprudence, also regarding the burden of proof, concerns the ground of gender (with age cases steadily expanding), the similar wording of the burden of proof provision across the protected grounds is bound to translate into similar lines of jurisprudence. The following analysis of the clarifications by the CJEU of the shared burden of proof under Article 8 of the RED is thus also relevant for cases on the other protected grounds. Furthermore, given the focus of this chapter on the jurisprudence of the ECtHR and considering the close interaction (and cross-fertilisation)

---

58 These factors are particularly visible in the practice of courts following the common law tradition and in the practice of international courts. For a discussion of the case law of the English courts, see T Thienel, above n 1, pp 567–568. The jurisprudence of the ICJ similarly shows a court requiring a degree of evidence that is proportionate to the seriousness of the allegations against states: ICJ, Corfu Channel (*United Kingdom v Albania*), Merits, 9 April 1949, ICJ reports 1949, 17; ICJ, Application of the Convention on the Prevention and the Punishment of the Crime of Genocide (*Bosnia and Herzegovina v Serbia and Montenegro*), Merits, 26 February 2007, 46 ILM 2007, 185, 241.

59 G Selanec, 'Burden of Proof in Antidiscrimination Cases: U.S. Insights into the CJEU Burden of Proof Doctrine', http://www.era-comm.eu/oldoku/Adiskri/03_Burden_of_proof/2014_Oct_Selanec.pdf, slide 21.

60 See also the extensive report by L Farkas and O O'Farrell, above n 11.

between the jurisprudence of the two highest European courts,[61] a closer look at the CJEU's jurisprudence is doubly warranted in this section.

By way of a preliminary point regarding the analysis undertaken here, it is appropriate to highlight that the shared burden of proof applies to both direct and indirect discrimination. The identification of criteria to determine a presumption of discrimination and a rebuttal of that presumption need to do justice to the respective 'natures' of direct and indirect discrimination. Hence, the identification of these criteria is intrinsically related to the ongoing discussion about the exact dividing line between direct and indirect discrimination.[62] While this distinction is relevant for all levels and areas of law, it takes on particular importance in EU law because of the fundamentally different justification scheme for direct versus indirect discrimination.[63] However, in international law generally, and as reflected in the practice of, inter alia, the ECtHR, the same justification scheme exists for direct and indirect discrimination. Consequently, the latter jurisprudence reflects less concern with the exact dividing line between these two concepts. Hence, for the analysis undertaken here, it is less appropriate to focus on demarcation questions between direct and indirect (racial) discrimination.[64]

The following analysis of the preliminary rulings under the RED will investigate whether and to what extent the CJEU has clarified the two phases of the shared burden of proof in relation to Article 8 RED, which stipulates in paragraph 1:

> Member States shall take such measures as are necessary, in accordance with their national judicial systems, to ensure that, when persons who consider themselves wronged because the principle of equal treatment has not been applied to them establish, before a court or other competent authority, facts from which it may be presumed that

---

61 I merely build here on the already abundant literature describing and analysing the relationship between the CJEU and the ECtHR, both from an overarching perspective and focused on non-discrimination law. For a few prominent examples of the former, see S Douglas-Scott, 'A Tale of Two Courts: Luxembourg, Strasbourg and the Growing European Human Rights Acquis' (2006) 43 *Common Market Law Review* 629; G Harpaz, 'The European Court of Justice and its Relations with the European Court of Human Rights: The Quest for Enhanced Reliance, Coherence and Legitimacy' (2009) 46 *Common Market Law Review* 105; FG Jacobs, 'Judicial Dialogue and the Cross-fertilization of Legal Systems: The European Court of Justice' (2003) 38 *Texas International Law Journal* 505. For an excellent example of the latter, see E Bribosia and I Rorive, Anti-discrimination Law in the Global Age', *EJHR*, 2015, http://www.philodroit.be/IMG/pdf/bribosiarorive_adinglobalage_jedh2015.pdf. Admittedly, there are also tensions and disagreements between the courts, as is captured inter alia in Jasper Krommendijk's chapter in this volume.

62 M Ambrus, M Busstra and K Henrard, above n 37, pp 176–178. See also L Farkas and O O'Farrell, above n 11, p 53.

63 FRA and European Court of Human Rights, above n 11, p 43.

64 For a paper which dedicates considerable attention to the exact dividing lines between direct and indirect discrimination in relation to questions of the allocation of the burden of proof, see K Henrard, 'Towards the Effective Protection against Racial Discrimination: Making up the Balance of the EU's Court of Justice's Guidance to National Courts regarding the sharing of the Burden of Proof', to be published in 2018 by Hart in a volume on *EU Anti-Discrimination Law Beyond Gender*, edited by U Belavusau and K Henrard.

there has been direct or indirect discrimination, it shall be for the respondent to prove that there has been no breach of the principle of equal treatment.

Turning to *Feryn* and *CHEZ*, the two substantive preliminary rulings on the RED so far, both rulings have been welcomed because of generous, teleological interpretation concerning the scope of application of the RED's prohibition of racial discrimination.[65] In this respect, the CJEU clearly adopted a teleological interpretation of the relevant RED provisions, an interpretation that furthers the RED's underlying aim of enhancing the effective protection against discrimination on racial grounds. In both cases, especially *CHEZ*, the CJEU did provide guidance to the national courts about the shared burden of proof. However, in neither case did the Court use all the opportunities it was given to clarify the uncertainties of the national courts in this regard.

4.2. *FERYN* AND *CHEZ*: SETTING THE SCENE

In *Feryn*,[66] the CJEU clarified that when an employer declares publicly that they will not recruit employees of a certain ethnic origin, this is bound to dissuade certain candidates from applying and thus actually hinders their access to the labour market. The fact that no identifiable victim comes forward and actually complains that he or she was not hired because of his or her ethnicity is immaterial in this respect.[67] The Court thus implicitly acknowledged that this public statement in itself constitutes 'less favorable treatment on grounds of racial or ethnic origin' and thus direct racial discrimination (Article 2(2)(a) RED), because the message it sends is bound to dissuade persons with that particular ethnic origin from applying at all. Continuing this logic, the Court also held that 'the existence of such direct discrimination is not dependent on the identification of a complainant who claims to have been the victim'.[68] Indeed, the fact that this public statement is made by one of the directors of the firm gives it such credibility – and thus force – that there may actually not be any applicants left to refuse on the basis of this discriminatory policy. The Court clearly opted here for a teleological interpretation of the RED, aimed at effective protection against racial discrimination.[69]

65 M Moschel, '17 Years of Race Equality Directive: A Mitigated Balance', forthcoming in U Belavusau and K Henrard (eds), *EU Anti-discrimination Law beyond Gender: Achievements, Flaws, and Prospects*, Hart Publishing, Oxford 2018. The analysis of the *Feryn* case builds on the one I developed in my Jean Monnet Working Paper 09/09: K Henrard, 'The First Substantive ECJ Judgment on the Racial Equality Directive: A Strong Message in a Conceptually Flawed, and Responsively Weak Bottle' (2009), 09 *Jean Monnet Working Paper*.

66 K Henrard, above n 65.

67 *Feryn*, above n 14, para 25.

68 Ibid.

69 In the process, the Court also had to justify this finding in light of Article 7 of the RED, confining the obligations of Member States to ensure that judicial or administrative

In *CHEZ*, a challenge was made against the practice of an electricity company that installed electricity meters in a district of a town, which is predominantly inhabited by Roma, at an inaccessible height of 6 to 7 metres, while in other parts of the same town the height was 1.7 metres. The company defended this practice because of the increased frequency in tampering with meters and unlawful connections in the district concerned.

The case has been welcomed as the first case in which the CJEU advanced the struggle of Roma communities against systemic discrimination by businesses and governments.[70] Importantly, the Court in *CHEZ* accepted that a non-Roma person can challenge a practice that discriminates against Roma when he or she is similarly affected by the measure. The Court underscored in this respect the fact that the prohibition of discrimination applies not to a particular category of persons, but by reference to the grounds mentioned. Consequently, it matters less that a claimant is not part of particular ethnic group as long as he or she suffers in the same way as a result of the measure taken. The CJEU's reading of the RED and its acceptance, in the words of the Advocate General, of victims by way of collateral damage[71] (following the Court's earlier reasoning in *Coleman*)[72] surely enhances the effective protection against racial discrimination. Again, the Court clearly opted for a teleological interpretation of the RED, which was aimed at furthering its overarching goal of countering discrimination on racial grounds.

In the earlier case of *Belov* concerning very similar facts, also implicating Roma, a paradigmatic example of a group suffering systemic discrimination, the CJEU had adopted a rather restrictive definition of 'court' in Article 267 of the Treaty on the Functioning of the European Union (TFEU). The resulting denial of the status of 'court' to the national equality body concerned had precluded the CJEU from ruling on the substance of the case.[73] While the reason why the Court did not take the opportunity offered by the *Belov* case remains uncertain,

---

procedures for the enforcement of the obligations under the Directive are available for instances with actual victims. In other words, the Court had to find a way to 'fill' the lacuna in the RED and overcome the ensuing internal inconsistency.

70 S Cox, 'When All the People in a District are Victims of Race Discrimination: CJEU Ruling in *CHEZ v CHEZ*' (2015) *EU Law Analysis*, http://eulawanalysis.blogspot.nl/2015/07/when-all-people-in-district-are-victims.html.

71 AG Kokott, Opinion in C-83/14, *CHEZ Razpredelenie Bulgaria AD v Komisia za zashtita ot diskriminatsia*, ECLI:EU:C:2015:170, para 58. The concept 'collateral damage' is used in international humanitarian law to identify 'damage to civilian targets', which is acceptable because it was not intentional, but rather an unintended side-effect; see also JD Ohlin, 'Targeting and the Concept of Intent' (2013) 35 *Michigan Journal of International Law* 81–82. However, the 'collateral damage' in casu refers to a prohibited species of (prohibited) discrimination.

72 Case C-303/06, *Coleman v Atteridge Law and Steve Law*, ECLI:EU:C:2008:415, para 56.

73 See also M Moschel, above n 65, pp 1433–1435.

the CJEU is correctly praised for tackling the complex questions surrounding systemic discrimination and its far-reaching effects in *CHEZ*.[74]

4.3. *FERYN*

In *Feryn*, the CJEU qualified the public statement by a director of the firm as a potential instance of direct discrimination, but failed to tie the facts of the case explicitly to the definitions of direct discrimination in the RED, and similarly did not answer the national court's questions about indirect discrimination.[75] The Court's reasoning about the shared burden of proof is arguably flawed because it failed to identify two separate potential instances of racial discrimination: one pertaining to the public speech and the other to the actual recruitment practice of the firm. Indeed, when the CJEU is serious about qualifying a particular public speech as a (potential) instance of direct discrimination in and of itself, irrespective of its actual impact, because of the strong dissuasive force towards a certain ethnic group, it is imperative to identify two distinctive instances of discrimination and to assess the shared burden of proofs for the speech instance separately. In other words and in terms of clarifying the shared burden of proof, the CJEU should have discussed the shared burden of proof twice: once for the speech instance and once for the practice instance of discrimination. There is actual best practice of some of the national equality bodies in this respect,[76] demonstrating that it indeed makes for clear and convincing reasoning when these two instances of discrimination are consistently distinguished in the argumentation.

The CJEU's failure to identify these two separate instances of discrimination resulted in confusing statements regarding the burden of proof and, more particularly, through the unprincipled and unclear incorporation of 'practice' elements in the shared burden of proof regarding the speech instance of discrimination. The Court qualified in paragraph 28 the public statement of one of the directors as constituting direct discrimination,[77] and in paragraph 31 as potentially amounting to a prima facie case of direct discrimination, since the statements concerned 'may constitute facts of such a nature as to give

---

74 AG Kokott in *Belov* had taken the opposite view regarding the standing of the national equality body; see M Moschel, above n 65.

75 The Court's assessment of the strong dissuasive force of a public statement by one of the directors of the firm could have been qualified as 'less favourable treatment'. Furthermore, the explicit statement that persons with a particular ethnic origin would not be employed arguably establishes a direct causal link with the protected ground, so that the statement concerns fits the definition of direct discrimination in Article 2.2.a of the RED.

76 For a more detailed analysis with references to examples from the Opinions of the Dutch Equal Treatment Commission (now the Netherlands Institute for Human Rights), see K Henrard, above n 65, pp 14–16.

77 *Feryn*, above n 14, para 28.

rise to a presumption of a discriminatory recruitment policy'.[78] Arguably, in paragraph 28 the Court was actually concerned with questions of definition, while only in paragraph 31 was it concerned with the shared burden of proof. Nevertheless, this sloppy reasoning is especially problematic in view of national courts' questions that express a fundamental unease and uncertainty about the distinction between 'discrimination' and 'a presumption of discrimination'.[79] In the end, the Court's reasoning on the shared burden of proof seems to limit the discriminatory speech to a prima facie case of racial discrimination only, while the firm could rebut this presumption inter alia 'by showing that the actual recruitment practice of the undertaking does not correspond to those statements'.[80]

More generally, the CJEU could have clarified the shared burden of proof and the related model of review better when it outlined the distinctive elements in both phases (created by the shared burden of proof) and also what needed to be 'proven' in each phase. More specifically, it could have clarified that as the public statement of the director in *Feryn* amounted to a prima facie case of discrimination, the firm needed to rebut this presumption. Since the limited exceptions for the prohibition of direct discrimination on racial grounds are clearly not applicable, Feryn could not rely on a reasonable objective justification. In other words, Feryn could only try to negate the presumption of discrimination in its attempt to persuade the Court that 'there has been no breach of the principle of equal treatment' (Article 8 RED).

Further guidance is surely welcome as to what could amount to a negation of this kind of presumption of discrimination. The strong dissuasive force of a public speech of one of the directors of a company arguably precludes that simply any type of evidence about the actual recruitment practice would be sufficient to rebut the presumption (and negate discrimination).[81] A credible public statement denouncing the discriminatory statement, explicitly distancing the firm concerned from this type of policy and practice, would arguably be essential to negate the presumption. Contextual elements regarding the way in which this statement is made and by whom (in the hierarchy of the firm) seem similarly relevant.

---

78 Ibid, para 31.

79 The Belgian Court of Appeal requested a preliminary ruling from the ECJ, consisting of six questions, which was reformulated and summarised by the ECJ as follows: 'The national court has requested the Court to interpret the provisions of Directive 2000/43 for the purpose, essentially of assessing the scope of the concept of direct discrimination in the light of the public statements made by an employer in the course of a recruitment procedure (first and second questions), the conditions in which the rule of the reversal of the burden of proof laid down in the directive can be applied (third to fifth questions) and what penalties may be considered appropriate in a case such as that in the main proceedings (question 6)', para 20.

80 Ibid, para 32.

81 See above (section 2), where it was argued that the kind of proof needed to rebut the presumption also depends on the strength of the prima facie case.

The CJEU added 'inter alia' and thus suggested that there would be other ways to prove that the firm had not breached the principle of equal treatment. However, it did not give any further indications on what these other ways would be.

If the CJEU would have indeed distinguished two separate instances of discrimination, how could it have applied the special allocation of the burden of proof to the speech and the practice instance of discrimination respectively? The public statement in *Feryn* can actually be said to amount to 'conclusive proof' of the speech instance of discrimination, which would not leave room for negation. Indeed, all the elements of (direct) discrimination are convincingly proven and thus the Court would not need to share the burden of proof to conclude to a finding of racial discrimination. Regarding the practice instance of discrimination, a public statement like the one in *Feryn* could additionally be considered as raising a presumption of directly discriminatory recruitment practice. However, as I argued earlier,[82] it is not self-evident what the rebuttal of this presumption through negation would require. Indeed, it is unclear how one can prove that one's actual recruitment practice does not use discriminatory selection criteria. Proving that one person of an ethnic background has been employed would arguably not be sufficient, since this does not necessarily mean that in other instances – or even in the vast majority of instances – racially discriminatory motives did not play a role. It would not seem reasonable to demand a review of all recruitment decisions ever taken. It seems similarly inappropriate to determine that a particular percentage of the personnel should have a (particular) ethnic background in order to rebut the presumption successfully. Clearly, further thought needs to go into defining what rebutting a presumption of a discriminatory hiring practice would mean. Additional case law, especially in the form of preliminary rulings of the CJEU, would be welcome.

Interestingly, in the meantime, the CJEU had the opportunity in the *Accept* case to refine its thinking about discriminatory statements regarding recruitment and the related sharing of the burden of proof in a case concerning homophobic statements by a patron of a football club.[83] *Accept* may not be a case on racial discrimination, but the factual setting is so similar to *Feryn*, while the provision on the burden of proof in the relevant directive (2000/78) is identical, that it merits examining whether and how the Court in *Accept* built on and developed its own reasoning in *Feryn*.

In *Accept*, the CJEU in several respects confirmed its reasoning in *Feryn*, while being more precise in the formulation used. In several respects, the judgment is to be welcomed. First, it is commendable that the CJEU maintained a teleological interpretation, where it acknowledged the potentially exclusionary

82 See K Henrard, above n 65, p 26.
83 *Accept*, above n 15.

power of mere speech, especially if it comes from someone who either has or is perceived to have the necessary power to back up the speech, such as in casu, a patron of the club. Indeed, a public statement about excluding particular groups of persons as potential recruits is acknowledged to possibly amount to a prima facie case of discrimination, without there being the need for an identifiable victim. The Court made it explicit that it is for the national court to ultimately assess the facts and decide whether or not a prima facie case is made.[84] Importantly, the facts of the case allowed the CJEU to clarify that even when the person making the statement is actually not legally capable of binding the club in recruitment matters, this does not bar the finding of a prima facie case, when and insofar as that person claims and appears to play an important role in the management of that employer. The Court furthermore identified two additional factors that the national court can take into account when establishing whether or not a prima facie case is made out, namely the perception of the public and whether or not the employer has clearly distanced itself from the statements concerned.[85] While the Court did not explicitly mention the dissuasive force of the public statement, the reference to the perception of the public arguably hints at the de facto impact of the statement.

The Court's analysis of the shared burden of proof in casu can be interpreted as implying a move to a more explicit recognition of a separate speech instance of discrimination. It is indeed striking that the CJEU's guidance about the rebuttal phase does not focus on proof of the actual recruitment practice, but rather on counter-speech and documents outlining the club's recruitment policy. According to the CJEU:

> a prima facie case of discrimination … may be refuted with a body of consistent evidence … such a body of evidence might include, for example, a reaction by the defendant concerned clearly distancing itself from public statements on which the appearance of discrimination is based, and the existence of express provisions concerning its recruitment policy aimed at ensuring compliance with the principle of equal treatment.[86]

Nevertheless, it needs to be acknowledged that the CJEU had actually 'precluded' an investigation into the actual recruitment practice of the defendant because of the risk of an interference with the right of privacy.[87] In other words, it remains

---

84 Ibid, para 50.

85 Ibid, paras 50–51.

86 Ibid, para 58. It should be noted that the Romanian High Court of Cassation and Justice in its decision 2224 relied heavily on the fact that the football club had indeed throughout the procedure distanced itself from the statements made by the individual 'patron'. For a summary, see http://www.equalitylaw.eu/downloads/3632-romania-high-court-confirms-rejection-of-the-action-of-accept-in-the-case-based-on-cjeu-c-81-12-pdf-97-kb.

87 *Accept*, above n 15, para 57.

to be seen whether in other 'public speech' cases the Court will continue to recognise a separate speech instance of discrimination, which is assessed separately from the 'actual practice' instance of discrimination.

The CJEU's reasoning could in any event be further improved if it would fully clarify the second phase (created by the shared burden of proof) by explicitly distinguishing between the two possibilities to rebut the presumption of discrimination, namely negation/refutation and justification. It can still be welcomed that the Court correctly talked about 'refutation' in relation to the burden of proof of the defendant,[88] which is in casu indeed the only real option to rebut the presumption.

4.4. *CHEZ*

In *CHEZ*, the CJEU arguably actively sought out opportunities to clarify the shared burden of proof. Notwithstanding the absence of any question (by the referring court) concerning the sharing of the burden of proof, the Court consistently added in its answers implications for the shared burden of proof.[89]

While the CJEU underscored that the ultimate application to the facts of the case needs to be done by the national courts, it actually provided very concrete guidance in several respects, also pertaining to the sharing of the burden of proof. Regarding the question on direct racial discrimination, the Court provided such concrete guidance on the first phase that it is hard to miss that the Court was actually persuaded that a prima facie case of direct racial discrimination had been made out. Indeed, the Court gave the national court no less than four hints indicating that it considered that the facts pointed to ethnic origin as a direct cause for the challenged practice, and thus to a prima facie case of direct racial discrimination. First, the Court highlighted that high meters were only placed in urban districts where the majority of the inhabitants are Roma.[90] Second, it opined that the company's assertion that damage and unlawful connections are perpetrated mainly by Roma 'could in fact suggest that that the practice at issue is based on ethnic stereotypes or prejudices'.[91] Similarly, the Court considered it significant that no proof was adduced about the actual damage and tampering in the district concerned.[92] Finally, it implicitly argued that the lack of individualised measures and the lasting nature of the practice again pointed to deep-seated prejudices against the group, which makes up the overwhelming majority in the district concerned.[93]

---

88 Ibid, paras 56–58.
89 *CHEZ*, above n 16, paras 77–85.
90 Ibid, para 81.
91 Ibid, para 82.
92 Ibid, para 83.
93 Ibid, para 84.

While the CJEU's answers were very concrete and tied to the facts of the case, it is possible to distil some more general pointers to a prima facie case of direct racial discrimination, more particularly indications that measures are taken based on prejudice instead of actual facts (and proof thereof), and (related) indications that measures are not really tailored but target a particular ethnic group as such. Regarding the rebuttal, the Court pointed out that in instances where the national court has concluded that there is a presumption of direct discrimination, the respondent would have to prove that the practice is exclusively based on objective factors unrelated to ethnicity.[94] Admittedly, the Court's reasoning about the rebuttal could have been more explicit and thus informative, inter alia by clarifying that while in principle two possibilities of rebuttal exist, namely negation/refutation and justification, in casu, only negation or refutation would be possible, since none of the limited exceptions to the prohibition of direct racial discrimination apply. Nevertheless, given the strength of the combined pointers towards a prima facie case of direct discrimination, a successful refutation by the respondent seems highly unlikely. In other words, in the event that the national court would follow the CJEU's hints and opt for the direct discrimination track, the CJEU's reasoning pointed towards a conclusion of prohibited direct discrimination.

The CJEU went on to highlight that if the national court would not find a prima facie case of direct discrimination, then a prima facie case of indirect discrimination should be considered.[95] If nothing else, this reasoning confirms that the Court considered the challenged practice to be deeply problematic. The Court's subsequent answers to the national court's questions about indirect discrimination showed how the facts of the case can also be translated in terms of an apparently neutral measure (adapting the height of meters to counter tampering and damage),[96] which has a disproportionate impact on Roma (the high meters only being installed in districts mainly inhabited by Roma).[97]

Interestingly, with regard to indirect discrimination, the CJEU's reasoning was most explicit and concrete in its guidance to the national court regarding

---

94 Ibid, para 85.

95 Ibid, para 105 reads: 'assuming that the referring court comes to the conclusion that it is not established that the practice at issue amounts to direct discrimination on the grounds of ethnic origin, it must be stated that the facts as found by that court permit the view to be taken that such a practice displays the characteristics required to constitute indirect discrimination'.

96 *CHEZ*, above n 16, para 106.

97 Ibid, para 107. Elsewhere the argument is made that the Court's reasoning could also reflect the preference for a two step model, especially in cases of systemic discrimination, where the dividing line between direct and indirect discrimination becomes murky. Nevertheless, as the Court does not make this two-track model explicit, it is not clear whether the Court would always favour to first try the direct discrimination track, or whether this order reflects the specificities of the case and the strong case the CJEU seems to be making for an instance of direct racial discrimination.

the rebuttal phase. The Court did not only specify in great detail what the defendant would need to provide proof,[98] but also handed to the national courts all the factors they should consider in the process. It underscored the notion that the company cannot simply hide behind so-called 'common knowledge', but needs to specify the actual damage it has sustained in the district and must demonstrate that, after 25 years, there would still be need for this practice.[99] The Court accepted that the practice might be considered suitable to reach the legitimate aim, but urged the national court to consider the possible presence of other suitable, less restrictive means (such as different type of meters).[100] For the proportionality review, the Court highlighted not only the widespread and long-standing nature of the practice at issue, but also its offensive and stigmatising effect.[101] In this respect, it brought to the attention of the national court the fact that other electricity companies used other techniques to combat damage and tampering.[102] In the end, the Court translated these numerous hints into a more outspoken conclusion, namely that 'the disadvantages appear disproportionate to the objectives pursued'.[103] Also in this respect it is possible to deduce from the concrete and case-specific elements put forward by the Court factors that are more generally relevant when evaluating attempts to rebut a presumption of indirect racial discrimination. More particularly, it appears very difficult to justify the disproportionate impact on a particular ethnic group when the measure is widespread and long-standing, not sufficiently tailored and not preceded by a search for less restrictive measures to attain a legitimate aim. In other words, in case the national court would opt for the indirect discrimination track, the CJEU's reasoning steered towards a conclusion of prohibited indirect discrimination.

The review of the preliminary rulings discussed here shows that the CJEU appears increasingly willing and ready to develop criteria regarding the sharing of the burden of proof, particularly about relevant factors for establishing a prima facie case of (direct) racial discrimination, and for assessing the rebuttal of a prima facie case of (indirect) racial discrimination. Further case law is eagerly awaited so that additional general indications and pointers both for the evaluation of the presumption of racial discrimination and its rebuttal can be identified.

As was already highlighted in relation to *Feryn* and *Accept*, and needs to be repeated for *CHEZ*, the CJEU's reasoning could be further improved (if it would fully clarify the second phase created by the shared burden of proof)

---

98 Ibid, paras 116–118.

99 Ibid, paras 116–117.

100 Ibid, paras 113–114, 120–122.

101 Ibid, paras 124–125.

102 Ibid, para 121.

103 Ibid, para 127.

by explicitly distinguishing between the two possibilities to rebut the presumption of discrimination, namely negation/refutation and justification.

5. THE ECTHR AND THE BURDEN OF PROOF IN RACIAL DISCRIMINATION CASES: A MIXED ACCOUNT

As the European Convention on Human Rights (ECHR) does not contain an explicit provision on the burden of proof – either a standard of proof or the allocation of the burden of proof – these matters are determined through the jurisprudence of the ECtHR.[104] A brief account of the general principles that can be gleaned from the Court's jurisprudence regarding the burden of proof is followed by a more extensive review of its case law on the allocation of the burden of proof in cases alleging racial discrimination. In the process, the Court's struggle to find the appropriate allocation of the burden of proof in cases on racially motivated crimes becomes apparent. This struggle is partly due to the intersection with criminal law and, more particularly, when (discriminatory) motive constitutes an element of the crime.

5.1. THE BURDEN OF PROOF PRINCIPLES BEFORE THE ECTHR

As was highlighted above, the proceedings before the ECtHR are governed by the principle of the free admission and assessment of evidence.[105] While it has been argued that the 'burden of production' does not apply to international judicial proceedings, in that the Court is not limited to the proof adduced by the parties,[106] it remains the case that 'the applicant must present facts which are supportive of his allegations by way of a beginning of proof in order to pass the admissibility stage'.[107]

Subsequently, at the merits stage, the practice of the ECtHR reveals a context-dependent approach to the burden of proof. It has stipulated that both the standard of proof (the level of persuasion necessary for reaching a particular conclusion) and the distribution of the burden of proof are 'intrinsically related to the specificity of the facts, the nature of the allegation made and the

104 D Harris, M O'Boyle, E Bates and C Buckley, *Law of the European Convention on Human Rights*, Oxford University Press, Oxford 2014, p 147.
105 Ibid.
106 T Thienel, above n 1, pp 546–547.
107 D Harris et al, above n 104, p 147.

Convention right at stake'.[108] However, these criteria are not systematically used and have not been explicitly applied to the facts of particular cases, thus clarifying the meaning of the expressions used. Nevertheless, these criteria are in line with the factors more generally identified in the practice of (international) courts, namely the seriousness of the allegations and the severity of the consequences of the finding of fact concerned.[109] The jurisprudence of the ECtHR has also been attentive to which party has effective access to evidence, and to the particular vulnerable position of persons in custody of public officials.[110] In these cases, the Court is ready to reduce the burden of proof on the applicant and put a more extensive burden on the respondent state; indeed, it has been applying the shared burden of proof in its jurisprudence.

The distribution of the burden of proof can also be related to the steps the ECtHR distinguishes in its analysis of alleged human rights violations. First, it establishes whether there has been an interference with the right at all and, subsequently, it reviews whether or not the interference is justified.[111] The burden of proof regarding the interference is on the claimant, who has to persuade the Court that an interference took place. Subsequently, the burden of proof shifts to the respondent state that has to persuade the Court that the interference is justified, in respect of the requirements of the limitation clause concerned.[112]

As the two phases of the shared burden of proof impose the burden of persuasion on different parties, these respective burdens of persuasion need to be satisfied to a particular standard of proof.[113] The ECtHR seems to focus its explicit discussions on the standard of proof on the burden of the applicant, and this is a standard of proof 'beyond reasonable doubt'.[114] While it can be argued that this standard is not the same high legal standard as in many criminal law systems,[115] it is still a very high standard, which is

---

108 *Nachova and others v Bulgaria*, nos 43577/98 and 43579/98, para 147, ECHR 2005. See also D Harris et al, above n 104, p 147 and see the analysis below.

109 T Thienel, above n 1, p 575. See also references above in n 61.

110 *Salman v Turkey*, no 21986/93, para 100, ECHR 2000.

111 This is nicely reflected in the Court's judgments, which consistently distinguish these steps with the respective headings, for the justification part further distinguishing between 'general principles' and 'application to the facts'. See also RCA White, 'Judgments in the Strasbourg Court: Some Reflections', 17 July 2009, ssrn.com/abstract=1435197.

112 D Harris et al, above n 104, p 147; T Thienel, above n 1, pp 551–552.

113 See also M Ambrus, above n 5, p 236.

114 The Court has used this standard ever since the Greek Case (European Commission, Report, 5 November 1969). While in these early cases the standard seemed to be specific to cases on Articles 2 (life) and 3 (torture), it has become the 'general' standard of proof: T Thienel, above n 1, pp 564–565. See also D Harris et al, above n 104, p 148.

115 Proceedings before the ECtHR are indeed not criminal in nature and instead concern state responsibility in terms of human rights obligations under the ECHR: T Thienel, above n 1, p 578.

heavily criticised.[116] Interestingly, the Court adds that this proof beyond reasonable doubt may 'follow from the coexistence of sufficiently strong, clear and concordant inferences or of similar unrebutted presumptions of fact'.[117] Admittedly, the latter statement does not concern the standard of proof, but rather the available methods of proof.[118] Nevertheless, the Court arguably adds this statement on inferences to show that the standard of proof is not unreasonably high.[119] Furthermore, focusing on 'inferences' in relation to the methods and the burden of proof facilitates working with presumptions of violations and thus a shared burden of proof.

5.2. HESITANT STEPS TOWARDS SHARING THE BURDEN OF PROOF IN CASES ALLEGING CRIMES WITH A RACIST MOTIVE

The principled acceptance by the ECtHR of the special allocation of the burden of proof is also visible in cases alleging racial discrimination. This is especially visible in relation to the prohibition of indirect discrimination, where the Court has gradually accepted the use of statistical evidence to establish a prima facie case of discrimination. Actually, this gradual coming to terms with the shared burden of proof went hand in hand with a very slow acceptance of the concept of 'indirect discrimination'.[120] Similar developments can be gleaned in relation to direct racial discrimination. For example, the Court has held in the *Timishev* case concerning traffic police officers who were ordered to bar entry to 'Chechens' that 'once the applicant has shown that there has been a difference in treatment, it is then for the respondent Government to show that the difference in treatment could be justified'.[121]

Interestingly, since 2000, the RED seems to exert a certain influence on the ECtHR's jurisprudence, even if the Court's actual reasoning is not explicit

---

116 AG Kokott, above n 1, p 217; T Thienel, above n 1, pp 576–587; F Tulkens, 'Commentaire' in H Ruiz-Fabri and JM Sorel (eds), *La Preuve Devant les Juridictions Internationales*, Editions Pedone, Paris 2007, pp 141, 146.

117 *Ireland v United Kingdom*, no 5310/71, ECHR 1978.

118 T Thienel, above n 1, p 576.

119 Ibid, p 577.

120 See, inter alia, R O'Connell, 'Cinderella Comes to the Ball: Article 14 and the Right to Non-discrimination in the ECHR' (2012) 29 *Legal Studies* 211, 222–23. In the range of cases in which Roma challenge the removal of their caravans on the basis of neutral rules as being discriminatory, because they disproportionately affect them, it is striking that the Court settles these cases in terms of Article 8 (right to respect for private life, family life and home), after which it tends to hold that no separate issue exists in relation to Article 14's prohibition of discrimination. See, inter alia, K Henrard, 'The European Court of Human Rights, Ethnic and Religious Minorities and the Two Dimensions of the Right to Equal Treatment: A Jurisprudence at Different Speeds?' (2016) 34-03 *Nordic Journal on Human Rights* 157.

121 *Timishev v Russia*, nos 55762/00 and 55974/00, para 57, ECHR 2005.

about it. Indeed, the directive's provision on the (shared) burden of proof features several times in the 'overview of relevant international law' in cases concerning alleged racial discrimination.[122]

However, the ECtHR has been more hesitant to share the burden of proof in relation to allegations of direct racial discrimination regarding discriminatory violence[123] ever since the Grand Chamber judgment in the *Nachova* case.[124] The Court had actually adopted in its first *Nachova* judgment a very promising ruling, in which it had established a prima facie case of racial discrimination, shifting the burden of proof to the government. The Chamber, considering that the particular evidentiary difficulties involved in proving discrimination called for a specific approach to the issue of proof, held that 'in cases where the authorities had not pursued lines of inquiry that had clearly been warranted in their investigation into acts of violence by State agents and had disregarded evidence of possible discrimination, the Court might, when examining complaints under Article 14 of the Convention … shift the burden of proof to the respondent Government'.[125] However, the Grand Chamber cautioned against this special allocation of the burden of proof in cases on alleged discriminatory violence. The special allocation would impose an impossible burden of proof on the government, namely the negative proof that no racial animus had informed the killings.[126] Furthermore, the Grand Chamber did not accept that flawed investigations as such were sufficient to constitute a prima facie case of racial discrimination. The Grand Chamber in *Nachova* started a new line of jurisprudence which distinguishes firmly between the procedural obligation to investigate properly such incidents on the one hand and the substantive obligation to refrain from discriminatory killings on the other.[127] Importantly, the Grand Chamber in *Nachova* did not reject sharing the burden of proof out of hand; it actually identified a set of relevant criteria for the use of the special allocation of the burden of proof, more particularly 'the specificity of the facts, the nature of the allegations made, and the Convention right at stake'.[128] Unfortunately, as highlighted before, the Court has not actually applied these criteria, let alone clarified them, either in *Nachova* or in subsequent cases. Often it did not even refer to these criteria at all.[129]

---

122 See the ECtHR cases discussed below.

123 See, inter alia, K Henrard, 'The Council of Europe at the Rescue of a Paradigmatic Case of Failed Integration?' (2011) 10 *European Yearbook on Minority Issues*, 269, 281–83.

124 *Nachova and others v Bulgaria*, nos 43577/98 and 43579/98, ECHR 2005.

125 Ibid, para 128.

126 Ibid, para 157.

127 Ibid.

128 Ibid, para 147.

129 See, inter alia, *Cakir v Belgium*, no 44256/06, ECHR 2009; *Soares and others v Romania*, no 24329/02, ECHR 2011. See also the discussion of the cases below.

In 2014, the ECtHR decided several cases on alleged discriminatory violence, several of which seemed to indicate that the Court was becoming more receptive towards the sharing of the burden of proof in such cases. Nevertheless, the following close scrutiny will reveal that the Court only shifted the burden of proof to the respondent state in cases in which the applicants could furnish extremely convincing (virtually conclusive) proof about the racial motive involved. Furthermore, the Court still does not apply the abovementioned (*Nachova*) criteria to the facts of the cases and has thus failed to clarify the meaning of these criteria. The review of subsequent cases reveals the ongoing preference of the Court to focus on the procedural obligation to investigate possible racist motives of violent crimes, without acknowledging implications of failures in that regard for the substantive obligation not to engage in or condone racist violence.

In 2014, the ECtHR was confronted with three cases of alleged discriminatory violence, one of which concerned alleged discriminatory violence by public authorities (*Antayev*);[130] the two others concerned complaints about a lack of protection by the public authorities against discriminatory violence by private parties (*Begheluri*[131] and *Abdu*).[132] Admittedly, *Begheluri* concerns discriminatory violence against Jehovah's Witnesses, a religious minority. Nevertheless, parameters that appear to influence the Court's evaluation of the prima facie phase in cases involving discriminatory violence against religious minorities are mutatis mutandis applicable for cases on racially discriminatory violence, given the extensive conceptual overlap between 'ethnicity' and 'religion'.[133]

Antayev and others v Russia concerned alleged racial violence against Chechens by police officers. The ECtHR established a prima facie case of racist violence by the police on the basis of a combination of direct and more indirect, contextual proof.[134] The Court actually had quite strong proof before it of racist violence by the police:[135] there was not only proof of biased internal police instructions stipulating that Chechens need to be treated in a special manner (confirmed by the use of a special task force for a minor offence), but there were also detailed allegations of racist abuse by the police officers concerned.

130 *Antayev and others v Russia*, no 37966/07, ECHR 2014.

131 *Begheluri and others v Georgia*, no 28490/02, ECHR 2014.

132 *Abdu v Bulgaria*, no 26827/08, ECHR 2014.

133 Admittedly, Jehovah's Witnesses are a religious minority without ethnic traits. Nevertheless, the Court is unlikely to develop different parameters for the identification of a prima facie case for racially discriminatory violence and discriminatory violence on religious grounds, exactly because of the conceptual overlap between ethnicity and religion.

134 *Antayev*, above n 130, paras 127–128.

135 For a similar case with strong proof of racial discriminatory violence and a finding of a prima facie case, see *Makhashevy v Russia*, no 20546/07, ECHR 2012.

Interestingly, the Court also seemed to return to its reasoning in *Nachova*, as in its establishment of the prima facie case of substantive discrimination, it attached considerable weight to the flaws regarding the special investigatory duty. Indeed, notwithstanding these serious indications, no investigations were conducted about possible racist motivation. The Court went on to find a violation of the prohibition of racial discrimination by Russia, as the government could not provide any (convincing) proof that the police violence was not tainted by discrimination.

Also, in *Begheluri*, the ECtHR was ready to accept a prima facie case of discrimination, while sending even stronger hints of a potential return to *Nachova* reasoning. This case concerned several instances of allegedly religious motivated violence against Jehovah's Witnesses by a group of Orthodox extremists. Notwithstanding the Court's distinction between a substantive and a procedural violation of the prohibition of discrimination, the assessment of both was rather intertwined. More particularly, in relation to the complaint about substantive racial discrimination by the police, the Court attached considerable weight to both contextual information about the systematic police tolerance of religious violence against Jehovah's Witnesses and the severe flaws concerning investigation and prosecution.[136] The Georgian government's defence that the complaint could not be substantiated was summarily dismissed by the Court, thus leading to a finding of prohibited racial discrimination.[137]

However, in *Abdu*, a case concerning discriminatory violence by private persons against (vulnerable) migrants, with many similarities with the *Begheluri* case, the ECtHR did not establish a prima facie case of racial discrimination by the police. Admittedly, there were no accounts of racist slurs by the police officers concerned, but there were numerous general reports about racist violence against migrants in Bulgaria and reports testifying about the structural problem of flawed investigations about alleged racist violence. In casu, the Court even highlighted the fact that the two alleged perpetrators were skinheads well known by the police and remarked that this heightened the investigatory duties of the authorities accordingly.[138] Nevertheless, the Court dismissed the complaint about the discriminatory motivation for the flawed investigation as manifestly ill-founded.

Hence, in both *Antayev* and *Begheluri*, the ECtHR seems to return to some extent to its reasoning in *Nachova's* Chamber judgment. The severe flaws regarding the investigatory duty and, more particularly, the duty to unveil possible discriminatory animus, combined with broader

136 *Begheluri*, above n 131, para 176.
137 Ibid, para 179.
138 Ibid, para 52.

contextual information, swayed the Court into accepting a prima facie case of discrimination (in the substantive sense). In *Abdu*, however, the Court was markedly more reticent to take into account the severe defects in the investigations, combined with broader contextual information of a systemic problem (and government inaction), and refused to acknowledge a prima facie case of discrimination (in the substantive sense).

While one can only speculate about the underlying reason for these differences, it would seem that the specificity of the available proof seems to be the most important factor. Indeed, in *Antayev*, the ECtHR was offered almost incontrovertible proof of racist police violence. The main difference between *Begheluri* and *Abdu* seems to be the absence of detailed information about racist slurs uttered by the police in the latter. Nevertheless, in *Abdu*, the Court could also have found a prima facie case of racial discrimination by the police, more particularly in view of the implication of skinheads with a record of discriminatory violence and strong contextual information both about the systemic violence against migrants and the systemic lack of investigation in discriminatory violence. Indeed, does a structural lack of investigation, and thus prosecution of racist violence, not qualify as condoning racist violence, and could this not be said to reflect a discriminatory attitude towards migrants among the police?[139]

Interestingly, in more recent cases on alleged racist violence,[140] the ECtHR's reasoning focused on the modalities and evaluation of the special investigatory obligation to unveil possible racist motives. It is to be welcomed that the Court seems to impose ever-stricter requirements for the fulfilment of this investigatory duty, while it scrutinises closely the way in which the national authorities employed national criminal law.[141] However, in most of these cases, the severe flaws regarding the special investigatory duty could also be related to possible prejudice and the discriminatory attitude of the public authorities. The Court even acknowledged this where it talks about the possibility of 'official acquiescence to or even connivance with hate crimes'.[142]

139 In *Eremia v the Republic of Moldova*, no 3564/11, ECHR 2013, the Court was willing to impute discriminatory intent to the government because the officials had been aware of the domestic violence against the complainant and had done nothing to protect her. See also D Petrova, 'Evolving Strasbourg Jurisprudence on Domestic Violence: Recognising Institutional Sexism', *Oxford Human Rights Hub: A Global Perspective on Human Rights*, 20 June 2013, http://ohrh.law.ox.ac.uk/evolving-strasbourg-jurisprudence-on-domestic-violence-recognising-institutional-sexism.

140 *MC and AC v Romania*, no 12060/12, ECHR 2016; *Sakir v Greece*, no 48475/09, ECHR 2016; *RB v Hungary*, no 64602/12, ECHR 2016; *Balazs v Hungary*, no 15529/12, ECHR 2015.

141 *MC and AC*, above n 140, paras 124–125; *Sakir*, above n 140, paras 70–72; *RB*, above n 140, paras 89–91.

142 *MC and AC*, above n 140, para 124; *Sakir*, above n 140, para 72.

Nevertheless, the ECtHR carefully avoided explicit evaluations of the possible substantive violation of the prohibition of racial discrimination, arguably demonstrating its ongoing reluctance to establish the related institutional racism.[143]

In the end, the ECtHR still seems fundamentally ill at ease with a shared burden of proof in cases concerning discriminatory violence. It only accepts a prima facie case when there is virtual 'conclusive proof' of racial discrimination or at least a strong combination of direct and more indirect contextual proof.

5.3. TENSION: CRIMINAL LAW PRINCIPLES AND SUSPECT GROUNDS

The ECtHR's apparent struggle with the shared burden of proof becomes visible in a particular type of case, namely cases in which there is an interaction with criminal law and, more particularly, where the racist motive constitutes one of the elements of the crime concerned. Indeed, criminal law does not lend itself to the sharing of the burden of proof due to the cardinal principle of the presumption of innocence, which triggers a particularly high standard of proof.[144] However, the ECtHR does not establish criminal guilt; it determines the responsibility of States parties in relation to their obligations under the ECHR to respect fundamental rights.[145] This also implies that the Court is not bound by the same stringent requirements regarding the standard of proof[146] and could work with the shared burden of proof.

A finding by the ECtHR that a state is responsible for racial violence is particularly serious and it will not want to conclude this too easily. Indeed, a survey of the practice of several domestic and international jurisdictions has

143 In *MC and AC*, the Court considered it no longer necessary to consider the substantive violation after having established a procedural violation of the prohibition of discrimination (para 126). In *RB*, the Court addressed the discrimination complaint within its analysis of Article 8 in itself. Admittedly, Balazs' complaint only concerned the procedural state obligations; it remains striking that the Court avoided acknowledging the numerous indications of institutional discrimination within the Hungarian police.

144 As the ECtHR recognises itself, e.g. *Barbera, Messegue and Jabardo v Spain*, no 10588/83, para 77, ECHR 1988. The extensive discussions and case law on the sharing of the burden of proof in the United States and elsewhere also concern civil law, and not criminal law. Nevertheless, it should be noted that even in criminal law at times, the burden of proof is shifted more towards the defendant: this shift is said to be sometimes justified where it is particularly difficult for a prosecution to meet a legal burden. See, inter alia, *Williamson v Ah On* (1926) 39 CLR 95, 113 (Isaacs J).

145 Articles19 ff and 32 of the ECHR.

146 For an extensive discussion of the potential origins of the current relatively high standard of proof adopted by the Court and what would be a proper standard of proof, see T Thienel, above n 1, pp 563–687.

clearly shown that 'the more serious the allegation, the more compelling must be the evidence to meet the standard of proof'.[147] While the latter statement concerns the standard of proof, it arguably also influences the sharing of the burden of proof and, more particularly, the identification of the criteria that determine the burden of persuasion for both phases. The applicant's burden to establish a prima facie case should not be too easy, in the sense that there should be sufficient indications of racist motivation. At the same time, the basic rationale of the shared burden of proof should neither be forgotten nor discarded. Indeed, the special allocation of the burden of proof is meant to alleviate the burden on the applicant, who is often faced with severe difficulties in terms of gathering direct proof.

Furthermore, the importance of an adequate protection against discrimination is arguably heightened in relation to so-called suspect grounds of discrimination, exactly the grounds that are often implicated in discriminatory violence. Differentiations on suspect grounds trigger heightened scrutiny by courts as they are considered 'a priori wrong and unacceptable'.[148] While this scrutiny pertains to the second phase (the justification phase), making it very difficult for the state to justify a prima facie case of discrimination,[149] it arguably also denotes a particular protection-worthiness of the victims. This in turn would plead for a shared burden of proof which does not impose an excessive burden on the applicant or alleged victim to establish a prima facie case. Nevertheless, as the special allocation of the burden of proof strives to bring (more) fairness, it should also not put an unreasonable burden on the respondent. In this respect, one has to consider the Grand Chamber's reasoning in *Nachova*, underscoring the difficulties in disproving racist motivations[150] and, more particularly, that motive did not play a role at all. Indeed, as long as racism influenced the practice/decision in some way, the majority of proper motives would not suffice to block the finding of a prohibited instance of racial discrimination.

Finding the fair allocation of the burden of proof in cases concerning discriminatory violence undoubtedly implies a complex balancing exercise, riddled with pitfalls, but one that needs to be engaged in.

---

147 Ibid, p 575, referring back to his extensive preceding analysis.

148 JH Gerards, 'The Discrimination Grounds of Article 14 of the European Convention on Human Rights' (2013) 13 *Human Rights Law Review* 99, 115.

149 See also JH Gerards, Intensity of Judicial Review in Equal Treatment Cases' (2014) 51 *Netherlands International Law Review* 135.

150 *Nachova*, above n 124.

6. CONCLUSION

Admittedly, delineating and identifying objective markers for a prima facie case is complex, especially in cases concerning racial discriminatory violence.[151] Nevertheless, developing such markers and criteria is critical to operationalise the shared burden of proof in discrimination cases. Accordingly, the ECtHR is invited to identify further parameters and relevant factors for the establishment of a prima facie case, which would not require the applicant to produce virtually conclusive proof, while also not imposing an impossible burden on the defendant to rebut the presumption.

Building on the existing judicial dialogue between the CJEU and the ECtHR, the latter Court is invited to have regard to the steadily developing jurisprudence of the CJEU. Admittedly, the latter jurisprudence does not concern cases on crimes with a racist motivation. Nevertheless, it is to be welcomed that the CJEU preliminary rulings and their often very concrete and case-specific factors allow for the deduction of more 'general' factors, both concerning the determination of a prima facie case of racial discrimination and the ways to rebut that presumption.

As the ECtHR is in principle willing to share the burden of proof, this recommendation is indeed of a more procedural nature. Nevertheless, as was highlighted before, this further identification of relevant markers and parameters is crucial to making the shared burden of proof a reality, while contributing to the effective protection against discrimination.

At the same time, it should also be recalled that the CJEU's jurisprudence on the shared burden of proof leaves room for further fine-tuning. Indeed, two suggestions for the development of the CJEU jurisprudence remain outstanding. First of all, in relation to public speech announcing discriminatory policies, it is imperative that throughout the Court's reasoning a distinction is made between two instances of discrimination, namely the 'speech' instance and the 'actual practice' instance of discrimination. Second, the CJEU should engage more in system reasoning, also regarding the rebuttal (phase) of the presumption of discrimination, so as to clarify the two different modalities this rebuttal can have, namely negation and justification respectively. Who knows, the enfolding jurisprudence of the ECtHR might also positively influence the CJEU, further strengthening the ongoing judicial dialogue.

---

151 See also OM Arnardóttir, 'Non-discrimination under Article 14 ECHR: The Burden of Proof' (2012) 51 *Scandinavian Studies in Law* 14, 17.

RETHINKING THE TWO MARGINS OF APPRECIATION

Oddný Mjöll ARNARDÓTTIR*

1. INTRODUCTION

The margin of appreciation doctrine is widely commented on, but commentators have nevertheless not been able to explain it to a satisfactory level of clarity.

* Dr Oddný Mjöll Arnardóttir (oddnyma@hi.is) is Judge at the Icelandic Court of Appeal and Research Professor at the University of Iceland. This chapter was originally published in open acess by Cambridge University Press. OM ARNARDÓTTIR, 'Rethinking the Two Margins of Appreciation' (2016) 12 *European Constitutional Law Review* 27 © The Author 2016. It was part of a research project on the margin of appreciation, funded by the Icelandic Research Fund and was drafted during visiting fellowships at iCourts, the Centre of Excellence for International Courts at Copenhagen University and at the European University Institute in Florence. An earlier version was presented at seminars at the University of Copenhagen (iCourts Centre) and the University of Oslo (MultiRights project). The author would like to thank George Letsas, Andrew Legg, Urska Sadl and the other participants at the seminars for their feedback; Gunnar Narfi Gunnarsson for assistance with case-law analysis; and anonymous reviewers for their helpful comments. For follow-up and more case law analysis related to the systemic margin of appreciation see OM ARNARDÓTTIR, 'The "procedural turn" under the European Convention on Human Rights and presumptions of Convention compliance (2017) 15 *ICON* 9 and OM ARNARDÓTTIR, 'Res Interpretata, Erga Omens Effect

Some works do exist that endeavour to theorise on the doctrine as such,[1] but the literature has generally been more focused on describing the different situations in which it may be applicable,[2] and the different factors that may influence it.[3] The literature theorising the doctrine also remains very eclectic and it seems that the only common themes that have emerged are that the doctrine has multiple forms and that the Court should do more to clarify its contours and underlying rationale.[4] Indeed, in 2012 it was argued that 'startlingly little' had been written on the conceptual elements of the doctrine, and with respect to offering a justification for it.[5] The more recent literature has been somewhat focused on arguing that certain aspects of the doctrine could be improved and/or better justified by developing assessment of the quality of domestic procedures as one of the key indicators for strictness or leniency of review,[6] or as tools to augment

and the Role of the Margin of Appreciation in Giving Domestic Effect to the judgment of the European Court of Human Rights' (2017) *EJIL*, 819.

1 Significantly G Letsas, 'Two Concepts of the Margin of Appreciation' (2006) 26 *OJLS* 705 and A Legg, *The Margin of Appreciation in International Human Rights Law: Deference and Proportionality*, Oxford University Press 2012, Ch. 2, 3, 7 and 8. See also Y Arai-Takahashi, 'The margin of appreciation doctrine: a theoretical analysis of Strasbourg's variable geometry' in A Føllesdal, B Peters and G Ulfstein (eds), *Constituting Europe: The European Court of Human Rights in a National, European and Global Context*, Cambridge University Press 2013, p 62 at p 82–102; and Y Shany, 'Toward a General Margin of Appreciation Doctrine in International Law?' (2006) 16 *EJIL* 907.

2 For example J Kratochvíl, 'The Inflation of the Margin of Appreciation by the European Court of Human Rights' (2011) 29 *NQHR* 324, 329–335 (norm application, norm definition, choice of means, other uses); S Greer, *The margin of Appreciation: Interpretation and Discretion under the European Convention on Human Rights*, Council of Europe Publishing 2000, pp 23–31 (democracy in crisis, balancing against public interest, balancing competing rights, positive obligations, adjectival discretion in defining exceptions, discrimination); S Greer, *The European Convention on Human Rights: Achievements, Problems and Prospects*, Cambridge University Press 2006, Ch. 4. See also Y Arai-Takahashi, above n 1, pp 69–78 (fact-finding, evaluating national law, evaluating human rights norms, balancing against public interest, balancing competing rights).

3 For example Y Arai-Takahashi, *The Margin of Appreciation Doctrine and the Principle of Proportionality in the Jurisprudence of the ECHR*, Intersentia 2002; E Brems, 'The Margin of Appreciation Doctrine in the Case-Law of the European Court of Human Rights' (1996) 56 *Heidelberg Journal of International Law* 240. Much of the literature on influencing factors is focused on specific Convention rights, see for example OM Arnardóttir, 'The Differences that Make a Difference: Recent Developments on the Discrimination Grounds and the Margin of Appreciation under Article 14 ECHR' (2014) 14 *HRL Rev* 647.

4 For example RStJ Macdonald, 'The Margin of Appreciation' in RStJ Macdonald, F Matscher and H Petzold (eds), *The European System for the Protection of Human Rights*, Martinus Nijhoff Publishers 1993, p 84; G Letsas, above n 1, p 706; Y Shany, above n 1, p 910; J Kratochvíl, above n 2, p 354; S Greer, above n 2, p 32; J Gerards, 'Pluralism, Deference and the Margin of Appreciation Doctrine' (2011) 17 *ELJ* 80, 114; P Popelier and C Van de Heyning, 'Procedural Rationality: Giving Teeth to the Proportionality Analysis' (2013) 9 *EuConst* 230, 248–249.

5 A Legg, above n 1, p 4.

6 The point was for example made by A Legg, supra n 1, p 70; and E Brems and L Lavrysen, 'Procedural Justice in Human Rights Adjudication: The European Court of Human Rights' (2013) 35 *Hum Rts Q* 176, 199–200.

the Court's review in cases where a wide margin of appreciation would otherwise be implied.[7] It has also been argued that such 'procedural review' could even in many situations replace the Court's 'substantive review' on the merits of a case, making the margin of appreciation doctrine redundant in these cases.[8]

Theoretical accounts focused on conceptualising the doctrine as a whole, however, remain few and far between. Recent key contributions of that genre are provided in the works of George Letsas and Andrew Legg, and the scope of this chapter will be focused on addressing the disagreement that exists between them on how the key element(s) or function(s) of the doctrine should be conceptualised.[9] For reasons that will be explained below, the starting point will be taken in Letsas' famous identification of a distinction between two concepts of the margin of appreciation, but a rethought conceptualisation will be suggested with different contours and a clearer dividing line between the two key elements of the doctrine. The aim of this chapter, therefore, is making the margin of appreciation doctrine more intelligible through relatively comprehensive theory building.[10]

The central argument presented is that the margin of appreciation consists of two distinct elements, which each relies on a different kind of rationale and has a different function. Specifically, it will be argued that the 'systemic' element is related to deference to other decision-making bodies for non-merits reasons, and that the 'normative' element is related to the Court's own assessment of merits reasons. The structure of the chapter is such that it will begin by restating Legg's disagreement with Letsas on the nature of the margin of appreciation. Here, it will also be pointed out how both of their work does not speak to some well-established key elements of the doctrine, and how it is also in need of rethinking in light of the Court's more recent case-law. The chapter, then, moves on to provide the rethought theoretical clarification of the two concepts of the margin of appreciation described supra, marrying observations from

---

7 See P Popelier and C Van de Heyning, above n 4, p 243; P Popelier, 'The Court as Regulatory Watchdog: The procedural approach in the case law of the European Court of Human Rights' in P Popelier, A Mazmanyan and W Vandenbruwaene (eds), *The Role of Constitutional Courts in Multilevel Governance*, Intersentia 2012, p 249 at p 265; and C Van de Heyning, 'No Place like Home: Discretionary space for the domestic protection of fundamental rights' in P Popelier, C Van de Heyning and P Van Nuffel (eds), *Human rights protection in the European legal order: The interaction between the European and the national courts*, Intersentia 2011, p 95.

8 J Gerards, 'The prism of fundamental rights' (2012) 8 *EuConst* 173, 197–199.

9 It should be noted that Y Arai-Takahashi, above n 1, has also recently aimed to theorise the doctrine as a whole, but he follows Letsas' dual conceptualisation of two margins of appreciation.

10 On legal theory building, see C McCrudden, 'Legal research and the social sciences' (2001) 123 *LQR* 632, 634; and M Van Hoecke, 'Legal Doctrine: Which Method(s) for What Kind of Discipline' in M Van Hoecke (ed), *Methodologies of Legal Research: Which Kind of Method for What Kind of Discipline*, Hart 2013, pp 14–15.

the case-law and the literature on margin of appreciation and subsidiarity with insights from moral reasoning and deference in the context of constitutional law.[11] It will also be pointed out how assessment under the systemic margin of appreciation logically precedes normative engagement by the Court, and it will further be argued that the distinction between the two margins has normative implications as the possibility of complete deference is only present under the 'systemic' element of the doctrine. Finally, it will be concluded that the rethought model for the two margins of appreciation is sound in theory and reflective of key elements in the Court's practice. It, thus, provides the keener understanding of the doctrine often called for in the literature and facilitates a normative assessment of the path the Court seems to be embarking on in its recent case-law through increased reliance on the quality of domestic procedures as a key element of the doctrine.

2. TWO RECENT CONCEPTUALISATIONS OF THE MARGIN OF APPRECIATION DOCTRINE AND THE CAUSE FOR A RETHINK

In his 2012 monograph, Andrew Legg provides a descriptive exposition of the case-law and argues that the doctrine of the margin of appreciation is justified by allowing the democratic formation of human rights norms at state level while retaining the international review of states' reasoning in support of the outcome; by the consent of contracting parties as a foundational element of international treaty law; and by deference to greater expertise when relevant.[12] Drawing on the philosophy of practical reasoning,[13] he also argues that the doctrine is characterised by assigning weight to 'external factors' relating to these elements (democracy, consensus, expertise). These, then, provide elements of second order reasoning functioning alongside first order reasons, which he argues are related to the nature of different Convention rights and the type of case at stake.[14]

---

11 The case-law analysis performed for this study reached all cases categorised as belonging to case reports and importance level 1 on the HUDOC database, pronounced as from 01.01.2006 until 01.04.2015. The search functions available on HUDOC were utilised in conjunction with the above criteria in search for the terms 'margin of appreciation' and 'require strong reasons to substitute'. Older judgments referred to by the Court or identified in the literature as important contributions to the development of the margin of appreciation doctrine were also consulted and relied upon as relevant.

12 A Legg, above n 1, p 58. He argues that the theory espoused 'closely corresponds to the practice', and 'enables a coherent exposition of the doctrine' p 18. As to the doctrine's legitimacy, a similar account can be found in e.g. P Mahoney, 'Marvellous Richness of Diversity or Invidious Cultural Relativism' (1998) 19 *HRLJ* 1.

13 See J Raz, *Practical Reason and Norms*, Oxford University Press 1999.

14 A Legg, above n 1, p 18 and 219.

On Legg's account the structure of the Court's reasoning is such that in making its judgments it relies on the first order reasons that relate to the substance or merits of a case, but also on the second order reasons referring to his three types of 'external' non-merits factors that influence the Court's assessment of the first order reasons.[15] Upon conceptualising the structure of the Court's reasoning in this way, he moves on to challenge the common understanding that the nature of the right or the type of case are also factors that influence the width of the margin. Instead, he argues that these are factors that affect the scope created for the functioning of the margin of appreciation proper.[16] On this understanding, then, the margin of appreciation has no role related to first order reasons on the merits or substance of the right in question. Different substantive elements related to first order reasons, such as the different interests at stake or the question of whether positive obligations are implied or not, create instead something that might be called 'a margin for the margin'. Legg also conceptualises the doctrine as exclusively located on the site of proportionality assessments in the Court's reasoning.[17] However, in order to do so, he collapses all the different stages and elements of the Court's pattern of analysis into an all-encompassing proportionality assessment that always engages the Court normatively on the merits of the case.[18] On this understanding, his second order reasons relating to the three influencing factors are never 'exclusionary' in the sense of excluding the Court's own assessments of the case before it.[19] The doctrine of the margin of appreciation, thus, is 'not to be understood conceptually as akin to non-justiciability'.[20]

15 Ibid, pp 8–9 and 196.

16 Ibid, p 200.

17 Ibid, p 37.

18 Specifically, A Legg states that any assessment of state conduct is in effect a proportionality assessment (Ibid, p 181), and that proportionality is more accurately conceptualised as a tool to define the contours of rights than as a tool for assessing interferences with rights (Ibid, p 178). This stance also leads to the approach that the distinction between proportionality assessments and definitions of the scope of rights is completely irrelevant (Ibid, pp 55, 66, 190). On the opposite position, arguing that there is an important distinction between the definition of the scope of rights and their application so defined, and that there is no place for the margin of appreciation with respect to the former, see S Greer, *The European Convention*, above n 2, p 212; and J Gerard and H Senden, 'The structure of fundamental rights and the European Court of Human Rights' (2009) 7 *ICON* 652. Legg's merger of different functions and analytic techniques in the Court's jurisprudence into 'proportionality' is not followed in the present chapter, as it does not reflect the different stages in the Court's reasoning accurately enough, and masks important differences in the function and rationale for the margin of appreciation doctrine as it applies to these different stages.

19 A Legg, above 1, p 19.

20 Ibid p 36. He nevertheless hints at possible unreviewability in the context of deference to UN Security Council Resolutions (Ibid, p 139) and argues that there is generally more reason for deference to international organisations than states (Ibid, p 144).

The point of Legg's work is to contribute to the debate on the justification of the margin of appreciation, and to theorise on the Court's structure of reasoning under proportionality from the perspective of the philosophy of practical reasoning. His conceptualisation of the doctrine is, in a sense, supportive or instrumental to that aim since the insistence upon a normative engagement by the Court is a key element of the justification offered for the doctrine. The argument is that since the Court is always free to reject the views of another decision-making body when it contemplates deference,[21] and since the margin of appreciation is always located on the reconceptualised all-encompassing proportionality assessment that engages the Court normatively,[22] the doctrine is justified. Were it otherwise, it would lead to an 'abdication of judicial responsibility' under the Convention.[23] This conceptualisation of the doctrine in the Court's jurisprudence, however, betrays the actual practice of the Court whereby, as we shall see, it often does give full deference. The Court can of course decide not to, which rescues that part of Legg's justificatory argument, which may also be taken to apply to those elements of the margin of appreciation that govern strictness of review under proportionality. But the insistence upon normative engagement does, for example, not hold with respect to the 'fourth instance doctrine', which is not tackled in Legg's descriptive case-law analysis. This element of the larger construct of the margin of appreciation doctrine applies when the Court is asked to reassess how national courts dealt with the establishment of fact or how they interpreted and applied national law.[24] When such issues arise the Court, as a general rule, categorically waives the jurisdiction to deal with them de novo. In cases of this kind, the Court for example expressly reasons that it 'must grant substantial deference'[25] or give 'due deference'[26] to the national courts, or that

21 Ibid, p 23.

22 Ibid, p 37.

23 Ibid, p 23. Correspondingly Legg refers to situations where the Court does not engage normatively as instances of 'servility' (Ibid, p 23) or 'obedience' (Ibid, p 137) to others, which he considers to have no place in the Court's jurisprudence.

24 On the fourth instance doctrine as synonymous with the margin of appreciation see J Christoffersen, *Fair Balance: Proportionality, Subsidiarity and Primacy in the European Convention on Human Rights*, Martinus Nijhoff Publishers 2009, pp 238–239. The Court, indeed, seems to use the two terms interchangeably, see for example *Koval v Ukraine*, no 65550/01, §118, ECtHR 2006, where the Court referred to the national court's margin of appreciation 'in the admission and assessment of evidence'. On the fourth instance doctrine generally, see M Dahlberg, '... It is not its task to Act as a Court of Fourth Instance': The Case of the European Court of Human Rights' (2014) 7 *EJLS* 84; Y Arai-Takahashi, above n 3, p 235; and European Court of Human Rights, Practical Guide on Admissibility Criteria (31.03.2011) http://www.dp-rs.si/fileadmin/dp.gov.si/pageuploads/RAZNO/Admissibility_guide_ENG.pdf.

25 *Beganović v Croatia*, no 46423/069, §78, ECHR 2009.

26 *Moskal v Poland*, no 10373/05, §56, ECHR 2009.

this 'is a matter which primarily lies within the competence of the domestic courts'.[27] In this respect, the Court relies on the argument that the domestic courts are 'better placed and equipped' to resolve questions of this kind,[28] and/or that it is 'not in a position' to do so itself.[29] The Court's rationale for this extensive deference, of course, is generally based on the fact that it is not set up with the competence or function of a higher court within the internal legal systems of the Contracting States, but only as a subsidiary mechanism for reviewing Convention compatibility. It, therefore, does not act as an appeals court ('fourth instance') for reviewing the quality of the domestic court's judgment under national law. It is, accordingly, not the Court's 'task' or 'role' to pronounce on questions of this kind,[30] and the result in most cases is that it leaves the task completely up to the national courts.[31] It is important, therefore, to avoid the mistake of taking Legg's work and argument for justifying the margin of appreciation as meaning descriptively/conceptually that the margin of appreciation always has the function that the Court engages normatively.[32]

In his well-known 2006 article titled 'Two Concepts of the Margin of Appreciation' George Letsas provided a very different conceptualisation of the doctrine. On his reading, the Court uses the margin of appreciation 'for both saying that the applicant did not, as a matter of human rights, have the right she claimed, and for saying that it will not substantively review the decision of national authorities'.[33] He coined the phrases 'substantive' and 'structural' margin of appreciation to describe this difference, and argued that the failure to distinguish between the two explains a lot of the confusion and controversy surrounding the doctrine.[34] Under Letsas' structural margin, the Court will defer to state authorities and refrain from reviewing their action on the ground that they are 'better placed' in the situation at hand. This concept is, therefore, supported by an argument from institutional competence, which he equates with the principle of subsidiarity, while noting that the principle does not only encompass a chronological or procedural priority for the national authorities, but also a normative one.[35] The substantive concept of the margin of appreciation

27 *Oao Neftyanaya Kompaniya Yukos v Russia*, no 14902/04, §559, ECHR 2011.

28 *Koval v Ukraine*, above n 24, §118.

29 *Marchenko v Ukraine*, no 4063/04, §48, ECHR 2009.

30 *Léger v France*, no 19324/02, §72, ECHR 2006.

31 The Court, however, retains the power to intervene and engage in its own assessments if the facts of the case reveal arbitrariness or manifest deficiencies in the way the domestic courts handled the relevant issues, see for example *Beganović v Croatia*, above n 25, §78 and 85.

32 Examples where the Court does not engage normatively seem to be interpreted by Legg as 'failure' and 'mistakes' (A Legg, above n 1, p 27 and 36). Cases that exhibit the well-established main approach of complete or almost complete deference to domestic courts' interpretation of domestic law, further, seem to be interpreted as exceptions (Ibid, p 173).

33 G Letsas, above n 1, p 706.

34 Ibid.

35 Ibid, p 720–722.

in Letsas' construction concerns the balancing of public and private interests under the Convention. The 'main idea' behind it, he argued, is simply making a 'very general and simple point about the limitability or non-absoluteness of the Convention rights'.[36] Explaining which categories of cases belong to which kind of margin, Letsas further argued that the structural element applies when the Court refrains from review on the basis that the issue is politically sensitive (notably under Article 15) and/or there is no consensus among the Contracting States,[37] while the substantive concept is at stake when reviewing limitations, exceptions or restrictions on rights.[38]

Letsas and Legg disagree not only on how to conceptualise the margin of appreciation doctrine, but also on what is the best theory of rights. Legg's account is based on interest-based theories of rights and the philosophy of practical reasoning.[39] His analysis revolves around the normative role of the margin of appreciation, and he sees it as almost synonymous with interpretation of rights.[40] The point of Letsas' article is, in a sense, opposite to Legg's bid for justifying the doctrine. It was intended rather to exhibit its normative emptiness and how the analysis of human rights questions needs to be normatively anchored in theories originating elsewhere; and to advance the Dworkinian reason-blocking approach as the preferred theory of rights.[41] As Letsas' conceptualisation of the doctrine is based on interpretivism, he does not set out to provide a systematic exposition of the Court's case-law like Legg. Indeed, he cautions that his account of the two margins of appreciation might not necessarily be 'the one that the ECtHR judges, one by one, share or have fully developed in their judgments'.[42] He nevertheless cites around 40 judgments to exhibit how his two conceptions of the doctrine are anchored in the case-law. Despite these case-law references, it is important not to make the mistake to think that Letsas' two concepts accurately capture the whole of the Court's practice under the margin of appreciation since he also does not tackle the case-law on the well-known 'fourth instance doctrine'.

Upon close analysis of the case-law, it is also difficult to detect a clear difference in kind between the margin of appreciation applied when balancing

---

36 Ibid, p 711 and 714.

37 Ibid, p 722 ss.

38 Ibid, p 710 ss.

39 J Finnis, *Natural Law and Natural Rights*, Oxford University Press 1980; J Raz, above n 13; J Raz, *The Morality of Freedom*, Oxford University Press 1986.

40 A Legg, above n 1, p 107: 'Much of this book relates to the interpretation of the treaties.'

41 G Letsas, above n 1, p 710 and 731–732. See generally R Dworkin, *Taking Rights Seriously*, Harvard University Press 1978.

42 Ibid, Letsas, p 706. Legal interpretivism is primarily based on Ronald Dworkin's body of work. In contrast with legal positivism it offers a constitutive explanation of legal rights according to which the practice of legal institutions is not determinative alone. Instead, and perhaps more importantly, moral principles have a fundamental justificatory role. See N Stavropoulos, *Legal Interpretivism*, Stanford Encyclopedia of Philosophy, Edward N Zalta ed., Summer 2014 Edition http://plato.stanford.edu/archives/sum2014/entries/law-interpretivist/.

interests in connection with highly sensitive or contested political and moral questions, which Letsas associated with his structural margin of appreciation,[43] and otherwise under limitable rights, which he associated with the substantive margin.[44] The Court's methodology of balancing all the relevant (merits and non-merits) reasons is, of course, the same in both types of cases, and the margin of appreciation therefore has the same overall function. However, as established by many a commentator and confirmed in the case-law analysis performed for the present study, the margin of appreciation is generally wider in the former situation.[45] This, however, is a difference of degree and not one of kind. A wider margin is, in fact, also generally implied when the Court balances interests in cases involving policy-making in the socio-economic sphere,[46] and in cases where the Court engages normatively with the balancing of competing individual interests,[47] but it is not altogether clear how such cases would fit in the overall scheme suggested by Letsas.

Subsequent to Legg's and Letsas' work, the Court has also devised new uses for the margin of appreciation doctrine in cases where two protected private interests collide and have to be balanced against each other under competing Convention rights. Their conceptualisations of the margin of appreciation seem incapable of capturing this important development, which exhibits the increased proceduralisation of the Court's review through the creation of presumptions

---

43 G Letsas, above n 1, pp 722–723.

44 Ibid, p 711.

45 For example under Article 8, see *A, B and C v Ireland*, no 25579/05, §233, ECHR 2010, on abortion legislation in Ireland; and *Evans v United Kingdom*, no 6339/05, §77, ECHR 2007, on the use of embryos. In the context of Article 9 and Article 2 of Protocol 1, compare the wide margin of appreciation applied in relation to religious symbols in the classroom in *Dogru v France*, no 27058/05, ECHR 2008 and *Lautsi and Others v Italy*, no 30814/06, ECHR 2011, and the narrower margin applied in relation to conscientious objection to military service in *Bayatyan v Armenia*, no 23459/03, ECHR 2011 or the dissolution of a religious community in *Jehovah's Witnesses of Moscow and Others v Russia*, no 302/02, ECHR 2010. See generally also J Schokkenbroek, 'The Basis, Nature and Application of the Margin-of-Appreciation Doctrine in the Case-Law of the European Court of Human Rights' (1998) 19 *HRLJ* 34; Y Arai-Takahashi, above n 3, pp 206–212 and A Legg, above n 1, p 86–88.

46 For example, under Article 8, the Court often refers to a wide margin of appreciation in relation to social or economic policy or technical issues, see for example *Şerife Yiğit v Turkey*, no 3976/05, §100, ECtHR 2010. A wide margin of appreciation is also habitually referred to in relation to substantive assessments under Article 1 of Protocol 1, see for example *Hutten-Czapska v Poland*, no 35014/97, §223–234, ECHR 2006, and *Velikovi and Others v Bulgaria*, no 43278/98, §179–180, ECHR 2007. Under Article 2 of Protocol 1, there is also a wide margin of appreciation for the 'setting and planning of the curriculum', see *Folgerø and Others v Norway*, no 15472/02, §84, ECHR 2007, and *Lautsi and Others v Italy*, above n 45, §69. See generally also J Schokkenbroek, above n 45, p 34; Y Arai-Takahashi, above n 3, p 214–215.

47 *Fáber v Hungary*, no 40721/08, §42, ECHR 2012, (balancing under Articles 10 and 11); *Palomo Sánchez and Others v Spain*, nos 28955/06 etc, §54, ECHR 2011, (balancing under Articles 8 and 10). Recently, the Court has even refrained from engaging normatively in cases of this kind, see infra.

of complete deference on substantive proportionality assessments in concreto (see infra). Legg's insistence that the doctrine is exclusively located on the Court's own proportionality assessments does not seem to make much sense in light of such judgments.[48] As they concern limitations on rights and balancing of competing interests, they would seem to belong to Letsas' 'substantive' concept of the margin of appreciation, which implies a more thorough 'substantive review'. However, as the Court is in effect saying that 'it will not substantively review the decision of national authorities'[49] in such judgments, they would also seem to belong to his 'structural' margin of appreciation, which he reserved for the most deferential case-law.

The contributions of Legg and Letsas are certainly important and strong in theory, but it cannot be denied that both have the weakness of not addressing the full extent of the Court's case-law under the margin of appreciation doctrine. Recent developments on the margin of appreciation, further, do not seem to fit within their conceptualisations of the doctrine. It seems appropriate, therefore, to revisit the issue of whether an internally consistent conceptual framework can be constructed whereby the many different elements of the margin of appreciation as it appears in the case-law of the Court can be understood as coming together at the level of (relatively) coherent legal doctrine.[50]

3. THE RETHOUGHT TWO MARGINS OF APPRECIATION: THE IDENTIFICATION OF TWO DIFFERENT FUNCTIONS FOR THE MARGIN OF APPRECIATION DOCTRINE IN THE CASE LAW OF THE COURT

Irrespective of any reservation regarding the completeness of the 'structural' and 'substantive' concepts of the margin of appreciation in Letsas' construction, he certainly seems to have pointed towards something real in the case-law. Other commentators have indeed also noted something similar. In fact, Letsas sought inspiration from RStJ Macdonald, who during his time as a judge at the ECtHR originally conceptualised the margin of appreciation doctrine as operating on a spectrum ranging from total deference indicating 'unreviewability', through intermediate positions, to the most stringent standard of justification in the Court's review, and conceptualised these two functions as those of 'reviewability'

---

48 Also, when discussing 'external factors' influencing the balancing of conflicting Convention rights Legg only addressed deference to the domestic legislature, but not to the domestic courts, see A Legg, above n 2, pp 83–85.

49 G Letsas, above n 1, p 721.

50 Due to the unclear and confused contours of the margin of appreciation, some authors have questioned whether it can be referred to as 'doctrine' proper, see S Greer, above n 2, p 32.

and 'justifiability'.[51] In the first comprehensive study of the development of the margin of appreciation in the case-law of the ECtHR, Howard Yourow also referred to the doctrine as a multifunctional tool, identifying two key functions; formal standards of deference on one hand and substantive interpretation on the other.[52] Further, in 2006, Yuval Shany argued that there was such a thing as a general margin of appreciation doctrine in international law and contended that it had two principal elements. While noting that international courts do not generally distinguish between them, he argued that the first element had to do with 'judicial deference', where international courts should refrain from reviewing national decisions de novo, and that the second element indicated 'normative flexibility', allowing different interpretations of the same norm depending on context.[53] Finally, Dean Spielmann, the president of the ECtHR, has recently presented his vision of the margin as having on one hand a 'normative' function, while on the other hand pursuing also a separate 'systemic' objective.[54] However, while arguing that a selection of recent judgments exhibits the systemic objective of the margin of appreciation, he does not set out to give the whole picture of the doctrine or to elaborate in a broader context the dividing line between the two different types of margin.[55]

A certain common ground on the existence of two key elements appears across all the above attempts at conceptualising the doctrine of the margin of appreciation, but there is no consensus or clarity on how to draw the line for dividing the systemic ('structural', 'reviewability', 'deference') and normative ('substantive', 'justifiability', 'normative flexibility') elements of the doctrine, or on how to identify and locate the two functions in the case-law. Macdonald, like Letsas, for example, speaks of total deference ('unreviewability') at the far end of the margin of appreciation spectrum, while Shany, like Legg, argues that total deference is not a possibility under the doctrine.[56] Similarly, Yourow links the

---

51 Similarly, he also argued that the confusion between the two functions was a problematic element of the case-law and that the distinction was more or less lost on the doctrine as it had evolved in the case-law of the Court, see RStJ Macdonald, above n 4, pp 84–85.

52 HC Yourow, *The Margin of Appreciation Doctrine in the Dynamics of European Human Rights Jurisprudence*, Martinus Nijhoff Publishers 1996, pp 195–196. Although categorised into four components, the two elements also appear indirectly in Arai-Takahashi's conceptualisation, see Y Arai-Takahashi, above n 3, pp 236–242. In subsequent work, he has adopted Letsas' dual conceptualisation as a heuristic tool, see Y Arai-Takahashi, above n 1, pp 90 and 94.

53 Y Shany, above n 1, pp 909–910, associating the former with norm-application, and the latter with norm-interpretation.

54 D Spielmann, 'Whither the Margin of Appreciation' (2014) 67 *CLP* 49.

55 Similarly, see the discussion by Judge Robert Spano of selected judgments as exhibiting the 'process of reformulating or refining the concepts of subsidiarity and the margin of appreciation', R Spano, 'Universality or Diversity of Human Rights? Strasbourg in the Age of Subsidiarity' (2014) 14 *HRL Rev* 487, 492.

56 RStJ Macdonald, above n 4, p 84; G Letsas, above n 1, p 706; Y Shany, above n 1, p 910; A Legg, above n 1, p 36.

weighing and balancing of claims and defences, in accordance with European consensus, to the normative or interpretational element of the doctrine, while Letsas, on the other hand, sees lack of consensus cases as the primary example of the structural margin of appreciation.[57] Letsas' concept of the structural margin also is not framed with reference to the Court's clearest examples of systemic deference under the 'fourth instance doctrine', and was conceptualised before the existence of Spielmann's examples of the Court taking a 'clear stance of principle' on the 'systemic' function of the doctrine.[58]

On the back of this literature, it can nevertheless be taken as established that there is consensus that there is some kind of a distinction between two different functions under the margin of appreciation doctrine. But the present confusion and inconsistency on the nature and contours of this distinction inevitably leads to the conclusion that while these works provide a good starting point, they do not sufficiently capture the whole of the margin of appreciation doctrine or the direction it is taking in the Court's more recent case-law. The time has therefore come to rethink and develop in a more holistic manner the way in which the two concepts of the margin of appreciation have been theorised, and to elaborate on their contours, interrelationship and underlying rationale. In the following, for reasons of clarity and specification from earlier works, Spielmann's terminology of a 'systemic' and a 'normative' function will be adopted.

3.1. THE TWO ELEMENTS OF THE PRINCIPLE OF SUBSIDIARITY

When aiming to rethink the margin of appreciation doctrine, it seems appropriate to note the well-established fact that it provides the doctrinal expression of the principle of subsidiarity. The two were first expressly united in the *Handyside* judgment where the Court reasoned that the former was a consequence of the latter,[59] and this understanding of the relationship between the two has since been carved in stone in the Court's case-law and in Protocol 15 to the Convention, which adds reference to the pair into the Convention's preamble.[60] It is beyond doubt, therefore, that subsidiarity provides the normative basis for the doctrine. The margin of appreciation should accordingly reflect the principle of subsidiarity.

The different elements of the principle of subsidiarity, tensions with the ideal of universal human rights and its development in national, European and

57 C Yourow, above n 52, p 195; G Letsas, above n 1, particularly pp 724–729.

58 D Spielmann, above n 54, p 63; G Letsas, above n 1, p 723.

59 *Handyside v United Kingdom*, no 5493/72, §48, ECHR 1976.

60 Protocol No 15 amending the Convention for the Protection of Human Rights and Fundamental Freedoms (adopted 24.06.2013) CETS No 213.

international law have all been elaborated on in the literature.[61] In the specific Convention context, the principle is most clearly expressed in Articles 1 and 19 ECHR, which stipulate that it is the primary responsibility of the Contracting Parties to secure the rights and freedoms defined in the Convention and limit the Court's task to ensuring the observance of their obligations under the Convention. Articles 13 and 35 ECHR, further, stipulate that individuals shall have an effective remedy before a national authority in cases of violations, and that all domestic remedies must be exhausted before a case can be brought before the ECtHR. Together these provisions express the fundamental elements of what has in the Court's practice become the larger construct of a Convention principle espousing the 'subsidiary nature of the international machinery for collective enforcement established by the Convention'.[62] More precisely, the Court has recently stated about itself that 'within the scheme of the Convention it is intended to be subsidiary to the national systems safeguarding human rights', and emphasised that '[s]ubsidiarity is at the very basis of the Convention'.[63]

In the abstract, the principle of subsidiarity 'divides decision-making in society, considering values of efficiency, liberty and justice.'[64] It represents the normative vision of agency that larger or more centralised units should not usurp functions that smaller or more local units are able to perform well enough. The underlying presumption is that, unless proven otherwise, smaller or local units are best suited to exercise power over their own affairs. Hence, the Court's habitual invocation of the principle, and the margin, in the terms that due to their 'direct democratic legitimation'[65] or 'direct knowledge of their society and its needs', the national authorities are 'in principle better placed' than an international court to perform the relevant assessments.[66]

---

61 See e.g. M Evans and A Zimmermann (eds) *Global Perspectives on Subsidiarity*, Springer 2014. For contributions in the field of international law see A Føllesdal, 'The principle of subsidiarity as a constitutional principle in international law' (2013) 2 *Global Constitutionalism* 37; D Shelton, 'Subsidiarity and Human Rights Law' (2006) 27 *HRLJ* 4; PG Carozza, 'Subsidiarity as a Structural Principle of International Human Rights Law'(2003) 97 *AJIL* 38; and WM Carter, 'Rethinking Subsidiarity in International Human Rights Adjudication' (2008) 30 *Journal of Public Law and Policy* 319. For contributions in the EU context see GA Bermann, 'Taking Subsidiarity Seriously: Federalism in the European Community and the United States' (1994) 94 *Colum LRev* 332; T Schilling, 'A New Dimension of Subsidiarity: Subsidiarity as a Rule and a Principle' (1995) 14 *YB EurL* 255; G de Búrca, 'The Principle of Subsidiarity and the Court of Justice as an Institutional Actor' (1998) 36 *JCMS* 217; and T Horsley, 'Subsidiarity and the European Court of Justice: Missing Pieces in the Subsidiarity Jigsaw?' (2012) 50 *JCMS* 267.

62 Case relating to certain aspects of the laws on the use of languages in education in *Belgium v Belgium*, nos 1474/62 etc, §4, ECHR 1968-IA.

63 *Austin and Others v United Kingdom*, nos 39692/09 etc, §61, ECHR 2012. For a recent review of the principle of subsidiarity as it appears in the case-law of the ECHR, see A Mowbray, 'Subsidiarity and the European Convention on Human Rights', (2015) 15 *HRLRev* 313.

64 D Shelton, above n 61, p 5.

65 *Hatton and Others v United Kingdom*, no 36022/97, §97, ECHR 2003.

66 *Stummer v Austria*, no 37452/02, §89, ECHR 2011.

It has been pointed out in academic commentary how the principle of subsidiarity in international human rights adjudication has a dual rationale that encompasses both functional and normative justifications.[67] The functional one is related to efficiency and competence as it recognises that smaller or local units closer to the events are better equipped to deal with them and accepts the limited resources at the Strasbourg Court's disposal. But there is also another functional concern behind the judicial restraint implied by the principle of subsidiarity. This is the simple fact of Contracting State consent as the foundation of Convention obligations and the relatively weak enforcement mechanism upon which the system rests, which calls for a certain amount of respect or deference to the Contracting Parties.[68] As the functioning of the Convention system depends very much on the extent to which the judgments of the Court are received as legitimate by the Contracting States, the language of subsidiarity provides a particularly effective legitimising strategy.[69] Normatively, however, the principle of subsidiarity when applied to human rights performance rests upon the rationale that it expresses respect for the self-determination of individuals, or groups of individuals through democratic processes.[70] As such it facilitates the pluralism and diversity associated with democratic society,[71] and recognises that there may exist different, but equally valid, ways of ensuring the same Convention rights. Subsidiarity, however, has always been 'a somewhat paradoxical principle' as it on one hand limits intervention from a larger or more centralised unit, while at the same time empowering it and justifying its action in those cases where the smaller or more local unit cannot or does not perform well enough.[72]

---

67 E.g. LR Helfer, 'Redesigning the European Court of Human Rights: Embeddedness as a Deep Structural Principle of the European Human Rights Regime' (2008) 19 *EJIL* 125, 128.

68 M Carter, above n 61, pp 319–320; RStJ Macdonald, above n 4, p 123.

69 PG Carozza, above n 61, p 40, refers to the principle as 'a conceptual and rhetorical mediator between supranational harmonization and unity, on the one hand, and local pluralism and difference, on the other.' See also J Raz, 'On the Authority and Interpretation of Constitutions: Some Preliminaries' in L Alexander (ed), *Constitutionalism: Philosophical Foundations*, Cambridge University Press 2001, pp 173–174 and 188–189, who highlights the legitimating function of 'non-merit reasons' when they are relied upon in the context of constitutional interpretation.

70 PG Carozza above n 61, pp 43–44. A Føllesdal, 'The principle of subsidiarity', above n 61, pp 61–62 focuses on the normative role of justifying or legitimising action on part of the international human rights regime, arguing that current state-centric versions of the principle are problematic and that a focus on individual's interests would be a more plausible way of imbuing the principle with normative force. See also A Føllesdal, 'Squaring the Circle at the Battle at Brighton: Is the War between Protecting Human Rights or Respecting Sovereignty Over, or Has it Just Begun?' in OM Arnardóttir and A Buyse (eds), *Shifting Centres of Gravity of Human Rights Protection Rethinking Relations between the ECHR, EU and National Legal Orders*, Routledge 2016, pp 189–204.

71 In the Court's own words, pluralism is 'indissociable' from a democratic society, see e.g. *Leyla Şahin v Turkey*, no 44774/98, §104, ECHR 2005.

72 PG Carozza, above n 61, p 44. A Mowbray, above n 63, p 340 notes how the principle of subsidiarity has indeed also been relied on by the Court to legitimate its judicial intervention

The complexity of the principle of subsidiarity and its twofold rationale is also reflected in the fact that it has different functions, as elaborated on by Paolo Carozza. He sees the principle as to a certain extent 'concerned with the distribution of competences among different levels of governance'[73] – as per the functional rationale – and to a certain extent as instrumental in explaining why international human rights law is 'still characterized less by fully articulated normative content than by the interpretive discretion that it leaves to states'[74] – as per the normative rationale. In a more concise form these dual functions may be referred to in the terms that the principle of subsidiarity regulates '*how* to allocate or *use* authority within a political or legal order'.[75] The principle of subsidiarity in theory, therefore, has a systemic dimension related to the distribution of competences and tasks, and a normative dimension that guides or justifies how authority is used, which accounts for the normative elasticity characteristic of the interpretation of international human rights norms.[76]

These different elements of the principle of subsidiarity have, however, not been made explicit in the Court's jurisprudence. When the Court refers to subsidiarity and the 'better placed' argument it may, therefore, be referring to either of the two conceptions of the principle; the systemic or the normative one. The same can generally be said about the Court's use of the margin of appreciation. As the margin of appreciation doctrine has evolved as an offspring of the principle of subsidiarity, both its functions nevertheless carry through to the doctrine. The margin of appreciation will, thus, take on different hues depending on whether it is employed as the expression of the systemic relationship between the national and supranational levels (who decides what and when), or whether it has a normative function when interpreting and applying the Convention within the scope of the Court's review as defined by this structural relationship (and how).

Looking at the different attempts at identifying and explaining the different functions of the margin of appreciation doctrine described supra, we can discern

---

when the domestic level has clearly failed, referring to *El-Masri v The Former Yugoslav Republic of Macedonia*, no 39630/09, ECHR 2012 regarding defects in fact-finding at the national level; and *Fabris v France*, no 16574/08, ECHR 2013 regarding clear disregard for well-established ECtHR case-law.

73 PG Carozza, above n 61, p 57.

74 Ibid, p 62.

75 A Føllesdal, above n 61, p 37 (emphasis added). In the EU context, GA Bermann, above n 61, pp 366–367 speaks of four functions; legislative function, interpretative function, a function of conferring legality, and a function in terms of confidence-building. All are in a sense sub-categories or consequences of the principle's key functions of governing the allocation or use of power.

76 In the Convention context, more specifically, Herbert Petzold actually already in 1993 identified that the principle of subsidiarity had taken on both connotations in the Court's case-law, see H Petzold, 'The Convention and the Principle of Subsidiarity' in RStJ Macdonald, F Matscher and H Petzold (eds), *The European System for the Protection of Human Rights*, Martinus Nijhoff Publishers 1993, p 49.

that even though they conceptualise the dividing line in different terms, they all straddle this difference between the systemic and the normative in one way or another. An explicit link with the two functions of subsidiarity is, however, generally absent.[77] Letsas is the first one to make that connection, via references to Petzold's work on subsidiarity. Curiously, however, he does not associate his substantive concept of the margin of appreciation with the principle of subsidiarity in its normative conception.[78] Unlike Carozza, who forges a link between the function of the margin of appreciation in the interpretative process and the normative element of the principle of subsidiarity, Letsas does not.[79] Instead, he seems to consider both elements of the principle of subsidiarity as reflected in his structural concept of the margin of appreciation.[80] It is submitted that the better way forward to providing a satisfactory explanation of the margin of appreciation in the case-law of the ECtHR is to bring understanding of how the principle of subsidiarity has a dual justification and function to bear upon our understanding of the margin of appreciation doctrine. We will proceed, therefore, on the understanding that the principle of subsidiarity and the margin of appreciation doctrine have a dual justification (functional and normative) – and that they have a dual function (the systemic distribution of competences between decision making bodies and the normative function of allowing pluralism and flexibility in the interpretation and application of rights). This difference is captured by employing the terms 'systemic' and 'normative' to describe each element.

3.2. SYSTEMIC NON-MERITS REASONS AND NORMATIVE MERITS REASONS

The distinction between the systemic and normative elements of the margin of appreciation doctrine is also important because different types of reasoning are logically relevant to each of the two elements. Conclusions on deference to others

---

77 RStJ Macdonald, above n 4, and Y Shany, above n 1, hardly mention subsidiarity, and while D Spielmann, above n 54, does, he makes no connection between the different functions of the principle and the different functions of the margin of appreciation. In 2002 Y Arai-Takahasi, above n 3, pp 236 and 239–240 discussed subsidiarity as related only to one of the four elements of the margin of appreciation he identified (balancing sovereignty; Convention mandated deference; 'fourth instance' doctrine and the principle of subsidiarity; and contested value-judgments). In 2013 he, however, presented an updated account, reflecting Letsas' conceptualisation of the link between subsidiarity and margin of appreciation, see Y Arai-Takahashi, above n 1, pp 90–94.

78 Subsequent works have not provided further articulation of this link either, see Y Arai-Takahashi, above n 3, pp 90 and 94.

79 PG Carozza, above n 61, pp 61–63.

80 G Letsas, above n 1, p 722, referring to chronological, procedural and normative priority alike as part of the rationale for the structural margin of appreciation.

under the systemic margin would focus on the characteristics and capacities of the other decision-making body, or the quality of its decision-making process, while own assessments under the normative margin would draw on the relevant substantive characteristics of the issue under consideration, such as the type of right at stake or the type of interests protected by it.[81]

These different types of reasoning correspond more or less to Raz's account of constitutional interpretation as legitimately consisting of two types of reasons. The first category is 'merits reasons', which relate to the normative substance or merit of constitutional provisions, but the latter consists of 'non-merit reasons' which relate to other (e.g. political or systemic) concerns that may also have a role to play.[82] While he argues that merits reasons are the most important ones in constitutional interpretation, he also submits that non-merits reasons may have a legitimating role and be relevant depending on context.[83] The more important merits reasons are first order reasons, but on Raz's account they nevertheless do not always defeat the less important secondary non-merits reasons. For example, the constitutional text might be interpreted differently from what would otherwise be required on the balance of merits reasons 'to placate a hostile legislature or executive, which may otherwise take action to limit the power of the courts or to compromise their independence'.[84] This depiction of the constitutional interpretative process, of course, presupposes normative engagement by an interpreter. According to Raz, however, non-merits reasons can also function as 'exclusionary'. Instead of influencing a decision on interpretation, such non-merits reasons may 'imply that one ought not to act on the balance of reasons' at all.[85] Raz's example of Ann, who decided not to decide on an investment option due to her tiredness, exhibits how this works. Here, Ann's tiredness was an exclusionary reason that simply cancelled any engagement with the merits of the investment.[86] Similarly, in the context of interpretation, if a non-merits reason is exclusionary, this means that instead of engaging with the balancing of all the (merits and non-merits) reasons relevant to the interpretation or application of a right, the interpreter simply does not engage normatively.

Like already mentioned, Legg conceptualises the margin of appreciation as exclusively related to his three types of 'external' non-merits reasons (democracy, European consensus, expertise) that influence the Court's assessment of the

81 See generally H Richards, 'Deference' (1964) 74 *Ethics* 135, 139.

82 J Raz, above n 69, pp 172 and 187.

83 Ibid, p 187. See also A Kavanagh, 'Deference of Defiance?: The Limits of the Judicial Role in Constitutional Adjudication' in G Huscroft (ed), *Expounding the Constitution Essays in Constitutional Theory*, Cambridge University Press 2008, p 190.

84 J Raz, above n 69, p 187.

85 J Raz, above n 13, p 41.

86 Ibid, p 37. See also EA Christodoulidis, *Law and Reflexive Politics*, Kluwer 1998, p 227.

first order merits reasons.[87] From the internal hermeneutic perspective, however, this conceptualisation of the margin and the structure of the Court's reasoning is quite problematic.[88] As the Court indeed not only locates the margin of appreciation on such non-merits reasons, but also on the consideration of various merits-based reasons, it simply does not reflect the case-law accurately enough.[89] Since both types of reasons are part of the Court's practice, the distinction between the systemic and normative elements of the margin of appreciation, as elaborated above, can provide the clarity missing from previous theoretical accounts of the margin of appreciation doctrine.

Exhibiting this distinction in practice the Court, for example, in *Dogru* emphasised that 'the role of the national decision-making body must be given special importance', and that the national authorities were 'best placed' to assess the situation (non-merits reasons under the systemic margin),[90] while also relying on the substantive rationale that the wearing of religious symbols on school premises could be a 'source of pressure and exclusion' and on the nature of the 'delicate relations between the Churches and the State' (merits reasons under the normative margin).[91] Similarly in *Folgerø*, it reasoned systematically that decisions on school curriculum involved 'questions of expediency on which it is not for the Court to rule' and which fell 'in principle within the competence of the Contracting States', while also reasoning normatively that no indoctrination can be involved.[92] As exhibited by these judgments, the 'better placed' argument or similar non-merits reasons are most often part and parcel of judgments where the Court engages on the merits.[93] The different rationales related to the

---

87 A Legg, above n 1, pp 8–9 and 196.

88 On the hermeneutic perspective see N MacCormick, *H.L.A. Hart*, Stanford University Press 1981, p 38; J Bell, 'Legal Research and the Distinctiveness of Comparative Law' in M Van Hoecke (ed), *Methodologies of Legal Research Which Kind of Method for What Kind of Discipline?*, Hart 2013, p 159.

89 Consider, for example, the following examples: *Evans v United Kingdom*, above n 45, §77 ('where a particularly important facet of an individual's existence or identity is at stake, the margin allowed to the State will be restricted'); *Dickson v United Kingdom*, no 44362/04, §77, ECHR 2007, ('The breadth of this margin varies and depends on a number of factors, including the nature of the activities restricted and the aims pursued by the restrictions'); *S and Marper v United Kingdom*, nos 30562/04 and 30566/04, §102, ECHR 2008, ('The margin will tend to be narrower where the right at stake is crucial to the individual's effective enjoyment of intimate or key rights').

90 *Dogru v France*, above n 45, §63 and 75 respectively.

91 Ibid, §71 and 72 respectively.

92 *Folgerø v Norway*, above n 46, §84. Although the Court identified other problems with the contested obligatory religious education course, it concluded that emphasis on Christianity per se, pursued in the context of no indoctrination, would fall within the State's margin of appreciation in planning and setting the curriculum, see §89. See also *Lautsi and Others v Italy*, above n 45, §62.

93 For an additional example see *Beganović v Croatia*, above n 25, §80, where the Court reasoned that 'provided that criminal law mechanisms are available to the victim' (merits reasons),

systemic and normative margins of appreciation, therefore, often interact. Such partial reliance on the national authorities' judgment should therefore only be taken as a factor influencing the Court's own interpretation and review, but not as substitute for it. In exceptional instances, however, systemic non-merits reasons can be relied upon as exclusionary reasons that result in the fact that the Court does not engage normatively on certain elements of the case before it.[94] This has most notably occurred in cases under the 'fourth instance doctrine' where the Court is asked to reassess the national courts' fact finding or interpretation of domestic law;[95] in the *Von Hannover (No. 2)* type of situation when it is asked to reconsider the proportionality assessments of diligent national courts when balancing interests under two equally protected Convention rights;[96] and in the *Boshporus Airways* type of situation when it is asked to assess the proportionality of 'directly applicable' measures of EU law that leave States no discretion in implementation.[97] We will now turn to examining cases involving exclusionary non-merits reasons in more detail.

3.3. COMPLETE AND PARTIAL DEFERENCE

Seeking a deeper understanding of the two different elements of the margin of appreciation, it is helpful to note that in moral reasoning, there is a difference between assuming the authority or competence to make a moral assessment and actually making one.[98] Deference, on one reading, is shown when the person or body in question does not assume the role of assessing a situation, and leaves it instead to some other person or body.[99] This does not necessarily have to mean that the person or body does not have the authority to assess the situation; it can also simply mean that they have chosen not to engage a vested authority.[100]

'the choice of the means to secure compliance with Article 3 in the sphere of the relations of individuals between themselves is in principle a matter that falls within the domestic authorities' margin of appreciation' (non-merits reasons).

94 The Court may, however, engage normatively on other elements of the same case, see for example *X v Finland*, no 34806/04, §216–222, ECHR 2012, where the Court categorically and completely deferred with respect to the interpretation and application of national law, but proceeded to the classic normative assessment under Article 8(2) of the quality of the law authorising interference (quality, accessibility and foreseeability).

95 For example *Koval v Ukraine*, above n 24, §115; and *Fedorenko v Ukraine*, no 25921/02, §27, ECHR 2006.

96 *Von Hannover v Germany*, nos 40660/08 and 60641/08, ECHR 2012.

97 *Bosphorus Hava Yolları Turizm ve Ticaret Anonim Şirketi v Ireland*, no 45036/98, ECHR 2005. (the 'ı' at the end of 'Yolları' is international).

98 H Richards, above n 81, p 135.

99 Ibid, p 138.

100 See president Spielmann's reference to parts of the doctrine as a tool by which the Court may 'waive' its power of review in D Spielmann, 'Allowing the Right Margin: The European Court of Human Rights and the National Margin of Appreciation Doctrine: Waiver or Subsidiarity of European Review' (2011–2012) 14 *Cambridge Yearbook of European Legal Studies* 381, 384.

More precisely, situations where a person or body does not assume the role of assessment at all can be referred to as instances of complete deference, or as indicating deference in the narrow sense. Under the Convention, this would mean that the Court simply proceeds on the basis of the assessment of the body deferred to. The term deference, to be sure, can also be taken to encompass partial deference where the opinions of others are taken into account as factors that influence own assessments of a situation.[101] In this latter instance, the assessment of others, as relevant under the systemic element, is a factor of variable strength in an overall assessment that also engages the normative element of the margin of appreciation. In the Convention context, the concept of deference is often used in this wider sense.[102] The common unqualified use of the term, however, is unhelpful for making sense of the margin of appreciation because it masks an important difference between the two elements of the margin of appreciation – the fact that non-merits reasons under the systemic element can theoretically be exclusionary and have the function that the Court does not assume competence vis-à-vis another decision making body to make a moral/judicial assessment at all (complete deference), while the normative element always implies substantive engagement by the Court.

Deference and own judgment, however, often intersect when making moral/legal assessments. Consider the example of a person saying 'I think Judy is right – in the long run it would not be good for any of us.'[103] It is readily apparent that this person combines deference to Judy's assessment and her own judgment of the underlying moral question to come to a conclusion. So too for the ECtHR, when it for example partly relies on the quality of the local decision-making process behind a particular national policy or action, and partly on its own normative proportionality assessment, to reach a conclusion on whether it is in violation of Convention standards.[104] The Court may also emphasise that

---

101 A Kavanagh, above n 83, p 186, explains how 'deference is a matter of degree depending on how much weight A assigns to B's judgment', which can range from situations of 'partial deference' to 'absolute or complete deference' (emphasis in original). This was described as the difference between 'deference as respect' and 'deference as submission' by D Dyzenhaus, 'The Politics of Deference: Judicial Review and Democracy' in M Taggart (ed), *The Province of Administrative Law*, Hart 1997, pp 279, 303. P Soper, *The Ethics of Deference: Learning from Law's Morals*, Cambridge University Press 2001, p 20, uses the analogy of requests and orders to describe the same difference. Similarly, see J Raz, above n 13, p 101. For the development of three categories of deference along the axis of 'submission' to own assessments in the context domestic law, see AL Young, 'In Defence of Due Deference' (2009) 72 *MLR* 554, 560–563.

102 A Legg, above n 1, pp 17 and 21 uses the concept of deference in this unqualified manner, and understands deference as always partial. See also for example J Kratochvíl, above n 2, p 327 and HC Yourow, above n 52, p 13.

103 Example taken from H Richards, above n 81, p 139.

104 See, for example, *Hatton and Others v United Kingdom*, above n 65. Compare paras. 122–127 (own proportionality assessment) and para. 128 (national decision making-process).

for reasons of 'direct democratic legitimation' and 'contact with the vital forces of their countries', the national authorities are 'better placed' than the Court to make the initial assessments in the case, while reasoning nevertheless that the relevant final evaluation of the Convention compatibility of the contested measure is the Court's.[105] Here again, the Court takes the assessments of the national authorities into consideration under the systemic margin, while also engaging itself under the normative margin. This kind of partial deference is, for example, exhibited in the *Dogru* and *Folgerø* judgments discussed supra. In such cases, the fact that the Court itself does engage normatively with the relevant substantive issue indicates that it nevertheless in the final analysis, exercises its authority under Article 32 ECHR to have the last say on the interpretation and application of Convention standards. Thus, while engaging the systemic and normative elements of the margin of appreciation alike and indicating partial deference in the wider sense, they do not indicate complete deference in the narrower sense. The rationales for deference (non-merits reasons) and own assessments (merits reasons), therefore, intersect in cases of this kind.[106] At the same time, the partial deference implied may have a legitimising effect in relation to the final outcome.

While being the most common situation, such partial deference engaging the systemic and normative elements alike is by no means the only possible result of applying the margin of appreciation doctrine. The Court may also in some instances defer completely to other decision makers as judgments under the 'fourth instance doctrine' exhibit (see supra). More recently, the Court has also devised a new use for the margin of appreciation doctrine in cases where two protected private interests collide and have to be balanced against each other under competing Convention rights.[107] When elaborating the margin of appreciation relevant to such assessments, and instead of relying on the classic approach of asserting its role to assess the reasons put forward by States in support of their action and performing its own proportionality review,[108] the Court stated that '[w]here the balancing exercise has been undertaken by the national authorities in conformity with the criteria laid down in the Court's case-law, the Court would require strong reasons to substitute its view for that

---

105 E.g. *Van der Heijden v Netherlands, no 42857/05,* §56–57, ECHR 2012.

106 A Kavanagh, above n 83, p 190, referring to this intersection of rationales to support the conclusion that both are part of the interpretative process in national constitutional law.

107 This group of cases is referred to by D Spielmann, above n 54, p 63, as exhibiting the 'systemic' objective of the doctrine. Commentators are only beginning to make sense of it, see Y Arai-Takahashi, above n 1, p 92, who briefly notes its existence in a footnote; and B Çali, 'Towards a Responsible Domestic Courts Doctrine? The European Court of Human Rights and the Variable Standard of Judicial Review of Domestic Court Judgments' in OM Arnardóttir and A Buyse (eds), *Shifting Centres of Gravity of Human Rights Protection Rethinking Relations between the ECHR, EU and National Legal Orders*, Routledge 2016.

108 For the classic approach, see for example *Lindon, Otchakovsky-Laurens and July*, nos 21279/02 and 36448/02, §45, ECHR 2007.

of the domestic courts'.[109] The Court has, therefore, created what can best be described as a presumption of complete deference to the national courts in situations of this kind. This presumption, however, is rebuttable. It 'presupposes that an effective legal system was in place and operating for the protection of the [relevant] rights',[110] and it is also further conditioned upon the national Courts having exercised due diligence in applying Convention principles, as developed by the Court, to the facts of the case. If they have, the Strasbourg Court will defer to their proportionality assessment, but if not the Court will step in and perform its own. This new approach was introduced and confirmed in four key judgments, which all concerned the balancing of Article 10 against Article 8. In *MGN*, *Von Hannover (No. 2)* and *Aksu*, after reviewing the quality of the national court's reasoning, the presumption of complete deference held.[111] Exhibiting the strength of the presumption, the Court in one of these judgments actually through its own assessment identified a problematic issue, but decided nevertheless that 'this element alone is insufficient for the Court to substitute its own view for that of the domestic courts.'[112] The *Axel Springer* judgment, however, lies at the other end of the spectrum. Here, the presumption of deference was referred to, but did not hold at all, and the Court performed the classic full de novo proportionality assessment under the Convention.[113]

109 *Axel Springer AG v Germany*, no 39954/08, §88, ECHR 2012; *Von Hannover v Germany*, above n 96, §107. This new approach was originally developed in slightly different language in *MGN v United Kingdom*, no 39401/04, §150, ECHR 2012, and *Palomo Sánchez and Others*, above n 47, §57.

110 *Aksu v Turkey*, nos 4149/04 and 41029/04, ECHR 2012.

111 *MGN v United Kingdom*, above n 109, §145–156, where the Court did 'not find any reason, let alone a strong reason, to substitute its view for that of the final decision of the House of Lords' (§155). The second case is *Von Hannover v Germany*, above n 96, §114–126, where the Court concluded on how 'national courts carefully balanced' the competing rights (§124), and how they 'explicitly took account of the Court's relevant case-law' (§125). Only in §120 did the Court add a minor own comment to the effect of confirming the assessment of the domestic court. The third case is *Aksu v Turkey*, id. As regards the facts of App. No. 4149/04, see paras. 69–77, where the Court was 'satisfied that [...] the Turkish courts made an assessment based on the principles resulting from the Court's well-established case-law.' Only in para. 70 did it add some limited own remarks when confirming the assessment of the domestic court.

112 *Aksu v Turkey*, above n 111, §86, see also §§84–85.

113 *Axel Springer AG v Germany*, above n 109, §§96–110. The Dissenting Opinion of Judge López Guerra, joined by Judges Jungwiert, Jaeger, Villiger and Palelungi, however, held that since the domestic courts had duly performed the required balancing exercise, 'none of the grounds which would justify a review by this Court of the judgments of the domestic courts are present'. Subsequently, the presumption of complete deference has been rebutted in situations where 'the national courts did not carefully balance the journalist's right to freedom of expression against the applicant's right to respect for his private life', see *Ion Cârstea v Romania*, no 20531/06, §38, ECHR 2014. Somewhat problematically, the Court may also sometimes refer to the presumption of Convention compliance, but apply the classic approach of its own proportionality review in part or in full, rendering the case-law on competing private interests somewhat confusing, see for example *Verlagsgruppe News GmbH and Bobi v Austria*, no 59631/09, ECHR 2012; and *Fáber v Hungary*, no 40721/08,

The above position of principle on competing rights in fact resembles the 'presumption of Convention compliance' established for EU law in the *Bosphorus Airways* judgment.[114] Here, and against the background of the Contracting State's obligations when EU law leaves it no discretion in implementation, the Court had to assess whether the impoundment of an aircraft according to EC Council Regulation no 993/93 was in violation of Article 1 Protocol 1. Like usually, the Court began its assessment by restating in general terms the key elements of the relevant Convention principles and the (wide) margin of appreciation applicable in similar situations.[115] But, interestingly, instead of proceeding on the classic approach and applying these principles in concreto to the facts of the case, the Court changed its analytical model. It stated that in situations where the respondent state is simply acting in 'compliance with obligations flowing from its membership of an international organisation to which it has transferred part of its sovereignty',[116] its actions are 'justified as long as the relevant organisation is considered to protect fundamental rights, as regards both the substantive guarantees offered and the mechanisms controlling their observance, in a manner which can be considered at least equivalent to that for which the Convention provides'.[117] Therefore, the Court held that when it comes to the conclusion – as it did for the EU – that such equivalent protection is provided, 'the presumption will be that a State has not departed from the requirements of the Convention when it does no more than implement legal obligations flowing from its membership of the organisation'.[118] It added that this presumption could be rebutted only if, 'in the circumstances of a particular case, it is considered that the protection of Convention rights was manifestly deficient'.[119]

In sum, all the examples discussed here ('fourth instance', competing rights under Articles 8 and 10, EU law) exhibit such a decisive reliance on systemic non-merits rationales that the result, under certain conditions, can be complete deference.[120] The distinction between such complete deference

ECHR 2012. For a fuller analysis of the relevant case law, see OM Arnardóttir, 'Organised Retreat? The Move from "Substantive" to "Procedural" Review in the ECtHR's Case Law on the Margin of Appreciation', European Society of International Law (ESIL) 2015 Annual Conference (Oslo), available at SSRN: https://ssrn.com/abstract=2709669 or http://dx.doi.org/10.2139/ssrn.2709669.

114 *Bosphorus Hava Yolları Turizm ve Ticaret Anonim Şirketi v Ireland*, no 45036/98, ECHR 2005.

115 Ibid, §§149–151.

116 Ibid, §154.

117 Ibid, §155.

118 Ibid, §156.

119 Ibid.

120 When originally introduced, concurring and dissenting judges expressed great unease over the move vis-à-vis EU law and competing rights, see id., Joint Concurring opinion of Judges Rozakis, Tulkens, Traja, Botoucharova, Zagrebelsky and Garlicki, paras. 3 and 4; *Palomo Sánchez and Others v Spain*, above n 47, Joint Dissenting Opinion of Judges Tulkens, Davíd Thór Björgvinsson, Jočiené, Popović and Vučinić, para. 10; and *MGN v United Kingdom*, above n 108, Dissenting Opinion of Judge Davíd Thór Björgvinsson, §5.

and own assessments is no stranger to legal thinking and has been identified as an important element of understanding doctrines of deference in the context of national law.[121] The EU preliminary rulings procedure is also an interesting example of how this distinction can work in practice, as the relevant legal rules clearly define the international court's role as limited to the provision of interpretative guidance (own normative engagement only on interpretation), while leaving the task of application of norms so interpreted to the national courts (complete deference on application in concreto).[122] It is somewhat surprising, therefore, that the literature on the margin of appreciation under the Convention has not paid much attention to it.[123] The difference between deference to others and own assessments is also important for the reason that resolving who has competence to decide logically precedes deciding the question of substance.[124] If the person or body contemplating whether to make a moral/judicial assessment decides it does not have or does not engage a vested authority at all, the matter ends there and no substantive assessment is made.

In conclusion it is submitted that the difference between full and partial deference, and the logical consequences thereof, can be better reflected under the margin of appreciation doctrine if it is more clearly conceptualised as entailing the systemic and normative elements as elaborated in this chapter. The rethought conceptualisation, thus, highlights how an increased focus on the systemic element of subsidiarity and margin of appreciation can have the practical result that the Court pronounces on the merits of fewer cases in concreto.[125]

121 D Dyzenhaus, above n 101; A Kavanagh, above n 83; AL Young, above n 101.

122 Article 267, TFEU. The use of the margin of appreciation in recent cases concerning the balancing of competing Convention rights has been described as resembling this structure of judicial decision-making, see OM Arnardóttir and Dóra Guðmundsdóttir, Speaking the Same Language? Comparing Judicial Restraint at the ECtHR and the ECJ' in OM Arnardóttir and Antoine Buyse (eds), *Shifting Centres of Gravity of Human Rights Protection Rethinking Relations between the ECHR, EU and National Legal Orders*, Routledge 2016. It should be noted, however, that the structure provided for in Article 267 TFEU has not always prevented the European Court of Justice from giving guidance so specific that it can be equated with full review, see T Tridimas, 'Constitutional review of member state action: The virtues and vices of an incomplete jurisdiction' (2011) 9 *ICON* 737, 739.

123 This distinction was, however, mentioned by R Spano, above n 55, p 494, who argued that the Court's role lies on a spectrum ranging from full de novo review of domestic decisions (as under Articles 2 and 3) to 'full and unlimited deference' (which he argues is uncommon, but may be at issue in difficult cases under Articles 6, 8–11, and Article 1of Protocol 1).

124 H Richards, above n 81, p 136; T Horsley, above n 61, p 281. See also J Gerards, 'Procedural review by the ECtHR – a typology' in JH Gerards and E Brems (eds), *Procedural Review in European Fundamental Rights Cases*, Cambridge 2017, p 127 at p 153, who argues that the omission of any substantive review is the 'full logical consequence' of increased attention to the quality of domestic decision-making processes in the Court's review model.

125 This is one of the obvious consequences of applying Janneke Gerards idea that 'procedural review' should always precede 'substantive review', making the latter redundant in some types of cases, see J Gerards, above n 8. While she argues that such an approach 'would reduce

This has obvious consequences for the Court's workload, but also for any normative assessment of how the Court wields its authority under Article 32 ECHR, which charges it with the judicial responsibility of deciding all matters concerning the interpretation and application of the Convention and its Protocols.

4. CONCLUSIONS: CALLING A SPADE A SPADE

4.1. THE CAUSE FOR A RETHINK

The literature on the margin of appreciation has hitherto not made a distinction between the systemic and the normative elements of the margin of appreciation doctrine as elaborated in this chapter. It has, in other words, generally not differentiated between deference to others for non-merits reasons and variable standards of review in the Court's own assessment of merits reasons. While a distinction of this kind was helpfully suggested by Legg, it was at the same time taken to the questionable conclusion that the margin of appreciation has no proper function in relation to merits reasons and inherently only relates to non-merits reasons, which also can never be 'exclusionary' in the form of preventing normative engagement by the Court. The literature is, further, generally focused on situations of partial deference where the systemic and normative rationales behind the margin of appreciation intersect, and the Court's normative role is engaged in concreto. This also applies to Letsas' well-known dual conceptualisation of the margin of appreciation. Even in the 'structural' conception, Letsas' approach is that the doctrine's function of limiting the powers of the Court only leads to the making of a qualified substantive judgment,[126] where it relies 'heavily, but not exclusively' on the national authorities' judgment, and the margin of appreciation functions to 'express the degree to which' this takes place.[127] On Letsas' construction, then, the two margins of appreciation both rely on merits and non-merits reasons alike, and perform very similar functions. Although they can be taken to express differences in degree with respect to the width of the margin of appreciation in situations of partial deference, it is hard to see the clear difference in kind.

---

the need to apply the margin of appreciation doctrine' (p 200), the Court itself seems to be embracing the doctrine as the mechanism through which to introduce it, see for example *Von Hannover v Germany*, above n 96.

126 G Letsas, above n 1, p 721 (on structural margin): 'I here refer to the tests employed to show whether interference with an individual right amounts to a violation under the various moral theories of human rights'.

127 Ibid, pp 721 and 722 respectively (emphasis added).

If a theory of the margin of appreciation is to perform the heuristic function legitimately expected of legal theories, it must reflect the Court's case-law as much as possible, and be able to tell us more about the different functions it performs and the different rationales that support them. With all due respect to the important contributions of Letsas, Legg and other commentators, it was therefore concluded that the time has come to rethink how the margin of appreciation doctrine has been conceptualised in the literature.

4.2. THE RETHOUGHT TWO ELEMENTS OF THE MARGINS OF APPRECIATION

Upon rethinking, it was concluded that the literature on the margin of appreciation doctrine has correctly identified two different functions for the doctrine, but that the lack of clarity and consensus on the dividing line between them, and on the consequences of the distinction, has hampered the development of a clear theoretical vision for the doctrine. Seeking to elaborate a theory focused on these two different functions, it was suggested that the two elements of the principle of subsidiarity, as elaborated in the literature, should be brought to bear on the doctrine. Accordingly, the margin of appreciation should be conceptualised as consisting of two elements. First is the systemic element, which like the systemic element of the principle of subsidiarity relies on a functional or pragmatic rationale related to the different competences of different actors in the European system for the protection of human rights, and has the function of influencing distribution of tasks between them. The second element is the normative one, which has a normative justification related to pluralism and flexibility and the function of influencing how rights are interpreted and applied. Drawing on insights from moral reasoning, it was also established how different types of reasoning are relevant to each element as the systemic element draws on non-merits reasons, while the normative element relies on merits reasons. It was also exhibited how this is, indeed, reflected in the case-law of the Court. Finally, and drawing on the literature on constitutional interpretation, it was argued that the distinction between complete and partial deference is important and should be brought to bear when theorising the doctrine. It was explained how the rethought two margins of appreciation are indeed capable of reflecting this difference as complete deference can only occur under the systemic element of the doctrine, which also logically precedes the Court's own normative assessment of a case. The rethought version of the two margins of appreciation presented herein, therefore, provides a grasp on the case-law where the systemic margin of appreciation is decisively relied upon; a grasp that theoretical accounts of the margin of appreciation have hitherto not been able to provide.

Defining the two elements of the margin of appreciation, it can be stated that the systemic one is related to deference to other decision-making bodies for non-merits reasons, and that the normative element is related to the Court's own assessment of merits reasons. In the former conception the margin of appreciation has a distinct systemic ('structural' or 'procedural') function related to the division of tasks within the European system for the protection of human rights, whereas the latter conception has a normative ('substantive') function and reflects pluralism and normative flexibility in the interpretation and application of Convention rights. The systemic and the normative elements of the margin of appreciation can intersect in various ways within the same case. In its purest or most extreme form, the systemic element of the margin of appreciation can exert such a strong influence on the Court's reasoning that the end result may best be described as complete deference to other actors in the European system for the protection of human rights on certain elements of a case. More often, however, it interacts with the normative merits reasons, resulting in partial deference. In such cases, a decisive reliance on the systemic rationale generally functions as an indicator for more lenient review.

The rethought version of the two margins of appreciation presented herein enables the clearer understanding of the doctrine so often called for in the literature. It is submitted, therefore, that it greatly enhances our chances of making sense of the Court's case-law, and the capacity for normative assessment of how the Court uses the powers vested in it. In the final analysis, it enables us to call a spade a spade instead of continuing to dabble in muddy waters.

ABOUT THE EDITORS

Emmanuelle Bribosia is Professor of Law and Director of the Centre for European Law at Université libre de Bruxelles, Belgium. Her research activities focus on international and European human rights protection, as well as on the right to equality and non-discrimination, with an emphasis on the interdisciplinary approach of these research themes. More details are available on her webpage: http://cde.ulb.be/member/prof-emmanuelle-bribosia/.

Isabelle Rorive is Professor of Law and Director of the Perelman Centre for Legal Philosophy at Université libre de Bruxelles, Belgium. Her research focuses on the theoretical and practical developments of the right to equality and non-discrimination, the migration of legal concepts between common law and civil law systems, the imprint of legal cultures on the development of law and judicial reasoning, and the human rights issues raised by the management of cultural pluralism. More details are available on her webpage: http://www.philodroit.be/_Rorive-Isabelle_?lang=fr.

As senior members of the European Network of Legal Experts in the Non-Discrimination Field and the Berkeley Comparative Anti-Discrimination Law Study Group, Emmanuelle Bribosia and Isabelle Rorive pursue many of their research projects in an international setting. In 2014, they jointly launched the Equality Law Clinic (http://equalitylawclinic.ulb.be) in the framework of the *Human Rights Integration* project. They both also act as Councillor at their University with regard to its diversity policy.

Ana Maria Corrêa is a PhD researcher at Université libre de Bruxelles, Belgium. She is attached to the Perelman Centre for Legal Philosophy. Her research focuses on the intersection of anti-discrimination rights and disruptive online platforms, and she adopts a comparative law perspective in her work. Her research is sponsored by the Capes Foundation. She joined the Equality Law Clinic in 2016–2017 and is a member of both the Council for European Studies and the Internet Society Association. More details are available on her webpage: http://www.philodroit.be/_Correa-Ana-Maria_?lang=fr.

www.ingramcontent.com/pod-product-compliance
Ingram Content Group UK Ltd.
Pitfield, Milton Keynes, MK11 3LW, UK
UKHW051920100926
8556IPUK00021B/1277